P9-EMC-069

Palgrave Macmillan Studies in Banking and Financial Institutions

Series Editor: **Professor Philip Molyneux**

The Palgrave Macmillan Studies in Banking and Financial Institutions are international in orientation and include studies of banking within particular countries or regions, and studies of particular themes such as Corporate Banking, Risk Management, Mergers and Acquisitions, etc. The books' focus is on research and practice, and they include up-to-date and innovative studies on contemporary topics in banking that will have global impact and influence.

Titles include:

The full list of titles available is on the website:
www.palgrave.com/finance/sbfi.asp

Palgrave Macmillan Studies in Banking and Financial Institutions
Series Standing Order ISBN 978–1–4039–4872–4

You can receive future titles in this series as they are published by placing a standing order. Please contact your bookseller or, in case of difficulty, write to us at the address below with your name and address, the title of the series and the ISBN quoted above.

Customer Services Department, Macmillan Distribution Ltd, Houndmills, Basingstoke, Hampshire RG21 6XS, England

HG
186
S3A53
2011
WEB

The Evolution of Nordic Finance

Steffen E. Andersen

palgrave
macmillan

© Steffen E. Andersen 2011

All rights reserved. No reproduction, copy or transmission of this publication may be made without written permission.

No portion of this publication may be reproduced, copied or transmitted save with written permission or in accordance with the provisions of the Copyright, Designs and Patents Act 1988, or under the terms of any licence permitting limited copying issued by the Copyright Licensing Agency, Saffron House, 6–10 Kirby Street, London EC1N 8TS.

Any person who does any unauthorized act in relation to this publication may be liable to criminal prosecution and civil claims for damages.

The author has asserted his right to be identified as the author of this work in accordance with the Copyright, Designs and Patents Act 1988.

First published 2011 by
PALGRAVE MACMILLAN

Palgrave Macmillan in the UK is an imprint of Macmillan Publishers Limited, registered in England, company number 785998, of Houndmills, Basingstoke, Hampshire RG21 6XS.

Palgrave Macmillan in the US is a division of St Martin's Press LLC, 175 Fifth Avenue, New York, NY 10010.

Palgrave Macmillan is the global academic imprint of the above companies and has companies and representatives throughout the world.

Palgrave® and Macmillan® are registered trademarks in the United States, the United Kingdom, Europe and other countries

ISBN 978-0-230-24155-8   hardback

This book is printed on paper suitable for recycling and made from fully managed and sustained forest sources. Logging, pulping and manufacturing processes are expected to conform to the environmental regulations of the country of origin.

A catalogue record for this book is available from the British Library.

Library of Congress Cataloging-in-Publication Data

Andersen, Steffen E., 1944–
   The evolution of Nordic finance / Steffen E. Andersen.
      p. cm. – (Palgrave Macmillan studies in banking and financial institutions)
   ISBN 978–0–230–24155–8 (alk. paper)
      1. Finance–Scandinavia–History. I. Title.

HG186.S3A53 2010
332.0948–dc22   2010033936

10   9   8   7   6   5   4   3   2   1
20   19   18   17   16   15   14   13   12   11

Printed and bound in Great Britain by
CPI Antony Rowe, Chippenham and Eastbourne

Contents

List of Tables

List of Schedules

List of Abbreviations

BG	Bikuben-Girobank
bn	Billion, i.e. thousand million
BoF	Bank of Finland, Finlands Bank, Suomen Pankki
BRFKredit A/S	Byggeriets Realkreditfond
CBK	Cristiana Bank og Kreditkasse
CHF	Swiss Francs
dcm	Daler copper mint
DEM	Deutschmarks
DFDS	De Forenede Dampskibsselskaber
DKK	Danske Kroner
DnB	Den norske Bank
DnC	Den norske CreditBank
EU	European Union
FED	The Federal Reserve System
FIM	Finmark
GBP	British Pound Sterling
GDP	Gross Domestic Product
GN	Great Northern (formerly Det Store Nordiske Telegrafselskab)
HEX	Helsinki Stock Exchange
KOP	Kansallis Osake Pankki
KSS	Konungariket Sveriges Stadshypotekskassa
KTAS	Kjøbenhavns Telefon Aktieselskab, TDC
LTCM	Long-Term Capital Management
NGL	Non-government loans
NOK	Norwegian Kroner
NORAS	Norges råd for anvendt samfunnsforskning
NOS	Norges Offisielle Statistikk
OECD	Organization for Economic Co-operation and Development
rd	Riksdaler species
SBGF	Statens Banksikringsfond
SBIF	Statens Bankinvesteringsfond
SDO	Særligt dækkede obligationer/specially covered bonds
SDS	Sammensluttede Danske Sparekasser
SEB	Skandinaviska Enskilda Banken
SEK	Swedish krona
SFS	Svensk Forfattningssamling

SKAB	Skandinaviska Kredit AB
SMEs	Small and medium-sized enterprises
STAB	Stockholms Tændstick AB
UBF	Union Bank of Finland, SYP
USD	US Dollar

Acknowledgements

First of all, it is my great pleasure to thank Birgit Hoffmeyer, occasionally my reluctant tennis partner in the distant past, for her patience and forbearance. Without her constructive criticism at the early stages of this project, it would never have materialized. Gustav Wedell-Wedellsborg, another friend since time immemorial, had the arduous task of reading some early drafts and saved me from embarrassing errors.

Secondly, I owe many thanks to all the colleagues and customers I have met during nearly 30 years of banking in the Nordic region. They include CFOs from the 200 largest Nordic corporations as well as fellow bankers from inside and outside the Nordic region, but they are too numerous to mention individually. They have all contributed to my knowledge of banking and corporate finance, and many of them have also stimulated my interest in the historical background and development of their respective institutions.

Thirdly, I am fortunate to have been assisted by a number of individuals and institutions, each of whom deserves my special thanks:

On the Danish mortgage institutions, I have received invaluable help from Realkredit Danmark (Karin Havers and Mogens Holm) and BRFkredit (Sickan Rasmussen). On Danish stock exchange matters, I am deeply grateful for the assistance given to me by the Copenhagen Stock Exchange, Ellen-Margrethe Soelberg and her colleagues, who found some delightfully illustrative specimens of information in the cellars of the Exchange. I am deeply grateful for the patience and help I have received from all of them.

On the role of central banks in the most recent crisis, I have benefited greatly from discussions with Jesper Berg, until recently Head of Department in Danmarks Nationalbank, and co-author of a book on the financial crisis (*Finansernes Fald*, 2009).

On banking matters, I am grateful to each of the Nordic Bankers' Associations, all of which have been most helpful. It was particularly illuminating to discuss the Swedish banking crisis experience with Mats Stenhammar and Christian Nilsson of the Svenska Bankföreningen.

In the Danish Bankers Association (Finansrådet) I have benefited from invaluable help from Klaus Willerslev-Olsen, Senior Vice President, and some of his colleagues, notably Birte Hansen, head of the library.

On Finnish financial history, I have been helped particularly by Professor Antti Kuusterä and Juha Tarkka, Advisor to the Board of the Bank of Finland. Their kind advice and the access they gave me to certain sections of the archives of the Bank of Finland has been invaluable. Kaija Erjanti, The Finnish

Bankers Association, has patiently answered several questions for me, for which I am deeply grateful.

Also, I should express sincere thanks to Aapo Nikunen, Timo Nyman, and Heikki Räty, my Finnish friends, all in various ways connected to the Finnish corporate and financial world. They have all assisted me in their own ways, not least by their interest and inspiration, as well as occasional translations from the not-so-easy Finnish language.

Monica Bergström, of the Helsinki Stock Exchange, deserves my deeply felt thanks for the statistical information she has provided to me.

In Norway, Norges Bank (Turid Wammen) helped me in several ways, for which I am seriously grateful.

To Søren Weis Dahl I am eternally grateful for his assistance with technical matters. Without his deep knowledge of text processing, this book would never have appeared. In addition, the long walks he has allowed me to take with Rolf, his dog, have provided me with opportunities to have long and almost uninterrupted philosophical discussions about the project.

Last, but not least, I must express a deeply felt gratitude to Vibeke, my wife for 38 years. She not only took upon herself to read through hundreds of pages, which were, eventually, never included in the book, but more importantly, she has bravely put up with all the inconveniences resulting from my preoccupation with the production of this book. Her understanding for my preoccupation has been truly remarkable.

Deeply felt thanks are also due to my late father, Svend Andersen, employed in Danmarks Nationalbank from 1942 to 1982, member of the Board of Governors 1963–1982, and president of the Copenhagen Stock Exchange, 1982–1985. My father greatly stirred my interest in history as well as economics and banking.

Any errors, misrepresentations, or misunderstandings are, of course, my sole responsibility.

Steffen E. Andersen

Introduction: What's It All About?

"Neither a borrower nor a lender be;
For loan oft loses both itself and friend,
And borrowing dulls the edge of husbandry."

(Hamlet, Act I)

The basic issue

In spite of Shakespeare's warnings, lending and borrowing belong to the oldest pursuits of the human race, almost as if it were some sort of sport. To the extent that this sport is not exercised exclusively on a man-to-man basis but through competing, professional intermediaries observing a few gentlemanly "rules of the game" – increasingly, and sometimes excessively, laid down in legislation – it can be said to represent capital market activities. The net effect of this "sport" has been real economic growth at a rate which could never have been achieved if all investments would have had to be financed only out of the savings of the investor, or if all lending and borrowing had had to be done exclusively on a direct man-to-man bilateral basis. Realizing the potential benefits of a multilateral collection of savings and an allocation of those savings to their "best" uses (however defined) is the task of the capital market.

This book intends to look at the development of the framework for capital markets in the Nordic area in an historical and conceptual perspective, and to look at these perspectives in a broad European context.

Another theme, which will be touched upon is the inherent conflicts of interest between capital providers and capital users. The question here is whether, or to what extent, regulations reflect the interests of the Antonios or the Shylocks of this world.

It will be seen that in the Nordic region capital markets emerged at least 100 years later than in the UK, and that even the fragmented pre-1871 Germany displayed many of the characteristics of a capital market 50–60 years before similar characteristics were evident in any of the Nordic countries.

1

One question which seems to come up naturally in this connection is to what extent the late industrialization of the Nordic region compared to the rest of North-Western Europe can be explained by the late emergence of capital markets in Scandinavia. It is tempting to argue that the rudimentary, incoherent, and fragmented framework for capital intermediation prevailing throughout the Nordic region until the final decades of the 19th century to some extent hampered, or at least did not facilitate, large-scale investments and industrialization. This question will be looked at to the extent that it is possible at all to discuss why something did not happen, or only happened with some delay. Minutes of board meetings deciding to give up investments because financing was not available, or available only on unacceptable conditions, are hard to come by in sufficient numbers to form a general pattern.

Norsk Hydro, a capital intensive producer of fertilizers and aluminium was founded in 1905 when financing was finally obtained, initially from the Wallenbergs in Sweden, but more permanently from Banque Nationale de Paris, which kept Norsk Hydro under foreign control until 1940. The foundation of Hafslund, now Norway's second largest energy company, is much the same story, except that in this case German banks supplied the financing. In Sweden, the railways built during the last quarter of the 19th century were mostly financed by German and British banks. The Finnish paper industry, one of the backbones of the Finnish economy, was not really developed until well into the 20th century, at least partially because the substantial investments required for efficient paper production could not be financed from the embryonic Finnish capital market, and in many years after WWII neither Denmark's nor Finland's international creditworthiness was beyond question.

On the other hand, it could perhaps be argued that an absence or scarcity of ideas or plans for large, capital intensive investments seemed to make the development of financial institutions rather futile, and provided incentives neither for private nor government initiatives. Over a prolonged period of time cause and effect probably ran in both directions. However, during shorter intervals, e.g. during the last 30–50 years of the 19th century, and during the first 10–15 years after WWII, it seems plausible that the "cause and effect" relationship was predominantly in one direction rather than the other. It seems possible that Norsk Hydro and Hafslund type of companies could have been founded 10–20 years earlier, that railway building in Sweden and Denmark could have flourished earlier, and that the Swedish iron manufacturing could have been reorganized into an efficient large-scale steel industry earlier than it actually did, if it had been easier to raise the necessary financing, or at least a major part of it, from local capital markets.

However, the relative industrial decline experienced by the UK during most of the 20th century clearly demonstrates that the existence of even a highly sophisticated capital market, although probably beneficial for economic growth, is far from a sufficient condition for such growth.[1]

Any clear conclusion to this discussion is hardly to be expected, since conclusions would very much have to be based on "what if" arguments.

It is difficult to approach the subject of capital markets without some reference to the intellectual framework provided first by Saint-Simon, the Utopian philosopher, who did not trust the financial markets to produce anything like a "just" allocation of resources. Such thinking was brought even more forcefully forward by Karl Marx, and further built upon by many later writers, cfr: "Die Dominanz der Banken über die Industrie als generelles Phänomen kapitalistischer Reproduktionszusammenhänge ... ist von Ökonomen und Historikern oft behauptet worden",[2] and, in direct reference to Marx: "Hier ist also die Herrschaft der Banken über die Industrie, die wichtigste Erscheinung der neuen Zeit, vorausgesagt, als noch kaum die Keime dieser Entwicklung sichtbar waren."[3]

Examples of dominance and exploitation by banks can probably be found somewhere, as well as merciless behaviour by other creditors. Some Shylocks have doubtlessly been successful in getting their pound of flesh. Unseen by Saint-Simon and his spiritual followers, other examples where unlucky capital suppliers have suffered at the hands of unscrupulous or over-optimistic borrowers are, however, probably equally, if not more, abundant. No student of economic history is unaware of cases where less than bona fide bonds and stocks have been issued to gullible – and even quite professional – investors. The unpaid debts of Charles V and his successors to the Fugger Bank in the 16th century, John Law's Mississippi scheme, and the notorious "South Sea Bubble" are certainly not the only cases in point. There are striking similarities between some of the railway and canal bonds issued in the 19th century by notorious "robber barons", and certain borrowings taken up by some telecommunication, IT companies, and others during the final years of the 20th century. The avalanche of "junk bonds" in the 1980s, and the "sub-prime" bonds in the early 21st century, to say nothing of the Enron case, are all examples in point. Among major Scandinavian cases, the notorious collapses of Kreuger (1932), Nordisk Fjer (1991), and Hafnia (1992) could be mentioned as cases where Shylocks have suffered at the hands of more or less unscrupulous Antonios.

---

[1]Some observers have suggested that the British capital market could to some extent be blamed for the relatively poor performance of British industry in the 20th century, cfr: F. Capie and M. Collins (1992) *Have Banks Failed British Industry?* (London), and W.P. Kennedy (1987) *Industrial Structure, Capital Markets, and the Origins of British Economic Decline* (Cambridge).

[2]V. Wellhöner (1989) *Grossbanken und Grossindustri im Kaiserreich* (Göttingen) p. 11.

[3]R. Hilferding (1910) *Das Finanzkapital* (reprinted by Europäische Verlagsanstalt, Frankfurt, 1968) p. 98.

Several spectacular bank crashes in the latest 800 years have also given rise to much debate about the integrity and diligence, or relative lack of the same, among bankers. It is unrealistic to expect this debate to stop in any near-term future, as banks will most certainly also crash in many years to come.

Malpractices as well as misfortunes have given rise to a broad range of regulations everywhere seeking in various degrees to protect either the Shylocks or the Antonios of this world, or at least to balance their mutually conflicting interests. A market completely void of any such "rules of the game" is no true market, and a market strangled in cobwebs of regulations is also no market. The elusive trick is to find the "right" balance of a moving target. Following each "crisis", the definition of the "right" balance will change.

Lessons from Italy, the Netherlands, and Prussia

The craftiness and misfortunes of the Italian bankers

> *"Go forth, try what my credit can in Venice do"*
> *"The Merchant of Venice", Act One.*

Quite apart from Shylock's misfortunes, the history of the famous Italian merchant-bankers is full of lessons, which have been taken to heart in the modern world only to a limited extent.

First, the Venetians understood that for a banking system to work, risks have to be taken. The four Venetian banking acts of 1318–1322 recognized that for a banking system to work properly, bank-to-bank transfers have to be accepted as settlement of debts (with the implied risks), that banks could keep only a fraction of their deposits as cash reserves (with the implied liquidity risk), and that banks had to maintain current accounts with other banks (with the implied "systemic" risk).[4] They also understood that banks require capital and trust, hence the requirement that bankers, in order to be licenced, were to be guaranteed for certain amounts by at least five other acceptable persons, who were not bankers. This proved, of course, in many cases to be insufficient. These are risks which have to be accepted, and which cannot be "regulated" away.

---

[4]For a description of the medieval and renaissance Italian banking system, see e.g. A.P. Usher (1932–1934) *The Origins of Banking* (*The Economic History Review*, Vol. IV, repr. 1964), or A.P. Usher (1943) *The Early History of Deposit Banking in Mediterranean Europe* (Cambridge, Mass.), and F. Chiapelli (ed., 1979) *The Dawn of Modern Banking* (Yale University Press), and R.C. Mueller (1979) *The Venetian Money Market: Banks, Panics, and the Public Debt 1200–1500* (The John Hopkins University Press), and R. de Roover (1963) *The Rise and Decline of the Medici Bank* (Harvard University Press).

Second, the sad histories of the Florentine house of the Frescobaldi, the Ricardi of Lucca, and the Grand Tavola di Bonsignori of Siena – all of the 13th century – showed the world the dangers of being excessively exposed to a few large clients. However, the Florentine Bardis, the largest of the medieval financial empires, was bankrupted 1346 for exactly the same reason as the earlier Italian houses, and so were the Medicis in the late 15th century. They all foundered from having exposed themselves excessively to Edward I, II, and III, the English kings, in their respective financings of the Welsh and Scottish campaigns in return for supposedly lucrative trading rights. The subsequent refusal by the English nobles to service the royal debts rang the death knell for the Italian bankers.

The third lesson is that credit, as Shylock would have agreed, should be backed by power.

Lenders lose if borrowers have a stronger position than creditors, politically, psychologically, and/or military – as demonstrated by the three English King Edwards, and vice versa. The contrast between the English Edwards and the contemporary Danish King Christoffer II (1319–1332) could hardly have been stronger. The Italian bankers were wiped out. The Holstein lenders to the Danish king took over the country. Shylock triumphed, for a while at least.[5]

Fourth, the fate of the Italian bankers shows the dangers of mingling different types of businesses. Their expected trading profits confounded a realistic evaluation of their credit risks. This aspect was reflected in Danish banking legislation 600 years later, when the Banking Act of 1930 forbade banks to engage in any other business than banking, cfr. Chapter 7.

Fifth, the continuous bank failures in Venice, Florence, and elsewhere in Italy and Spain caused the respective governments to take strong actions. In Venice, the City formed the Banco della Piazza di Rialto (1587), largely copied from the Banca di San Giorgio in Genoa (1408). The purpose of the new bank was to replace the private banks, which had by now virtually disappeared.[6] Its activities were to take deposits repayable on demand, make account-to-account transfers (giro business), settle bills of exchange, and offer occasional minor loans to the government.[7] It was forbidden to do any commercial lending.

---

[5]Count Gerhard III of Schauenburg, the largest creditor, who in 1326 had taken over the peninsular of Jutland for himself and his direct heirs in settlement of debts, was assassinated in 1340 by representatives of the borrower.
[6]R.C. Mueller (1997) *The Venetian Money Market, 1200–1500* (The John Hopkins University Press) pp. 579–86, gives a chronological list of the Venetian bankers between 1225 and 1550, and a list of approximately 50 banks which failed between 1327 and 1500.
[7]Cfr. G. Luzzato (1964) *Les Banques Publiques de Venise*, in van Dillen (ed.) *History of the Principal Public Banks* (Frank Cass & Co. Ltd). Details of this bank are not known, since most of its archives have been lost.

The example set by the Netherlands

"Guilded tombs do worms enfold"

"The Merchant of Venice", Act Two

In 1609, the Banco della Piazza di Rialto in Venice was used as a model by the City of Amsterdam, where a mechanism was strongly wanted to alleviate the problems caused by the multitude of different currencies circulating in the Netherlands. The Venetian model was developed and refined, but the basic structure of what came to be the Amsterdam Wisselbank ("Exchange Bank") was identical to the Rialto Bank.[8] It was not endowed with any other capital than what was gradually built up from retained earnings, but it was guaranteed by the City of Amsterdam. It accepted non-interest bearing deposits in all currencies, kept them on accounts in one common currency, the Guilder (purely an accounting unit), repaid the deposits in a currency of the depositor's choice at a rate of exchange to the guilder decided by the Bank, made account-to-account transfers, settled bills of exchange, but did not discount them, traded currencies and precious metals, made occasional loans to the City, and, in principle, nothing else except occasional funding for the Bank van Leening. For more than 100 years the Amsterdam Wisselbank remained the most venerable financial institution in Europe. Part of its success can also be explained by the fact that all bills of exchange exceeding 600 guilders (since 1643, 300 guilders) were required by law to be settled over accounts with the Wisselbank. This meant that nearly all of Amsterdam's multitude of merchants had to have accounts with the Wisselbank. Its balance sheet and P&L accounts were kept absolutely secret, which probably added to its aura.

In addition, the City set op the Bank van Leening, which was to act as a small-scale lender and pawn broker to the City's business community, and which was funded mainly with interest-bearing bonds and deposits, and occasional borrowings from the Wisselbank.

In the long run, the Wisselbank did not work. Tempted by profits or status, or pressured by customers, the bank managers engaged the bank in commercial loans with first the Dutch East India Company, and later other business. When the collapse of the East India Company in 1797 forced the Wisselbank to open its books, the Bank turned out to be a guilded tomb full of worms. Overexposed to both the East India Company and to the virtually bankrupt City of Amsterdam, the Wisselbank was finished. It lived a dormant life for some years and was finally closed in 1819.

---

[8]Cfr. J.G. van Dillen (1964) *The Bank of Amsterdam* in J.G. van Dillen (ed.) *History of the Principal Public Bank* (Frank Cass & Co. Ltd) pp. 79–125. See also M.'t Hart, J. Jonker & J.L. van Zanden (1997) *A Financial History of The Netherlands* (Cambridge University Press) pp. 45–51.

While the Amsterdam Wisselbank was still going strong it was copied in several European cities, including Tilburg, Hamburg (the Hamburger Bank, 1619), and Nürnberg. Since they were all guaranteed by their respective cities, they became known as "public banks". A similar bank was created in Stockholm, the Palmstruch Bank of 1656, cfr. Chapter 1. Thus, Venice came to Stockholm via Amsterdam and Hamburg.

The lesson from Prussia

In the late 18th century a number of regional financial organizations, "Land-wirtschaftliche Kreditinsitute", for short, "Landschaften", were created in Prussia, Posen, Schlesien, and Pommern for the purpose of making cheap credit available to the large landowners. They will be given a short description[9] here because they served as an inspiration for the Danish and Swedish mortgage associations, which came to play central roles in their respective capital markets in the 19th and 20th centuries (cfr. Chapters 3 and 6).

The first wave of regional organizations, "Die Fünf Alten", grew up in the years 1770–1788. A second wave of similar institutions followed in the 19th century, intended also for minor landowners.

They were not completely identical in all respects, but the main characteristics of these (first wave) institutions were:

1. They were associations of borrowers in a specific region indicated by the name of the association. Membership of the associations was restricted to the landed nobles in each of the respective regions. In four of the "fünf alten" membership was automatic (i.e. being a nobleman with an estate exceeding a certain size automatically implied membership of the respective Landschaft). Membership implied joint liability for the obligations of the Landschaft, whether the member had a loan or not.

2. The associations had no paid in capital of their own, (except in two cases,[10] and except for reserves they built up), and they did not do business for profits. They were pure service organizations. They "arranged" credits; they did not lend, and they did not take deposits. They were definitely not banks.

3. The size of the credits arranged was purely a question of the estimated value of the land offered as collateral, as estimated by the Landschaft.

---

[9]The description of the Landschaften is based on H. Mauer (1907) *Das Landschaftliche Kreditwesen Preussens* (Strassbourg), and on A.F. Bergsøe (1839) *Motiveret Udkast til en Creditforening for Danske Grundbesiddere* (Forfatterens Forlag, Kjøbenhavn).

[10]According to A.F. Bergsøe (1839) King Wilhelm II paid in a capital sum of 200,000 Thaler, at 2 per cent interest, to each of the Schlesige and West-preussische Land-schaften, but not to any of the others. *Motiveret Udkast til en Kreditforening for Danske Grundbesiddere*, pp. 8 and 11. This is not mentioned by Mauer.

The borrower would then receive fixed interest "Pfandbriefe" (mortgage deeds) in nominal amounts corresponding to one half of the estimated value of the land (in some Landschaften two-thirds). The borrower could sell the Pfandbriefe himself, or he could ask the Landschaft to sell them on his behalf.

These Pfandbriefe became quite popular on the Berlin Stock Exchange.

4. For the end-investors, the Pfandbriefe represented a claim against the Landschaft.

5. The joint liability among the members implied that the Landschaft could claim any missing interest payments from all the other members, in case a foreclosure on the defaulting borrowers did not bring in the amount owed to the Landschaft.

   In the unlikely case that the Landschaft could not pay the holder of the Pfandbrief, the investor could try to collect his claim directly from the borrower, since the mortgage deeds carried the text: "Pfandbrief, welcher auf das im Kreise X gelegene Gut Y ausgefertigt worden"[11] (the "Spezialgarantie"), and if that did not work, the joint liability would come into play, so that the Pfandbrief holder could claim his money from all or any of the members of the Landschaft (the "Generalgarantie"). Opinions have differed on the question whether borrowers were liable to the full extent of all of their assets or only to the extent of their mortgaged property (i.e. only joint or both joint and personal liability).[12] This issue was never put to the test.

6. There was never any fixed amortization plans. In principle, the loans were perpetuals, but the borrowers could always repay, partially or in full, at their option.

   This was asymmetrical. The Pfandbriefe could be called at six-months notice (or immediately for small amounts). In principle, this could cause liquidity problems for the Landschaft, but it was assumed that investors' demand for Pfandbriefe would roughly match redemption calls from other Pfandbrief holders, so that no problems would emerge. This assumption actually proved correct (apart from the effects of war disruptions 1806–1814, when the Prussian government had to rescue several of the Landschaften). This asymmetry was modified in the 1830s in connection with the introduction of amortization plans.

A discussion of definitions

What is a "capital market"?

In the present study, the focus is on "organized capital markets".

---

[11] H. Mauer (1907) *Das Landwirtschaftliche Kreditwesen Preussens*, p. 4.
[12] H. Mauer (1907) *Das Landwirtschaftlich Kreditwesen Preusseens*, p. 4 (n. 1).

An "organized capital market" is here defined as follows:

An organized capital market is a market existing for the purpose of connecting capital suppliers to capital users in a framework characterized by

1. The existence of professional intermediaries who perform this function as their main activity, who offer a broad variety of financial contracts and services, and who account for this activity separately from any other activities they may be doing.
2. The existence of a sufficient number of capital suppliers, intermediaries, and capital users, i.e. market participants, in the market to ensure a satisfactory degree of competition among the market participants.
3. The existence of a secondary market for financial contracts (typically, but not necessarily, stock exchanges).
4. The existence of a reasonable regulatory framework regulating (a) the mutually opposing interests of the suppliers and users of capital, and (b) the intermediaries for the purpose of safeguarding a generally sound financial system, and (c) the flow of capital between various sectors of the economy.
5. The existence of a framework ensuring a reasonable degree of transparency in the market.

Thus defined, there is evidence that capital markets emerged gradually in certain places on the Continent in the second half of the 18th century (particularly Amsterdam), and in England early in the 19th century.

The frequent use of words like "satisfactory" and "reasonable" in a definition, which is supposed to be precise is, of course, not entirely satisfactory, but there seems to be no way around the "fact" that several aspects surrounding this subject are a matter of degree and subject to personal opinions.

Two final general comments:

First, capital markets can only work in a predominantly monetary economy, since financial assets and liabilities are expressed in monetary terms, although history does have some examples to show where contracts have been expressed in monetary terms but settled in kind. In Europe, the economies changed from being predominantly based on barter into predominantly monetary economies during the Middle Ages,[13] although this was far from a smooth, continuously forward moving process.

In the Nordic region it happened much later. Although in Denmark the first coins were minted already in 986, minting of Danish coins was

---

[13] "The forward market in money ... could only exist where there was already a highly-charged economy. Such was the case by the thirteenth century in Italy, Germany, and the Netherlands." F. Braudel (2002) *The Wheels of Commerce* (Phoenix Press) p. 51 (Translated from *Les jeux de l'Echange*, 1979).

discontinued in the early 14th century, and it was not until after the Reformation that the use of coins became widespread. Even in 18th-century Denmark, many transactions were settled in kind. In Finland, a tax reform as late as 1840 provided for tax payments in kind (although the tax liability was expressed in money), but the monetization process is difficult to follow statistically.[14] Also in Sweden, the monetization process did not really gather momentum until the second half of the 19th century, following the expansion of the banking networks, cfr. Chapters 4 and 6.

Secondly, a distinction is quite commonly made between the "capital market" and the "money market", where the former is usually defined as the market for credit instruments having a remaining maturity exceeding one year, and the latter less than one year. For several reasons this distinction will generally not be used here. One reason is that maturity transformation is a central function of the capital market, so what may be short term for the capital provider may end up as long term for the capital user (or the other way round), and another is that many long-term instruments carry variable rates of interest, thereby serving some of the functions of short-term instruments. Finally, the one year criterion is a purely arbitrary one without any logical justification.

What is a "bank"?

"That which we call a rose
by any other name would smell as sweet"

"Romeo and Juliet", Act Two

Among "professional intermediaries", banks are probably the most common entities. The problem is that that which we call a "bank" can take many different shapes, and some of them are "banks" in name only.

In this study "banks" are defined as legal entities which regularly take deposits on current accounts from the general public for the purpose of lending the funds thus collected to members of the general public for a broad variety

---

[14]"Tyvärr är det inte möjligt att med statistiska mätinstrument följa denne monetäriseringsprocess. Men några uppgifter kaster ljus över skeendet. Gennom en skattereform bestemtes år 1840 att varje skatterubel skulle omfatta 3 kappar säd, 3 pund smör, 3 pund talg och et penningbelopp länsvis väkslande från 5 til 24 kopek." N. Meinander (1962) *Penningpolitik under etthundrafemtio år* (Finlands Bank), p. 16. SEA's translation: "Unfortunately, it is impossible to follow this process of monetization by statistical means. However, certain information does throw some light on the development. A tax reform in 1840 stipulated that every tax ruble should be equivalent to 3 cups of seed, 3 pounds of butter, 3 pounds of lard, and a money amount between 5 and 24 kopeks, depending on county."

of purposes, which offer money transfer services, and which have these activities as their main business.

Thus defined, Glass-Steagall type "investment banks", brokers, fund managers, leasing and factoring companies, old-fashioned savings banks, banques privées, and traditional mortgage institutions (but possibly building societies), are not "banks", but this does not, of course, imply that such institutions are not capital market institutions. It only means that they should probably not be subject to standard banking regulations. Their presence as separate institutions is not essential for the existence of a capital market. But in case they do not exist in a given market place, the implication of the proposed definition of a capital market is that the activities of such absent institutions should be taken care of by the "banks" (or other financial institutions) in the market in order for a "capital market" to exist.

There is plenty of evidence that "banks" in the sense of the proposed definition have existed in the Mediterranean at least since the mid-13th century, but in the Nordic region not until 1656, cfr. Chapter 1.

The definition of a "bank" is of some importance, because of the implication it has for the type of business organization, which is subject to banking legislation and regulation. Until about the mid-20th century, regulations in most western countries distinguished between commercial banks, savings banks, and other financial institutions. In modern times, however, EU regulations have, in some respects, e.g. capital requirements, abandoned all differentiation between different types of financial institutions. This is not necessarily a very constructive approach, as discussed in the concluding chapter. Different roses do have different smells, and some plants bearing the outer appearance of roses, are revealed, upon closer inspection, not to be roses at all.

What is a "stock exchange"?

> *"What news on the Rialto?"*
>
> *"The Merchant of Venice", Act One*

Originally, places like the Rialto were just centres for the exchange of gossip and the concluding of occasional commercial transactions.

In the present study, a "stock exchange" is defined as follows:

A stock exchange is a legal entity, whose management has the authority to

(a) give access to securities traders satisfying specific criteria with respect to experience, integrity and financial standing, and

(b) allow the listing of standard securities satisfying specific criteria regarding type and quality of the issuer, and

(c) keep a record of all activities on the exchange, and make this information available to the general public without delay, and
(d) enforce specific rules and regulations regarding trading practices and information on the current affairs of the issuers, to the extent such information may reasonably be assumed to have an impact on the price of the listed securities.

Thus defined,[15] stock exchanges did not really exist anywhere before the early 19th century, although several European stock exchanges claim to date from the 16th or 17th centuries.[16] Until then they were essentially just meeting places providing some shelter against foul weather, and places where anybody could sell almost anything to anybody on whatever conditions agreed upon between buyer and seller.

Politicians often express the view, and sometimes take steps in the direction, that industrial growth can somehow be enhanced if the access to a stock exchange for potential issuers of bonds or shares could be eased, i.e. if the quality requirements could be relaxed. Sometimes special stock exchanges for small- and medium-sized enterprises (SMEs) have been created as a result of such political wishes, often under the headline of "industrial policy". Politicians also wish that stock exchange listed securities should be safe investments for widows, orphans, and other unprofessional investors. These two objectives are difficult to combine, and efforts to do so have so far not succeeded.

---

[15]Other definitions are, of course possible. A fairly recent definition reads: "Stock exchange: A market where specialized intermediaries buy and sell securities under a common set of rules and regulations through a closed system dedicated to that purpose. Only when all those criteria are met can it be said that a stock exchange has come into existence, and nowhere was that true in the 18th century, including London." R. Michie (1999) *The London Stock exchange. A History* (Oxford University Press) p. 3.

A slightly older German definition reads: "Börse: Die regelmässige Zusammenkunft von Käufern, Verkäufern und Vermittler zum Handeln in Wertpapieren ... die nach Menge und Qualität genau betstimmt sind, an einem bestimmten Ort. Die Börse ist eine ständige Einrichtung mit der Aufgabe, Angebot und Nachfrage marktmässig zusammenzuführen durch die Festsetzung von Preisen (Kursen), die möglichst viele Geschäfte zur Erfüllung bringen." Brockhaus Enzyklopädie, 1967.

The difference between these two definitions is quite striking. Michie's definition stresses the specialization of the activity under a specific set of rules, whereas the German definition stresses the purpose of balancing supply and demand through an equalization of prices, and mentions nothing about rules and regulations.

There is, however, no conflict between these two definitions. They just stress different aspects of the nature of a stock exchange. The definition suggested above tries to capture all of these different aspects.

[16]E.g. Bruges, 1409, Antwerp, 1460, Lyons, 1462, Amsterdam, 1430, etc., cfr. F. Braudel (2002) *The Wheels of Commerce* (Phoenix Press. Originally: "Les jeux de l'Echange", 1979) p. 99.

Politicians, capital suppliers, and market analysts also have an insatiable demand for information. Listed companies everywhere have, therefore, been met with ever increasing demands for all sorts of information regarding anything which might have an impact on the stock market price. This demand for a more or less constant flow of information has led many listed companies to retire from the stock exchange, particularly minor companies which cannot afford the luxury of having special "investor relations departments".

Since providing services, which are paid for, is the objective of modern stock exchanges it is hardly surprising that some of them have gradually been transformed from originally informal meeting places, first into public monopolies (often set up by royal decree), and later into profit-seeking listed companies competing strongly against each other for more listings, trading, new issues, and services. Clearing and custodial services, once the tedious domain of banks or specialized institutions, are now also being offered by some stock exchanges.

1
Sweden-Finland, ca. 1650–1817: Wilderness Replaced by Confusion

"All the world's a stage,
And all the men and women merely players,
They have their exits and their entrances…".

("As you like it", Act II)

1.1 An overview: The changing structures of political and financial power

Between ca. 1640 and 1810, Sweden had its entrance and its exit as a Great Power. In the beginning, Sweden's military adventures brought it the status of a Great Power in the north and the Baltics at Denmark-Norway's expense. The conquests included the southern provinces of today's Sweden, taken from Denmark-Norway (1657–1660), and much of the eastern and southern rims of the Baltic Sea.

However, disastrous battles in today's northern Germany (Fehrbellin, 1675) and Ukraine (Poltava, 1709), two wars against Russia in the 18th century, unsuccessful participation in the Prussian Seven Years War, and another Russian War in 1808–1809 ended Sweden's status as a Great Power. Finland, a Swedish province since the Middle Ages, was lost to Russia in 1809.

In the middle of the political upheavals of the 17th century, Sweden also made its entrance in financial history, when Europe's first note-issuing bank was formed in Stockholm in 1656, 38 years before the foundation of the Bank of England. However, in contrast to some other European countries, the idea of banking did not really catch on, neither in Sweden-Finland nor in Denmark-Norway. It took 80 years from the formation of the first bank in a Nordic country till another bank was founded (Copenhagen, 1736), and from then it took another 37 years until a third Nordic banking institution was born (Diskontkompaniet, Stockholm, 1773). Sveriges Riksbank was the only one of these banks which survived the Napoleonic Wars, so by 1830, Sweden was no closer to having a "capital market" than the case had been 174 years before.

It could be discussed at length, without any conclusion, whether the very limited circulation of money throughout this period made banking unrealistic, or whether the absence of banks inhibited the spreading of a monetary economy.

With only about 1.4 million inhabitants in 1720, and roughly 2.5 million in 1815, plus some 300,000–400,000 in Finland, Sweden-Finland was thinly populated. Stockholm's population remained about 75,000 throughout the 18th century, somewhat less than Copenhagen's 100,000 (in 1800).

1.2   The problems

1.2.1   Expensive wars

The wars referred to above, including four wars against Denmark-Norway, were expensive. The time-honoured method of looting and plundering the occupied territories could pay some of the costs of the mercenaries, but this solved only part of the problem. War-faring had become increasingly capital intensive as the use of more and heavier guns and larger naval vessels accelerated. Guns and other equipment, pensions to retired and wounded Swedish officers and their widows, all had to be paid for from domestic sources.

1.2.2   Capital intensive chartered trading companies

As in other countries, including England, The Netherlands, and Denmark-Norway (cfr. Chapter 2), several chartered trading companies were formed in Sweden to bring back riches from the newly discovered far-away corners of the world, including Generalhandelscompagniet (1626), Afrikanska Kompagniet (1649). Ostindiska Compagniet (1731), the largest and most successful of them, commonly known as "Söderkompaniet", was dissolved 1813. An impression of the size of its operations can be gleaned from the size of its warehouse in Göteborg, which now houses the Göteborg City Museum.

With the exception of "Söderkompaniet", all of these companies failed after relatively few years of operation, mostly because of lack of capital. They were financed in the typical fashion of the 17th century, i.e. vessels were acquired by groups of investors, who financed each expedition separately, and who reaped the profits upon completion of an expedition and the sale of the goods brought home. It was not until 1753 that "Söderkompaniet" was endowed with a "permanent" share capital.[1] By this time a "permanent" share capital had been customary for more than 100 years in both the Dutch and the English East India Companies.

Anyway, not very much is known about the financing and the results of these companies until the mid-18th century. They were shrouded in deep

---

[1]Cfr. T. Frängsmyr (1976/1990) *Ostindiska Kompaniet* (Förlags AB Wiken) p. 30. The supply of a permanent capital had been provided for on a voluntary basis in the second charter of 1746, but was not made compulsory until the third charter of 1766.

secrecy, and upon the completion of each expedition, the books were burnt, at least in the case of "Söderkompaniet" until 1753.

From the accounts of the Riksbank it can, however, be seen that these trading companies were not financed in any significant way from the only bank existing in Sweden. Financing was obtained directly from shareholders, occasionally the king, and from foreign sources.

1.2.3   The fragmented iron industry

The problem with the iron industry was that it was operated by large numbers of independent miners, each with special government-issued permits, but with only the personal savings of each individual miner as capital. In the middle Ages, this was no problem, but as time went by problems intensified. Financing requirements increased not only because of larger production volumes and the seasonal nature of the business, i.e. working capital, but also because of new production techniques involving larger hammers and more power, i.e. investment financing.

Lack of financing was widely felt to be a problem and has been seen as a major reason for a slow development of the Swedish iron and steel industry, cfr. this verdict (SEA's translation): "The small-scale cottage industry nature of the production was without question the greatest weakness of the older Swedish iron manufacturing ... It is evident that ... it developed slowly because of the insufficient capital base of the petty operators."[2] In 1695, a tax roll counted 412 iron works ("bruk") and 327 owners.

1.2.4   The costly Göta Canal

For centuries it had been a great dream to connect Sweden's west coast with Stockholm by a canal. However, each time a plan had been presented, it was rejected because of lack of capital.

Finally, in 1809, the decision was made to go ahead with the Göta Canal. The driving force behind the project was Baltzar von Platen, the son of a Prussian officer, who had joined the Swedish army in 1746. Having studied canal projects at home and abroad for ten years, he was asked by the government to work out a detailed proposal and cost estimate for a Göteborg-Stockholm canal. The result was the formation in 1810 of the Göta Canal Ab under a royal charter, and with v. Platen as its president.

The cost estimate presented by v. Platen did not include all costs. He feared that the full cost estimate would have killed the project. For the same reason he resisted proposals to build a wider and deeper canal with bigger locks, which would have made the project much more useful. Given

---

[2]Boëthius & Kromnow (1947) *Jernkontorets Historia*, I–III (Jernkontoret, Stockholm) bd. I, p. 463.

the government's reaction in 1815 to the escalating costs, v. Platen's fears appear quite realistic.[3]

Indeed, opinions differed substantially over the merits of this canal. It was argued loudly that it would absorb a disproportionate amount of scarce capital to the detriment of other and probably more profitable or useful purposes.[4]

The canal took 22 years to be completed. The costs ended up at Rd 10.4 million against the original estimate of only 1.5 million (silver value, i.e. fixed prices). Nearly one-third of this amount was provided by private shareholders, and most of the rest by government grants. About 10 per cent was debt, which was written off gradually between 1817 and 1842.[5]

The project was planned as a private enterprise, and it soon had a capital of a dimension so far never before seen in Sweden ("... ett kapital av för vort land förut okända dimensioner"),[6] but its capital requirements proved too big for the non-existent Swedish capital market.

1.2.5   The confusing currency system, and limited monetary economy

Although money circulation was very limited outside the major coastal towns in the 17th and 18th centuries, coins did circulate in a fairly confusing currency "system" developed, and developing, over time.

Between the time of Gustav Wasa (1523–1560) and the currency reform of 1776, the "system" was essentially based on the "riksdaler species" (rd) containing approximately 25 grams of fine silver (not much different from other European main coins at that time). This coin did, however not circulate except in cross-border transactions. Gold ducats were also occasionally used in foreign transactions, worth about two rd. In daily domestic transactions, the "daler silver mint" was used (if money was used at all) with a silver content, which declined steadily over time. In the mid-17th century, it would take approximately 1½ daler silver mint (dsm) to buy one rd, but in 1776, when the dsm was abolished, one rd would cost about three dsm. The most widely used coin was the "daler copper mint" (dcm), originally with an official value of half the dsm, but between 1665 and 1776 one-third of the dsm (official value). By 1803, it had dropped to 1/18 rd.[7]

---

[3]S. Bring (1922) *Göta Kanals Historia*, I–II (Uppsala) bd. I, pp. 94–8.
[4]S. Bring (1922) *Göta Kanals Historia*, I–II (Uppsala) bd. I, pp. 126–8.
[5]S. Bring (1922) *Göta Kanals Historia*, bd. I, p. 126 and Bilaga.
[6]S. Brisman (1924) *Sveriges Affärsbanker*, I–II (Svenska Bankföreningen, Stockholm) bd. I, p. 37.
[7]The description of the currency system is based on S. Brisman (the Riksbank's official chronicler) *Sveriges Riksbank 1668–1918*, bd. 1–5 (Stockholm, 1918–1931) bd. 1, pp. 33–7, and bd. 5, p. 141; bd. 2, p. 376; bd. 5, pp. 141–5.

The official exchange rates between the rd, the dsm, and the dcm were fixed from time to time by royal decrees, the "Mynt Placat", with the penalty of death for violations. There is, however, no evidence that the death penalty was ever applied. Market exchange rates often differed strongly from the official rates.

The copper mints, usually produced as mint plates with several mints on them, were quite impractical to use. One rd in copper mint weighed 2.7 kilos. The "system" was in dire need of improvement.

1.3   Responses and actions

1.3.1   Bringing in foreigners, sale of crown land, and copper mining

The foreigners

It is difficult to over-estimate the importance of foreigners in the economic and financial development of Sweden in the 17th and 18th centuries. In the words of E. Heckscher, the distinguished Swedish economist and historian (SEA's translation): "... the enormous foreign recruitment to the Swedish nobility during the "Great Power Period" consisted in very important cases precisely of foreign lenders to the Crown ... Presumably, this was a rather important assistance to enable the country to shoulder the heavy burdens of war."[8] A few examples will illustrate the point:

It was no coincidence that Willem Usselinx, the Dutchman who took the initiative to form the above-mentioned Generalhandelskompagnie, had settled in Göteborg in 1624. Göteborg was a very new town (official "birthday" 1621), and had attracted numerous Dutchmen from their war-torn home country. In fact, Göteborg was almost a Dutch colony. The first City Council consisted of seven Swedes, one Scotsman, and ten Dutchmen.[9]

Louis de Geer (1587–1652) was another particularly noteworthy Dutchman. He had made a fortune for himself from trading in all kinds of armoury, and from arranging loans to those who would buy it from him. In the 1620s he was probably the largest supplier of hardware to the Swedish army and a big lender to the Swedish king. In 1627 he obtained Swedish citizenship, and the king, unable to repay the loans, granted him a monopoly on arms deliveries, and large tracts of land and iron mines, including Finspång, a well-known cannon foundry, and Åkers Styckebruk, another iron foundry known for cannon production since 1584 (and still existing). In 1641 de Geer was elevated to the Swedish nobility.

The brothers Jacob (1623–1690) and Abraham (1625–1678) Momma (ennobled Momma-Reenstierna) originating from the Netherlands, became large

---

[8]E. Heckscher (1949) *Sveriges Ekonomiska Historia från Gustav Vasa* (Stockholm) p. 276.
[9]L. Magnusson (2002) *Sveriges Ekonomiska Historia* (Prisma, 3. ed. Stockholm) p. 142.

owners of land and mines. They were shipbuilders, shipowners, and textile manufacturers, and, of course, lenders to the Crown.

An investigation[10] into the major Stockholm merchant houses of the 18th century found that at least 15 out of the 26 houses investigated had been founded by merchants originating from the Netherlands, Germany, England, or Scotland. The names included the Grill family, the Jennings, Robert Finlay, Jean Henri Lefebure, Thomas Tottie, Schön, Falck, etc.

Sale of Crown land

Crown land was a source of revenue in several ways. It produced rent as long as the Crown owned it, and it produced income when the Crown sold it, which the Crown did on a large scale in the mid-17th century.

Copper mining

The copper mine at Falun, commonly known as "Stora Kopperberg" was a major source of Crown income since the Middle Ages, and particularly in the 17th century. The mining and smelting techniques had been learnt from immigrated German miners.[11]

The mine was operated as a sort of co-operative, but was in 1347 made subject to strict regulations and certain privileges.[12] The Crown gave up its direct ownership in the early 17th century, but continued to levy large duties on the miners.

When the copper production at Falun peaked in the latter half of the 17th century with an annual production of about 2,000 tons, it accounted for about one-half or two-thirds of all copper mined in Europe.[13]

---

[10]K. Samuelsson (1951) *De Stora Köpmanshusen i Stockholm 1730–1815* (Doctoral thesis, Ekonomisk-Historiska Insitutet i Stockholm) pp. 24–45.

[11]Cfr. S. Kristiansson (1997) *Strömningar till och från Stora Kopparberget. En studie i påverkansfaktorer* (Stora) pp. 58 and 66.

[12]The earliest known document relating to the Stora Kopperberg dates from 1288, and describes a transaction whereby the bishopric of Västerås exchanged 1/8 of the mine for certain other properties. This document, (original kept in the National Archives with a copy on display at the Falun Museum) is evidence of a the system of part-ownership and has tempted some observers over time to proclaim Stora Kopperberget the world's oldest joint stock company. It did not, however, have any other resemblance than co-ownership to a joint stock company. There is no evidence of limited liability or central management, even if for purely practical reasons the miners had to practice a certain co-operation.

[13]According to *Svensk Uppslagsbok*, Malmö, 1947–55, it was two thirds. In his *Strömningar till och från Stora Kopperberget*, 1997, S. Kristiansson quotes Erik Odhelius, the 17th-century mining scientist, who concluded around 1690 that the Swedish copper production was as large as the combined production in the rest of Europe (p. 82), but in the 1690s the Falun production was already past its peak.

The copper exports were mainly paid for with bills of exchange issued by Amsterdam merchant-bankers, and such bills would be used to make payments nearly all over Europe. In the words of E. Heckhsher (SEA's translation): "In this way, copper was the basis for the continuous bills of exchange operations, or kite-flying ("växelrytterier"), which were centred in Amsterdam but which stretched all over central Europe from Riga to Hamburg and Lübeck, and further to Frankfurt a.m. and Nürnberg. To a large extent, this was the way the requirements of the Swedish armies were met in the foreign fields ... So, the significance of copper for covering the constant needs of the Great Power of Sweden for foreign payments was evident."[14]

By the early 19th century, the mine at Falun had been depleted. It continued as mainly a forest industry company, exploiting its vast forests in the Falun area. In 1888, it was reorganized into a joint stock company, and in the late 20th century it discarded the "Kopperberg" from its name, calling itself just "Stora". In 2000, it merged with Enso Gutzeit, the large Finnish forest industry group, which then became Stora Enso, one of the world's largest paper producers.

1.3.2   The role of the merchants and the iron industry

A large part of the business of the big Stockholm and Göteborg merchant houses was tightly interwoven with the iron industry. The respective roles of the merchants and the iron manufacturers were closely inter-connected.

Basically, the iron manufacturers ("brukspatronerna" or "bruksägarna") had fairly stable relationships with particular merchants, to whom they delivered their contractually pre-agreed volumes of (mostly) iron rods during the summer and autumn period. The merchants would usually pay for these deliveries in advance, once a year, for the following year's deliveries. The advances were usually secured with pledges over the future deliveries. From around 1740 onwards, the iron trade was essentially concentrated on about 30–40 merchants in Stockholm and Göteborg, who were supplied by 300–400 iron works, nearly all located in mid-Sweden ("Bergslagen").

In this way one of the most important functions of the merchants was to act as a sort of banker to the mine owners.[15] The iron industry needed the credits, and there were few other sources of credit in the amounts and duration required by the manufacturers.

The system had the consequence that most of the iron works owners became highly dependent on their respective merchants. They depended on the merchants both for the sale of their production, and for prepayments for that production. They were nearly always in debt to the merchant houses. The

---

[14]E. Heckscher "Sveriges Ekonomiska Historia från Gustav Vasa", Stockholm, 1949, p. 275.

[15]"... men allra mest köpmannens funktion som en sorts bankförbindelse för bruk och bruksägare". K.-G. Hildebrand (1987) *Svenskt Järn. Sexton- och sjuttonhundratal Exportindustri före industrialismen* (Jernkontorets Berghistoriska Skriftserie 20) p. 149.

debts were supposed to be repaid by the deliveries, but in many cases deliveries fell short of contractual obligations, and the debts mounted. In many cases the merchants seized the mines and production facilities in settlement of the debts. Thus, a number of the biggest merchant houses also became "brukspatroner". In the words of K.-G. Hildebrand, the iron industry historian (SEA's translation): "Among those who acquired iron works in the 1700s, the large Stockholm and Göteborg merchants had a particularly prominent position ... the granting of credits to the owners was not rarely the natural way to a – planned or unplanned – acquisition; there were always some owners of iron works who had problems with their business and could not pay."[16]

A number of Stockholm and Göteborg Shylocks greatly enhanced their fortunes this way.

The merchants mainly refinanced themselves through merchant-bankers in Amsterdam, or the Amsterdam Wisselbank, until the second half of the 18th century, when this business was mostly taken over by London houses.

1.3.3 Palmstruch's Bank, or Stockholm's Banco: The first bank in the Nordics, 1656–1667

Hans Wittmacker, born 1611 in Riga by Dutch parents, had travelled widely and knew the Amsterdam Wisselbank and the Hamburger Bank quite well, when he settled in Stockholm in 1647.

He was soon appointed to a high-ranking position in the Kommercekollegie ("Ministry of Commerce and Economic Affairs"). In 1651, he was ennobled under the name of Johan Palmstruch.

One of Palmstruch's ideas was to improve Sweden's messy currency and payment "system" through the creation of a bank, just as this had been the original idea behind the Amsterdam Wisselbank (cfr. the Introduction).

Thus, in 1652, Palmstruch addressed a proposal to the government in which he argued that the difficulties could be overcome "... mit ... einrichtung einer Wechsel Bancq, umb nach der Venetianer, Amsterdamer, Hamburger etc. gebrauch undt weise."[17] Palmstruch had fully understood that the bank would need only little cash, since any money taken out by bakers or grocers would return as new deposits within a few weeks: "... Dass wenige Kupfergeld, so etwan dieser oder jener zur teglichen ausgabe zu seiner Hauss- oder Hoffhaltunge auss der banck möchte nehmen, ... wurde doch, wo nicht in der ersten, doch gewiss in der 2. 3 oder 4:ten woche, beij Beckern, Hökern etc. eingesamblet, beij summen wiederumb in die Banco kommen ...."[18]

---

[16]K.-G. Hildebrand (1987) *Svenskt Järn. Sexton- och sjuttanhundratal Exportindustri före industrialismen* (Jernkontorets Berghisatoriska Skriftserie 20) p. 142. Also see this source, pp. 131–46, for a description of the ownership structure of the iron works.
[17]Quoted from Palmstruch's proposal, reprinted in Brisman (1918) *Sveriges Riksbank 1668–1918*, bd. I–V (Stockholm 1918–1931), bd. I, bilag II, pp. 19–21.
[18]As footnote 17.

Otherwise, the money would stay in the bank, and payments would be made through account-to-account transfers like in Venice, Amsterdam, and Hamburg.

It will be noticed that facilitating access to credit for commerce and industry was not a motive for the proposed bank. Instead, easing of payments and savings on the use of copper were the driving forces.

In 1656 Palmstruch and his associates received two charters for 30 years to operate two banks – an exchange/deposit bank and a lending bank, i.e. just like in Amsterdam and Hamburg.[19] Since the two charters were issued simultaneously, in favour of identical persons, they will be described together. Having stated the main purpose of the bank(s) in the preamble of the charters – to support the value of the copper mint – and having cited the Amsterdam and Hamburg banks as examples,

(SEA's translation: "Our own domestic copper mint should hereby be brought up to its correct and proper value, and ... for this purpose our Commissioner, our beloved, noble and well borne Johan Palmstruch has most humbly offered and tendered ... to establish and operate in our realm and provinces certain exchange banks like in other cities, notably according to the Amsterdam and Hamburg ways and examples."),[20] the charters go on to the specifics.

The main conditions of the charters were as follows:

1. The charters created a 30 years monopoly for Palmstruch and his associates. The two banks were to be operated separately.

    Since the charters were given to identical groups of people, the division into two banks was purely fictional. The bank(s) soon became known as "Stockholms Banco".

    Like in Amsterdam and Hamburg, the charters did not foresee any paid-in capital for either of the banks.

2. The exchange bank should work like the Amsterdam Wisselbank, i.e. overdrafts were forbidden (penalty 3 per cent, like in Amsterdam). Other lendings were, in principle, allowed (primarily intended for the loan bank) but only against full collateral. Deposits would be received without interest. There would be fees for withdrawals and for account-to-account transfers (like in Amsterdam).

3. Unlike Amsterdam, there was no requirement that bills exceeding a certain amount had to be settled over accounts in the exchange bank, and consequently there were few merchant account holders. However, taxes and other payables to the Crown were to be paid into the exchange bank.

---

[19]The full text of both charters have been reprinted in Brisman (1918) *Sveriges Riksbank 1668–1918*, bd. 1–5 (Stockholm, 1918–1931), bd. I, bilag IV.

[20]The Palmstruch Exchange Bank Charter, *Sveriges Riksbank 1668–1918*, bd. I, bilag IV, p. 26.

4. The loan bank could receive deposits, including deposits from the exchange bank, and pay interest. Collateral for loans could, in principle, consist of almost anything, except quickly perishable goods.
5. Outside the charters it was decided that the profits were to be split with 50 per cent to the Crown, 25 per cent to the City of Stockholm, 12.5 per cent to Palmstruch, and 12.5 per cent to his associates (who apparently contributed with nothing but their names). It was, essentially, a government institution, and the government appointed a "super inspector" (överinspector) to supervise the operation.

The bank opened for business in July, 1657. The volume of deposits never reached any significant volume. By 1660 they peaked at the modest level of some 400,000 rd, according to a letter from Palmstruch. Precise figures do not exist since no balance sheet was drawn up until 1664, and very little accounting material has survived.[21]

Stockholms Banco had a short life. Luck – an indispensable ingredient in all banking business – ran out in the shape of the 1660 Mynt Placat (the "currency decree", cfr. 1.2.5 above). The 1660 Mynt Placat stipulated an exchange rate between copper mints and silver-based mints, which had the effect that depositors withdrew all their copper mint deposits from the bank in order to melt them down. Through absolutely no fault of the bank's management it ran into an acute liquidity crisis.

Under these dire circumstances Palmstruch came up with an idea which has made his name immortal in the history of money, banking, and finance.

When his bank could not repay its depositors with metal, he gave them a piece of paper, "kreditivsedlar" ("credit notes"), representing cash. The bank note had been born, in the year of the Lord, 1661.[22]

What made these pieces of paper different from the receipts or "certificates of deposit" which had previously been circulating as means of payment elsewhere, including Venice, Amsterdam, and London, was that they were issued in round amounts without necessarily representing a claim against any specific deposit. Palmstruch soon found that he could lend virtually unlimited amounts funded by these instruments, the issue of which was limited only by the willingness of the receivers to accept them as money. The government was the largest borrower and thus the largest user of the "kreditivsedlar".

The temptation to issue them in excessive volumes soon became irresistible. When the market became flooded with paper money, the holders of this paper began to ask to have it cashed. In 1664 the game was over.

---

[21]Brisman (1918) *Sveriges Riksbank 1668–1918*, bd. I, pp. 43–4.
[22]"There can hardly be any doubt that 'kreditivsedlarna' are to be regarded as the world's first fully developed monetary notes issued by a bank." (SEA's translation) from Brisman (1918) *Sveriges Riksbank 1668–1918*, bd. I, p. 61.

An inquiry was arranged (1667), and Palmstruch was found guilty of fraud and sentenced to prison and execution if he could not redeem the losses (approximately 140,000 dsm) which, of course, he could not. He had not used the project to enrich himself. After four years in prison he was pardoned. A few months after his release, he died (1671).

Palmstruch's trial was slightly reminiscent of that of Shylock vs. Antonio, as well as the Castello case in Barcelona.[23] There was less interest in real justice than in satisfying public opinion. Later and more sober views on Palmstruch's offence are that he was guilty only of lack of control, careless accounting (normal in those days), and some miscalculations of interest and exchange rates. The holders of the bank notes were redeemed by the government, like in most later bank rescues.[24]

1.3.4   Sveriges Rijksens Ständers Bank (1668–),[25] and Riksgäldskontoret

The unfortunate fate suffered by Stockholms Banco did not blind the government to the advantages of having an institution where citizens could make deposits and which could make money transfers in a simpler way than carrying heavy loads of coins around. If lending could also be done in a safe manner, so much the better, but this was seen as a separate issue.

So, in 1668 King Karl XI (1660–1697) issued a Royal Decree,[26] in which he declared that since he had always appreciated the bank as highly useful to himself, the whole Realm, and its citizens (in that order), he would now ask the Riksdag, i.e. the Assembly of the Representatives of the Estates, to organize a Bank on the conditions briefly outlined below. Although amended a couple of times, it was not fundamentally changed during the next 198 years.

---

[23]In response to the many bank failures in the 14th century, the Catalan government had decided to behead bankowners, who could not satisfy demands for cash withdrawals. This was actually practiced, so in 1360 Fransech Castello was beheaded in front of his bank, cfr. P. Spufford (2002) *Power and Profit* (Thames & Hudson) p. 40, and A.P. Usher (1943) *The Early History of Banking in Mediterranean Europe* (Cambridge, Mass.) pp. 239–42.

[24]For a description and evaluation of the trial, see Brisman (1918) *Sveriges Riksbank 1668–1918*, bd. I, pp. 75–80.

[25]The archives of Sveriges Riksbank have been remarkably well preserved and formed the basis for the first history of the Bank, by F. Silverstolpe ("Berättelse om Banco-Wärket i Sverige") in the years 1783–1802 in seven handwritten folio volumes totalling 7,842 pages, plus 34 quarter volumes of copied documents, and a special history of Palmstruch's Bank.

[26]The royal decree ("Kongl. May:tz Nådige Fösäkring gifwen Rijksens Ständer, på några wilkor och Fördelar til Banckens Bästa", September 17, 1668), a document which outlines in 11 relatively short articles the main points for the (renewed) bank, reprinted in Brisman (1918) *Sveriges Riksbank 1668–1918*, bd. I–V. bd. 1, bilag VII, pp. 78–81.

The formal status of the Riksbank

In contrast to Stockholms Banco, no charter was given to any individual person or group of individuals. The Bank was to be placed directly under the control of the Assembly of the Estates (the nobility, the burghers, the clergy, and the farmers).[27] There is no doubt that it was a public sector institution. The Estates guaranteed the deposits (as the City of Amsterdam guaranteed the deposits in the Wisselbank), but it was not under government control, and there was no paid in capital.

The reason why the Bank was placed under the control of the Estates rather than the Crown/government was that the government had, through its excessive borrowings from Stockholms Banco, been at least partly responsible for its failure. It was recognized that it was not healthy to let a government have too easy access to money. The result was that the Riksbank and the government continuously squabbled over loan requests, but until 1741 (cfr. below) the Bank successfully resisted efforts by the government to force it to undertake unlimited inflationary war financing based on paper money.

Since it was placed under the control of the Estates ("ständerna") it was named " Sveriges Rijksens Ständers Bank", referred to here as the "Riksbank".

In contrast to Stockholms Banco, there was never any direct mention that it should have a monopoly. It is unclear if applications from anybody to set up a rival bank would have been approved (probably not), and to form a bank without royal approval was, of course, unthinkable.

The Riksbank took over the remaining assets and liabilities of the defunct Stockholms Banco, but since it was organized under a new Charter, and under a new form of "ownership" and supervision, there is little doubt that the Riksbank should be regarded as a new bank rather than a reorganization of its predecessor.

Although formally two separate banks – the Exchange Bank and the Loan Bank, just like the Amsterdam and Hamburg banks, and just like the Stockholms Banco – with separate managements and accounts – there was never any real doubt that they were regarded both then and later as essentially one bank. Several phrases in both the Charter and the much more detailed "Ständers Förordning" refer to "banco werket", i.e. the "banking operation", in the singular, not plural. Only in a few exceptional situations did the formal division into two separate banks have any practical consequences.

Thus, the 11-article Royal Charter covers both banks, but mentions the Loan Bank in only three of these articles, and only on minor points. The Exchange Bank appears to have been considered the more important of the two halves.

---

[27]Originally, the Fourth Estate, the farmers, did not want to take any responsibility for the Bank, or be part of the guarantee issued by the Estates in favour the depositors. They did not join the party until late in the 18th century.

The operation of the Riksbank

Its capital consisted of accumulated undistributed profits. Accounting for doubtful loans ("Conto di Memoria") started in 1699 with a minor amount kept unchanged until 1707 when a small increase was made. No major increase was made until 1731.

All crown revenues in the shape of customs, duties, excise, and rent were to be paid into government accounts in the Bank (slightly expanded compared to Stockholms Banco). In contrast to the Amsterdam Wisselbank there was, however, no requirement that bills exceeding a certain minimum amount had to be settled over accounts with the Bank. Therefore, nobody felt any strong urge to keep accounts with the Bank.

Finally, the Bank would operate the Mint on behalf of the Crown, clearly an inspiration from Amsterdam.

With 76 articles, the Bank Regulation[28] issued by the Estates only five days after the above mentioned Royal Decree was considerably more detailed. The main points can be summarized as follows:

1. Like in Amsterdam, Hamburg, and the Stockholms Banco, this Exchange Bank was explicitly forbidden to undertake any lending whatsoever (Art. VIII, SEA's translation): "Under no pretext whatsoever can any part of the monies and the means of the Exchange Bank be touched or attacked by the Commissioners, or be used or employed in commerce or trade, but always and un-removed remain on deposit in that place, so that the owner can command and withdraw it according to his own good will."

   Lending in the shape of overdrafts was just as forbidden as for Amsterdam Wisselbank, the Hamburger Bank, and Stockholms Banco, and punished in identical way: "Then som mehra assignerar än han hafwer i avance, skal til straff erläggia 3 pro Cento af alt thet övriga han assignerat hafwer..." (Art. XXX). Even the level of the penalty was copied from Amsterdam.

   Clearly, it had to have a profile distinguishing it from the Stockholms Banco, although bad loans were not the reason for the demise of that bank.

   Real life, of course, turned out rather differently. Most of the deposits were lent to the Loan Bank, thereby helping it to fund its normal commercial lending business. This was probably the plan from the beginning, but like in Amsterdam, the truth had to be kept secret from the public in order to gain the confidence of depositors.

2. The bank's accounts were to be kept in the four different currencies/mints, which were current in Sweden at the time: ducats, riksdaler species (rd), daler silver mint (dsm), and daler copper mint (dkm), cfr. 1.2.5 above.[29]

---

[28]Sweriges Rijkes Ständers Beslut och Förordning i Stockholm, Dat. Den 22 September Åhr 1668, reprinted in Brisman (1918) *Sveriges Riksbank 1668–1918*, bd. I, pp. 82–103.

[29]Amounts mentioned in this chapter are mostly in dsm, as calculated and presented in Brisman (1918) *Sveriges Riksbank 1668–1918*, until 1776, when the dsm was abolished. After 1776, amounts are in rd.

The strange thing is that in spite of the explicit intention to copy the Amsterdam Wisselbank, one of the most fundamental functions of that bank was not copied. The background for the establishment of the Wisselbank was the perplexing number of different currencies circulating in the Netherlands at the time, and deposits in the Wisselbank were essentially all changed into a unit of account (Florin banco) when made. So, every single deposit and withdrawal automatically involved an exchange of currencies. In Stockholm that was not the case. In 1644 a decree had been issued that all contracts were to be fulfilled in the currency in which they had originally been made, and this also applied to the Riksbank. Thus, deposits made in dkm could only be withdrawn in dkm, and loans made in dsm had to be repaid in that currency. Few exchange transactions appear ever to have taken place in the Exchange Bank, and it had to maintain and watch its liquidity in all of the above-mentioned four different currencies, as in Palmstruch's bank. It was an "Exchange Bank" in name only.

3. In the Exchange Bank, no interest was paid on deposits, like in Amsterdam.
4. According to Art. XXXXIV (SEA's translation) "... there is no better way to avoid the great misuse and usury ... being practiced than to have a well organized lending bank, and this would also help making use of all the capital which would otherwise lay around fruitlessly but which could, with good collateral, be employed by such a bank with royal permission, and so it was found necessary to continue the business of the Loan Bank."

   The tone of this text suggests that the existence of a loan bank is only accepted with some reluctance, and only to avoid the worse evil of widespread usury.
5. The lending business was regulated by several articles, the first of which (Art. L) looks rather strange by modern standards. It states that the commissioners should not look at the personal qualities or conditions of the borrowers ("... vthi sielfwe vthläningarne intet Personerne eller någon theras wilkår anse ..." but they should accommodate each and every one so long that the means of the Bank could afford and allow it ("... men hvar och en thermedh accomodera, så wijda Bankens medel thet kunna tåle och admittera ...").

   All loans had to be fully secured by collateral which could consist of nearly anything except perishable goods (... "ofördärfweligt" ...). The allowance for chattel mortgages was, however, not much used, much to the regret of the iron manufacturers.

   Mortgages turned out to become by far the most important sort of collateral, but also a source of many problems and heavy losses. It often turned out that identical properties had been mortgaged to several different lenders, or they had been sold, burnt or fallen into general decay or disrepair. Therefore, it was also stipulated that mortgage loans should be guaranteed by a third person. This explains why these loans were never popular with anybody. In any case, prospective mortgage borrowers found it increasingly difficult to find willing guarantors.

Most of the borrowers were members of the nobility, civil servants and minor tradesmen. Very few of the larger merchant houses or the iron manufacturers ("brukspatroner") were found among the Loan Bank's clientele. The iron manufacturers ("brukspatronerna") found it almost impossible to borrow from the Bank because it was extremely reluctant to accept iron rods or the iron works ("bruk") as collateral.

6. Interest was initially fixed at 8 per cent for loans exceeding 400 rd copper, but for smaller loans it could be up to 10 5/32 per cent. However, it was regarded as desirable that the rate could later be reduced to 6 per cent ("... dock skulle Rijksens Ständer giärna see, at wärket thet första möijeligit wore, kunde således menageres thet interesset til 6 pro Cento kan blifwa modererat ...") with a proportionate reduction of the other rates.

It soon turned out to become a problem for the Riksbanks's liquidity management that it was not free to set interest rates according to supply and demand. Whenever market rates differed too much from the rates stipulated for the Riksbank, it was either flooded with deposits or drained.

The tradition for considering interest rates a politically sensitive issue is as old as lending itself, and has not yet abated, although interest rates are, of course, prices just like all other prices.

7. It appears particularly noteworthy that for this Bank, which claims to be the oldest central bank or note-issuing bank in the world, it was strictly forbidden to issue any sort of paper which could be used as money, cfr. Art. LXXI (SEA's translation): "Since a large misuse and swindle has occurred through credit notes, no such notes or any other notes which could look like them may hereafter be used by this bank ('wärk') ... but are totally abolished and forbidden."[30]

Reality turned out somewhat differently. Both the Exchange Bank and the Loan Bank issued various certificates (three different types) mainly intended for use in their administration and internal control in connection with the making of deposits.[31] These certificates, or "notes", got into the hands of depositors – mainly as "certificates of deposit" – and then started circulating as means of payment. The circulating volume of these forms reached an amount of roughly half the deposit volume about 1708.

In 1726, the government instructed all public offices to accept the notes issued by the Riksbank as settlement of payables, taxes, duties, etc, thereby making the notes legal tender.

8. Like elsewhere in Europe, including the Amsterdam Wisselbank, the financial status of the bank was considered a state secret revealed only to Secrete

---

[30]"Såsom igenom Creditiff Zedlar för thetta ett stort missbruk och oreda är förelupen; altså skola inga sådane Zedlar eller andra, som ther til kunna hafwa lijknelse ... här effter i thetta wärket brukas, men aldeles wara afskaffade och förbudne".
[31]For a brief description of the nature of these forms, see Brisman (1918) *Sveriges Riksbank 1668–1918*, bd. I, pp. 132–7.

Uttskottet (the "Secret Committee" of the Assembly of the Estates), which dealt with confidential matters of state.

Table 1.1 shows how the Riksbank developed until 1817:

Table 1.1   The Riksbank, Main Balance Sheet Figures, 1670–1817, Selected Years (1670–1776: '000 dsm. 1776–1803: '000 rd.)

	Deposits			Equity	Loans	
	Loan Bank	Exchange Bank	Total		Crown	Total
1670	210	165	375		21	236
1700	3,728	864	4,593		156	3,881
1709	8,659	421	9,080		5,967	9,708
1720	6,890	1,276	8,166	1,443	6,842	8,689
1730	5,735	3,124	8,878	3,281	7,185	8,727
1736	5,281	2,559	7,840	2,476	6,524	10,674
1740	4,535	10,615	15,150	3,534	9,422	10,600
1750	5,448	14,188	19,636	10,197	15,481	25,798
1762	9,549	49,582	59,131	23,219	42,970	79,226
1776	5,782	50,019	55,801	42,945	49,861	76,812
1776	1,251	8,358	8,734	9,746	8,050	12,656
1803	5,345	3,101	8,486	3,798	1,865	11,805
1817	1,027	24,526	25,553	6,703	8,763	26,930

Source: S. Brisman (1918) *Sveriges Riksbank 1668–1918* (Stockholm, 1918–1931, Bd. I–V) bd. I &II (bilag), and bd. V (bilag).

Note: In 1776, the dsm was abolished and replaced by the rd at approximately 6.2 times the value of the dsm. Therefore, the 1776 figures are shown in both currencies.

Consolidated figures for the two "halves" were not produced before 1743. In the source, loans refer to the Loan Bank, and equity is shown as common for both halves. The equity has been calculated by K.G. Simonsen, an employee of the Riksbank's Statistical Department in the early 20th century, as accumulated profits, cfr. *Sveriges Riksbank*, bd. V, Bilag, pp. 2–33. The figures are not a consolidated balance sheet in a book-keeping sense.

"Deposits" include notes. After 1736 notes make up the major part of the deposit amounts shown.

Table 1.1 shows that the Riksbank's development between 1668 and 1817 fell in five periods of alternating expansion and stagnation, or even contraction.

1668–1709: Expansion

By 1700, the number of deposit accounts had reached nearly 3,000, about the same as in the Amsterdam Wisselbank and twice the number in the Hamburger Bank, which did not accept deposits from foreigners, and total deposits in the Riksbank were about 46 per cent of the amounts deposited with the Wisselbank.[32] This would have been impressive if it had not been for the large tax-collection accounts. Most accounts were quite small. Assuming one account per account holder, it appears that about 5 per cent of Stockholm's inhabitants had an account with the Riksbank around 1700, which was roughly the same ratio as in Venice and Bruges 300 years earlier, where 10–11 per cent of the grown up male population is estimated to have had a bank account.[33]

1709–1736: Stagnation and decline

The decline was initially caused by the news of the disastrous defeat at Poltava, which resulted in a classic run on the Bank. In the subsequent years, the stagnation resulted from the differences between the interest rates it was allowed to use, and the "market rates". By 1730, the number of borrowers had dropped to 90.

1738–1762: Renewed expansion

Sweden's Russian wars in the 1740s and 1750s were, to a large extent, financed by borrowings from the Riksbank. This sparked a flooding of the country with paper money and debasement of the silver mint (dsm), culminating in the suspension of convertibility of notes into metal and an end to all lending by the Bank in 1762.

1762–1803: Stagnation

The Riksbank in "sleeping mode", preoccupied with the management of its portfolio of mortgage loans, government loans, and the withdrawings of its excessive note circulation.

The 1776 currency reform replaced the dsm with the riksdaler species (rd) as the currency standard, and reintroduced convertibility, financed by two large loans taken up by the Riksbank in Genoa and Amsterdam, but it failed to make the Riksbank resume its lending activities.

In 1789, the government responded by recreating the Riksgäldskontor ("Government Debt Office"), an idea first used in the 1720s to sort out the government debts from the Great Northern War. The Riksgäldskontor now emerged as an important lender to the government, financed by note-issues ("riksgäldssedlar"), which flooded the country during the next 20–30 years.

1803: Revival

When also the riksgäldssedlar had become practically worthless, the Riksbank was revived and instructed to mop up the riksgäldssedlar and replace them with its own notes.

---

[32]Cfr. E. Heckscher (1964) *The Bank of Sweden in its Connections with the Bank of Amsterdam* in v. Dillen (ed.) *History of the Principal Public Banks* (F. Cass & Co. Ltd) p. 173.
[33]Cfr. P. Spufford (2002) *Power and Profit* (Thames & Hudson) p. 40.

This reactivation was also intended to provide funding for the discount houses (cfr. 1.3.7 below), which, after 1810, mainly meant indirect financing of the construction of the Göta Kanal (cfr. 1.2 above and 1.3.7 below).

Table 1.2 shows the composition of the riksbank's non-government loan portfolio 1743–1810:

Table 1.2   Composition of Riksbanken's Non-government Loans, 1743–1810

1743–1776: '000 dsm *1776–1810: '000 rd,* *Annual averages*	*Total non-government loans (NGL)*	*Of which secured by mortgages*	*Mortgage loans in % of NGL*	*Loans to discount houses*	*Discount house loans in % of NGL*
1743–1745	3,223	1,944	60.2		
1754–1756	21,150	16,283	76.9		
1764–1766	30,991	25,914	83.7		
1775–1776	27,770	24,289	87.5		
1776	5,189	4,046	80.0	426	8.2
1785–1787	5,581	3,366	61.6	400	7.2
1796–1798	3,743	2,601	70.1	456	11.8
1803–1805	8,511	3,179	38.1	4,217	48.8
1808–1810	12,658	2,958	23.4	6,270	53.2

Source: Brisman (1918–1931) *Sveriges Riksbank 1668–1918*, bd. V, Bilag (K.G. Simonsson).

During the first 140 years of its existence Sveriges Riksbank had allocated, willingly or otherwise, some 70–80 per cent of its lending to the Crown and other government agencies, and most of the remaining 20–30 per cent to mortgage loans. Some of this loan volume may have been for business purposes, but otherwise the conclusion is that only some 5–10 per cent of the Bank's lending was done against chattel mortgages, which had originally been seen as a primary objective for the Bank, cfr. the Royal Charter and the Bank Regulation issued by the Estates. This does not necessarily mean that the Bank's business loans were totally insignificant. A few merchant houses did obtain quite large loans from time to time. In the final quarter of the 18th century, 7–10 of the large Stockholm merchant houses were the beneficiaries of some 40–50 per cent of the Bank's non-government, non-mortgage and non-discount house loans,[34] but this was still only about 5 per cent of the Riksbank's total loan volume. This, of course, also means that for the other hundreds of larger or smaller businesses the Bank had no significance as a source of finance. It is apparently unclear how much these bank loans accounted for in the total financing raised by these 7–10 iron exporters.

---

[34]Cfr. K. Samuelsson (1951) *De Stora Köpmanshusen i Stockholm 1730–1815* (Ekonomisk-Historiska Instituttet i Stockholm) pp. 174–6.

The world's oldest central bank?

Sveriges Rijksens Ständers Bank has traditionally been called the world's oldest existing central bank, or the world's oldest existing note issuing bank.[35] Such claims depend on the definition of both "central banks" and "bank notes".

The forms initially issued to its depositors were not intended as bank notes, since this was forbidden by its Charter. The Bank of England started issuing notes several years before the Riksbank's notes were officially declared legal tender in 1726.

The concept of a "central bank" is of much more recent origins, and the criteria for being a "central bank" are not inextricably connected with neither state ownership nor note issuing. Since about the time of WWI, "central banks" can broadly be defined as note-issuing banks, which do not compete with private sector banks for commercial business of any sort. Sveriges Riksbank was a commercial lending bank for most of the 19th century, and retained mortgage lending until 1913, and competed for private deposits until the 1880s (cfr. Chapter 6). The Bank of England (the issuing department), the German Reichsbank, and a few others had become almost central banks several years earlier.

What can truthfully be said is that Sveriges Riksbank is the oldest existing one of those banks, which, during the late 19th and early 20th centuries, gradually developed into "central banks".

The irony is that the Riksbank was originally planned as a commercial bank, for the purpose of collecting savings from the general public and facilitating credits to the business community, and it was forbidden to issue bank notes or anything like it. Some 60–70 years after its foundation it had ended up as the completely opposite: a bank based almost entirely on bank notes, with the government as its single largest client, and of very little use to the business community, and with a large mortgage-lending business.

1.3.5   Manufakturkontoret and Manufakturdiskonten, 1739–1878 (The "Office for Manufacturing" and the "Discount House for Manufacturers")

In line with the prevailing mercantilistic thinking of those days, the foundation of Manufakturkontoret in 1739 was intended to assist and subsidize the

---

[35]E. Heckscher "The Bank of Sweden is the oldest bank of the world still in existence …" Heckscher (1964) *The Bank of Sweden* in van Dillen (ed.) *History of the Principal Public Banks*, p. 161, or I. Nygren "… inte bara den första sedelutgivande banken i världen utan … också med sin karaktär av statsinstitution ursprunget till världens första centralbank …" I. Nygren (1985) *Från Stockholms Banco till Citibank* (Liber Tryck AB, Stockholm) p. 14.

Prof. Brisman was more modest, and quite correct, when he wrote: "Den er även den enda av de offentliga bankerna från denna tid, som står kvar ännu i våra dagar." *Sveriges Riksbank 1668–1918*, bd. I, p. 151. SEA's translation: "It is even the only one of the public banks from those days which still exists."

development of particularly the textile industry. For unknown reasons the mining industry was outside the scope of Manufakturkontoret's activities.

The idea was that this new Office should buy up and distribute raw materials, pay out premiums to particularly successful manufacturers, extend loans, and make prepayments to manufacturers. The means came from special extra duties of 7–15 per cent levied on certain goods. In addition, it could borrow from the Riksbank. The Office was supervised by the resourceful Gustav Kierman (of whom more will be said in 1.3.6 below).

Manufacturers could borrow up 75 per cent of the value of their finished goods, which were taken as collateral – many of which were produced primarily for the purpose of obtaining a credit,[36] because the valuation of the goods was generous, and at 4 per cent the interest was low compared to the Riksbank's 5–6 per cent, and the unregulated market's 10–15 per cent.

In 1757 Manufakturkontoret was supplemented with the creation of Manufakturdiskonten, which represented a real novelty in the Swedish credit market. In contrast to the Riksbank and the Jernkontor (the "Iron Office" cfr. 1.3.6 below), it did not restrict itself to lending against collateral in the form of warehoused goods. It introduced the discounting of bills. This meant lending without physical collateral, which was a new concept in Sweden at this time. The discounting could be had for up to a certain percentage (usually 15–25 per cent) of the value of the previous year's production, and for maturities up to nine months.

As a "capital market institution" Manufakturkontoret and Manufakturdiskonten had less quantitative significance than the Riksbank. During the 1770s and 1780s some 300–400 borrowers enjoyed the services of Manufakturdiskonten, and outstanding loans reached a level of some rd 500,000 (less than 5 per cent of the Riksbank's non-government loans). However, from 1817 onwards its activities were greatly expanded, and it has, therefore, often been called "an 18th century institution with its biggest significance in the 19th century".[37]

In 1766, its activities, including Manufakturdiskonten, were taken over by Kommercekollegiet ("Ministry of Commerce"). In 1878, the Manufaktur Diskont was dissolved.

1.3.6   Jernkontoret (the "Iron Office"), 1747–

During the 1730s, the credit demand from the iron industry was desperate. A most humble memo ("Ödmiukaste Memorial") from the ironworks owners ("brukspatronerna") to the Riksdag, dated June 30, 1738, reveals the sentiment in the iron industry at the time (SEA's translation): "... the present hardship and depression of the iron industry derives particularly from the all

---

[36]Cfr. S. Brisman (1918–31) *Sveriges Riksbank 1618–1918*, bd. II, p. 154.
[37]Cfr. I. Nygren (1985) *Från Stockholms Banco till Citibank* (Liber Förlag) p. 27.

too great shortage of money in this country ... and equally humbly the owners of the iron works suggest to the most worthy Estates of the Realm that Riksens Ständers Banque must be the foremost conduit and most appropriate mechanism for countering the lack of money through loans of capital against properties and real goods ... since trade is declining, and mines are at the utmost brink of their downfall because of lack of credit in the country".[38]

In spite of this frantic appeal for more ample credit facilities, nothing was done in the short run.

One of the problems which had to be overcome, was the mutually opposing interests of the manufacturers ("brukspatronerna") and the iron merchants, and those who were both (cfr. 1.2.1).

In a supreme effort to create unanimity among the various interested parties, a grandiose dinner party for 40-odd people was held in October, 1747. The bill has been preserved. It ran to dcm 3,052 plus cakes for dcm 525, i.e. a bit more than the annual salary of the general manager of the Riksbank. The drinks consumed on this occasion comprised 148 bottles of wine, and 18 large bowls of punch.[39] It worked. Agreement was finally reached. The king signed the statutes of the Jernkontor (the "Iron Office") in December, 1747.

The basic principles of the new Iron Office were that it should buy iron in the market when prices were particularly low, and that it should extend loans to manufacturers and traders to cover their interest costs for loans from the Bank. The loans would be secured by the iron products.

The operations of the Iron Offices were to be financed by a payment to the Iron Office of 2 per cent of the value of the iron delivered, the "jernkontorsdaler" ("Iron Office Daler"). In addition, the Iron Office was granted a – modest – line of credit in the Riksbank at an artificially low rate of interest (3 per cent). Thus, a very close co-operation between the Bank and the Iron Office was foreseen from the very beginning.

Close co-operation among various institutions was the order of the day, which also implied double or even treble positions or functions of a relatively limited number of individuals. The fates of the above mentioned Gustav Kierman, 1702–1766 (cfr. 1.3.4) and Jean Henri Lefebure (1708–1767), an immigrant Huguenot, illustrate the implications.

---

[38]"... at Järnhandelens nu warande twång och förtryck besynnerligen härrörer af den alt for stora penningebrist som är i landet ... och i lika ödmiukhet understält Riksens Höglofl. Ständer, om icke Riksens Ständers Banque må wara den förnämste tillgång och tillräckeligaste medlet til penningenödens förebyggande, genom Capitalers lån uppå fastigheter och reelle effecter ... då handelen liksom aftyner, och Bergswärcken äre på yttersta bredden af sin undergång, förmedelst penningebrist inom landet ...." The letter is reprinted in Brisman (1918–1931) *Sveriges Riksbank 1668–1919*, bd. II, Bilagor, pp. 57–60.

[39]Cfr. B. Boëthius & Å. Kromnow (1947–1968) *Jernkontorets Historia*, 1–3 (Jernkontoret, Stockholm) Del I, p. 202, where a detailed description of this dinner is given.

Gustav Kierman was the leading figure of the Burgher Estate and chairman of the Banking Commission of the Estates, as well as a member of the Riksbank's board ("bankfullmägtig"). He was also one of the largest commercial borrowers of the Bank. In addition, he was a shipowner and one of the largest iron exporters, and had considerable interests also in iron manufacturing. He would, therefore, benefit particularly from the assistance of the Iron Office, and he played a crucial role in the founding of that institution, and became one of its board members. Jean Henri Lefebure was the owner of several iron works, Sweden's fifth largest iron exporter, and a board member of the Iron Office as well as its largest borrower. The private businesses of both Kierman and Lefebure naturally implied that they had large foreign exchange operations of their own.

Simultaneously with the foundation of the Iron Office, a new Växelkontor ("Exchange Office") was set up for the purpose of supporting the exchange rate against foreign currencies (a vain attempt, of course). Initially, it was considered only natural that the Bank, the Exchange Office, and the Iron Office should all take advantage of the knowledge, experience, and connections of people like Kierman and Lefebure, who were both appointed to take charge of the new Växelkontor. It is obvious that these mixings of public and private responsibilities would imply conflicts of interest and, ultimately, lead to fateful suspicions of manipulations and malpractices.

The new Exchange Office needed money to support the exchange rate. With Kierman and Lefebure on the boards ("fullmägtige") of both the Iron Office and the Exchange Office, a big loan (dcm 200,000) from the Iron Office to the Exchange Office proved not too difficult to arrange in 1749, in return for the "mutual services the Exchange Office and the Iron Office could offer each other".[40] The same year Plomgren, another centrally placed merchant, borrowed dcm 230,000 (approximately 73,000 dsm) from the Iron Office. By these transaction the resources of the Iron Office had been nearly exhausted, so by 1750 the mine and ironworks owners ("brukspatroner"), much against their expectations, had still seen almost none of the lending capacity of the Iron Office. Ten years later this had hardly changed at all.

As a "capital market institution" the Iron Office remained quite small, even compared to the modest amounts of "business loans" extended by the Riksbank (SEA's translation): "Since the Iron Office did not base its banking business on any systematic taking of deposits, the Fund was not of a magnitude which could play any decisive role in the financing of the iron industry."[41] It also meant that the Iron Office could not help the mine and ironworks owners to the extent originally envisaged, and that the "brukspatroner" remained under the financial power of the large trading houses in Stockholm and

---

[40]Cfr. Boëthius & Kromnow (1947–1968) *Jernkontorets Historia* (Jernkontoret, Stockholm) Del I, pp. 246–8.

[41]Cfr. Boëthius & Kromnow (1947) *Jernkontorets Historia* (Jernkontoret) Del I, p. 561.

Göteborg. "Thus, the iron works remained left to satisfy their credit requirements from the individual trading houses." (SEA's translation).[42]

Kierman's and Lefebure's numerous public and private interests finally caught up with them. Their fates were akin to that of Johan Palmstruch, (cfr. 1.3.1 above), except that for Kierman and Lefebure there was no reprieve. They had too many enemies in the opposition party (mösserne, the "Caps"), and when in 1765 the "Caps" gained the majority in the Riksdag they found Kierman and Lefebure guilty of fraud, and condemned them to a one month diet of "water and bread" followed by prison for life. They were accused of having swindled the Växelkontor for dsm 6 million through the triangular exchange operations between Jernkontoret, Växelkontoret, and their own businesses. Although the amount was later reduced to 1.5 million there was no way Kierman and Lefebure could repay it. The truth of the matter remains unresolved, but it is not difficult to see how things could get somewhat mixed up.

Water and bread, not of modern standards, turned out not to have been a healthy diet. Both of them died a few months after the end of their prescribed diet.

After Lefebure's death it was discovered that he owed the Jernkontor the vast amount of dsm 500,000. It took his heirs 75 years to clear this debt.

Thus, the Jernkontor failed to fulfill its originally intended task, which was to provide financial assistance to iron works owners in difficult financial conditions and under pressure from hard-nosed merchant lenders.

The Jernkontor was more of service to the Shylocks than to the Antonios.

1.3.7 Diskonterna (the "discount houses"), 1773–1817

Since neither the Manufakturdiskont nor the Jernkontor had solved the problems created by the Riksbank's inactivity after 1762, thoughts and plans kept rumbling.

After many deliberations and reports, a 15-year charter was finally issued in 1773 for a group of worthy persons to form and operate a privately owned credit institution named Stockholms Diskontkompanie, to be based on bill discounting. The driving force behind the final plan was Johan Liljencrantz (1730–1815), Gustav III's "finance minister".

Stockholms Diskontkompanie was based on the following principles:

Liabilities:
- a share capital of rd 400,000, with joint liability among shareholders;[43]
- a credit from Riksbanken of rd 100,000 at 3 per cent interest;
- borrowings/deposits received from the general public.

---

[42]Cfr. Boëthius & Kromnow (1947) *Jernkontorets Historia* (Jenkontoret) Del I, p. 412.
[43]Limited liability was still an almost unknown concept. It is thought to have applied in the Bank of England, the Bank of Ireland, the Royal Bank of Scotland, and the Bank of Scotland, but the opinion has also been expressed that only a bankruptcy among these institution would have cleared up this question, cfr. E.T. Powell (1966) *The Evolution of the Money Market 1385–1915* (F. Cass & Co.) pp. 302–3.

Assets:
- discounted bills, without collateral, maximum rd 5,600 per borrower, at 6 per cent prepaid interest;
- cash.

As defined in the Introduction, it will be seen that the Stockholms Diskont-kompanie was actually a bank. It took deposits from the general public, it operated on the principle of fractional reserves (although no particular cash reserve was stipulated), and it lent money to just about everybody, although according to its charter it could only discount bills issued by "business men", and there was a maximum amount for each individual borrower. In real life, neither of these limitations was strictly observed, except perhaps, in the beginning. The borrowers included civil servants and officers as well as merchants, shopkeepers, landowners, etc.[44]

Also, it is noteworthy that for the first time in Sweden it was officially recognized that it might be a good idea for a bank to be founded with a certain amount of capital – this had been recognized in Denmark already in 1736 (cfr. Chapter 2).

Receipts issued by the Diskont for deposits would circulate as means of payment. Their attraction was that they were interest bearing, and that, since they could be used for making payments, people did not suffer any loss of liquidity by making deposits.

In addition, the Diskont could issue assignments of its deposit with the Riksbank. Such assignments also circulated (and were also interest bearing) and became very popular as means of payment.

The Stockholm Diskontkompanie was so successful that, when the charter expired in 1788, the Crown wanted to have the profits and the borrowing opportunities for itself, not least because of the newly declared war against Russia. So, in 1787, the Stockholm Diskontkompanie was replaced by the government owned Generaldiskontkontor based on identical principles – which were equally disregarded.

Their main features of the diskonter are summarized in Schedule 1.1.

Göteborg

The first discount house in Göteborg did not get its charter prolonged at expiry for the same reason that it was not renewed for Diskontkompaniet in Stockholm, so it was wound up. Instead, an interim discount house was created with a charter, which could be revoked at six-months notice. In return for accepting the interim solution, the Riksgälds- kontor demanded a share in any profits exceeding a certain minimum.

Inspired by the success of all the discount houses, the Göta Kanalkompanie also found that it could support its financial needs by establishing a discount

---

[44]Details of the first 15 years of the life of the Stockholms Diskont are unknown, since no archives for this period have been found, cfr. S. Brisman (1924) *Sveriges Affärs-banker*, I–II (Svenska Bankföreningen, Stockholm) bd. I, p. 7.

Schedule 1.1   The Discount Houses, 1773–1817 (Amounts in '000 riksdaler species (Rd))

Name, year, and duration of charter	Ownership	Capitalization	Initial Riksbank loan	Other comments
Diskontkompaniet, 1773–1788	Private until 1787	400	100	Taken over by the government 1787, and wound up 1788–1814.
Generaldiskont-Kontoret, 1787–1803	Government			Continued existing business of Diskontkompaniet.
Diskontverket med Rigsgäldssedlar, 1798–1803	60% government, later 80%	250		Created by the Riksgälds-kontoret.
Riksdiskontverket, 1803–	66.6% government			Did not take deposits. Operated by the Riksbank.
Diskontverket I G'borg, 1783–1795	Private	135.4	50	Level of deposits ca. 100 most of its life.
G'borg Diskont II, 1797–1802. Charter revocable at 6 months notice.	Private, but profit-sharing with government	100	50	No archives survive. Intended as a temporary institution.
G'borg Diskont III, 1802(04)–1817	Private	200	200	Expanded the business of its predecessor. Wound up 1817–1820.
Malmös Diskont, 1803(04)–1817	Private	100	100	Overextended itself with bad loans. Wound up 1817–1848 at a cost to the government of Rd 430.
Göta Kanals Diskont, 1810–1817	Göta Kanal company	0	800	Kanal Kompaniet its largest borrower. Wound up 1817–1848 at a cost to the government of Rd 914.
Åbo Diskont 1805(6)–1808	Private	150	150	Died from the Russian attack 1808.

Source: S. Brisman (1924) *Sveriges Affärsbanker*, I–II (Svenska Bankföreningen), bd. I, pp. 1–60.

house. So, almost immediately upon the incorporation of the Canal Company in 1810, it founded a discount house, the Göta Kanals Diskont, but in contrast to the others, without any capital of its own. The Göta Kanals Diskont became a large-scale lender to the Canal Company itself, and to its shareholders. The optimism surrounding the canal project also induced the Riksbank to grant it a credit of no less than 800,000 rd which meant that Göta Kanals Diskont soon became larger than the Göteborg and Malmö houses combined. At the end of the day, it also meant that it was wound up with a larger loss than the two others combined.

The 1800–1804 changes

In the years 1800–1803, the government decided to encourage the formation of new discount houses in cities, which were populous and had good business activities ("... avlägsna, folkrika, och näringsfulla städer ...").[45] Operations in Göteborg and Malmö started in 1803–1804, and Åbo (Turku), in 1807. Shares in the Åbo Diskont were in strong demand, but only in Stockholm, where 23,000 of the 30,000 shares were sold.

The lending business allowed for the new discount houses did not differ from the previous principles. The maximum amount per borrower was not strictly observed ("... iakttoks icke strängt ... det fanns de, som fått närmere 300,000 rd."[46]

Table 1.3 below shows the approximate amounts and balance sheet compositions of the discount houses in the later stage of their lives:

Table 1.3   The Discount Houses: Main Balance Sheet Figures, 1806–1817

'000 Riksdaler	1806	1810	1814	1817
Malmö Diskont				
– Capital: 100. Riksbank loan: 100				
– Deposits	838	2,184	2,559	2,303
Total assets/liabilities	1,038	2,384	2,759	2,503
Göteborg Diskont III				
– Capital: 200. Riksbank loan: 200				
– Deposits	786	1,656	1,558	796
Total assets/liabilities	1,186	2,056	1,958	1,196
Göta Kanals Diskont				
Capital: 0. Riksbank loan: 800	–			
Deposits		2,343	5,429	3,472
Total assets/liabilities		3,143	6,229	4,272

Source: Brisman (1924) *Sveriges Affärsbanker*, bd. I, p. 244, combined with SEA's assumptions.
Assumptions: All profits distributed. No changes in original Riksbank credits.

---

[45]Brisman (1924) *Sveriges Affärsbanker*, I–II (Svenska Bankföreningen, Stockholm) bd. I, p. 17.
[46]Brisman (1924) *Sveriges Affärsbanker* (Svenska Bankföreningen) bd. I, p. 29.

The discount houses in Malmö, Göteborg, Åbo, and Göta Kanals Diskont competed vigorously for deposits in Stockholm, but the government did not allow any of them to undertake any lending business in Stockholm. This was kept strictly as a monopoly for the Riksbank – after the revival of that bank in 1803 – and the Riksdiskontverk, which was operated by the Riksbank.

The end of diskonterna, 1812–1817

The Russian attack in 1808–1809 was the death knell for the Åbo Diskont, and spread nervous jitters in Malmö, and even in Göteborg. The Malmö and Göteborg diskonter were temporarily saved by the Riksbank, but in 1812–1817 several factors combined to spell the end of the discount houses.

Among the major reasons for the eventual dissolution of the discount houses were both the usual post-war companions of consecutive inflation and deflation, and individual cases in both Malmö and Göteborg of disproportionately large single exposures.[47] In addition, the business models of the discount houses were at a strong disadvantage when market interest rates increased far above the rates they were allowed to charge.

Initially (1808), the Riksbank/Riksdiskonten was instructed to extend unlimited help ("... utan minsta begränsning lämna all den hjälp, som behövdes"[48]). The support was given on conditions implying that the diskonter had lost their independence.

The role of "Lender of Last Resort" was played also at the later stages of this period, but in the end it was decided to wind up the diskonter (1817).

The role of "Lender of Last Resort" was not adopted because the Riksbank considered itself a modern central bank, but probably because of the close connections between the Riksbank and the diskonter embodied in the large credits extended to them by the Riksbank. These credits would be lost in case of an uncontrolled collapse of the diskonter.

The reason why it took 30 years to wind up the Malmö and the Kanal Diskonter, at considerable costs to Riksbanken, was that their main "assets" were loans to the Göta Kanalkompanie.

The end of diskonterna implied that by 1817, Sweden was no closer to having a "capital market" than was the case just after the opening of Stockholms Banco 160 years earlier.

About one dozen of pension funds had also emerged as suppliers of medium- or long-term capital, but these funds were all quite small because each of them was reserved for special groups of beneficiaries (officers, clergymen, civil

---

[47]The Malmö Diskont lost ca. 600,000 rd on just three exposures, which had been kept hidden from the auditors, cfr. Brisman (1924) *Sveriges Affärsbanker*, bd. I, p. 56.
[48]Brisman (1924) *Sveriges Affärsbanker*, I–II (Svenska Bankföreningen, Stockholm) bd. I, p. 33.

servants, etc.), and most of them were also restricted to limited geographical areas (Stockholm, Värmland, etc.)

It was not until 1830 that Sweden again could boast of two simultaneously existing active banks.

1.4   The stock exchange

Since merchants needed to meet in order to do business, they had for a long time agreed to meet in the area below the doorstep of the Tyska Kyrkan ("the German Church") in Stockholm, close to the Stortorg. No records have survived evidencing exactly when this practice started, but since some of the merchants meeting at that place were German Hanseatic merchants, the practice must have started no later than the early 17th century, and possibly already in the 14th century.

By the mid-18th century it was found that it might be good for business if a meeting place was constructed, which could provide some protection against rain and snow. In 1756, a petition was sent to the Representatives of the Estates for permission to collect funds for the construction of an exchange building. The king approved that for a number of years a special duty was levied on the imports of a number of luxury goods, and that the proceeds of this duty should be applied towards the construction of an exchange building on the Stortorg.

By 1776, the building was completed, and became the property of the City of Stockholm. It was, however, far from a "stock exchange" in the sense of any of the definitions discussed in the Introduction. There were absolutely no rules or regulations. Anybody could trade anything, and so they did.

2
Denmark-Norway in the Age of Globalization, 1736–1814

"I hold the world but as the world,
a stage, where every man must play a part."

("The Merchant of Venice", Act One)

2.1   An overview: From prosperity to bankruptcy

In the financial world, Denmark started playing its formal part in 1736, when the first bank in the dual monarchy of Denmark-Norway was born. The following 75 years clearly demonstrated the extent to which Denmark-Norway was subject to the political and economic winds blowing on the global stage.[1] The great Northern War (1709–1720) had indirect links to the Spanish War of Succession, and the fate of the dual monarchy in 1814 was a direct consequence of the Napoleonic wars.

Politically, Denmark-Norway's main objective was to stay out of the conflicts between England and France. This succeeded until 1801, but it did not last. England, fearing that the Danish navy might eventually fall into Napoleon's hands, made a pre-emptive strike against Copenhagen (1801). This, of course, pushed Denmark-Norway into Napoleon's camp, which made the English attack Copenhagen again in 1807, ultimately leading to the separation of Norway from Denmark (1814).

Commercially, Denmark-Norway was not far behind England and the Netherlands in its efforts to set up royally chartered trading companies and trading posts in Africa and the Far East.

Colonies and trading posts were established in India (Tranquebar, 1620 and Frederiksnagore, 1755), on the Ivory Coast (1658–1660), and in the

---

[1]The phrase "globalization" may be new, but Norwegian vikings settled in Canada in the 11th century, Chinese silks had been brought to Europe since the 13th century, and Magellan's vessels circumnavigated the world 1519–1522, almost 500 years before the phrase "globalization" was coined. The concept of "globalization" may remain a matter of degree and definition, but it is far from a new phenomenon.

West Indies (St. Thomas, 1666, St. Jan, 1717, and St. Croix, 1733). Danish commerce thrived from the far eastern trade as well as from the notorious "triangle trade" made possible by this globalization, exploited by both royally chartered and private trading companies.[2] Most of the wealth created in Denmark-Norway in the 18th century was the result of trade with the Far East, Africa, and the West Indies. The number of warehouses flanking Copenhagen's harbour, now converted into hotels, office and apartment blocks, bear witness to the significant volumes of trade passing through Copenhagen in those years, later known as the "Flourishing Trading Period".

None of the large commercial enterprises – private or royally chartered – survived the debacle of the Napoleonic wars – except as more or less empty shells.

Financially, Denmark went through alternating periods of strengthened and weakened government finances reflecting the changing international conditions. The costly mobilizations in the 1740s, the early 1760s, and in the 1790s produced very severe financial strains, and from the mid-1790s onwards the government finances gradually deteriorated, until they collapsed completely with the notorious "State Bankruptcy of 1813", cfr. 2.3.2.

A hundred years after the first bank had been formed in Denmark, there was still only one bank, and Denmark-Norway was not much closer to having a "capital market" than in 1736.

2.2   The problems

With respect to the "financial system" and "capital market" in the 18th century, the main problems after ca. 1735, were

- The large navy and army, required ever increasing amounts of money, particularly in the 1760s and in the early 19th century;
- Financing the increasingly capital-intensive trading companies, private as well as royally chartered, required the collection of savings from all corners of the dual monarchy. Although some of the trading companies became very profitable, the business required huge investments in ships, warehouses, and working capital, and in some periods there were big problems, e.g. the early 1780s;

---

[2]The most prominent names were, i.a. Niels Ryberg (one of the richest men in Denmark in the 1770s), Fabricius de Tengnagel (whose father originated from Holland), Joost v. Hemert (who had unsurmountable problems after 1782), Chr. Duntzfelt, Constantin Brun, whose imposing town mansion can still be seen in Copenhagen's centre, Frederick de Coninck, of Dutch origins, Erich Erichsen, whose town mansion later served as the head office of the Københavns Handelsbank (now part of Danske Bank), Pierre Pechier, a notorious gambler whose red brick town mansion has, since 1871, served as the head office of Danske Bank, and several others.

- Financing the rebuilding of Copenhagen after the fires of 1728 and 1795, and the bombardment by the English in 1807;
- The lack of financial institutions. It seems puzzling that the government did not, until 1736, try to collect savings in a more structured and organized manner, e.g. through some sort of a bank, government sponsored or otherwise. After all, a bank had existed in Sweden since 1656, and the glorious examples of the Amsterdam Wisselbank, the Hamburger Bank, and the Bank of England, as well as a number of other public banks on the Continent, were well-known;
- Financing the government deficits, particularly in 1810–1813, when the government went bankrupt.

2.3   Responses and actions

2.3.1   The royally chartered trading companies

During the 17th and 18th centuries 15–18 trading companies, i.e. 15–20 per cent of all chartered trading companies founded in Europe in this period (depending on definitions) were founded in Denmark-Norway with royal charters and a number of royally granted privileges – mainly exclusive rights to trade in certain geographical regions. Roughly ten of these companies were engaged in trade with the Far East, Africa, or the West Indies. Six smaller companies were primarily engaged in fishing and whaling in the North Atlantic.

From a capital market perspective, the main aspects about these companies, could be summarized as follows, although the companies were far from identical on all these points:[3]

1. The Crown usually supplied a major part of the share capital. Ministers and senior civil servants also contributed, more or less voluntarily. The king would normally appoint the directors, whatever the amount of the royal shareholding. The number of shareholders would normally be 150–300. The shares were transferable, but otherwise shareholder rights were virtually non-existent, at least in the earlier companies.

---

[3]Sources:
Ole Feldbæk (1986) *Danske Handelskompagnier 1616–1843, Oktrojer og interne ledelses-regler* (Selskabet for Udgivelse af Kilder til Dansk Historie, København).
R. Willerslew (1942–1944) "Danmarks første Aktieselskab", *Historisk Tidsskrift* (HT), 10–16.
P.P. Sveistrup (1942–1944) "Det Danske Vestindiske Handelsselskab", *HT*, 10–16.
K. Glamann (1949) "Studier i Asiatisk Kompagnis Økonomiske Historie 1732–1772", *HT*, 11–12.
Rasch & Sveistrup (1948) *Asiatisk Kompagni i den florissante Periode 1772–1792* (København).
K. Klem (1970) *Det kgl. Østersøisk-gueniske Handeelsselskab* (Handels-og Søfartsmuseets Årbog).

2. In most cases, the capital would consist of a relatively small "permanent" capital and additional capital collected for each expedition. This additional capital would usually be distributed to the shareholders upon completion of an expedition. However, there were several variations on this theme. In at least one case (Afrikanische Compagnie, 1659), no capital could be taken out during the lifetime of the charter. In some cases the supply of "additional" capital was voluntary while in other cases it was compulsory under the threat of forfeiture of the already paid in capital, e.g. Ostindische Compagnie, 1670–1729, and Vestindisk-guineisk Kompagni, 1671–1754.

3. Book-keeping in the "Italian style" was first prescribed in 1659. For comparison, the double entry book-keeping method had been introduced in the English East India Company already in 1600.[4]

Det Kongeligt Octroyerede Danske Asiatisk Kompagnie (Asiatisk Kompagnie, or "Asiatic Company"), 1732–1843, was the largest, most long-lived, and most successful of the Nordic trading companies.[5]

With respect to shareholder rights and corporate governance it represented a vast step forwards compared to nearly all of the earlier royally chartered companies. Thus, the top management was elected directly by the shareholders (§22 of the Charter).[6] In fact, the Asiatic Company, not the 1616 Ostindische Compagnie,[7] should have the honour of being called "Denmark's First Joint Stock Company".

---

[4]Cfr. W.R. Scott (1912/1951) *The Constitutional and Financial History of Each of the Chief Joint-Stock Companies from 1553 to 1720*, Vol. I–III (Gloucester, Mass., 1912, reprinted, Peter Smith, N.Y., 1951).

[5]The only other Nordic companies, which might compete for the label "largest Nordic" were the Swedish Asiatic Company and the Stora Kopparberg. No financial records for the former have survived, cfr. Chapter 1, and the latter had a very special ownership structure making it difficult to define as a "company" until much later. Anyway, "size" is difficult to define also for the Danish Asiatic Company, because turnover and profits were subject to huge variations from year to year depending on the irregular completion of expeditions. From its accounts it appears that at its peak (ca. 1772–1782), the Asiatic Company had some ten vessels at sea simultaneously, probably the best measurement of its "size".

The Company's head office and warehouses on the eastern shore of Copenhagen's harbour now form part of the Foreign Ministry's blocks of offices.

[6]The charters and conventions of all the chartered companies from the 17th and 18th centuries have been reprinted and commented upon by O. Feldbæk (1986) *Danske Handelskonpagnier 1618–1843, Oktrojer og interne Ledelsesregler* (Selskabet for Udgivelse af Kilder til Dansk Historie, København).

[7]R. Willerslew, who labelled the 1616 Ostindische Compagnie "Denmark's first joint stock company" (*Historisk Tidsskrift*, 10–16, 1942–1944) seems to be aware of no other criteria for a joint stock company than the principle of limited liability. That this principle applied emerges only indirectly from the fact that when the company encountered severe financial problems, no efforts were made to collect more capital from the shareholders.

The number of shareholders grew from about 150 in 1732 to 270 in 1753.[8] With the royal family and two other shareholders initially controlling nearly 25 per cent of the capital, the ownership structure was quite concentrated, possibly an indication that raising the capital was not easy.

At first, the two largest shareholders were Mr. Desmerciéres and his father, with a combined shareholding of approximately 15 per cent. Mr. Desmerciéres was a wealthy civil servant immigrated from France. He was the illegitimate son of the second largest shareholder, Count Gyldensten, a celebrated courtier. Born Jean Henri Huguetan, he made a fortune from profiteering in France, and later had to flee both France, the Netherlands, and England with a bunch of furious creditors sharp on his heels, before he arrived in Denmark in 1711 with a large fortune. He endeared himself to the kings Frederik IV (1699–1730) and Christian VI (1730–1746), i.a. by graciously financing the construction of the Christiansborg Palace in the 1730s – the second of the four castles on that site. He was elevated to the ranks of nobility under the name of Gyldensten. Father and son were also deeply involved in the creation of Denmark-Norway's first bank a few years later.[9]

Table 2.1 shows how the assets were financed.

The immediately striking feature – compared to a modern trading company – is the completely dominating role played by equity financing until about 1780.

Table 2.1   Asiatisk Kompagnie: Composition of Liabilities, Selected Financial Year-Ends

Rd '000	31.03, 1744	31.03, 1764	31.03, 1783	11.04, 1806
Circulating Fund	1,274	2,309	N.A.	N.A.
Continuing Fund	503	600	N.A.	N.A.
General Capital Account	N.A.	N.A.	2,400	2,400
Retained earnings			2,099	0
Bank debt			654	
Other domestic liabilities	25	257	2,752	7,554
Foreign debts		1,010	1,871	345
Total	1,802	4,176	9,776	10,299

Source: Asiatisk Kompagni's archives, Rigsarkivet (National Archives). As from 1797, the balance sheet date was changed from March 31 to April 11.

---

[8] Cfr. K. Glamann (1949) "Studie i Asiatisk Kompagni's økonomiske historie 1732–1772", *Historisk Tid sskrift*, 11–12.

[9] Mr. Desmerciéres died without issue, but he had a sister who eloped to Sweden with the son of the Spanish ambassador to Denmark. Their descendants, named Gyldensten, still own Count Gyllensten's renaissance manor house and estate.

The equity

For each new voyage, the shareholders had to supply a "circulating fund", in proportion to their shareholdings, the "continuing fund". The "circulating fund" would be repaid to the shareholders, together with their proportionate share of the profits upon the completion of a voyage and the sale of the cargo.

Similar principles were followed by several other companies, but not by all. When the Charter was renewed in 1772, the two "funds" were combined into a "General Capital Account" of rd 2.4 million. No new capital was raised in this connection. The implication was, however, that the traditional repayment of the "circulating fund" upon completion of a journey was stopped.

From a capital market perspective, the motivation for this stock-splitting and writing-up of the capital is of some interest. Before the stock-splitting, the shares were too expensive for "ordinary" citizens, and the king wanted to widen the market for the shares.[10]

The domestic liabilities

The almost non-existence of domestic borrowings until the 1770s is particularly striking. When additional capital was required in the 1760s, it was found abroad.

The Copenhagen Bank (founded 1736, cfr. below) was in no way an important source of credit to Asiatisk Kompagnie (in sharp contrast to the roles played by the Bank of England and the Amsterdam Wisselbank in the financing of respectively the English and the Dutch East India Companies). During the approximately 70 years of the Company's active life, less than 20 year-end balance sheets show any borrowings from the only bank in Denmark at the time. The Copenhagen Bank did not have the capacity to supply the amounts of credit required by the large trading houses, cfr. Tables 2.2 and 2.3.

Table 2.2 shows the composition of the domestic liabilities at selected year-ends.

The "Tranquebar" account came into existence after 1777 when the Government took over the administration of the Indian colonies in Tranquebar and Bengal from the Company. The Company then had to pay for the use of the facilities in the colonies.

---

[10]"For at lette adgangen til Deeltagelse i Compagniet for Dem af Vore Medborgere, som ikke have været i stand til at anskaffe sig en Actie i det forrige Compagnie formedelst Deres Höye Værdi, og for at give leilighed til en större Circulation i Handelen, maae enhver af de 1600 Actier, som det forrige Compagnie bestoed af, giöres til 3 nye Actier, saa dette nye Compagnie nu kommer til at bestaae 4800 Actier, og hver Actie at beregnes til 500 Rdaler, eller Compagniets heele Fond 2,400,000 Rixdaler, som omtrent er deres Virkelige Værdie, for saa vidt som endnu kand sees." Quoted from the 1772 Konvention ("Management Instruction") as reprinted in O. Feldbæk (1986) *Danske Handelskompagnier 1616–1843* (København) p. 149.

Table 2.2   Asiatisk Kompagnie: Composition of Domestic Liabilities at Selected Year-Ends

Rd '000	1781	1783	1790	1797	1806	1815
Tranquebar	33	317	1,731	1,630	2,642	955
The bank	382	654			113	
Miscellaneous creditors	315	1,904	3,204	1,146	2,113	415
Other	555	531	677	667	2,687	671
Total	1,285	3,406	5,612	3,443	7,555	2,041

Source: As for Table 2.1.

According to the year-end figures, the borrowings from the Bank never constituted more than 5–7 per cent of total liabilities, and were mostly zero. The reason why the substantial increase in domestic debts from the late 1770s onwards bypassed the only domestic bank completely will be seen from the description of the bank below.

By far the major part of the "Miscellaneous creditors" consisted of an account set up in 1782, "Conto pro diverse Creditorer", representing a sort of "commercial paper" sold directly by the Company to domestic investors, usually in denominations of rd 1,000 each, issued to bearer. The maturity could be up to three years. The 1806 figure includes a small amount of bills of exchange.

The foreign borrowings

The changing pattern of the foreign credits is another striking feature emerging from Table 2.1 above. Between 1797 and 1806, when most of Europe was at war, borrowings from abroad dropped significantly.

The foreign borrowings consisted partly of minor bilateral trade credits from approximately 30 different names mostly in Amsterdam, Hamburg, Altona, and London, and occasionally in Paris, Stockholm, and Dantzig. The other part of the foreign borrowings consisted of five fairly large medium-term "bond loans", totalling approximately rd 2.9 million, issued to investors in Amsterdam and Antwerp in the years 1764–1805, and 1807 in Hamburg, and booked in the Company's accounts under the label "Account for miscellaneous foreign creditors for monies borrowed in Holland" (Conto pro diverse udenlandske Creditorer for Optagne Penge udi Holland, resp. Antwerp/Amsterdam/Hamburg).[11]

The two latest loans (1805 and 1807) were issued by the Asiatisk Kompagnie on behalf of the Crown suggesting that in this period the company's credit-worthiness was seen as better than that of the Crown, even at this stage

---

[11]*Source*: The Asiatic Company's archives, Rigsarkivet (National Archives). The Company's accounts are very well-preserved.

when the Company's reserves had been depleted. The Crown was sliding towards bankruptcy.

2.3.2 Denmark-Norway's first bank

Several banking projects were aired in the 17th and the early 18th century, all copied in more or less detail from the Amsterdam Wisselbank or the Hamburger Bank. Only one of them ever got so far as to obtain a charter, but for unknown reasons the project never got off the ground.[12]

In Denmark-Norway at this time, as in Sweden-Finland, it appears that any attempt to set up a bank-like operation would require royal approval. This is understandable if a contemplated bank was supposed to enjoy royal privileges of some sort, and without such privileges no bank was considered realistic. All existing banks had so far been established either by government initiative and ownership or with royal charters. Other "banks" had so far been "only" merchant or goldsmith businesses, which had gradually migrated into deposit-taking and lending. Money-lenders existed, but they lent their own money, and probably borrowed very little for the purpose of lending.

Den Kiöbenhavnske Assignation – Vexel – og Laane- Banque (the "Copenhagen Bank", since 1791 known as "Kurantbanken")

The foundation[13] of the first bank in Denmark-Norway grew out of a number of circumstances, the most apparent of which seem to have been:

- the need for capital to rebuild Copenhagen after the Great Fire in Copenhagen in 1728;
- mercantilistic policies, aiming at accelerating investments in manufacturing equipment (water mills, roads, etc), besides the above-mentioned trading companies;
- the succession of King Christian VI to the throne in 1730, triggering major changes in the government and the creation in 1735 of the "General Landets Økonomi-og Kommercekollegium" ("General Ministry of Economics and Commerce"). A central figure in this new ministry was Jean

---

[12]An application from Abraham Tongelo, a Dutchman who had settled in Copenhagen in 1611, was rewarded by King Christian IV with a banking charter in 1624 (SEA's translation): "... to conduct true exchange, lending, payments and other merchant banking." ("... at holde rigtige wexell, lone, betale og anden kiøbmandz bencke." Here quoted from A. Nielsen (1903) "Danske Bankprojekter fra Tiden før Kurantbankens Oprettelse", *Nationaløkonomisk Tidsskrift*, (København) p. 581. Tongelo's application included a copy of the charter for the Hamburgische Bank.

[13]The birth of the Bank has been examined by Dr. Erik Rasmussen (1950–1952) in: "Kurantbankens oprettelse", *Historisk Tidsskrift* (København) 11–13, pp. 137–75, which includes a one page summary in English.

Henri Desmerciéres, the above-mentioned son of Count Gyldensten, who seems to have brought the formation of a bank to the top of the agenda.

The new bank, born in 1736, was a very different animal from the Amsterdam Wisselbank and Hamburger Bank type of institution, which had been contemplated over the previous 112 years. It therefore also did not at all look like the 68 years older Swedish Bank ("Riksbanken", cfr. Chapter 1). In fact, it was born with a strong resemblance to the Bank of England. Like the Bank of England, it was a private joint stock company, based primarily on the issue of bank notes and a paid in capital.

According to the Regulations of the Bank (§§12–13), giro business was planned like in Amsterdam, Hamburg, and Stockholm, but since there were very few deposit accounts, this business never materialized:

The constitutional documents of the new bank consisted of (1) the Kongelig Octroy (the "Royal Charter") issued by the king, dated October 29, 1736, describing the bank's privileges, (2) the Banco-Reglement og Anordning (the "Bank Regulation"), dated November 5, 1736, laying down the main principles for conduct of the Bank's business in 22 articles, and (3) the Banco-Convention og Foreening Imellem Interessenterne udi den Allernaadigst octroyerte Kiöbenhavnske Banque (the "Bank Convention and Shareholder Agreement of the Graciously Chartered Copenhagen Bank") giving a more detailed description of the business the bank was intended to do (26 articles).

There is no doubt that the new Bank was a "bank" according to the definition suggested in the Introduction.

During most of the 18th century, the Bank was known as the "Kongeligt oktroyerede Bank" or simply as the "Københavnske Bank".

The main points of the three constitutional documents[14] were:

The charter and privileges

The preamble states that (SEA's translation): "... a bank adapted according to the circumstances of this city and these Kingdoms can be most useful for the benefit of commerce and manufacturing as well as for the maintenance of a safe and lasting credit system. Because of our most gracious and constant concern for the general well-being of our dear and loyal subjects, and for no other reason, we have ... with much pleasure and our most royal consent ... given the following privileges."

---

[14]A handwritten original of the Charter, signed and sealed, has been preserved in the National Archives (RA), where a small fragment of a contemporary copy printed in German Gothic letters is also kept. A transcript of all three documents in Danish, undated, is kept in the Århus State Library. From the quality of the paper and its layout, which is identical to the printed German/gothic fragment in the RA, it may be assumed that it is probably not much younger than the RA fragment.

In other words, the officially declared purpose of the Bank was to supply the business community with credit. Real life turned out quite differently, as the government's credit demand gradually "crowded out" the commercial sector.

The most important privilege was, of course, the irrevocable right to set up the bank in the first place, and to let the commissioners ("Commissarier"), elected by the shareholders, have a free hand in the running of the bank's affairs. The Charter did not state specifically that the Bank would enjoy a monopoly (in contrast to Palmstruch's Bank in Stockholm 78 years before, cfr. Chapter 1), but it would probably have been unrealistic for anybody else to try to obtain similar privileges.

The Bank opened for business in March the following year, managed by seven board members, elected by the shareholders, who were required to have at least ten shares in the Bank each, i.e. an investment of rd 5,000, and who were paid an annual salary of rd 400 (Convention, §11).

The share capital and the shareholders

The biggest problem, as seen by the founding fathers, was to raise the required capital.[15] The rd 500,000 share capital, decided by Count Gyllensten, was seen as the maximum amount that could realistically be expected to be raised. The collection period was foreseen to stretch over four years.

To everybody's surprise and relief, the entire capital was subscribed in a few days.

The largest shareholders were Count Gyllensten and Mr. Desmerciéres, his son, who between them took 10 per cent of the total. A total of 34 persons had a combined shareholding of 511 shares, but had less than 50 per cent of the votes because of the voting rights limitations. The number of shareholders totalled 285.[16]

The voting limitations were introduced at the insistence of the merchants who feared, correctly, that the Crown and its representatives would end up as the largest shareholder group.

The 1762–1763 increase of the share capital to rd 2.5 million was undertaken to facilitate the Bank's financing of the military expenses in connection with the expected war against Russia, and the 1766–1767 reduction to rd 600,000 was decided because of a planned reduction in the Bank's lending volume, when it was apparent that the war would not materialize.

---

[15]"Det problem, som først maatte rejse sig, ... var, om det ville være muligt at tilvejebringe den nødvendige aktiekapital. Det var da ogsaa det spørgsmaal, Gyldensteen først beskæftigede sig med." E. Rasmussen (1950–1952) "Kurantbankens Oprettelse" (*Historisk Tidsskrift*) 11–13, p. 152.

[16]E. Rasmussen (1950–1952) "Kurantbankens Oprettelse", *HT*, 11–13, pp. 167–8.

The bank notes

According to the Charter (§7) the notes issued by the Bank should be considered ready money by everybody everywhere in the King's lands. However, they could always be demanded converted into coin on any working day ("... Banquens Billetter, eller Banco-Sedlerne, ... skulle over alt i Vores Riger og Lande, have deres fri og ubehindrede Löb og som reede Penge gaae fra Haand til anden, indtil deres Belöb udi Myndt in Natura i Banquen affordres ... paa ... alle Sögne Dage ... Og i hvorvel ingen particulaire af den anden bör være forbunden samme imod sin Vilje at antage, saa ville Vi dog Allernådigst, at de udi Contributioner, samt Told og Consumption, og i alle Vores Indkomsters og Forpagtningers Oppebörsel og Afgift, udi Vores Riger og Lande, ligesom reede Penge bör imodtages ...").[17] This meant that the bank notes were legal tender.

Convertibility was suspended between 1745 and 1747 because of large note issues caused by preparations for war against Sweden. Convertibility was suspended again in 1757 because of preparations for war against Russia. It was never re-established in the 56 remaining years of the Bank's lifetime.

The deposits and depositors

No efforts seem to have been made to collect deposits. No interest was paid on deposits. It took more than 25 years to acquire 50 depositors, and during those 25 years the four largest depositors accounted for 60–80 per cent of the total deposits.[18]

The largest depositors in that period were the king, other government agencies, and after 1762, H.C. Schimmelmann, the finance minister. Throughout the lifetime of the Bank, government agencies were the dominating depositors in the Bank.

Towards the end of the Bank's life, the number of depositors had grown to about 200, a far cry from the 3,000 depositors enjoyed by the Stockholm Bank (which paid interest on deposits).

The lending business

All loans had to be for amounts of minimum rd 100 (Regulation, §14 and Convention, §18), have a maturity normally not less than one month, and not exceeding six months, and interest always to be paid in advance (Convention, §18). All loans had to be secured with acceptable collateral, i.e. all sorts of merchandise (Convention, §17), which were not considered subject to rapid loss of value. Fish, wines, and spirits were expressly mentioned as unacceptable.

---

[17]Quoted from the above-mentioned (fn. 14) printed version kept in the State Library in Århus.
[18]Cfr. The Bank's year-end balance sheets in the National Archives.

The attitude towards fixed property as collateral seems to have been curiously ambivalent. Each of the three constitutional documents addressed this issue, but they reflected widely different attitudes ranging from sanguine positive to sceptical negative. The issue was not solved until the 1762 capital increase, when an amendment clarified that fixed property was perfectly acceptable as collateral. The ambivalence was rather strange considering that one of the reasons advanced for creating the bank in the first place was to provide finance for the rebuilding of Copenhagen after the great fire of 1728.

Otherwise, the lending activity was only restricted by the Commissioners' perception of the "markets" willingness to accept the notes issued by the Bank, and a general lending guideline in the Convention's §17 (SEA's translation): "Concerning more loans, all of which cannot really be specified here, it will be up to the good judgement and foresightedness of the Commissioners, on the one hand that they do not lend the Bank's money, and particularly not large amounts, except against the best possible security, and not to others than such as those to whom they would entrust their own means, but on the other hand, that they are not too difficult, which could hamper the Bank's income and functioning, which it is otherwise hereby sought to enhance for everybody's benefit."[19] This admirably sums up the basic dilemma of all banks since ancient antiquity, or before. Nobody has yet found the miracle answer to this dilemma (Basel II and III are certainly no solution, just a re-phrasing of the dilemma).

Interest was initially decided to be 5 per cent p.a., but with a strong request to reduce it as soon as possible, cfr. the Charter, §20). The request worked. The interest rate was reduced to 4 per cent already before the Bank opened (Convention, §17). To see interest as a market price like any other market price has occasionally been a problem even 250 years later.

Since interest rates in the unregulated "markets" at this point of time were usually somewhere between 6 and 12 per cent, the Bank was clearly intended as a "cheap" source of credit (still, in Amsterdam and Hamburg credits could be had at 3–4 per cent, and the Dutch East India Company paid only 2 per cent for its credits from the Amsterdam Wisselbank, at least in some periods, and the Stockholm Bank charged 3–6 per cent depending on the circumstances, cfr. Chapter 1).

As a supplier of credit to the business community, the Bank did, during the first 10–20 years of its life, perform as planned. When the government started having financial problems, it did, eventually "crowd out" the business

---

[19]"Angaaende flere Udlaan, som ikke egentligen alle her kand specificeres, da ankommer det paa Banco Commissariernes gode Jugement og Forsynlighed, at de ikke paa den eene siide udlaaner Banquens Penge, og i særdeleshed anseelige Capitaler, uden imod mueligste og beste Sikkerhed, og ikke til andre end saadanne, som de ville betroe deres egne Midler til, og paa den anden Side dog derhos ikke ere alt for difficile, hvilket kunde hindre Banquens Indkomme og den Roullering, som man til det almindelige Beste herved söger at befordre."

community (cfr. the balance sheet figures, Table 2.3. Also, it will be seen from the Asiatisk Kompagni figures that the Bank was never of a size which could adequately service the larger trading companies. If the Copenhagen Bank had been Asiatisk Kompagnie's only source of credit, the Bank's exposure to this borrower would have exceeded its equity, even after the 1762 capital increase.

When Russia's hostility towards Denmark in early 1760s led to the mobilization of a large army, and brought the Danish government finances to its knees, a contact was somehow established with Carl Heinrich Schimmelman (1724–1782), a shrewd financial wizard who had made a fortune for himself procuring arms for the Prussian army, and who had settled in Hamburg as a proficient financier. This able man was brought to Copenhagen as "Schatzmeister", and was soon after effectively the monarchy's "finance minister". Through his contacts in Hamburg and elsewhere, he succeeded in arranging a number foreign short- and long-term loans to the Crown, the Bank, and, occasionally, some of the chartered trading companies.

The assassination of Szar Peter III in 1762 ended the threat of war, and friendship with Russia was restored. It now became imperative for Schimmelman to try to bring the Bank's balance sheet back to order. He wanted the Bank to survive as a secure future source of credit for the Crown. Besides, he was a major depositor and shareholder in the Bank. So, in 1765, an agreement was made between the government and the Bank that the Crown would repay all its debts to the Bank (over a brief period), and that the Bank would limit its loans to its approximately 450[20] private sector borrowers to a maximum of rd 3 million, of which a handful of the major trading companies accounted for more than half. The Bank had lost its independence, and had become an instrument of the government's financial policies. In this connection the Bank's share capital was reduced to rd 600,000, cfr. above.

Needless to say, the Crown did not keep its promises, nor did or could the Bank.

Table 2.3 gives a general view of the Bank's development.

The nationalization

The taking over of the Bank by the Crown in 1773 has been the subject of much gossip.

The official story[21] is that since the Bank had become an instrument of government policy anyway, it would make sense for the government to

---

[20]Cfr. H. Chr. Johansen (1968) *Dansk Økonomisk Politik i Årene efter 1784* (University of Århus, doctoral thesis) bd. I, pp. 121–2.

[21]As told by E. Rasmussen in his doctoral thesis (1955) *Kurantbankens Forhold til Staten 1737–73* (Københavns Universitet) pp. 221–37. Rasmussen did not believe in the "shady" story. Considering the sloppy way the Bank's accounts were kept and the fact that certain accounts were kept secret from the auditors, a fact Rasmussen was fully aware of, it seems a bit strange that Rasmussen dismissed the "shady" story so readily. However, there is no proof.

Table 2.3   The Copenhagen Bank's Balance Sheet: Main Figures, Selected Years, 1738–1812 (Rd kurant '000)

Year end	Assets			Total assets and liabilities (gross)	Liabilities		
	Loans to				Equity	Notes (net)	Deposits
	Crown agencies	Private sector	Cash				
1738	–	661	264	931	292	385	255
1757	243	2,310	55	2,611	551	1,926	134
1762	7,700	3,500	25	10,138	675	5,330	378
1767	3,109	1,967	146	7,224	539	4,512	168
1772	6,477	3,171	84	7,723	708	6,046	345
1790	7,474	9,487	830	32,913	660	15,583	1,643
1805	20,554	1,277	125	32,902	99	20,666	2,416
1810	(16,944)	950	58	51,152	–	43,422	7,730
1812	(15,436)	818	82	98,916	–	85,046	13,870

Sources: The Bank's archives, the National Archives, E. Rasmussen (1955) *Kurantbanken's Forhold til Staten 1737–1773* (Copenhagen University, doctoral thesis) pp. 25–33, and J. Wilcke (1929) *Kurantmønten 1726–88* (København), 1927, and same (1929) *Specie-, Kurant- og Rigsbankdaler 1788–1848* (København).

The amounts of loans to Crown agencies shown for 1810 and 1812 are in brackets, because they are misbooked in the Bank's main balance sheet books (National Archives) from which they are taken. The true amounts are close to the amounts shown for notes.

have complete control over the Bank, and the Crown would enjoy the dividends from the Bank. The only issue would be to decide on a reasonable price for a take-over.

The shady story, as spread by later historians,[22] is that a large amount of Crown debts to the Bank was recorded only in secret protocols, and that, if these assets had been known to the shareholders, the price of the shares would have been considerably higher than the price actually agreed upon. This is the story, which has survived.[23] According to this version, the motive for the plan (i.e. Schimmelmann's plan) should have been that since Schimmelmann's private financial affairs (tobacco, rhum, and sugar in the Caribbean colonies, shipping, and gun manufacturing for the army) were inextricably interwoven with those of the government, he could gain much from the freedom of maneuvering, which government ownership of the Bank could provide him in his capacity as finance minister and in his private commercial dealings with the government. He would be dealing

---

[22]First put into writing after the Bank's demise in 1813, and most forcefully voiced by M.L. Nathanson (1837–1844) *Historisk-statistisk Fremstilling af Danmarks National- og Stats-Husholdning* (Kjøbenhavn, 2nd edn) pp. 401–9.

[23]See e.g. J. Wilcke (1927) *Kurantmønten 1726–1788* (Kjøbenhavn) p. 337, and E. Olsen (1962) *Danmarks økonomiske historie siden 1750* (Københavns Universitet) p. 243.

with himself. For the Crown, the incentive was that the debts recorded in the "secret protocols" would be eliminated, and the Bank could be acquired at a lower price than otherwise.

No such "secret protocols" have ever been found. This, of course, is no proof that they never existed. Indisputably, both Carl Heinrich Schimmelmann, and Ernst Heinrich Schimmelmann (1747–1831), his son, appointed "finance minister" shortly after his father's death in 1782, would have had a strong motive and plenty of opportunity to destroy any such evidence. Nobody else had so much direct influence over the Bank in the 40 years between the nationalization of the Bank orchestrated by the elder Schimmelmann in 1773, and the closing of the Bank by his son in 1813.

If true, the younger Schimmelmann might have learned a lesson, which certainly was to his benefit in connection with the Crown's taking over of two of the chartered trading companies in 1784 and 1786, at prices highly advantageous to the shareholders, including the finance minister himself.[24]

In 1827, E.H. Schimmelmann was rewarded for his services to the country by being made foreign minister of the (now reduced) monarchy, a position he held until his death in 1831.

The end

After the visits to Copenhagen by the English admirals Parker and Nelson in 1801, and a second visit in 1807 by other English gentlemen, Copenhagen and the Danish navy had to be rebuilt. This was expensive, and most of the financing was done by Crown borrowings from the Kurantbank, which meant printing paper money without limits. Between 1810 and 1812 the volume of notes issued by the Kurantbank had trebled. In 1812, it quintupled. In the words of a later observer, the notes were like big, white snowflakes. They were dissolved, when they hit the ground.[25] In 1813, the notes lost nearly all their remaining value. Between 1807 and 1813 the value of the rd "kurant", i.e. the currency in circulation, dropped from about 70 per cent of the rd species (i.e. the silver coin) to 0.7 per cent.[26]

In 1813, reality had to be faced, and Ernst Schimmelmann decided on a currency reform, which implied the dissolution of the Kurantbank, and that holders of debt instruments, including bank notes, would get their money back in the shape of new money to be issued by a new bank – the state-owned

[24]Cfr. P.P. Sveistrup (1942–1944) "Det Danske Vestindiske Handelsselskab", *HT*, 10–16, pp. 420–6, and K. Klem (1970) *Det Kgl. Østersøisk-guineeiske Handelsselskab* (Handels-og Søfartsmuseets Årbog).

[25]"Sedler ... der havde det tilfælles med den virkelige Tøsnes store Fnugger, at den opløstes, idet den nåede Jorden." Marcus Rubin (1892) *1807–14. Studier til Københavns og Danmarks Historie* (København) p. 258.

[26]Cfr. P. Thestrup (1991) *Mark og skilling, kroner og ører. Pengeenheder, priser og lønninger i 350 år* (Rigsarkivet/National Archives) p. 13.

Rigsbank – in amounts depending on the date of the respective claims, and depending on the debtor. The Crown's creditors could choose between settling their claims with one-sixth of their face value, or accept low-interest perpetual government bonds at full-face value, but of doubtful real value.

Within five years, the Rigsbank was to be replaced by a new privately owned bank.

This was the Currency reform, forever after known as the notorious Danish State Bankruptcy of January 5, 1813.[27]

2.3.3 Other "organized" lending institutions

During the last quarter of the 18th century, a number of government lending offices were created for various purposes. From the brief descriptions given below it will be seen that these offices did not have the effect of creating a "capital market" in the sense that borrowers were given the opportunity to choose between different competing lenders to obtain the best possible solution to their individual financing problems. With the exception of two institutions, the Generalmagasinet and the Danmark-Norges Speciesbank, the other three offices had very narrow and specific purposes, and they never achieved a size to make them significant sources of credit. In spite of their names, they were not "banks".

The *Banque Comptoire* was created 1773 mainly to support the exchange rate. It also made occasional loans to distressed companies, e.g. in the 1782 "mini-crisis". Dissolved 1817. The *Kongelige Creditkasse* was created 1786 to assist farmers with long-term loans. Closed 1816. *Depositokassen*, was created 1799 to assist distressed companies. Dissolved 1813. All of these offices were funded mainly with credits from the Copenhagen Bank.

Generalmagasinet

In the spirit of the prevailing mercantilistic thinking, the Generalmagasin was created in 1737–1738 for the purpose of acting like a wholesaler, which offered some finance to its clients. It was far from a "bank".

The office was funded by government grants, borrowings from the newly created Copenhagen Bank, and by more or less forced loans from civil servants.

It was not successful. Good products were sold by the manufacturers directly in the market, while bad products were sold to the Generalmagasin (there is a strong resemblance to the similar Swedish institution, cfr. Chapter 1).

Closed in 1771.

---

[27]The Decree of January 5, 1813 ("Forordning om Forandring i Pengevæsenet for Kong-erigerne Danmark og Norge, samt Hertugdømmerne Slesvig og Holsteen"), the Currency Reform, has been reprinted in Danmarks Nationalbank (1968) *Dansk Pengehistorie*, bd. 3 (bilag, v. K. Mordhorst) pp. 217–20 and is analysed in *Dansk Pengehistorie*, bd. 1, pp. 100–7, by K.E. Svendsen, and by Sv. Å. Hansen (1960) *Pengevæsen og Kredit 1813–1860* (Kreditforeningen af Grundejere i Fyens Stift) pp. 64–70.

Danmark-Norges Speciesbank, 1791

Danmark-Norges Speciesbank was established in 1791 as a private joint stock company with a share capital of rd 2.4 million species. The plan was that it should take over the lending activities of the Copenhagen Bank. It was, therefore, not a competitor or a supplement to the Copenhagen Bank, but planned as a replacement.

It was the creation of this "bank" that made the Copenhagen Bank be known as the "Kurantbank" (issuing "kurant notes", or "current notes", i.e. sub-par inconvertible money), in order to differentiate it from the "species bank", which could issue convertible notes up to an amount of 1.9 times its silver holdings.

Because of the very cautious lending policies necessitated by the silver coverage requirements, there was no way it could satisfy demand. By 1800, its lending volume had reached a level equal to approximately half of that of the Kurantbank it was supposed to replace. Credit demands after 1800, particularly from the Crown, could only be satisfied from the Kurantbank, which was not hampered by tedious concerns about silver holdings, and whose lending activities were consequently reactivated.

The Species Bank was taken over by the Crown in 1813, and dissolved in 1817.

2.3.4   The "market" for long-term capital, insurance companies, and the first mortgage credit institution: Kreditkassen for Husejere i Kjøbenhavn

None of the above mentioned institutions (except Den Kongelige Creditkasse) offered any long-term loans, except in the sense that short-term loans could, in principle, be prolonged. However, some private, or semi-private (i.e. royally chartered) insurance companies or pension funds did invest in medium- or long-term bonds secured with mortgages over fixed property. These institutions were primarily:

- *Kjøbenhavns Brandforsikring*, founded 1731, as a result of the great fire of 1728, with a share capital of rd 300,000. In 1784 it had assets of rd 1,463,000[28] primarily invested in Copenhagen mortgages. Had to be reconstructed after the fire of 1795.
- *Det Kongeligt octroyerede Kjøbenhavnske Brand-Assurance-Kompagni på Varer og Effekter* (fire insurance for goods), founded 1778 with a share capital of rd 300,000. Its assets were mainly placed in government bonds.
- *Den Almindelige Enkekasse* ("Widows' General Pensionfund"), established 1775. It made long-term loans of rd 100,000–250,000 annually during the 1780s.[29] Wound up 1845.

---

[28]H. Chr. Johansen (1968) *Dansk økonomisk Politik efter 1784* (Århus Universitet, doctoral thesis) bd. I, p. 138.
[29]H. Chr. Johansen (1968) *Dansk økonomisk politik efter 1784*, p. 138.

Finally, there was the *Kreditkassen for Husejere i Kjøbenhavn*, the first mortgage institution in the Nordic area, founded 1797 for the purpose of financing the rebuilding of Copenhagen after the Great Fire in 1795. The idea of how to organize the financing of a reconstruction of one-third of the town was entirely new in Denmark, if not elsewhere in continental Europe. As the name suggests, its lendings were restricted to properties in central Copenhagen.

The Kreditkasse was funded partly with a paid in capital of rd 300,000 (like some of the Prussian Landschaften), but mostly with bonds issued "on tap" as loans were disbursed. They carried a nominal interest of 4 per cent. In addition, a number of private individuals had issued guarantees (against a fee), and the king had graciously agreed to guarantee the bonds with an amount up to Rd 300,000 (discontinued for bonds issued after 1816). The loans and bonds had unlimited maturities, so that Crown guaranteed bonds were still circulating by the end of the 19th century. The Crown guarantee never had to be called.

Legally, it was a non-profit association of creditors, in contrast to the Prussian Landschaften and the later Danish mortgage associations, which were associations of borrowers.

The bonds were negotiable, but since nobody could know whether a satisfactory secondary market for the bonds would develop, the bondholders had the right, until 1813, to call the loans at any time, just as the borrowers could repay the loans at any time. There was no fixed amortization plan, and the borrowers were jointly liable for the Kreditkasse's obligations, like in the Landschaften.[30]

Kreditkassen for Husejere i Kjøbenhavn survived until 1975, when it merged into BRFkredit A/S.

2.4   The stock exchange

2.4.1   The stock exchange building "Børsen"[31]

This Copenhagen landmark building with its sandstone ornaments and dragon tail spire, known since its construction in the years 1619–1640 as "Børsen", was conceived by King Christian IV as a personal investment. The king

---

[30]The history of this institution has been described in "Kreditkassen for Husejere i Kjøbenhavn 1. Marts 1797–1, Marts 1897", Kjøbenhavn, 1897. This centenary memorial script was kindly made available to SEA by BRFkredit.

[31]A full official history of the Copenhagen Stock Exchange has never been written. The latest and most comprehensive "History" is J. Werner "Børsen", 1915, which is, however, mostly a history of the building. Also, V. Lorenzen (ed.) "Grosserer-Societetet", Copenhagen, 1942, a celebratory book published by the Grosserer-Societet (the "Merchants' Guild") on the occasion of its bicentennial birthday and the 125 year birthday of the "Committee of the Merchants' Guild" contains useful information on the Stock Exchange, although the book primarily deals with the Guild and its presidents through the ages.

personally paid for it, and let the space to merchants who used the ground floor to warehouse all sorts of commodities, while the first floor was used as offices and shops.

Between 1738 and 1785,[32] a number of rooms in the east end of the building were used by the Copenhagen Bank, which owned the building from the middle of the century until 1813, when it again became Crown property. The presence of the Copenhagen Bank in the building obviously cemented the place as Copenhagen's financial centre.

In 1855–1857 the building was sold to Grosserer-Societetet (the Merchants' Guild), which has owned it ever since.

Throughout the 17th and 18th centuries, and well into the first half of the 20th century, the Exchange was primarily a commodities exchange. The question is how and when the place changed into a "stock exchange" as defined in the Introduction.

2.4.2   The royal decrees of 1808[33]

On December 22, 1808, three royal decrees were issued defining most of the formal framework for the Stock Exchange until 1920. They replaced three earlier royal decrees,[34] which regulated the activities of brokers ("mæglere"), the use of bills of exchange, and a certain formalities regarding the conduct of business on the Stock Exchange. The 1808 decrees retained much of the substance of the earlier decrees, but were much more detailed.

Their main points were:

"Forordning for Mæglere i Kiøbenhavn" ("1808 Mæglerforordningen")

("Decree for Brokers in Copenhagen", the "1808 Broker Decree")

According to §5 of this decree,[35] brokers were grouped into four different classes: Commodity brokers, bill brokers, shipbrokers, and assurance brokers. A broker

---

[32]In 1785 the Bank had a new building erected adjacent to the south side of stock exchange building. This building was the home of the Copenhagen Bank and its successors (Rigsbanken and Nationalbanken i Kjøbenhavn) until 1878, when it was demolished, and the Bank moved into its "modern" premises in the shape of a Florentine style palace in Holmens Kanal, demolished about 1970 to be replaced by the present marble palace of Danmarks Nationalbank.

[33]The said decrees are published in: "Kronologisk Register over de Kongelige Forordninger og Aabne Breve samt andre trykte Anordninger som fra 1670 af ere udkomne." Kiøbenhavn, 1812 - - -, kept in the "Royal Library" (Kgl. Bibliotek), Department for Economics.

[34] 1: Forordning af 16 April, 1681, om Commerciens og Navigationens Befordring, saa og Vexel-Retten;

2: Forordning af 26 Januar, 1684, om Mæglernes Articler i Kjøbenhavn ("Mæglerforordningen");

3: Børs-Ordonnance til Negotiens Nytte af 18 Juni, 1692.

[35]An original of this Royal Decree, has miraculously survived – in poor condition – in the cellars of the Copenhagen Stock Exchange, which kindly let SEA take a photocopy.

could, in principle obtain a licence for all four classes except that commodity and shipbroking could not be combined.

One of the most important aspects of this decree (and the 1684 Broker Decree) was that it applied only to "mæglere" (brokers), later "vexelmæglere", who were pure middlemen and could trade absolutely nothing for their own account. "Vekselerere" (stockbrokers) were, essentially, wholesaler-merchants who had specialized in the trading of financial assets and could trade anything, also for their own account. Socially, they were worlds apart from the brokers, even if the brokers were respected and often quite wealthy citizens. The distinction between "vexelmæglere" and "vekselerere" – corresponding to the distinction between jobbers and stockbrokers on the London Stock Exchange – continued until 1920.

Brokers were sworn by the City Executive upon recommendation from the Grosserer-Societet (the "Merchants Guild").

A new responsibility of the brokers was introduced by §20, which required the brokers to issue a weekly price list for commonly traded commodities, bills of exchange, species coins, discount rates, shares, and assurances in co-operation with the merchants of the town ("Ligesom det herefter skal være en fælleds Pligt for samtlige Stadens Mæglere, eengang hver Uge, efter nærmere Overenskommelse med Stadens Handlende, at besørge en nøiagtig Priis Courant paa Vexler og Speciesmynt, samt Disconto og Actiers Priis, tilligemed Assurancepræmierne …").

Thus, *the first official price list for Danish securities was born*,[36] but because of the troubled times and the irregularity of transactions, the first official price list did not appear until May 12, 1810.[37] It comprised six shares and ca. 10 bonds.

"Anordning om Børsens Holdelse i Kiøbenhavn" ("Børsanordningen")

("Decree on Stock Exchange Procedures" the "Stock Exchange Decree")

Compared to the 1692 Exchange Ordinance, the most important new elements were (1), the provision for a royally appointed Børs-Commissaire ("Stock Exchange Commissioner") and (2), a specification of the type of assets which could be auctioned on the Stock Exchange premises.

The task of the Commissioner was primarily to supervise the auctions, to ensure that they were conducted orderly according to the rules, and to prevent any unauthorized persons from participating in the proceedings of the Exchange. The only indication of a definition of "unauthorized persons" was a mentioning of beggars and other people without legitimate interest in the stock exchange business.

---

[36]Actually, a rescript dated February 27, 1787, had already requested an official price list to be made out by the brokers twice a week. However, this list appeared only with highly irregular intervals, and listed only foreign bills of exchange.

[37]J. Werner "Børsen", 1915, p. 94.

The specification of assets which could be auctioned on the Exchange read (SEA's translation): "Merchandise and commodities, ship and accessories, ship participations, shares, bills of exchange and other negotiable securities, and other instruments of debt." There was very little which could not be traded.

("Placat, hvorved Forordningen om Commercien for Danmark og Norge af 4. aug. 1742 i visse Dele nærmere bestemmes og indskærpes".
(Commerceforordningen af 1808")

("Public notice whereby certain parts of the Decree on Commerce in Denmark and Norway, dated August 4, 1742, are more precisely defined and stressed".
"The 1808 Commerce Decree")

The 1742 Decree[38] was a lengthy document giving detailed instructions on the nature and quantities of goods, which could be traded by wholesalers, and by various categories of retailers respectively. The significance of the Decree for the capital market was only indirect through the status it gave to the wholesalers, who were later given a central role in the appointment of brokers ("mæglere") and the production of the official price list of the Stock Exchange in co-operation with the brokers. The special status given to the wholesalers was signified by the order they were given to select a president and two vice presidents (the "Elders") representing the merchants in discussions with the government. It was, in fact, a "lobby group" set up by act of law. It was, initially, a very loosely connected group, without any formal framework, later to become known as "Grosserer-Societetet"[39] (the "Merchants' Guild").

The combined effect of the three decrees of 1808 was very close to establishing the Copenhagen Stock Exchange as a "real" stock exchange in the sense of the definition proposed in the Introduction. December 22, 1808, could very well be proclaimed the "birthday" of the Copenhagen Stock Exchange.

However, in Copenhagen the commodities exchange was not separated from the stock exchange until well into the 20th century. Until the mortgage bonds had established themselves in the market, the Copenhagen Stock Exchange remained primarily a commodities exchange.

Whether the Copenhagen (and London) stock exchanges could be seen as distinct legal entities in the early 19th century, is doubtful. They had grown up from a particular set of circumstances and habits, in contrast to some other exchanges (e.g. Berlin, Oslo, and Helsinki), which had been created by government decisions.

---

[38]"Forordning af 4. aug. 1742 om Commercien for Danmark og Norge, til sammes desto bedre Befordring og bestandige Fortgang, samt for god Orden og Skik derved at holde."
[39]Most of the wholesalers recognized the inadequacy of this and in 1790 organized "Grosserernes Nøjere Forening" ("The more particular association of merchants") with formal bye-laws. Originally, it comprised 39 of Copenhagen's ca. 50 largest merchant houses.

2.4.3 The securities traded on the stock exchange

Since the mid-18th century, some journals made occasional mentions of shares having been traded on the Stock Exchange, and from 1759 such information usually included prices of the traded shares.[40]

In the second half of the 18th century, the trading activity was dominated by shares in about 10–15 companies – the Copenhagen Bank, the Species Bank, ca. 8 chartered trading companies, a few sugar refineries and insurance companies, and two Norwegian mining companies, but not all of these simultaneously. In the early 19th century a large volume of government bonds began to dominate the scene, and nearly all of the shares of the chartered trading companies disappeared.

Asiatisk Kompagni was the only one of the chartered trading companies, which survived the war period. This, of course, reduced the share trading to almost nothing for many years. When the concept of an "official price list" was introduced (1808/1810, cfr. above), it listed only six shares (three insurance companies, a brewery, a sugar refinery, and the Asiatic Company), seven assorted government or government related bonds, and bonds issued by the Kreditkasse for Husejere i Kiøbenhavn.[41]

The main activity for the "vekselerere" (whose number had swollen from ca. 60 in 1790 to about 200 in 1810), "mæglere", captains, and shipping agents who thronged the Stock Exchange Building in the early 19th century, was trading commodities. Particularly grain and gossip.

---

[40]Cfr. B. Stancke (1971) *The Danish Stock Market 1750–1840* (Institute of Economic History, Copenhagen University) which gives a detailed review of share prices recorded on the Stock Exchange in this period.

[41]Cfr. A.v. Benzon (1944) *Fondsbørsen og Kreditforenings Systemet* in Th. Kristensen (ed.) *Haandbog i Kredit og Hypotekforeningsforhold* (Odense) pp. 551–2.

3
Denmark, 1818–1918: A Dismembered Country

"The fire seven times tried this,
Seven times tried that judgement is
That did never choose amiss"

("The Merchant of Venice", Act II)

3.1 An overview: Rising from the ashes

Politically, the Danish governments chose amiss on a number of occasions between 1800 and 1864. Some of these decisions led to rampant inflation, bankruptcy of the Crown, and the loss of Norway (cfr. Chapters 2 and 5), and in 1863–1864 other errors of judgement led to the loss of the duchies of Schleswig and Holstein.[1] However, strong liberal sentiments dominated most political decisions until the end of the century, and after the setbacks of the loss of Norway, and the general European agricultural depression of the 1820s, relative prosperity was eventually restored.

Economically and commercially, the 19th century was characterized by a gradual restoration of orderly government finances since about 1840, and growing demand for agricultural products from England and Germany. This led to improved prices and to accelerated growth of Danish exports and incomes. Exports to England and Germany soon more than compensated for the market lost in Norway.

---

[1]Denmark's 1849 Constitution did not apply to the duchy of Schleswig, a fact which strongly hurt the romantic and nationalistic feelings prevailing at the time. This was amended in the 1863 Constitution. However, to make it applicable to Schleswig but not to Holstein would be a gross violation of the 1460 agreement by which the two duchies could never be separated, and none of them could ever be more closely connected to Denmark than the other. It could not, of course, be made applicable in Holstein, which was a member of the German Federation, and which just "happened" to have the Danish king as its duke. So, it was decided to introduce the amended constitution in Schleswig, in spite of the complications. Bismarck, the Prussian chancellor, chose to consider the matter a causa belli.

Table 3.1   Indicators of Industrialization and Urbanization

	Total population '000	Urban population in % of total	GDP contribution in per cent from		
			Manufacturing	Agriculture	Other
1860	1,600	24	19	43	38
1880	1,969	28	16	42	42
1900	2,450	38	21	28	51
1915	2,921	41	19	29	52

Sources: Danmarks Statistik, as presented in H. Chr. Johansen (1985) *Dansk Økonomisk Statistik*, vol. 9 of *Danmarks Historie*, 1–9 (Gyldendal, København) pp. 107 and 388–411.

Although income from services, shipping, and construction ("Other") increased faster than the rest of the economy, Denmark remained fundamentally an agricultural country well into the 20th century. The fact that urbanization progressed faster in Denmark than in the other Nordic countries does not change this conclusion, and can probably be explained by the fact that Denmark is smaller and more densely populated than the three other Nordic countries, and that an increasing share of the agricultural products was treated and developed in the cities (e.g. tinned foods and beer). The timing of Denmark's industrialization has been discussed intensively.[2] The consensus seems to be that the industrial "breakthrough" did not happen until the 1890s, or even later. The fact is that the GDP contribution from manufacturing did not overtake the agricultural contribution until the 1930s. In Sweden, this happened already before WWI.

Thus, Denmark displays the paradox of a relatively slow and late industrialization combined with a fast and extensive urbanization. By 1900, Copenhagen, the largest Nordic city, had 400,000 inhabitants, a quadrupling over 100 years.

The institutional framework of the "capital market" remained nearly unchanged until the middle of the 19th century. In 1845, like in 1737, there was only one bank. The only additions to the scene were a mortgage institution, which was active only in the centre of Copenhagen (cfr. Chapter 2), and about ten tiny savings banks of no consequence as capital market institutions.

From about 1850, however, the financial sector grew faster than in the other Nordic countries, and Hamburg ceased to be the dominating source of credit to the commercial and agricultural sectors. As from about 1875,

---

[2]See e.g. Sv. Å. Hansen (1969) *Early Industrialization in Denmark* (Copenhagen), O. Hornby (1969) *Industrialization in Denmark and the Loss of the Duchies* (Scandinavian Economic History Review, vol. XVII, no. 1), and R. Willerslev (1952) *Studier i dansk industrihistorie 1850–1880* (Copenhagen), and A. Nielsen (1944) *Industriens Historie i Danmark* , bd. I–3 (Copenhagen). Prof. Sv. Å. Hansen argues convincingly that no breakthrough happened until the 1890s.

Denmark satisfied most of the criteria for having a capital market as defined in the Introduction.

Between 1813 and 1873 the currency was the rigsbankdaler (rbd), 1854 re-named rigsdaler (rd), with half the silver value of the old rigsdaler (i.e. 12.64 gr. of fine silver). Joining the gold standard in 1873, the rigsdaler was replaced by the krone (0.44803 gr. of fine gold), with two kroner equal to one rigsdaler.

For ease of comparisons, all pre-1873 amounts in this chapter have been restated in kroner (DKK).

In 1873, Denmark and Sweden entered the Scandinavian Currency Union, in which one DKK equalled one Swedish krona (SEK), and the two currencies were legal tender in both countries. In 1877, the Currency Union was joined by Norway.

The Scandinavian Currency Union broke up during WWI.

3.2   The problems

The problems, from a capital market perspective, were – as elsewhere – the financing needs generated by a relatively fast changing nature of the economy. The fact that industrialization came slowly and late to Denmark did not mean that capital spending was insignificant.

Tenant farmers bought their farms from the large landowners, and farming became mechanized. Table 3.2 below shows the growing ratio of gross fixed investments and savings to gross domestic product. From the 1890s onwards, these ratios seem to have been higher in Denmark than in the other Nordic countries (cfr. Chapters 4, 5, and 6).

More than 1,000 dairies and slaughterhouses were built in the 1880–1900 period, and between 1876 and 1918 agricultural fixed gross

Table 3.2   Gross Domestic Product and Gross Fixed Investments, Selected Years, 1860–1914

Average of years	Gross domestic product million DKK	Gross savings in % of GDP	Gross invest-ment in % of GDP	Average of years	Gross domestic product million DKK	Gross savings in % of GDP	Gross invest-ment in % of GDP
1860–1863	486	15	14	1895–1898	1,098	15	19
1867–1868	643	9	11	1900–1904	1,399	19	21
1876–1877	802	12	13	1907–1910	1,811	18	20
1880–1882	843	11	12	1912–1914	2,344	20	17
1888–1890	929	10	12				

Source: Sv. Å. Hansen (1983) *Økonomisk Vækst i Danmark*, bd. I+II (Københavns Universitet), bd. II, Tables 3 and 7.

investments varied between 15 and 30 per cent of total fixed gross investments.[3]

In the first half of the 19th century, gross fixed investments were at a relatively low level, but in spite of accelerating capital spending, Denmark actually emerged from the 1860s as a net creditor country – helped by a large lump sum payment as compensation for the abolition of the Sound Toll in 1857. However, towards the end of the 19th century and in the early 20th century, investments took an almost feverish pace, substantially outstripping domestic savings, and large foreign borrowings were made. It has been estimated that 20–25 per cent of the investments made between 1870 and 1907 were financed with foreign borrowings.[4]

The foreign borrowings were not quite unproblematic. The mortgaging of fixed property to German insurance companies, and the taking over of other Danish assets by German lenders was cause for some concern, just as it was a discomforting experience that when Denmark contemplated an increased import duty on French wine to protect the weak balance of payments, the French government threatened to close the Paris Stock Exchange to new issues of Danish bonds.[5]

3.3   Responses and actions

3.3.1   Financing agricultural investments and railways

Dairies and slaughterhouses

There can be little doubt that the formation of the co-ops greatly facilitated the financing of the fairly large investments in mechanical dairies and slaughterhouses in the last two decades of the 19th century. The personal liability of the members for the loans taken up by the co-ops made them seem acceptable credit risks for the young and small banks and savings banks.

The first co-operative in Denmark was a consumer co-op, formed 1866, but in contrast to the rest of Europe the expansion of the co-ops in Denmark happened almost exclusively with producer co-operatives. Thus, 1,050 of the 1,100 dairies built between 1882 and 1899 were co-ops.[6] Between 1887 and 1899, 30 slaughterhouses were built, 25 of which were co-ops.[7]

---

[3]Cfr. Sv. Å. Hansen (1983) *Økonomisk Vækst i Danmark* (Københavns Universitet, Inst. for Økonomisk historie) 3. udg. bd. II, Tables 7 and 8, pp. 267–72.

[4]H. Chr. Johansen (1985) *Danmarks Historie, 1–9*, bd. 9, *Dansk Økonomisk Statistik 1814–1980* (Gyldendal, København) p. 91, and Sv. Å. Hansen (1983) *Økonomisk Vækst i Danmark* (Københavns Universitet) bd. I, p. 309.

[5]Sv. Å Hansen (1983) *Økonomisk Vækst i Danmark*, bd. I–II (Københavns Universitet) bd. I, 3, udg., p. 310. Norway had a similar experience, cfr. Chapter 5.

[6]L. Buch (1960) "Investeringerne inden for Mejerierne og Slagterierne", *Nationaløkonomisk Tidskrift*, p. 132.

[7]Since the 1990s, 93–7 per cent of all dairy products and slaughters have been produced by just two co-ops, Arla (dairy products) and Danish Crown (meat).

Table 3.3 illustrates how the ca. DKK 25 million dairy investments undertaken in the years 1882–1899 were financed:

Table 3.3   Dairy Investments and Their Financing, 1882–1899

Source of finance	Million DKK		%	
Co-op capital paid in	ca.	2.0	ca.	7
Loans from savings banks	–	18.0	–	73
Banks	–	2.5	–	9
Mortgage associations	–	0.5	–	2
Other	–	2.5	–	9
Total	ca.	24–25		100

Source: L. Buch (1960) "Investeringerne inden for Mejerierne og Slagterierne", *Nationaløkonomisk Tidsskrift*, pp. 131–43.

The average capital outlay per dairy was about DKK 22,000, not by itself a very large amount, but as seen from Table 3.3 most of the financing came from the savings banks, which had average levels of deposits around DKK 600,000–700,000 in the 1880s, cfr. Table 3.7 below, and which also supplied the working capital to the dairies. Most of the rural savings banks would have 3–5 dairies among their customers, and thus were heavily exposed to this sector.

Slaughterhouses were slightly different because they were much more capital intensive. The average slaughterhouse was five times as expensive to set up as the average dairy, and the 30 slaughterhouses built in the years 1887–1899, cost a total of ca. DKK 4 million.[8] However, also in these cases the savings banks were the main source of finance, including working capital.

Railways

Railways were started in Denmark when in 1844 the government was persuaded by a business organization, Industriforeningen, (as from 1910 Industriraadet, "The Federation of Danish Industries") to grant a concession to a newly founded company, Det Sjællandske Jernbaneselskab A/S, to build a railway between Copenhagen and Roskilde, a 30 km stretch of flat land with no natural obstacles.

The cost had originally been estimated at ca. DKK 2 million, but ended up at roughly 4 million. It was decided to form Det Sjællandske Jernbaneselskab with a share capital of DKK 3 million. The only problem was to raise the

---

[8]L. Buch (1960) "Investeringerne inden for Mejerierne og Slagterierne", *Nationaløkonomisk Tidsskrift*, pp. 136–8. Out of 13 slaughterhouses examined by Buch, eight had used savings banks only, three had used both banks and savings banks, and two had used only banks.

capital. The government would have nothing to do with it. Neither the usefulness nor the profitability of the project was evident to the government.

Only 15 per cent of the shares could be sold in Denmark. The rest was sold in Germany, mostly in Hamburg.[9] So, in 1847, the first railway in any of the Nordic countries was inaugurated with trumpet fanfares and much curiosity.

The difficulties encountered in raising the necessary capital, and the unexpectedly high construction costs, meant that the planned extension of the railway to Korsør was postponed for about five years. It was built by an English engineering company, which also arranged the financing, mostly through a share issue in London (GBP 535,000, or approximately DKK 5 million).

The big issue, fiercely discussed for more than 15 years, was the plan for a railway in Jutland. It was recognized that the Danish capital market would be unable to absorb the amount of shares and bonds which would have to be issued, if this project was left to private investors. The volume of circulating bonds and shares would be increased by 50 per cent compared to the pre-1848 volume, and that would "crowd out" other borrowers.[10] At this time, three new mortgage institutions were just being started, the government had substantial borrowing requirements, and the Municipality of Copenhagen was about to launch a large new bond loan on the market. There was no "room" for more bond issues.

Eventually (1859), a contract was signed with a large English engineering company, to build and finance the railway at construction costs estimated at around DKK 40 million, 75 per cent of which was financed with Sterling bonds. A company was formed with a share capital of DKK 5 million, planned to be sold in London by the engineering company. This proved impossible, so the engineering company had to keep the shares.

In 1869, the engineering company was severely short of cash, so the Danish government acquired the shares in the Jutland railway company and eventually formed a state company (De Danske Statsbaner) owning and operating all the trunk lines, while several provincial feeder lines were organized as private companies.

By the late 1860s and in the 1870s, investments in railway systems and their maintenance had become a major expense for the government, absorbing 10–20 per cent of annual government revenues.[11]

By the end of the century, the railway net had been largely completed. This had been achieved with only relatively small amounts having been raised from the domestic capital market. Germany and England were the largest capital suppliers, and the government was the borrower and provider of most of the residual capital.

---

[9]Cfr. *De Danske Statsbaner 1847–1947* (Generaldirektoratet for Statsbanerne, 1947).
[10]Cfr. *De Danske Statsbaner 1847–1947*, p. 47.
[11]Cfr. *De Danske Statsbaner 1847–1947*, p. 75, and Danmarks Statistik.

3.3.2   New banks

Nationalbanken i Kjøbenhavn, 1818 (re-named Danmarks Nationalbank in 1936, the central bank)

Like Portia's second suitor at Belmont, the men of 1813–1873 focused on silver.

As part of the 1813 Currency Reform, it was decided that the Rigsbank was to be converted into a private bank as soon as possible in order to restore confidence in the currency. So, on July 4, 1818, the king signed a 54-paragraph royal charter for the new bank, valid for 90 years. The reason for the unusually long charter period was that it was realized that it would take many years for the Bank to achieve its primary goal of establishing a sound monetary system with convertibility into silver.

The main points of the Charter were[12] (SEA's translation, with a few comments):

§1:   "The Bank, which shall bear the name of Nationalbanken i Kjøbenhavn, is to be recognized as a private company, which, separately from Our finances, shall be governed by men to be elected and appointed .... We give for Ourselves and Our successors the Royal promise that no command from Us or Them shall ever influence the management of the Bank, which is to be bound alone by its Charter and Regulations ..."
This promise has been kept even if modified by the 1936 Act, cfr. below.

§3:   "The Bank's foremost objective is and will be to establish and secure a safe monetary system in the country ("... befæste et sikkert pengevæsen ..."). To that end it will endeavour with all means at its disposal ... to restore and maintain the silver par value of the Rigsbank notes taken over from the Rigsbank ...."
This paragraph was what gave the Bank a status very close to a "central bank" in a modern sense. However, to the Bank itself, its commercial activities remained its most important objectives and dictated several of its future decisions, cfr. below. The Bank referred to §3 when it suited its purposes.

§5:   "The ... purpose of the Bank is to promote the money circulation by loans and discounts in order to facilitate production, commerce, and trade; and by the opening of folio accounts and accepting deposits to keep entrusted means in safe custody ...".

§6 and §7:   The Bank's capital ("Grundfond") would consist of the "bank mortgage" ("Bankhæftelsen"), i.e. the 6 per cent first priority mortgage on the 1802 tax valuation of all private fixed property, except that for

---

[12]The Charter has been reprinted with comments in A. Rubow (1918) *Nationalbankens Historie 1818–1918*, bd. I–II, bd. 1, 1818–1878 (Nationalbanken i Kjøbenhavn) pp. 67–114.

agricultural properties this was reduced to 1 per cent because of the steep fall in agricultural incomes after 1815.

In return for this mortgage, the property owners became owners of the bank (§11), but share certificates were not issued until 1836.

In addition, there was a small amount of voluntarily paid in capital.

There was a strong incentive to pay the mortgage to the Bank, even when this had to be done in silver equivalent, because the property owner would then not have to pay the $6^{1}/_{2}$ per cent mortgage interest and would also receive 4 per cent dividend on the amount of his ownership of the Bank.

§§22–26: Stipulations regarding the lending and deposit business. Loans could be offered against good collateral. Maximum maturity was six months, but prolongations were possible. Interest was negotiable up to maximum 6 per cent p.a.

Interest on bill discounting had been freely negotiable since 1799 because of the international character of this business. There was neither minimum nor maximum maturities for the bills.

Deposits could be received in current accounts (folio) as well as notice. Interest was negotiable.

In 1857, interest rates were completely deregulated, but already next year maximum rates were re-introduced on credits secured by fixed property (4 per cent p.a.). Ceilings on mortgage loans were maintained until 1942, except for mortgage institutions, cfr. below.

§§28–41: Concern the management of the Bank. It was to have a board of 15 self-supplying directors (initially elected by a special committee), who would appoint four governors. A fifth governor would be appointed by the king. The governors were responsible for the day-to-day management of the Bank. In addition, the king would appoint a Royal Bank Commissioner ("Kongelig Bank-Kommissær") who would act as a link between the government and the Bank. Originally, this was the Minister of Justice. He had a right to be present at meetings of the governors, but he had no vote (this arrangement is still valid, except that in modern times the position of "Kongelig Bank-Commissær" has usually been held by the minister for economic affairs).

The shareholders had no rights other than receiving dividends from the moment convertibility had been restored (1845). Experience from the Bank of England had shown that shareholder elected directors could sometimes be overgenerous to their electors to the detriment of the Bank.[13]

---

[13]Rubow (1918) *Nationalbankens Historie 1818–1918*, bd. I–II (Kjøbenhavn), bd. I, p. 106.

§42:   "Nationalbanken shall be and remain the only institution in Denmark entitled to issue representative means of payment ..." (... "repræsentative Betalingsmidlers Udgivelse").

Similar promises had been made to Kurantbanken, Danmark-Norges Speciesbank and to Rigsbanken, in contrast to the Swedish Riksbank, cfr. Chapters 1 and 6.

The promises made in this Charter were made by a monarch who enjoyed absolute power,[14] and such promises were, of course, always subject to the whims of whoever was in power. In the case of Nationalbanken, the promises were actually kept.

Table 3.4 below shows the development of the Bank's lending business.

Table 3.4   Lending by Nationalbanken i Kjøbenhavn, 1818–1918, Selected Years (Amounts in million DKK)

Year	Discounted bills	Loans against securities	Mortgage loans	Government loans	Holdings of bonds & stocks	Other	Total million DKK
1818	1.9	16.2					18.1
1835	1.8	5.9					6.4
1857	30.0	13.5	11.8		0.7	0.2	56.0
1895	16.7	10.1	4.7		16.8	20.0	68.3
1906	31.4	14.5	2.3		4.7	7.9	60.8
1915	55.0	11.5	1.5	11.2	26.7	17.9	91.2
1918	42.5	15.4	1.3	108.5	28.2	25.1	221.1

Sources: 1818–1899: A. Rubow (1918) *Nationalbankens Historie 1818–1908* (Nationalbanken i Kjøbenhavn) Bilag XII.
1900–1918: *Dansk Pengehistorie*, bd. I–IV (Danmarks Nationalbank, 1968) bd. III, Bilag, v. K. Mordhorst.

Note: The "Total" column is the total of the six columns shown. Not included in the above figures are the Bank's holdings of gold, cash, and balances with domestic and foreign banks.

The figures clearly demonstrate the credit squeeze in the 1818–1835 period, when the country's only bank cut its outstanding loan volume to one-third of its 1818-level in order to accumulate silver, restore the notes to their par value against silver, and to reintroduce silver convertibility.

The acute credit needs of the 1820s and early 1830s were partly met with lendings directly by the government to both small and large landowners, as well as loans (including long term) from the rapidly growing number of

---

[14]Formally, the Danish kings held absolute power between 1660 and 1849 (in Schleswig until 1864).

savings banks, but the amounts were small. The main source of credit was bills of exchange drawn on Hamburg merchant bankers[15] and banquiers.

In the 1830s the Bank reluctantly opened two provincial branches, and later in the century, three more.

By 1836, the notes had regained their par value against silver, and the Bank embarked upon a highly expansionary credit policy – until the mid-1850s – led by a new group of governors, who included the legendary L.N. Hvidt (1835–1856) – a merchant and shipowner, who was also chairman of the Grosserer-Societet (1842–1856), president of Sparekassen for Kjøbenhavn og Omegn, the country's largest savings bank, and royally appointed stock exchange commissioner (1808–1816).

The Bank was less keen on collecting deposits, which were regarded as unstable and dangerous funds. It did not pay interest on such deposits. In fact, it charged fees for accepting call deposits, just like the Amsterdam Wisselbank. It paid interest only on larger amounts deposited at notice by various government agencies, municipalities, and savings banks.

Table 3.5 below shows the liabilities of the Bank:

Table 3.5   Liabilities of Nationalbanken i Kjøbenhavn, 1818–1918, Selected Years (million DKK)

Year	Note circulation	Government deposits	Other deposits	Equity	Solvency ratio	Total million DKK
1818	55.6					
1835	28.4					
1857	43.6					
1895	76.5					
1905	119.0	5.8	6.2	34.0	19.8%	167.5
1915	220.4	7.9	16.7	36.4	17.2%	211.9
1918	372.4	76.6	105.3	42.1	7.1%	596.4

Sources: Note circulation 1818–1875: Rubow (1918) *Nationalbankens Historie* bd. I, Bilag IX. 1876–1918: Danmarks Nationalbank (1968) *Dansk Pengehistorie* bd. 3, Bilag II. Same for the other liabilities.

When the bank's charter was about to expire (1908) the Social Democrats in the Rigsdag tried, unsuccessfully, to introduce a stronger degree of government control in the new charter. In 1907, a new charter was enacted for 30 years, essentially unchanged from the 1818 charter. Even the share capital (DKK 27 million) remained unchanged.

---

[15]It was often said at the time that Denmark had two capitals: Copenhagen, the political, cultural and social capital, and Hamburg, the materialistic one, cfr. Sv. Å. Hansen (1960) *Pengevæsen og Kredit 1813–1860* (Fyens Stifts Kreditforening) p. 124.

The Nationalbank and the government did, however, forge closer links a few years later, when new actors had taken over in both the Ministry of Finance (E. Brandes) and at the Nationalbank (M. Rubin). The background was the 1908 Banking Crisis (cfr. below). The outcome was an agreement made in 1913 between the Ministry of Finance and the Nationalbank that the latter should be the government's exclusive bank. In the future, the government (the Ministry of Finance) would have a current account only with the Nationalbank, and this account could have credit as well as debit balances. As a compensation to the other banks, which hereby lost important deposits, the Nationalbank offered to rediscount bills from those banks at a rate 0.5 per cent lower than its normal rediscount rate.[16] The Nationalbank was now closer to becoming a "central bank".

Table 3.4 above shows the relative decline of the Bank's commercial business, particularly the mortgage loans, as lendings to the government expanded. The Nationalbank did, however, continue to discount private commercial bills of exchange until after WWII, and to offer deposit accounts to private individuals until the late 1960s.

Other banks

Tired of having to send bills to Hamburg for discounting, and having asked the Nationalbank in vain to set up branches in the main provincial cities, a group of merchants established their own bank in Odense, Fyens Disconto Kasse A/S, in 1846. This was the first case in Denmark of a bank being formed without a royal charter or any government initiative. They just did it. The initiators did, however, ask for the privilege not to have to pay stamp duties, and this request was partially granted. The bank was started with a share capital of DKK 1 million and, as the name suggests, bill discounting was intended as its main business.

Over the next ten years 13 other provincial banks were created in much the same way, but none of them was anywhere near the size of the Fyens Disconto Kasse, which accounted for 22 per cent of the combined share capital of these banks by 1860.[17] They were small institutions, operating only in and around the provincial towns in which they had been created. However, in several of these provincial towns, a strong competition developed between the local banks and the local savings banks, at least for other business than bill discounting.

In Copenhagen, the Nationalbank also did not quite satisfy the demand for bill discounting and other bank services. It was restrained by its need to observe the silver coverage of its note issues, and it did not see deposit

---

[16]Cfr. Sv. Å. Hansen (1968) *Perioden 1818–1914* in *Dansk Pengehistorie*, bd. I–III (Danmarks Nationalbank) bd. I, p. 390.

[17]Cfr. E. Cohn (1957) *Privatbanken i Kjøbenhavn gennem Hundrede Aar* (Privatbanken) p. 69, where all the names and their respective amounts of share capital are given.

taking as much of an alternative way of funding loans. After the mid-1850s, the lending activities of Nationalbanken declined.

Against this background, the first major Copenhagen bank project[18] was launched in 1857 and started operations under the name of *Privatbanken i Kjøbenhavn,* deliberately contrasting it to *Nationalbanken i Kjøbenhavn* – although the latter was, in principle, also a privately owned bank, albeit under a royal charter.

The launch of Privatbanken was successful because the project was backed by 12–15 of Copenhagen's heavyweight merchants as well as by three of the country's largest landowners. They proposed a bank with a share capital of DKK 8 million, of which the proponents would supply DKK 1 million. Thus, it would be almost as big as the 14 existing provincial banks combined.

Asked by the Minister for the Interior, the Nationalbank expressed grave concerns about the proposed bank, as with some earlier proposed banking projects in Copenhagen. In the opinion of the Nationalbank, there was absolutely no need for any new bank, and the fact that the proposed statutes of the new bank did not state that it would not engage in shipping, industry, and general commerce convinced the Nationalbank that the proposed bank would be an unstable, or even dangerous, copy of the "credit mobiliers" which were having big problems in France at this time. The proponents protested that they had absolutely no such intentions.

The minister understood that the Nationalbank was jealously guarding its de facto Copenhagen monopoly, just like the Bank of England and Banque de France had previously done, and granted (most of) the requested exemption from stamp duties.

The only remaining problem was to raise the share capital. This problem turned out to be serious. The proponents underwrote the DKK 1 million as planned, but only with some difficulty was another DKK 3 million raised. Thus, Privatbanken i Kjøbenhavn was started in late 1857 with only half of its planned share capital. The share capital had been provided by just over 500 shareholders, 19 of whom had a combined holding of approximately one-third of the total, and none of whom had more than 3 per cent.[19]

Two general managers were employed. One of them, Carl Frederik Tietgen (1829–1901) became Denmark's undisputed greatest businessman for the next 25 years. When he died, an obituary in one of the leading daily newspapers read: "C.F. Tietgen is dead. The country's leading figure is dead. He towered

---

[18]By 1856, two other banking institutions existed in Copenhagen: One was "Central-kassen", a minor operation resulting from the 1831 transformation of a commercial company into a nondescript financial institution (mostly just receiving deposits from provincial savings banks) and managed by Nationalbanken, and Kjøbenhavns Private Laanebank, set up in 1854, and absorbed by Landmandsbanken in 1922.

[19]Cfr. E. Cohn (1957) *Privatbanken gennem hundrede Aar* (Privatbanken) p. 93.

above us all ... He shaped the development of our society for more than half a century ..."[20] He was only 28 years old when he was appointed, but if he was young in limbs he soon proved to be old in judgement.

Tietgen had ideas which differed from those of the directors, but after a few years and a few successes the directors had become convinced that Tietgen's strategy was fine. Privatbanken was turned into something close to a credit mobilier or a Gründerbank, much in contrast to the original plans. From the mid-1860s and for the following 20 years Privatbanken under Tietgen's guidance helped create at least 20 industrial and commercial companies,[21] and in that process also revolutionized the Danish joint stock company system by making the one-share-one-vote principle generally accepted (nearly all previous companies had had voting limitations of some sort).

However, Privatbanken does not appear to have been a "real Gründerbank". It seems that Privatbanken normally acted only as a place for subscription for shares, and that it did not itself invest in the shares of the companies it launched, or even underwrite the share issues.[22] In contrast, Tietgen would often, together with some of the Privatbank directors, personally pick up some of the shares. Tietgen, and those of the board members who followed his example, became very rich from this activity.

In a number of cases, Tietgen would also join the board of the companies he floated. Privatbanken would, of course, be the main banking connection for all of these companies.

The main reason for Privatbanken's relatively slow growth towards the turn of the century was the decision not to open branches in the provinces. The strategy was to act as the Copenhagen correspondent for the provincial banks and savings banks. In this respect Privatbanken followed a strategy also taken by the Stockholms Enskilda Bank. In the 20th century, this strategy proved not to be the winning one.

---

[20]"C.F. Tietgen er død. Landets Førstemand er død ... Han skabte vort Samfunds Udvikling i mere end et halvt Aarhundrede ..." Obituary in "Politiken", here quoted from O. Lange (2006) *Stormogulen. C.F. Tietgen – en finansmand og hans tid* (Gyldendal, Copenhagen) p. 17.

[21]Many of these companies still exist, albeit in a somewhat different shape, e.g. De Danske Sukkerfabrikker (the original core of today's Danisco), GN Great Northern (originally Det Store Nordiske Telegrafselskab), DFDS, Tuborg – de Forenede Bryggerier (merged with Carlsberg 1969), and TDC (for which the original core was Tietgen's Kjøbenhavns Telefon Aktieselskab, or KTAS). Privatbanken was the first in Denmark to have a telephone installed, so its phone no. was 1 (gradually expanded to 11 11 11 as time went by, until an entirely new system was introduced in the late 20th century).

[22]Cfr. A. Nilsen (1923) *Bankpolitik*, bd. I–II (H. Hagerups Forlag, Copenhagen) bd. 1, p. 322, where Tietgen's memoires are referred to on this point. Both Cohn and Lange are strangely silent on this matter. It would require some very deep digging in the archives to investigate this question. The immediately available accounts are too summary to cast any light on the issue.

In the meantime, Tietgen's position had created both envy and opposition. Another group of people more closely connected to the agrarian circles set out to form a competing bank which would be of more use to the landowners than Tietgen's industrially oriented bank. The result was the creation of "Landmandsbanken", which grew to be the largest Nordic bank in the 1910–1923 period.

The initiator of the plans for this bank was Niels C. Frederiksen (1840–1905), economist and professor at the university of Copenhagen, politician, and a large landowner. He was an energetic, restless, and entrepreneurial man, constantly on the move to something else, but unfortunately with no interest or patience for the tedious details of management, control, or accounting. Having first worked for the formation of the new bank and joined its board of directors, he left the board after one year in disagreement over strategy. He then concentrated on his own affairs and went bankrupt twice.

One of N.C. Frederiksen's acquaintances was a Joseph Michaelsen (1826–1908), economist and editor of a couple of magazines. A low ranking civil servant in the Mail Department, he did not seem very well positioned to be a co-founder of a new bank, but through his journalistic activities he had many useful contacts in political and financial circles, and among the large landowners. When asked by N.C. Frederiksen whom they should contact to assist them with their plans for a new bank, Michaelsen was in no doubt. The essential man to have on board was Gottlieb Abrahamson Gedalia (1816–1892), a well-known and colourful banquier and stockbroker with many contacts abroad and with a highly successful broker firm dealing in i.a. American, Russian, and Egyptian bonds. He was, however, somewhat mocked on the stock exchange for his bad manners and faulty way of speech (having been brought up mostly in Hebrew), and for his vanity, which had made him buy the title of "baron" from the republic of San Marino. His many foreign contacts had earned him the position of Consul General for Portugal, and when in 1870 a new king had to be found for Spain's vacant throne, the French ambassador to Denmark asked him if he could suggest a Nordic prince.

Having made a fortune from an earlier railway investment in western Denmark, he had tried in vain to form a credit mobilier type of bank, so he grasped enthusiastically at the new opportunity. However, following a disagreement with the rest of the directors he left the board after only a few months to pursue his own interests. Once more he went into railway financing, but this time it bankrupted him.

These were the three unlikely men who boarded the boat in 1871 to create *Den Danske Landmandsbank, Hypothek- og Vexelbank*, a name suggesting some familiarity with the German "Hypothek und Wechselbanken". However, Frederiksen and Michaelsen succeeded in gathering a fair number of large landowners with sufficient interest in the project, but with insufficient money and knowledge of banking.

The birth process was fraught with difficulties,[23] including disagreements over the composition of the board of directors, the name of the new bank, and the main focus of its business.

The biggest problem was, as usual, to find the money to capitalize the new bank. It was soon agreed that it should have a share capital of DKK 12 million – the decision on this amount might have been influenced by the fact that the Privatbank had increased its share capital to DKK 12 million a few months earlier. The large landowners were expected to subscribe a substantial amount, but at the end of the day they had provided a paltry DKK 1 million.

This was where Gedalia proved his worth. He used his sales talents, and methods which would have been unacceptable today, to form a consortium consisting of himself and his connections in Berlin and Hamburg,[24] which underwrote DKK 8 million.

Thus, Den Danske Landmandsbank was born as, essentially, a German bank in Denmark.

In the longer run, the German ownership declined, since the German shareholders rarely used their subscription rights, which were gradually bought by the Bank. By the end of the century the German shareholdings were negligible. The Bank's planned DKK 12 million share capital was fully paid-in by 1875 and doubled in 1886. The shares were accepted on the Stock Exchange's official price list in July 1875.

There were two reasons for the "Hypothek" department of the Bank:

First, the landowners wanted a facility from which they could raise long-term mortgage loans without having to accept the joint liability characterizing the mortgage associations, cfr. below. Secondly, they disliked the way the mortgage associations disbursed their loans because of the uncertainty of the final proceeds.

The bonds issued by the Hypothek department were to be secured by the mortgages and the Bank's share capital, and it would disburse its loans in cash, not in bonds.

Initially, the Hypothek department was a big success, but in the longer run it could not compete with the mortgage associations. Since the turn of the century, only the section for municipality loans was active (but the mortgage bonds kept circulating for many years).

---

[23]Cfr. J. Schovelin (1921) "Den Danske Landmandsbank, Hypothek- og Vekselbank, 1871–1921", published by the Bank on the occasion of its 50th anniversary, which gives a detailed description of the people involved and the birth process.

[24]The German underwriters were the well-known F.W. Krause & Co. (Berlin) and Johann Berenberg, Gossler & Co. (Hamburg), and Union Bank, Berlin. Cfr. Schovelin (1921) *Den Danske Landmandsbank, Hypothek og Vekselbank, 1871–1921 A/S* (Kjøbenhavn) pp. 177–91.

After some 30 years, the use of the name "Hypothek- og Vexelbank" was discontinued, and the Bank became known as "Den Danske Landmandsbank" (commonly known as "Landmandsbanken"), since 1976 "Den Danske Bank af 1871", and after the big 1990 merger just "Danske Bank".

The difficult problem of finding a capable general manager for the Bank was solved by Gedalia. In 1855 he had employed a 16-year old apprentice by the name of Isak Moses Glückstadt (1839–1910), whom he ten years later dispatched to Kristiania (Oslo) to sort out his problems in Norway. Glückstadt's efforts succeeded. He stayed in Kristiania, profitably expanding Gedalia's Norwegian business until 1870, when he was headhunted to become general manger of Den norske Creditbank. Gedalia proposed Glückstadt as general manager for the new Landmandsbank. It turned out to be an excellent choice.

In sharp contrast to Privatbanken, Glückstadt decided that Landmandsbanken should start almost immediately to build up a branch network. From a capital market perspective, this had two effects: First, it created competition to the local provincial banks and savings banks, and secondly, it made Landmandsbanken grow quite fast, particularly from the late 1890s onwards, and enabled it to finance larger transactions than would otherwise have been the case, including arranging or participating in foreign government loans.

Around 1880 Landmandsbanken had already overtaken Privatbanken in terms of total assets and equity, cfr. below.

In the meantime, Kjøbenhavns Handelsbank A/S ("Handelsbanken"), the fourth of the Copenhagen main banks, had been established (1873) at the initiative of David Baroch Adler (1826–1878), the banquier who had originally assisted Tietgen with the creation of Privatbanken, but who had been outmaneouvered by Tietgen in the board of directors. Adler was also a politician (member of the Folketing, the "lower chamber" 1864–1869, and of the Landsting, the "upper chamber", 1869–1878), and the co-founder of both a provincial bank and a provincial mortgage association.

Like Landmandsbanken, Handelsbanken also started immediately to build up a countrywide net of branches, and overtook Privatbanken around the turn of the century, cfr. below.

The structure of the Danish banking world around 1900

With the establishment of the Copenhagen Handelsbank, the Danish banking scene had acquired the structure it was to keep for the next 117 years with the three main banks completely dominating the scene, the Nationabank with a dwindling commercial role, and then a multitude of quite small metropolitan and provincial banks. Table 3.6 illustrates the relative positions by 1917 (market shares measured in respect of bank loans totalling DKK 1,989 million).

Table 3.6   Relative Positions of the Four Main Banks in 1917 (Million Kroner)

	Share capital	Reserves	Deposits	Total loans	Market share	Total assets	Solvency ratio
Nationalbanken	27	8.4	97	158	8%	448	7.9%
Privatbanken	36	7.9	336	288	14%	385	11.4%
Landmandsbanken	100	25.0	769	825	41%	941	13.3%
Handelsbanken	40	13.7	442	424	21%	519	10.3%

Source: Danmarks Nationalbank (1968) *Dansk Pengehistorie*, bd. I–IV, bd. III (Bilag, v. K. Mordhorst), and Danmarks Statistik (1969) *Kreditmarkedsstatisik*, Statistiske Undersøgelser nr 24.
Note: The solvency ratio used here is calculated as the equity as a percentage of total assets.

By 1917, the Landmandsbank had already been the largest Nordic bank for some years as a result of its phenomenal growth rate since the 1890s, achieved not least through its rapidly growing foreign business.

3.3.3   Savings banks and the Savings Banks Act of 1880

Having had a rather slow start with first a very small savings bank intended only for the peasants and other employees of the Holsteinsborg estate and ten years later another savings bank for Copenhagen and suburbs, the movement accelerated during the 1830s and 1840s, as shown in Table 3.7, which compares the development of the savings banks with that of the banks.

Table 3.7 shows the usual pattern of large numbers of small savings banks and fewer but larger banks. Further, the growth of total savings banks deposits came almost exclusively from the increasing number of savings banks. Their average size remained almost constant. While financing co-ops was an impor-

Table 3.7   Banks and Savings Banks, and Their Deposits, 1852–1918, Selected Years (Amounts in Million Kroner)

Year	Banks (excluding Nationalbanken)			Savings Banks		
	Number of banks	Total deposits	Deposits pr. bank	Number of savings banks	Total deposits	Deposits pr. savings bank
1852	1	1	1.00	38	21	0.55
1860	15	13	0.87	57	56	0.98
1870	18	27	1.50	168	118	0.70
1876	40	71	1.78	401	221	0.55
1900	86	310	3.60	516	454	0.80
1915	141	1,077	7.63	513	995	1.94
1918	152	2,669	17.56	514	1,472	2.86

Source: Danmarks Staistik (1969) *Kreditmarkedsstatistik*, Statistiske Undersøgelser nr. 24.

tant business for the rural savings banks (cfr. 3.3.1 above), it was also common practice in the early years to place most of the funds on deposit with the Nationalbank or the Privatbank.

Sparekassen for Kjøbenhavn og Omegen (est. 1820), which had among its founders one of the governors of Nationalbanken, placed its funds exclusively with Nationalbanken at 5 per cent interest, paying 4 per cent to its depositors. This was simple and transparent business. There was, however, some debate internally in the Sparekasse whether it should contemplate lending to private individuals. A protocol from a meeting of directors reads (SEA's translation): "Much could be said in favour of lending them (i.e. the deposits) to private individuals, but that would imply a book-keeping system entirely different from that of the savings bank proper, it would increase the responsibility and workload of the directors, without benefitting the depositors."[25] This policy was standard for most savings banks until some time around mid-century.

However, these practices changed, and the savings banks started offering short-term loans to private individuals against all sorts of collateral, including real estate, and to place funds in Nationalbank shares, government bonds, and, from the mid-1850s, mortgage bonds. Some even started discounting bills. In a protest against this "urbanization" of the savings banks two new savings banks were started in the 1857, Bikuben and Den Sjællandske Bondestands Sparekasse,[26] which would concentrate on the social and agricultural origins of the savings banks movement.

The changing business profile of the savings banks is clearly seen from Table 3.8:

Table 3.8   The Changing Asset Composition of Savings Banks, 1835–1859

Year	Percentage of Total Assets				Total Assets	
	Government coffers	Loans	Securities	Cash and bank deposits	%	Million DKK
1835	63	5	–	32	100	4.6
1845	31	40	5	24	100	12.3
1850	21	58	4	18	100	17.4
1859	0	82	13	4	100	55.6

Source: Sv. Å. Hansen (1960) *Pengevæsen og Kredit 1813–1860* (Fyens Stifts Kreditforening) p. 170.

---

[25]Here quoted from Sv. Å. Hansen (1960) *Pengevæsen og Kredit 1813–1860*, p. 158.
[26]The chairman of Bondestanden's Sparekasse was a certain Mr. C. Alberti, who was also Minister of Justice, and the son of one of the founders of the savings bank. In 1908 he confessed that he had embezzled a very large amount (DKK 14 million) from the savings bank. He spent nine years in jail.

The Savings Banks Act of 1880

By 1880, when more than 400 savings banks had come into existence without other formalities than a registration with the Ministry for the Interior, the government decided that legislation was needed, and a law was passed the same year[27] to take effect as from January 1, 1881. This Savings Banks Act was laudably brief (13 paragraphs), but also left many questions unanswered, some not clearly addressed until the passing of the Savings Bank Act of 1937 (cfr. Chapter 7). The substance of the 1880 Savings Banks Act was:

§§1–3: The Minister for the Interior would appoint a "Savings Bank Inspector", reporting to the Minister. Existing savings banks had to submit their statutes to this Inspector for approval, together with a list of their board members. No new savings banks could be set up without approval from the Inspector. The statutes had to describe, i.a. the saving bank's business plan, proposed interest rates, deposit terms, lending policies, allocation of profits, and remuneration of directors.

§§4–7: Stipulations concerning accounting and auditing. Annual and quarterly accounts to be submitted to the Inspector.

§8: The Inspector could order a savings bank to close down, if its reserves and 5 per cent of the deposits had been lost.[28]

§§9–10: Stipulations concerning winding up and registration.

§11: The Savings Banks Act did not apply to banks defined as institutions paying dividends to founders, guarantors, and shareholders, and which discounted bills of exchange. Such institutions were not allowed to call themselves "savings banks", unless they had so far also conducted "savings bank business".

Comments:

First, there was no requirement for any paid-in capital. Usually, savings banks were created by groups of people who would act as guarantors for the obligations of the savings bank, and who would receive a fixed remuneration in return (e.g. 3 per cent p.a). Part of the guarantee was sometimes paid up in cash and would earn normal interest.

Second, this Act was the first formal attempt to establish a distinction between banks and savings banks. Later savings banks acts sharpened this

---

[27]Lov nr. 64 af 28. Maj, 1880, om Spare- og Laanekasser ("The Savings Banks Act of 1880"). The discussions leading to the savings banks and banking acts passed between 1880 and 1937 have been analysed by Prof. P.H. Hansen (January 2001) "Bank Regulation in Denmark from 1880 to World War Two", *Business History*, vol. 43, pp. 43–68.

[28]This stipulation was copied in the Swedish Savings Banks Act of 1892, cfr. Chapter 6.

distinction, cfr. Chapter 7. Apparently, §11 defines "banks" as dividend paying institutions, whereas the profits (if any) generated by savings banks were not to be distributed. This would seem to mean that banks were joint stock companies – for which there was no legislation at this point of time – whereas savings banks were some other unspecified type of legal entity. The only indication of a difference of activities is the mention of the discounting of bills,[29] which according to §11 was regarded as "banking business", although some savings banks actually also discounted bills, at least until 1937.

On the liabilities side, the confusion was no less. Offering savings accounts and time deposits was – almost generally – considered savings bank business, but several banks also offered such accounts. Call deposits, current accounts, and overdraft facilities, on the other hand, was considered banking business, but savings banks increasingly also offered such accounts.

On these questions, the 1880 Savings Bank Act was of little help. Banks and savings banks had been co-operating and supporting each other until about 1870, but thereafter competition between the two groups intensified. The atmosphere grew increasingly tense, and the problems were not resolved until the passing of the Banking Act of 1974 (cfr. Chapter 7).

3.3.4 The mortgage associations and the Mortgage Associations Acts of 1850, 1861 and 1897

The acute shortage of credit in the 1820s and 1830s (cfr. above) caused several proposals to be made during these years. The most noticeable result was the 147-page report[30] made by A.F. Bergsøe, who had been commissioned by the government to study some mortgage credit institutions created elsewhere in Europe. Bergsøe's report and recommendations were clearly inspired by the "Landschaften" he had studied in Prussia. Bergsøe's highly detailed report and its (mostly) well-argued proposal were received with a great deal of scepticism in government circles. There were doubts about the realism of the plan to issue bonds without government guarantees, and fears that farmers might be tempted to indulge in excessive indebtedness. Therefore, it took 11 years before the proposal was turned into action.

---

[29]§11: "Denne Lov kommer ikke til Anvendelse paa Banker eller lignende Penge-institutter, hvorved Deltagelse i Udbytte og Overskud er forbeholdt Stiftere, Garanter eller Aktionærer, eller som drive Vexelomsætning. Slige Pengeinsitutter maa ikke kalde sig Sparekasser ..."

[30]A.F. Bergsøe (1839) *Motiveret Udkast til en Creditforening for Danske Grundejere* (Kjøbenhavn) cfr. the Introduction, p. 7.

Action came in the shape of the Mortgage Association Act of June 20, 1850.[31] It was a model of brevity with just seven paragraphs. Its basic substance was that applications for setting up mortgage credit associations would be approved on certain conditions, and that they would be granted the following privileges:

a)   exemption from stamp duties;
b)   the right to arrange foreclosures on defaulting debtors without otherwise normal court proceedings;
c)   the right to make loan agreements at interest rates exceeding 4 per cent p.a.
and
d)   funds held in trust on behalf of widows, underaged, public offices, etc. could be placed in bonds issued by the associations.

The conditions to be fulfilled in order to be granted these privileges can be summarized as follows:

a)   minimum total loan amount (loan applications) of DKK 2 million within an area where the directors of the association could be expected to have sufficient knowledge of the properties offered as collateral, and where they could exercise control;
b)   loans not to exceed 60 per cent of the estimated value of the property;
c)   circulating volume of bonds never to exceed remaining debts to the association;
d)   all members of the association (the borrowers) to be jointly liable for the obligations of the associations with 100 per cent of the value of their mortgaged property (implying that the mortgage had to be a first priority mortgage) and personally liable for their own loans with all of their asset;
e)   the bonds issued by the associations to be negotiable and issued to bearer (or to name), and for a minimum amount of DKK 100;
f)   the loans to be amortizing with a percentage to be decided by the association; by implication, the amortizations were to be used for redemption of the circulating bonds by lottery.

Comments:
It will be noticed that

–   no capital injections were required for these mortgage associations;
–   the rate of amortization was left open;

---

[31]Lov om Oprettelse af Creditforeninger og Laanekasser for Grundejere af 20. Juni 1850.

- neither call options for the bondholders nor early repayment options for the debtors were mentioned (in spite of Bergsøe's lengthy discussions on these subjects);
- borrowers were personally liable with all their assets for their own borrowings. In respect of their joint liability they were liable only with their mortgaged property;
- neither reserve fund nor administration contributions were mentioned in the Mortgage Association Act, in spite of Bergsøe's recommendations. This, as well as amortization rates, was left to the individual associations to decide for themselves. Modest reserves were, however, built up partly by issuing the bonds in amounts 2–4 per cent lower than the corresponding mortgage deeds issued by the borrower to the association, and partly by current reserve fund and/or administration contributions (usually 0.5 per cent p.a.).

The strongest resemblance to the Prussian Landschaften lay in the right of the borrowers to borrow exclusively on the value of their property without any evaluation of their general creditworthiness, the joint liability of the borrowers, in the fixing of a maximum mortgage percentage, in the limiting of the outstanding bond circulation to the amount of debts to the association, in the disbursement mechanism (disbursement in bonds for the borrower to sell), nominal interest on the bonds identical to the nominal interest on the mortgage deeds, and in the institutions' character of non-profit associations of borrowers. In these characteristics, the Prussian and Danish mortgage institutions were worlds apart from the English building societies and the French centralized system.

The biggest differences compared to the Landschaften were the absence of the call option, which the Prussian bondholders originally had, later modified, and the absence of any identification in the bonds of the precise property which served as primary collateral for the bond.

The association would hold the private mortgage deeds issued by the borrower, and the association would issue bearer bonds representing the portfolio of individual mortgage deeds in its possession.

For the buyer of the mortgage bonds, the risk was spread over a large number of borrowers. Over the following 40 years, 14 mortgage credit associations were created. They differed mainly with respect to their geographical area of operation and the types of property they could lend against.

From a capital market point of view, it was regrettable that because of this specialization, there was practically no competition between these institutions. However, as time went by, this lack of competition in mortgage finance was to a large extent alleviated by competition from the savings banks, cfr. Table 3.8 above. During the second half of the 19th century mortgage finance had become an increasingly important business for savings banks, particularly in rural districts and provincial towns.

During the 1850s and 1860s the development of the mortgage institutions was slow, mainly because it was found difficult to find buyers for the bonds.[32] The Stock Exchange was not interested in these new and unknown papers, so the mortgage institutions tried to assist their borrowers with efforts to persuade banks, including the Nationalbank, and savings banks to pick up the bonds. Efforts to sell the bonds in Hamburg were generally unsuccessful. However, after some years the mortgage bonds found general acceptance, until 1861 when difficulties for two institutions in Jutland gave cause for some concerns. In these two cases, the rising property prices during the 1850s caused the respective institutions to make much too optimistic valuations. One of them went bankrupt[33] with heavy losses for the bondholders. The other one was wound up with substantial costs to the jointly liable borrowers.

These two institutions (and one of the secondary mortgage institutions, which had problems in 1930–1931 (cfr. Chapter 7) were the only cases in the ca. 160 year history of the Danish mortgage credit associations where serious problems have been experienced, and in only two of these three cases did the bond holders suffer losses.

The difficulties of these two institutions together with a new idea that bonds should be issued in series open for a limited period caused a revision of the Mortgage Association Act in 1861. The main purposes of the idea of issuing bonds in specific series were partly to make the final maturity of the bonds more easily predictable, and thereby make them more attractive for investors, and partly to limit the joint liability of the borrowers to the series in which they had their loans. Series would be kept open for one to three years, and then closed, and a new series would be opened.

Another amendment introduced by the 1861 Act was that henceforth, new mortgage institutions could only be created by act of law. There were serious doubts that more than the four institutions then existing were needed or beneficial.

Nine institutions were set up by act of law between 1861 and 1920, two of which set up in 1880 particularly for smallholders. Bonds issued by these two institutions were denominated first in Reichsmarks and later in Sterling, and interest payments were guaranteed by the government. They were sold in substantial volumes in Berlin and London. This was in the days of the gold standard, when foreign exchange risks were considered negligible.

---

[32]Cfr. T. Glud (1951) *Kreditforeningsinstitutionen i Danmark* (De Danske Kreditforeninger) pp. 41–2, and p. 50.

[33]Cfr. T. Glud (1951) *Kreditforeningsinstitutionen i Danmark*, pp. 50–2, and O. Hjelm (1944) *Ny Jydske Kjøbstad-Creditforening* in Th. Kristensen (ed.) *Haandbog i Kredit- og Hypotekforeningsforhold*, I–II (Odense) bd. I, p. 302.

The next step in the development of the Danish mortgage credit system was the Second Priority Mortgage Act of 1897.[34] The background was that in Copenhagen (and presumably in other larger cities as well) a substantial borrowing requirement had emerged in connection with the rapid growth of the urban population. Much of this borrowing was undertaken as second priority mortgage deeds placed bilaterally at high interest rates and with call options. In 1895 a group of entrepreneurial people set up an organization intended to improve the conditions for second priority mortgage credit, but because of the restrictions imposed by the 1861 Act, they could not issue bearer bonds, and they were not exempt from stamp duties. However, they went ahead with their plan, and they did succeed in placing a few bond loans. They applied to the Ministry for the Interior to receive official recognition and privileges. After two years of haggling, an approval was given by the Ministry of Finance for what came to be known as "hypotekforeninger" to issue bearer bonds secured by mortgages between 60 and 75 per cent of the value of the mortgaged property. The Ministry for the Interior had wanted to have nothing to do with it. Therefore, there was also no Inspector, as for the first priority institutions. In the opinion of the ministry, this would have conferred too much of an official recognition or perhaps even moral responsibility for these bonds in which the ministry had little faith.[35] Between 1897 and 1936, nine "hypotekforeninger" were founded, six for urban properties and three for agricultural properties, all in different cities and rural areas.

Everything went well,[36] and as from July, 1898, the second priority bonds were officially quoted and traded on the Copenhagen Stock Exchange (the first priority mortgage bonds had been officially quoted since the 1860s, and the Kreditkasse for Husejere since the beginning of the century). The effective interest on the second priority bonds was only marginally higher than on the first priority bonds (0.25–0.5 per cent p.a.).

3.4 The size of the financial sector, 1860–1914

The result of the formation of the savings banks, the banks, and the mortgage institutions, as outlined above, was an almost explosive growth in the financial sector. Table 3.9 illustrates the development.

---

[34]Meddelelse af Stempelbegunstigelser til Laaneforeninger mellem Grundejere af 18. Dec. 1897 (udfærdiget gennem Finansministeriet).
[35]Cfr. B. Gjessing (1944) *De Danske Hypotekforeningers Historie* in Th. Kristensen (ed.) *Haandbog i Kredit- og Hypotekforeningsforhold*, I–II (Odense) bd. I, pp. 102–5.
[36]Except that in the 1931–1933 depression one of the hypotekforeninger ran into severe difficulties, and the bondholders had to accept a 20 per cent reduction in their interest and capital claims, cfr: H.A. Dal (1944) *Ny Jydsk Land-Hypotekforening* in Th. Kristensen (ed.) *Haandbog i Kredit- og hypoteksforeningsforhold* (Odense) bd. I, pp. 479–81.

Table 3.9 Relative Composition and Growth of the Credit Stock, 1860–1915

	National-Banken	Commercial banks	Savings banks	Mortgage institutions	Insurance companies	Total	Total, million DKK	Index	Total, in per cent of GDP
	Per cent of total credit stock								
1860	27	11	22	34	7	101	184	100	40
1870	19	14	29	31	8	101	297	161	45
1880	9	21	25	38	7	100	608	330	72
1890	5	18	26	45	7	101	1,062	547	110
1900	3	23	22	46	7	101	1,770	961	134
1910	1	25	17	49	7	99	3,428	1,860	178
1915	2	31	(15)	45	7	100	4,552	2,473	158
	Per cent of GDP								
1860	10	5	9	13	3	40			
1870	8	6	13	14	4	45			
1880	6	15	18	28	5	72			
1890	5	19	28	50	8	110			
1900	4	30	30	61	9	134			
1910	5	44	30	88	11	178			
1915	3	49	24	71	11	158			

Sources: Loans from banks, savings banks, mortgage institutions, and insurance companies, as for Tables 3.4 and 3.7. GDP: Danmarks Statistik.

Notes:
1. Bonds issued by the first priority mortgage institutions accounted for 95–97 per cent of the mortgage bond volume before 1910, and 90–95 per cent in the years 1910–1915.
2. The amounts shown in the column "Total" cannot be seen as the net position of the financial sector towards the non-financial sector, since mortgage bonds were increasingly held by the other financial institutions.

In spite of the reservations necessitated by the double counting referred to in note 2 above, Table 3.9 clearly shows a growth rate of the financial sector much faster than that of the economy as a whole, ca. 3.5 per cent p.a. against ca. 6.25 per cent p.a. There is no doubt that financial intermediation was Denmark's fastest growing industry between 1860 and the outbreak of WWI.

Table 3.9 also clearly demonstrates the large changes in the relative positions of the various types of financial institutions.

3.5   The stock exchange: A small world

During the lean years between roughly 1815 and 1845, there was little activity on the Copenhagen Stock Exchange.

Institutionally, the recruitment of brokers was made more formal through the formation in 1817[37] of "Grosserer-Societetets Kommite", among whose responsibilities it was to advise the government on current commercial affairs, including the appointment of brokers of all four types (cfr. the 1808 "Broker Decree"), and supervision of the Stock Exchange. Also, whole-salers[38] ("grosserere") were now required to be members of the Grosserer-Societet.

Securities trading on the Stock Exchange was negligible in this period. The only securities traded were government bonds, and shares in the National-banken (after 1836), a couple of insurance companies, and the dormant Asiatic Company (cfr. 2.3.1).

Price fixings took place on Fridays through informal discussions among the brokers.

The price list dated November 15, 1845,[39] comprises seven bond issues (including two Norwegian and one Swedish), and ten shares, with offer and bid prices, and eleven done transactions ("giort til").

In 1857, the stock exchange building was acquired from the Crown by the Grosserer-Societet, which has owned it ever since.

The second half of the century was rather different.

Institutionally, the price fixings were changed into formal auctions, conducted by a designated "vekselmægler", during which the securities were announced one by one, and offer and bid prices were noted, and trades recorded. Official price fixings now also happened on Tuesdays, and unofficial

---

[37]The formation of this Committee was requested by the government by the "Anord-ning of April 17, 1817, angaaende Handelsberettigede m.v."

[38]Wholesalers were defined as merchants with a wealth corresponding to at least the value of half of an average ocean-going vessel.

[39]A newspaper cutting with this price list has miraculously survived in the cellars of the Copenhagen Stock Exchange, which kindly let SEA have a copy.

prices could be quoted on the days in between. Since 1854, the newspapers brought the prices daily.[40] Bids and offers could only be made by members of the stock exchange, i.e. "veksellerere" and "vekselmæglere" authorized according to the 1808 decree, who had this activity as their main business.

However, the two groups of securities brokers, the "veksellerere" and the "vekselmæglere" (cfr. 2.3.1) kept squabbling over their respective privileges and responsibilities. A temporary solution was found in 1876, when the Grosserer-Societetets Kommite and the two groups of brokers agreed on the creation of a price fixing committee, "Vekselmæglernes of Veksellerernes Kursnoteringsudvalg", which became the ultimate authority on prices, and on the acceptance to or rejection from the price list of specific securities. In 1888, this was supplemented with a formal document[41] describing the criteria for acceptance to the price list. The document specifies that apart from a prospectus, for whose correctness the issuer is responsible, domestic bonds are admitted only if issued by public authorities, institutions or companies (... "offentlige Autoriteter, Instituter eller Selskaber") and foreign bonds only if negotiated and payable in Copenhagen. The bonds and shares must be issued in the interest of the public ("... være udgivne i offentlige øjemed ...") or for commercial or industrial purposes, and their amounts will have to be of a size sufficient to make them continuously traded on the Stock Exchange ("... Genstand for stadig Omsætning paa Børsen ...").

If the 1808 decrees did not mark the "birth" of the Copenhagen Stock Exchange in the sense of the definition proposed in the Introduction, then the combination of the 1876 and 1888 agreements certainly did, even if the commodity trading did not move out of the Stock Exchange until much later. Grain trading stayed on the Stock Exchange until the middle of the 20th century.[42]

It will be noticed that after 1808, the Copenhagen Stock Exchange had a number of features in common with the London Stock Exchange. Both were entirely self-regulating organizations, and in both cases membership was purely personal, and in neither place could banks trade directly. On these points the London and Copenhagen exchanges differed substantially from the German exchanges, and from the Stockholm, Oslo, and Helsinki Stock Exchanges.

---

[40]Cfr. Th. Kristensen et al. (1944) *Håndbog i Kredit- og Hypoteksforeningsforhold*, I–II (Odense) p. 556.

[41]"Regler med Hensyn til Optagelse af Værdipapirer paa den ordinære Kursliste", issued by Grosserer-Societetets Komite og Vexelmæglernes og Vexellerernes Kursudvalg, December 10, 1888.

[42]"Børslivet præges i vore Dage fortrinsvis af Kornbørsens Mænd og af Fondsbørsen ..." Aa. v. Benzon (1944) *Fondsbørsen og Kreditforenings Systemet*, i Th. Kristensen (ed.) *Haandbog i Kreditforeningsforhold*, p. 548. ("In our days, life on the Exchange is dominated by the men of the grain exchange and the securities exchange ...") (SEA's translation).

Other institutional changes included the 1857 "Commerce Act" ("Næring-sloven"), which relaxed the conditions for becoming a wholesaler ("grosserer"), and made it easier to become a broker, whereby their number increased from about a dozen in the first half of the century to 22 veksellerere, 33 veksel-mæglere, and 19 combined commodity brokers and vekselmæglere in 1871.[43]

In the second half of the 19th century, the number of bonds and shares issued and traded on the exchange increased significantly, cfr. Table 3.10.

Table 3.10 shows that trading activity on the exchange was quite limited until early in the 20th century. The increased trading volume in 1905–1908 demonstrates the "bubble" of those years. The figures also show the post WWI "bubble" and the subsequent slump.

The slow turnover rate of bonds in particular is an indication that most of the trading took place outside the Stock Exchange.

Most of the increase in the share circulation was caused by the formation of banks and, later, a number of steamship, railway, and industrial companies. The growth of the bond circulation was primarily the result of the activities of the mortgage institutions, but government bonds and municipality bonds (including a few Norwegian and Swedish issues) also counted.

Table 3.10   Bond Circulation and Trading Volumes on the Copenhagen Stock Exchange, 1893–1921

Annual averages	Circulating mortgage bonds, DKK million	Stock Exchange Turnover DKK million		Total, DKK million	Total turnover in % of GDP
		Bonds	*Shares*		
1893–1895	539	4.5	23.9	28.6	2.9
1896–1898	672	4.7	30.2	34.9	3.2
1899–1901	764	16.2	23.7	39.9	3.0
1902–1904	948	19.9	35.3	55.4	3.8
1905–1907	1,165	22.0	104.4	126.4	7.8
1908–1910	1,452	20.0	99.5	119.5	6.5
1911–1913	1,715	22.1	245.6	267.7	12.4
1916–1918	2,032	68.7	525.0	593.7	14.8
1919–1921	2,221	137.0	309.1	446.1	6.0

Sources: Bond circulation: Danmarks Statistik: *Kreditmarkedsstatistik*, Statistiske Undersøgelser nr 24, 1969.
Trading volumes: Danmarks Statistik: Statistisk Årbog, relevant years.
Note: For the turnover, the source does not distinguish between mortgage bonds and other bonds. Turnover in per cent of GDP refer to the middle year in the indicated interval. Same for circulating bonds.

---

[43]Cfr. J. Schovelin (1921) *Den Danske Landmandsbank, Hypotek- og Vekselbank, 1871–1921* (Den Danske Landmandsbank) p. 247.

4
Finland, 1809–1917: A Changed World

Yesterday this day's madness did prepare,
To-morrow's silence, triumph, or despair;
Drink! – for you know not whence you came nor why;
Drink! – for you know not why you go nor where!
(From the 12th century "Rubaiydt of Omar Khayyám",
as translated by E. Fitzgerald, 1857)

4.1 An overview: From Swedish province to Russian Grand-Duchy, and to independence

In 1808, the Finns could hardly foresee that yet another Swedish-Russian war would change Finland from a Swedish province to a Grand-Duchy of the Russian Empire in 1809, nor that Russia would accept, in 1917, that Finland broke out of the crumbling Empire to gain full sovereignty, nor that this would immediately be followed by a bloody civil war.

The political and monetary turmoil resulting from the Napoleonic wars and the transition to the state of a semi-autonomous part of the Russian empire, the agricultural depression of the 1820s, the Crimean war, and the disastrous famine in the 1860s leading to mass emigration all combined to make Finland's economy languish for the first two-thirds of the 19th century. Finland's population actually declined by nearly 100,000 in the second half of the 1860s to around 1.6 million. However, rapid growth over the following 40 years increased the population to about 3.1 million when independence was achieved.[1]

Although most of the Swedish legal framework remained in force in Finland for most of the 19th century, Finland's new status as a Russian Grand-Duchy implied fundamentally new conditions for the development of Finnish financial institutions. During most of the century, Finland

---

[1]Statistics Finland (2005) *Statistical Yearbook.*

92

enjoyed a fair degree of domestic autonomy, governed by a Senate chaired by the Russian Governor General, who also appointed the senators, but decisions regarding the currency circulation and financial institutions in Finland were taken in St. Petersburg. The new political reality also caused the capital to be moved from Åbo[2] to Helsingfors (1812–1819), although Åbo had three times as many inhabitants as Helsingfors at that time. The official reason was that Helsingfors had a citadel and was easier to defend, but the real reason was that Åbo was considered too much steeped in Swedish traditions and attitudes, and was inconveniently close to Stockholm.

The slow process of industrialization is reflected in the relatively small urban population (in both absolute and relative terms): In 1880, the urban population was approximately 174,000, or ca. 8 per cent of the whole population. By 1900, these figures had grown to 340,000 and 12 per cent, respectively, and by 1910 to ca. 467,000 and 15 per cent,[3] much less than in Sweden and Denmark, but not much different from Norway.

It will be noted that gross capital formation increased its share of gross domestic product over the 40 years shown in Table 4.1, but less so than in Denmark in the same period, cfr. Chapter 3. A substantial part of the investments was financed from abroad. In 1893, the long-term gross foreign debt was 83 million finmark, or 16 per cent of GDP. In 1900 these figures had

Table 4.1   Gross Domestic Product and Capital Formation, 1860–1900

	Residential construction	Other investments	Total investments, million finmark	Total investments in % of GDP	GDP, million finmark
	Million finmark				
1860	13	18	31	11	282
1870	15	29	44	12	336
1880	14	28	42	10	427
1890	18	51	69	13	525
1900	27	101	128	15	812
1913					1,348

Source: R. Hjerppe, M. Peltonen & E. Pihkala (1984) "Investment in Finland 1860–1979", *The Scandinavian Economic History Review*, vol. XXXII, p. 43. GDP: R. Hjerppe & E. Pihkala (1977) "The Gross Domestic Product of Finland 1860–1913", *Economy and History*, vol. XX: 2.

---

[2]For the pre-1917 period the old Swedish city names will be used, since they were universally used at the time. For the post-1917 period, the modern Finnish names (Helsinki, Turku, Viipuri, Tampere, etc.) will be used.
[3]G. Modeen (1930) "Byggnadsverksamheten i städerna åren 1921–28", *Ekonomiska Samfundets Tidskrift, Ny Serie. Häfte 17*, p. 2.

increased to 169 million finmark and 20 per cent respectively.[4] Around the turn of the century some 25 per cent of the capital spending was financed by foreign borrowings.

4.2   The problems

The fabric of Finland's political and economic framework in the 18th and 19th centuries was scarcely conducive for the development of a "capital market" at the same pace as in Sweden and Denmark.

The main problems in this respect were:

1. Limited penetration of money circulation outside the coastal towns and, to the extent that money did circulate, it consisted of the simultaneous circulation of Swedish and Russian money until 1842.
2. Rudimentary transportation facilities until late in the 19th century, particularly in the long winter months. In the second half of the 19th century, the desire for railways, canals, and other capital intensive investments accelerated, but these investments required finance on a scale which nobody had yet tried to organize in Finland.
3. One-sided economy based mainly on forest products. Between 1880 and 1914, the share of Finland's exports consisting of forest industry products increased from about 53 per cent to about 71 per cent.[5]
4. Many trading and financial links with Sweden were severed after 1809. The Åbo branch of Sveriges Riksbank, and the Åbo Diskont were both closed (cfr. Chapter 1), and Swedish creditors reclaimed their money from Finnish borrowers.

The development of a "banking system" definitely came 80–90 years later in Finland than in Sweden, and nearly 20 years later than in Denmark. There can be little doubt that the 1809 transfer of political power to St. Petersburg delayed the emergence of local Finnish banks.

Even if Finland had generated savings on a scale sufficient to finance the big infrastructure investments in addition to other current investments, there was, until late in the century, no way to collect the savings and channel them into large projects. Instead, the savings were kept locally to finance only small-scale capital spending.

---

[4]Hjerppe, Peltonen & Pihkala (1984) "Investment in Finland 1860–1979", *The Scandinavian Economic History Review*, vol. XXXII, p. 45.
[5]Cfr. H.E. Pipping (1969) *I Guldmyntfodens Hägn. Finlands Bank 1878–1914*, vol. II of Pipping's official history of the Bank of Finland (Finlands Bank, Helsinki) p. 30.

4.3 Responses and actions

4.3.1 The Bank of Finland

The foundation and intended purposes

After the closure of the two above-mentioned Swedish banking offices the need for a bank was so strongly felt that already before the Peace Agreement had been signed, plans for a new bank were discussed at length[6] in both the Landtag (the Assembly of the Estates), the Senate, and in special committees. The discussions were muddled, because nobody knew precisely what to aim for. A copy of the Åbo Diskont, based on private shareholders, was considered quite unrealistic. When the Åbo Diskont was formed in 1805, most of the shares had been sold in Stockholm (cfr. Chapter 1).

Finally, the czar instructed the local government to form a new credit institution, copied from the Stockholm Bank and the Banque de France, and that its main purposes should be to[7]

1. assist with the repayment of mortgage debts owed by Finnish landowners to Swedish creditors;
2. assist with the financing of agricultural and commercial investments, and
3. promote and organize the circulation of money in the country – and, in that connection, to replace the Swedish riksdaler with rubles.

The final results, negotiated directly between Gustav Armfeldt, the Finnish ambassador to the Imperial Court, and Czar Alexander I, were formally laid down in "Hans Kejserliga Majestäts Nådiga Reglemente för Wäxel – Låne-och Depositions Contoiret i Storfürstendömet Finland",[8] dated December 12, 1811, the official "birthday" of the Bank of Finland.

In 1817, the name was modified to "Storfürstendömet Finlands Vexel-, Depositions- och Låne-Banque". Finally, in 1867, the name was officially declared to be "Finlands Bank", "Suomen Pankki" or the "Bank of Finland" (BoF).

---

[6]A detailed review of these discussions is given in H.E. Pipping (1961) *Från Pappersrubel till Guldmark. Finlands Bank 1811 –1877*, vol. I of Pipping's official history of the Bank of Finland (Finlands Bank, Helsinki) pp. 39–66.
[7]Cfr. Pipping (1961) *Från Pappersrubel till Guldmark. Finlands Bank 1811–1877*, p. 56.
[8]"His Imperial Majesty's Gracious Regulations for the Exchange-, Lending-, and Deposit Office in the Grand Duchy of Finland".
The original of this document can be seen in the library of the University of Helsinki, and is summarized by Pipping (1961) *Från Pappersrubel till Guldmark* (Finlands Bank) pp. 54–66.

The main features of the bank were:

a) Ownership.
Based on the experience with the Åbo Diskont (cfr. Chapter 1), there was no illusion that shares in any such venture could be sold in sufficient amounts either in Finland or in Russia. Therefore, and because the new masters wanted to be able to keep an eye on the project, it was decided to place the BoF directly under the ownership of the local government (the Senate), and that His Imperial Majesty should be the bank's top authority. The top managers were appointed by the czar.

It differed from the Banque de France by not being a joint stock company, and from the Stockholm Bank by being placed under the government (the Senate), and not under the Landtag (Assembly of the Estates).[9] It also differed from the Swedish Riksank by not being divided into two "halves", a "loan bank" and "an exchange/deposit bank", in the tradition of Venice, Amsterdam, and Hamburg (cfr. the Introduction and Chapter 1).

b) Capitalization.
The prudence of capitalizing the bank was recognized, in sharp contrast to the Swedish Riksbank (cfr. Chapter 1). However, nobody had a clue as to which amount of capital would be required. Proposals varied between 500,000 silver rubles and 1 million,[10] which was seen as the maximum amount that could realistically be expected.

In the end, the Senate consented to supply an injection of one million paper rubles, i.e. 500,000 silver rubles,[11] which formed the "grundfond" ("basic fund"), also known as "primitivfonden". The Contoire kept pressing the Senate for more capital, but the auditors told the Contoire to relax, since, in their view, "there was no reason to increase lending in a country with so little industry".[12]

c) Funding.
It was decided that the BoF should issue notes for large as well as small denominations (kopeks) in order to satisfy the demand for currency for

---

[9]The Assembly of the Representatives of the Estates did not convene between 1809 and 1863, but this was hardly foreseen in 1811.
[10]In 1811, the silver ruble was equivalent to approximately 2/3 of the Swedish silver rd (species), i.e. one Swedish silver rd. species equalled nearly 1.5 silver ruble. Pipping (1961) *Från Pappersrubel till Guldmark*, p. 38.
[11]The 1:2 ratio between silver and paper rubles was almost the market rate in 1811, and stipulated in the Reglemente for the Contoire. Most of the following 30 years it varied between 3 and 4 paper rubles to one silver ruble. Pipping (1961) *Från Pappersrubel till Guldmark*, pp. 72 and 80.
[12]"... det fanns inte anledning, sade de, att öka utlåningen i ett land med så litet industri." Pipping (1961) p. 82.

daily use, and that they could circulate alongside the larger denomination Russian paper rubles in a fixed rate of exchange (1:1).

The deposit business was limited to the receipt of payments owed to the government (taxes, etc.), and term deposits. No interest was paid, and deposits never amounted to very much.

d) Lending.

Short-term lending was done with maturities of 6–12 months. The borrowers would primarily be farmers, workmen, shopkeepers, etc, paying interest at 5 per cent p.a. A maximum amount per loan was fixed at 10,000 paper rubles, like in the Swedish diskonter. Collateral requirements were strict, and the total amount of these loans was capped at the level of the circulating small denomination notes.

Solving the refinancing problems of the large landowners, whose mortgage loans were being reclaimed by the Swedish creditors, was one of the primary objectives of the BoF. These refinancings also carried 5 per cent interest, were repaid in equal instalments over 20 years, were capped at a maximum of 15,000 rubles per loan, and were secured by first mortgages. The total volume of the long-term loans was capped at an amount equal to the bank's equity. Until 1840 these loans represented 70–80 per cent of the BoF's total loan volume.[13]

An institution operating on the principles summarized above would scarcely seem to constitute a "bank" as defined in the Introduction.

It did take deposits, but only on a very modest scale, and not really from a broad range of people, and it did not actively solicit deposits. It also did lend money, but again not really to any broad circle of customers, and with odd quantitative limitations. Anybody with large-scale borrowing needs for business purposes, other than refinancing of land mortgages, still had to go to money lenders at home or abroad (mostly Stockholm, St. Petersburg or Hamburg). It was more of an administrative mortgage office than a real "bank".

This conclusion is further supported by the initial use of the word "Contoire" in its name rather than "Banque" as proposed by the Assembly of the Estates. The word "Contoire" was used precisely in order to point out the limited scope intended for the new institution.[14]

---

[13]Pipping (1969) *I Guldmyntfodens Hägn. Finlands Bank 1878–1914* (Finlands Bank, Helsinki) pp. 109–10.
[14]"Benämningen (contoire) var uppenbarligen avsedd att reducera institutionens rang, och den motsvarade något så när de inskränkta möjligheter den hade under de närmast följande decennierna". Pipping (1961) *Från Pappersrubel tillGuldmark. Finlands Bank 1811–1877* (Finlands Bank, Helsinki) p. 56.

On August 14, 1812, the new institution, located in Åbo, opened its doors to the public. The choice of Åbo was not much to the liking of Gustaf Armfelt, whom the Czar had appointed the institution's first General Manager. According to this very able man, Åbo was a city worthy of being put on fire and reduced to ashes, and it was inhabited by negligent civil servants, lazy professors, legally minded merchants, and foul scoundrels.[15]

If so, it was in some contrast to what had been recommended in one of the preparatory reports, which had concluded (SEA's translation) that what was required was men experienced in banking, and who had been accustomed to handle their own affairs and those of others with cautious care, and who were by nature thrifty, and known for their honesty and frugal way of living.[16] It appears doubtful if any modern banker can satisfy these requirements.

Armfelt did not, however, need to worry for too long. Already in 1812 the Czar Alexander I had decided that the capital of his new Grand-Duchy, and therefore the BoF, should move to Helsingfors (cfr. 4.1). It took a few years for suitable buildings to be erected, but in the autumn of 1819, the Bank closed in Åbo and opened up in Helsingfors. To be present in both cities was beyond contemporary imagination.

The role of the "bank" as a capital market institution up, 1811–1840

The main feature of the BoF's operations was the weird system of the separate "funds", each organized with its own purpose and quantitative limitations, and in some cases with subsidized interest rates. By the mid-century about a dozen different "funds" had been created. One such "fund" had e.g. been set up to alleviate the debt burden of landowners, who suffered from the depressed agricultural conditions in the 1820s, and two other funds were earmarked to finance "productive investments".

In most cases these funds were the result of requests from influential pressure groups, e.g. large landowners, craftsmen, civil servants, etc. This shows the extent to which the "system" was a case of a political administration, rather than a "market mechanism". The loan conditions would differ between some of these funds, but would be identical for all borrowers

---

[15]"Får man tro Gustav Mauritz Armfelt, var ämbedsmannauselheten i Åbo enorm, och konseljen ansåg han mest bestå av 'trähuvuden'. Staden var en 'håla', en 'kåk' värdig 'att påtändas och läggas i aska' och den befolkades av 'försumliga tjänstemän, lata professorer, juridisk sinnade köpmän och stygga käringar'". Pipping (1961) *Från Pappersrubel till Guldmark*, p. 54.

[16]"Det krävdes män med insikt och erfarenhet i bankärenden, som blifvit tillwande att med försigtighet vårda egna och andras medel, af naturen böjda för sparsamhet och inskränkt lefnad, kända för redlighet och strenga seder", Pipping (1961) *Från Pappersrubel till Guldmark*, p. 59.

from a particular fund, regardless of the different circumstances of the individual borrowers.

Interest rates, repayment schedules, allocation of loans for different purposes, and maximum amounts of individual loans were all subject to political decisions taken in St. Petersburg or by the Senate. This was "selective credit policy" in its extreme although, of course, this expression did not exist at the time.

In addition to the above-mentioned lending activities of the Bank, lendings previously offered directly by the Senate were also transferred to the Bank in the 1820s. These were mainly minor personal loans of a "social" nature, but falling in three different categories, one of which was non-interest bearing.

From Table 4.2 it is seen that between 1824 and 1840 the loan volume hardly grew at all. Between 1812 and 1835 the number of new loans given from the "Basic Fund" totalled an average of 12 loans annually, and "Small Denomination Fund" had 374 loans outstanding by 1840.[17] As a capital market institution, the Bank of Finland was not a very impressive animal in this period.

The Bank was not the only lending institution at the time. Other lenders included a number of public and semi-public institutions, benevolent organizations, foundations, etc, all of which needed to place funds at interest (e.g. Allmänna Brandstodsbolaget and Civilstatens änka- och pupilkassa). They advertised their offers in newspapers published with more or less regular intervals. According to the definitions discussed in the Introduction, such lenders would, however, not be considered part of the "organized" capital market. The volume of such loans has been estimated to exceed

Table 4.2   Lending Volumes by the Bank of Finland, Selected Years, 1813–1840

'000 paper ruble	Basic fund	Small note fund	Agri-cultural fund	Manu-facturing fund	Total "own" loans	Government loans 3 different groups	Total
1813	400	109			509		509
1820	1,181	898			2,079		2,079
1829	1,670	709	55	101	2,535	1,480	4,015
1840	2,237	394	194	187	3,012	1,228	4,240

Source: Pipping (1961) *Från Pappersrubel till Guldmark. Finlands Bank 1811–1877* (Finlands Bank) Exhibit 2, p. 511.

---

[17]Pipping (1961) *Från Pappersrubel till Guldmark* (Finlands Bank, Helsinki) p. 117.

the loans made by the Bank of Finland.[18] Otherwise, people and institutions with money to spare temporarily, usually made deposits with Commerce Bank or e.g. Sterky & Son, the banquiers, both in St. Petersburg. By early 1840, the Bank was less of a bank than the Åbo Diskont had been. It satisfied the definition of a bank only to a limited extent. Some of the Italian merchant-banking houses of the renaissance period were closer to satisfying the definitions of a bank discussed in the Introduction, than was the Bank of Finland in early 1840.

The Charter of 1840

The inadequacy of BoF's 1811 Charter persuaded Czar Nicolai I to sign a new 161 paragraph Charter on April 21, 1840. The main changes were:

1. The money standard was to be silver rubles, based on a loan from the Russian government.
2. Swedish notes and coins were declared illegal as from 1842.
3. Short-term lending could be offered by the Bank against a wider range of collateral than before.
4. The Bank could now discount also domestic bills of exchange, at 4 per cent discount.
5. The Bank now had specific permission to take deposits, against 4 per cent interest. However, it still took deposits only for certain round amounts, and only time deposits with three days notice.
6. Branches were opened in five cities.

The system of lending from individually earmarked "funds" continued. The 1840 Charter still included detailed rules for maximum total loan amounts for various purposes, specific rates of interest and maturities for individual types of loans, as well as detailed rules for the sort of assets which could be accepted as collateral, and the valuation of such assets. Not much was left to the discretion of the management.[19]

However, from 1840 onwards, the Bank was, after all, closer to being a "real" bank than before, although in many respects it looked like a mixture of a pawn broker, a savings bank and a mortgage institution.

---

[18]Cfr. Pipping (1961) *Från Pappersrubel till Guldmark. Finlands Bank 1811–1877* (Finlands Bank) p. 116.

[19]Pipping gives an example resulting from the long list of the types of assets which could be accepted as collateral: "Ett tryckeri i Wasa vägrades kredit ... med motiveringen att det varken var ett 'fabriks- eller manufakturverk'". SEA's translation: "A printer in Wasa was refused a credit for the reason that it was neither a 'factory nor a manufacturing business'". Pipping (1961) *Från Pappersrubel till Guldmark* (Finlands Bank) p. 149.

Between 1840 and 1858, BoF's lending more than quadrupled. The two main reasons were partly the rapidly rising demand for loans from the fund created for mortgage loans for urban properties, and partly the bill discounting, which shot up sharply in 1858 after the passing of Finland's first Bills of Exchange Act in that year.

The reforms of the 1860s and 1870s

Between 1840 and the late 1870s, the BoF gradually developed into a real capital market institution. The transformation of Finland's financial scene during the 1860s and 1870s owes a lot to Johan Vilhelm Snellman (1806–1881), a central figure in Finnish culture, politics, and finance. Born in Åbo, and after much travelling in Europe, he settled in Helsingfors where he became a professor in philosophy.[20] Eventually, Snellman became a member of the Senate and head of the Senate's Finance Committee ("finanschef", 1863–1868). In the latter capacity, Snellman prepared the introduction of the finnmark and its separation from the Russian ruble, which had been severely undermined by the Crimean War. The separation of the Finnish monetary system from the collapsing ruble probably helped speeding up the development of a private banking system in Finland.

The main steps in this development were:

1. The original opposition of the BoF to the setting up of private commercial banks[21] was, finally, ended. However, in a last "rear-guard action" the Bank decided (1859) to actively develop its deposit-taking business, and to introduce overdraft facilities, for the clear purpose of making private banks superfluous.[22]
2. After much discussion, it was decided in 1877 to switch the ownership ("garanti och vård"[23]) of the Bank of Finland from the Senate to the Representatives of the Estates,[24] like in Sweden. The purpose was to give

---

[20]Snellman's efforts to promote the Finnish language and Finnish culture became a decisive factor in the recognition by the rest of the world of Finland as a distinct nation in 1917.

[21]In this respect the BoF did not differ from the Bank of England, the Banque de France, Nationalbanken i Kjøbenhavn, Sveriges Riksbank, or Norges Bank, cfr. Chapters 2, 3, 5, and 6.

[22]"Finlands Banks verksamhetsfält hade utvidgats 1859 i klart syfte att göra privata banker obehövliga." Pipping (1961) *Från Pappersrubel till Guldmark* (Finlands Bank, Helsinki) p. 451.

[23]"Guarantee and protection", §1 of the 1877 Reglemente (repeated in 1895), Pipping (1969) *I Guldmyntfodens Hägn. Finlands Bank 1878–1914* (Finlands Bank, Helsinki) p. 305.

[24]In 1863, the Representatives of the Estates (the "Landtag") started convening again from time to time (in 1867, 1872, and 1875, etc.).

the BoF substantially more autonomy, although its governor was still appointed by the czar.

3. In 1874, the administration of the "funds" managed by the BoF on behalf of the Senate since the 1820s were returned to the Senate. Also, the BoF gradually dissolved its own "funds", so that by the mid-1880s the "compartmentalization" of the BoF's lending had ended. Repayment of existing loans and winding up of the old system did, however, drag on for about 30 years.

4. In 1860, Finland was allowed to introduce the markka (finnmark) at the rate of four markka to one ruble. In 1865 the markka was made convertible into silver.

5. As from July 1, 1878, the finnmark changed to the gold standard at a rate of one gold mark = one French gold franc.

The lending facilities managed by the Bank of Finland on behalf of the Senate between the 1820s and 1874 were, also after their return to the Senate, "... characterized mainly by the running of an unco-ordinated system of funds".[25] There does not seem to have been much "market mechanism" in the allocation of these funds, which totalled quite significant amounts. Although new regulations issued in 1900 stipulated that these funds could only be lent to cities and local authorities, the number of private borrowers seems to have retained an almost equal share of such loans.[26]

Table 4.3 shows the development of the lending volumes of the BoF from its own funds and the government's funds in proportion to total lendings from banks and savings banks. The relative insignificance of the savings banks is also seen (the difference between the fourth and fifth column).

Commercial or "central bank"?

By 1917, the Bank of Finland had already for some years displayed a number of the characteristics associated with central banks:

a. The wording of § 1 in the 1875 Reglemente defining as the objective and task of the BoF to ensure "... stadga och säkerhet i landets penningeväsen, samt att befordra och underlätta penningomsättningen landet." (to ensure "... stability and reliability in the country's money

[25]Y. Blomstedt (1976) *Valtiokonttori 1875–1975* (Med svensk resumé: "Statskontoret 1875–1975", with an English summary) (Statskontoret, Helsinki) p. 185.
[26]Y. Blomstedt (1976) *Valtiokonttori 1875–1975* (Statskontoret, Helsinki) p. 187.

Table 4.3   Lending Volumes by the Bank of Finland and the Government, Selected Years, 1860–1914

				BoF and Government loans in % of	
Year	BoF's own funds	Government funds	Total	Total bank loans	Total loans from banks and savings banks
	Million marks				
1860	24	13	37	100	93
1870	17	13	30	63	56
1880	19	16	35	52	43
1890	42	22	64	42	37
1900	59	33	92	35	27
1905	56	28	84	20	15
1910	92	31	123	18	15
1914	91	(45)	136	(17)	(12)

Sources:
BoF's and government lendings: Pipping (1961) *Från Pappersrubel till Guldmark*, pp. 511–13, Pipping (1969) *I Guldmyntfodens Hägn*, p. 433, and K. Vattula, ed. (1983) *Suomen taloushistoria*, Historial Statistics, vol. III (Helsinki) pp. 340–1.
Bank lendings: Pipping (1969) *I Guldmmyntfodens Hägn*, pp. 435–6. The figures exclude correspondents and bond holdings.
Savings banks: K. Vattula, ed. (1983) *Suomen taloushistoria*, Historical Statistics, vol. 3 (Helsinki) pp. 334–43.
Figures in brackets are partly SEA's estimates.

system, and to promote and facilitate the circulation of money in the country.")[27] This is the classic task of a "central bank".

b. Its role as guardian of the country's reserves of silver (1865–1878) and gold (1878–1914). Also a classic task of a "central bank".

c. Its legal status. Guaranteed and protected by the Estates, based on a special charter, a monopoly of note-issuing, and a governor appointed by the czar – all of which are today usual but not indispensable features of a "central bank".

---

[27]Here quoted from Pipping (1969) *I Guldmyntfodens Hägn* (Finlands Bank) pp. 236 and 302. According to Pipping it is impossible to trace the origins of the quoted wording, because the working protocols have been lost. However, §3 of the 1818 Charter for Nationalbanken i Kiøbenhavn had an almost identical wording: "Bankens ... Bestem-melser er ... at virke frem til at befæste et sikkert Pengevæsen i Landet ... og ... at fremme Pengeomløbet ..." (Here quoted from the Charter as reprinted in A. Rubow (1918) *Nationalbankens Historie*, vol. I, pp. 70–1.

Other features of the BoF – also long after WWI – were distinctly atypical, or even in direct contrast to the regular responsibilities of a "central bank", in particular:

d. The Bank's commercial activities in direct competition with the private banks and savings banks. In government circles it had been pointed out that the Bank was losing market shares to the private banks. Between 1880 and 1908 its share of outstanding bank loans had been reduced from 54 per cent to 11 per cent,[28] a completely irrelevant consideration for a central bank. In the 1890s it increased its branch network to 13 branches in order better to compete with the private banks. This was also reflected in the BoF's 1877 Charter, defining the Bank's business areas as: "The Bank of Finland issues bank notes, buys and sells gold and silver, bonds and government paper, Russian and foreign bills of exchange and payment orders, grants monetary loans and overdraft facilities, and receives monetary deposits" (SEA's translation).[29]

e. The Bank did not play any leading role in setting interest rates, and was not really a "banker for the banks".[30] It mostly followed the moves made by the private banks – at least until the early 20th century. In fact, around the turn of the century the BoF tried to introduce an interest rate agreement among all the banks[31] in order not to have to face too much interest rate competition.

In the hectic years around 1914, when some ten Finnish banks got into serious trouble, the Bank of Finland was conspicuously inactive. Five of these banks went bankrupt, and the others were taken over by other banks in privately organized arrangements. Both the Nationalbanken i Kjøbenhavn and Norges Bank played much more active roles in similar circumstances in the first decade of the 20th century.

The conclusion is that before WWI the Bank of Finland was less of a "central bank" than several other future "central banks", even if they all displayed a mix of commercial and central banking functions and features.

---

[28]Cfr. Pipping (1969) *I Guldmyntfodens Hägn* (Finlands Bank) pp. 387–8.

[29]"Finlands Bank utgifver sedlar, köper och försäljer guld och silfver, obligationer och statspapper, ryska och utländska växlar och invisningar, beviljar penningelån, och kassekreditiv, samt emottager penningeinsättningar." Pipping (1969) *I Guldmyntfodens Hägn* (Finlands Bank, Helsinki) p. 304.

[30]Cfr. N. Meinander (1962) *Penningpolitik under etthundrafemtio år. Finlands Bank 1811–1961* (Finlands Bank) pp. 51–2.

[31]CFr. Pipping (1961) "När blev Finlands Bank en Centralbank?", *Ekonomiska Samfundets Tidskrift*, 3. s, p. 241.

4.3.2 Financing the Saima Canal and the first railway

The biggest project to be financed around the mid-19th century, when the BoF was still the only bank in the country, was the Saima Canal linking the large lakes in eastern Finland to the Gulf of Finland. Completed in 1856, it had taken several years to build at a cost of around 1 million silver rubles. It was financed mainly through a domestic bond issue, to which His Imperial Majesty, the Czar Nikolas I, graciously gave his consent. The Grand-Duchy was the borrower, and the BoF arranged the issue. The 3.6 per cent coupon long-term bonds were originally intended to have fairly large denominations, but they proved difficult to place. Eventually, they were issued in denominations as low as 50 rubles ("Saima notes") in order to increase their popularity, and the BoF had to keep at least 10 per cent of the issue on its own books, implying that the issue had essentially flopped. The "capital market" did not have the capacity for this investment. The small denomination notes had a certain circulation as means of payment.

In 1862, the first railway was completed, running ca. 100 km north from Helsingfors to Hämeelina, from where it was extended to St. Petersburg in 1870.

Railway construction accelerated during the following decades. Between 1880 and 1910 the annual railway investments averaged about 7 million Marks plus a similar amount in maintenance, repairs, and supplementary expenses.[32] Most of the necessary capital was found abroad by the government through the Bank of Finland's connections to banking houses[33] in London, Germany, and Paris (e.g. Rothschildt, Bleichröder, Deutsche Bank, Norddeutsche Bank, Crédit Lyonnais, and Société Générale).

The European railway mania of the 1850s came to Finland with some 30–40 years delay.

4.3.3 Savings banks and Finland's Hypotekförening

The savings banks and the 1895 Savings Banks Act

Like everywhere else, the savings banks in Finland came many years before the commercial banks and, like elsewhere, they were more numerous, and much smaller than the banks.

In 1822 and 1825 the first two savings banks were founded in Åbo and Helsingfors, respectively, only a few years later than the first savings banks in the three other Nordic countries.

---

[32]Cfr. Pipping (1969) *I Guldmyntfodens Hägn* (Finlands Bank, Helsingfors) pp. 37–8.
[33]Cfr. H.E. Pipping (1969) *I Guldmyntfodens Hägn*, pp. 197–205 regarding the foreign loans, including railway loans, raised by the Bank of Finland particularly through Rothschildt (Frankfurt) and Bleichröder (Berlin).

The idea to set up savings banks in Finland must primarily be ascribed to two men: Carl David Skogman (1786–1856) and John Jacob von Julin (1787–1853).

Born in Finland, Skogman made a brilliant career as a Swedish civil servant. He was instructed to produce a report on the English and Scottish savings banks. This report – "Underrättelse om så kallade Besparings-Banker" – published 1819, included a proposal for a savings bank in Stockholm and became the basis for the start of the Swedish savings banks (cfr. Chapter 6).

Julin was brought up in commerce and was a successful businessman. In 1822, he acquired the Fiskars business, including 70,000 hectares of land. Through his travels abroad he had become acquainted with the English and Scottish savings banks, and with Skogman's report. Julin's deeply felt philanthropic and humanitarian interests resulted in a proposal for the establishment of savings banks in Finland, based on the principles introduced by Skogman in Sweden.

The first Finnish savings bank was founded in Åbo in 1822, when 93 persons had provided a "grundfond" ("capital base") of 3,935 paper rubles. By the end of 1823 it had 195 accounts with balances totalling ca. 20,000 rubles.[34] Although Swedish money dominated the currency circulation in Åbo, the Åbo Savings Bank did business only in rubles. The by-laws, largely copied from the Stockholm Savings Bank, prescribed limitations on interest rates, deposit and withdrawal amounts. The by-laws of the Stockholm Savings Bank, stipulating that deposits could be received from persons of both genders and primarily persons from the working or serving classes, had in Åbo been modified to "persons of humble means" ("mindra bemedlade personer").

The management of the Åbo Savings Bank was free to grant loans as they saw fit, as long as the collateral was beyond doubt. Loan applications from people in the process of starting up a business would be given preferential treatment.

The savings bank established in Helsinki in 1825 had by-laws largely copied from the Åbo Savings Bank. Only 2,809 paper rubles could initially be collected for the capital base.[35]

The main differences between the Åbo and the Helsingfors savings banks were that in Helsingfors, Swedish currency was also accepted, and that in Helsingfors the general managers were held personally responsible for any

[34]Urbans (1963) *Sparbankväsedet i Finland, 1822–1922* (Vammalan Kirjapaino OY, Helsinki) p. 80. This work also provides brief biographies of C.D. Skogman and J.J. von Julin.
[35]A. Hästesko (1926) *Helsingfors Sparbank 1826–1926* (Helsingfors) p. 5.

losses the savings bank might incur from its lendings.[36] This provision was copied more or less directly in several of the later Finnish savings banks.

The Helsingfors Sparbank soon became the leading Finnish savings bank, cfr. Table 4.4.

During the following 16 years no other savings banks were formed in Finland. The attitude seems to have been to wait and see how the two first savings banks performed. The savings banks network did not become countrywide until the turn of the century, much in contrast to the other Nordic countries.

Table 4.4 below illustrates the slow growth of the Finnish savings banks sector in the 19th century and the rapid growth after the turn of the century:

Table 4.4   The Development of the Finnish Savings Banks, 1823–1915

Year	Number of savings banks	Total savings bank lendings	Total savings bank deposits,	of which Helsingfors Savings Bank %	Number of savings bank accounts	Average balance per account. Mark
		Million mark				
1823	1	..	0,02	–	..	..
1850	3	..	1,95	37	..	..
1870	39	6	6,38	16	15,200	420
1880	111	14	14,45	13	36,470	396
1900	192	77	77,62	13	14,081	550
1910	376	223	228,00	10	291,603	782
1915	419	331	360,00	8	383,164	940

Sources: R. Urbans (1963) *Sparbankväsendet i Finland 1822–1922* (Helsinki) pp. 440–6 (Number of savings banks, accounts, and Deposits).
A. Hästesko (1926) *Helsingfors Sparbank 1826–1926* (Helsinki) Exhibit, pp. 19–22.
K. Vattula (1983) *Suomen taloushistoria*, Vol. 3, "Historical Statistics" (Helsinki) pp. 334–43.
Note: Savings banks statistics are virtually non-existing prior to the 1870s.

Comparing Table 4.4 with the corresponding figures from Denmark and Sweden shows that the savings bank sector in Finland grew more slowly and never reached a relative position comparable to those reached by the savings banks in Denmark, Norway, and Sweden.

The sharp increase in the figures between 1910 and 1915 was mainly due to inflation, which accelerated quickly after 1913.

---

[36]"Direktionen är genom erhållen decharge för sin förvaltning likväl icke frikänd från den oundvikliga skyldigheten att ersätta förluster härrörande af utlåningar ..." §10, Reglor för Helsingfors Sparbanksinrättning, as reprinted in A. Hästesko (1926) *Helsingfors Sparbank 1826–1926* (Helsinki) p. 9.

In 1895, it was decided to introduce a Savings Bank Act. Like in Sweden, the first Savings Banks Act came much later than the first banking act, in this case 32 years later. The Finnish Savings Bank Act was largely copied from the three-year older Swedish Savings Bank Act.[37] The main stipulations were:

1. The §1 defined "savings banks" as (SEA's translation) "... a money-organization ('penninginrättning') having the right to accept deposits from the general public and to repay them at notice, and without any rights for the initiators to profit from these activities".
2. In contrast to Sweden, municipalities could be recognized as initiators. In Denmark it does not seem that this idea ever occurred to anybody.
3. The capital ("grundfond") had to be minimum 10 per cent of deposits.
4. A government Savings Banks Inspector would be appointed to oversee the savings banks – an inspiration from Denmark.

In contrast to Denmark, there was no attempt in the Savings Bank Act, however vague, to make a formal distinction between "banking business" and "savings banks business", but there was an understanding in Sweden as well as in Finland that savings banks should not engage in "more general banking" ("vidsträktare bankrörelse"[38]), and would neither discount bills, receive call deposits, nor offer overdraft facilities.

Finlands Hypoteksförening

The creation of mortgage institutions in Prussia, Poland, and elsewhere in the Baltics did not pass unnoticed in Finland where, in the 1850s, there was only one bank, and where the borrowing requirements accelerated.

In 1858, a pamphlet titled "Om Hypoteks-föreninger" ("On Mortgage Associations") appeared, written by Henrik Borgström (the Younger). Borgström was the son of a highly successful Helsingfors merchant, who had worked in the newly founded Stockholms Enskilda Bank. The result of his pamphlet was that the Senate issued a decree "angående vilkoren och allmänna grunderne för hypotheksföreninger i Finland" ("ordinance concerning the conditions and general basis for mortgage associations in Finland"). Active in the formation of both Finland's first commercial bank, the Hypoteksförening, and the stock exchange (cfr. below), the younger Borgström might well be called the "father of the Finnish capital market".

---

[37]Out of the 31 paragraphs, no less than 21 had an identical, or partially identical, wording to the corresponding paragraphs of the Swedish Savings Banks Act, cfr. R. Urbans (1963) *Sparbankväsendet i Finland 1822–1922* (Vammalan Lirjapaino, Helsinki) p. 212.
[38]Urbans (1963) *Sparbankväsendet i Finland 1822–1922* (Helsinki) p. 214. Negative experience in Danish savings banks was quoted as a reason.

Long discussions ended in the decision to create a central mortgage association, in contrast to the Danish decentralized system. Its purpose would be to offer medium- and long-term loans to farmers against first ranking mortgages on agricultural property, based on bonds sold at home and abroad. It started operations in 1861 with Borgström (t.Y.) as its first general manager.

Like the Prussian Landschaften and the Danish mortgage associations, it largely matched the terms on its assets and liabilities, and therefore did not have any liquidity problems. Initially, it also had joint liability among the borrowers like the Prussian, Swedish, and Danish associations.

Guaranteed by the Grand-Duchy of Finland and with higher coupon rates than bonds of similar maturities issued elsewhere, the bonds were easily sold abroad.

The domestic "market", however, proved to have a limited capacity, even if some benevolent foundations and a couple of insurance companies could pick up certain amounts. Consequently, the bonds traded at prices down to 82 per cent of face value.[39] Efforts to stimulate demand were closely connected to the foundation of Finland's first privately owned bank and reflected the very limited market for bonds in Finland.[40] The BoF had refused a request to commit itself to buying the bonds at any particular price or in any particular volume.

A similar mortgage institution, Städernes Hypoteksförening, was formed in 1893 but never grew to any significant size. In addition, the larger banks formed bond issuing mortgage departments of their own.

4.3.4   The private banks

In Finland, private banks developed late and slowly. The first one was approved in 1862, the next two in 1872 and 1889 respectively. In the 1890s, the foundation of banks speeded somewhat up, so that by the end of the 19th century, Finland could boast of no less than ten banks, and 13 on the eve of WWI.

In 1862, after several years of public discussions and rejected banking projects, the Bank of Finland and the Senate finally gave in and approved the by-laws for Finland's first privately owned commercial bank. It was probably no disadvantage that the Bank of Finland governor, the strongest opponent to competition, had died the year before, and that the above-

---

[39]Cfr. H. Pipping (1962) *Bankliv Genom Hundra År*, the official history of Föreningsbanken (UBF, Helsingfors) p. 32.

[40]The small size of the Finnish bondmarket can e.g. be illustrated by the fact that in the late 19th century only ca. 5.5 per cent of the assets of the Finnish insurance companies consisted of bonds, while the corresponding figure was 37 per cent for the Swedish insurance companies, cfr. N. Meinander (1962) *Penningpolitik under etthundrafemtio år* (Finlands Bank) p. 42.

mentioned Henrik Borgström (t.Y.) was personally acquainted with the Senate finance minister ("finanschefen"). The Senate's approval was given on May 21, 1862, but for ten years only (as for the Swedish "enskilde" banks). It was duly renewed in 1872, 1882, and 1892. Thus, Finland's first private bank had been born, named Föreningsbanken, or Union Bank of Finland (UBF), until 1886 with note-issuing rights.

In contrast to Denmark and Sweden at this time, establishing a bank was not just a question of asking for relief from certain stamp duties and having the proposed by-laws approved. In the Grand-Duchy, this was still a matter for decision at the highest possible political level, just like in Sweden in 1658 and in Denmark in 1736. In this respect, the Banking Acts of 1866 and 1886 made no substantial changes.

Henrik Borgström (t.Y.) played a central role in the preparation of UBF and its activities. Already in 1859 he had issued a pamphlet titled "Penningställingen år 1859 och privatbanker" ("The Monetary Situation in the Year 1859 and Private Banks"). Borgström's idea was to combine the abovementioned Hypoteksförening with an agricultural bank, but this idea was eventually given up. However, Borgström's original proposal was reflected in the by-laws of the new bank, which stated the bank's purpose to be to support Finland's agriculture, industry, and commerce.[41] To this end it was also decided that up to half of the new bank's share capital could be paid in with bonds issued by Hypoteksföreningen. Borgström (t.Y) became the first general manager of UBF, a position he had no difficulty combining with his simultaneous position as general manager of Hypoteksföreningen.

The original plan was to collect a share capital of 6 million finmark proved over-ambitious, and the end the Bank had to contend itself with 3 million, a decent amount compared to those of other banks founded in this period. It was more than twice as much as the amounts raised for Stockholms Enskilda Bank in 1857 (1 million kroner, or the equivalent of about 1.4 million finmark, or for Skandinaviska Kreditaktiebolaget in 1864 (0.5 million kroner = 700,000 marks). However, in Sweden share capital was being raised for several other banks at the same time, all over the country, so there was a much stronger competition for the funds.

Also, at this stage neither the first Banking Act nor the first Companies Act had yet been passed, so the question of limited liability for the shareholders was not crystal clear (cfr. 4.5).

---

[41]Cfr. G. Åhman (1942) "Strukturförändringar i affärsbankernas rörelse", *Ekonomiska Samfundets Tidskrift, Ny Serie, Häfte 56*, p. 55, and Pipping (1962) *Bankliv Genom Hundra År*, (UBF) p. 36, which pictures the first page of the by-laws, which read: §1, "I ändemål att underlätta penningrörelsen för Finlands jordbruk, industri och handel bildas ett aktiebolag under namn av 'Föreningsbanken i Finland' ... §2, Bolagets grundkapital utgör tre millioner mark ..."

At the beginning, UBF had about 1,000 shareholders. The five largest shareholders, including Borgström father and son (1,000 shares combined), took a total of about 9 per cent of the shares.[42] There were, in other words, no dominating shareholder(s).

It was, from the beginning, planned that the bank should develop a nationwide branch network, and this was done quite speedily. By the end of its first operating year it already had ten branches, and by the eve of WWI, the number had swollen to more than 60.

Kansallis-Osake-Pankki, or the "National Joint Stock Bank" (KOP), Finland's largest bank for much of the 20th century was a product of the rising wave of nationalism, which emerged with increasing force during the last quarter of the 19th century.

The main characters in the founding process were Otto Stenroth (1861–1931), later chairman of the Bank of Finland and the first foreign minister of independent Finland, and August Hjelt (1862–1919), later vice-chairman of the Senate's Department of Finance.

They met initially (1889) in absolute secrecy[43] for fear of counter measures from the existing banks, and organized other secret meetings all over the country where trusted "Fennomen" (nationalist Finns) were asked to subscribe the 2.5 million mark share capital, which had been decided upon. The subscription was a great success, and on September 12, 1889, the concession was granted by the Senate. On October 12, the first meeting of shareholders and directors was held in the mirror hall at the Hotel Kämp. The doors were opened for business in February 1890.

Because of its chosen nationalistic stance, the new bank (KOP) had a rather special problem in its early days. The problem was that few of the "technical" banking expressions existed in the Finnish language, so the staff had to whisper the Swedish words until the necessary Finnish vocabulary had been developed, and the staff and clients had got used to it.

However, the growing nationalistic sentiments had the effect that the Finnish-speaking part of the population preferred to bank with KOP, while the Swedish-speaking clientele generally preferred Föreningsbanken (UBF) or the Bank of Helsinki (absorbed by UBF in 1986).

Thus, it soon became general knowledge that e.g. Wärtsilä, Nokia, Ahlström, and Kymene (now UPM-Kymene) would have UBF as their main bank connection, while e.g. Neste, Enso-Gutzeit (now Stora Enso), and Rauma-

---

[42]Cfr. Pipping (1962) *Bankliv Genom Hundra År* (UBF, Helsingfors) pp. 40–3.
[43]Cfr. J. Vesikansa (1989) *Kansallis-Osake-Pankki A Hundred Years* (KOP, Helsinki) p. 9.

Repola would have KOP as their main bank.[44] This segmentation of a limited banking market according to linguistic preferences, and the implied limitation of the competition among the banks was, of course, unfortunate from a capital market point-of-view.

From the very beginning it was clear that the new bank (KOP) should have a nationwide network of branches, and the first five branches opened already in the first year of operation.

The early development of large branch networks by the Finnish banks headquartered in only one or two cities besides Helsingfors and the absence of minor provincial banks was a feature, which strongly contrasted Finland to the pattern of the banking landscape spreading in the three other Nordic countries. In 1900, Finnish banks could boast of a total of 104 branches, and by 1915 this figure had increased to 181 spread over 76 cities and villages. The few provincial banks, which did emerge, were soon either absorbed by the Helsinki banks or went bankrupt or were dissolved for similar reasons.[45] In the three other countries a few large banks domiciled in the respective capitals grew up and gradually developed countrywide branch networks, but in addition a large number of minor provincial banks with a small number of branches in their respective regions of operation also appeared and thrived relatively well – in Denmark and Norway more than a hundred (cfr. Chapters 5 and 7).

The dominating position of the three main private banks is clearly seen in Table 4.5, although the smaller banks did increase their share of the banking market from slightly less than 10 per cent in 1885 to about 22–24 per cent in 1914. The Finnish banking scene was developing into even more of an "oligarchy" than was the case in the three other Nordic countries.

---

[44]Cfr. J. Ojala, J. Eloranta & J. Jalava (2006) *The Road to Prosperity. An Economic History of Finland* (SKS, Helsinki) p. 115. This issue disappeared, of course, when UBF and KOP merged in 1996 to become Merita Bank. KOP virtually never used the Swedish version of its name, "Den Nationale Aktiebank", just as Föreningsbanken rarely used the Finnish version of its name "Suomen Yhdyspankki", or SYP. However, in the 1950s a major revolution happened in UBF, when it was decided that the minutes of the board meetings, so far written in Swedish, would in the future also be written in Finnish. The language issue was a subject of great controversy in the top management of the bank in the 1940s and 1950s, and had direct implications for the appointment of Rainer von Fieandt as its general manager, because many of the Swedish-speaking board members considered von Fieandt a representative of the national Finnish mentality and hostile to the Swedish community, cfr. T. Vihola (2000) *Penningens Styrman. Föreningsbanken och Merita 1950–2000* (Jyväskylä) p. 84. Anyway, in 1945 von Fieandt was appointed general manager of UBF, and in 1955 he was appointed Governor of the Bank of Finland.
[45]Cfr. Åhman "Strukturförändringar i affärsbankernas rörelse", *Ekonomiska Samfundets Tidskrift, Häfte,* 56, 1942, pp. 59–65.

Table 4.5   The Development in the Number and Lendings of the Private
Banks, 1866–1915

	Number of banks	Outstanding loan amounts, million finnmark				Bond holdings	Total, million finnmark
		UBF	NB	KOP	Others		
1865	1	17	–	–	–		17
1870	1	18	–	–	–		18
1875	2	27	9	–	–		36
1880	3	19	13	–	–	11	43
1885	3	26	17	–	5	14	62
1890	6	33	30	9	17	15	104
1895	6	40	49	21	22	24	176
1900	10	76	73	60	60	23	292
1910	13	165	105	160	139	26	595
1915	13	171	137	185	(165)	(30)	(690)

Sources: Number of banks: G. Åhman (1942) "Strukturförändringar i affärsbankernas rörelse",
Ekonomiska samfundetstidskrift, Ny Serie, Häfte 56, p. 59.
Outstanding loan amounts: UBF and NB: Pipping (1962) *Bankliv Genom Hundra År* (UBF) p. 413.
KOP (1940) *Kansallis-Osake-Pankki 1889–1939* (Helsinki) pp. 84, 111, 143, 181. NB (Nordiska
Banken) was merged with UBF soon after WWI.
Total & bond holdings: Pipping (1969) *I Guldmyntfodens Hägn* (BoF, Helsinki) p. 435.
Others: The difference between "Total" excluding bond holdings and the sum of UBF, NB, and
KOP.
Note: Excluding correspondents.
Information of bond holdings by individual banks not available.
Figures in brackets are SEA's estimates based on the known growth rates for the three main
banks.

This did not, however, mean that the Finnish scene was completely
without competition. After the opening of the UBF, the Helsingfors Savings
Banks lost deposits to the new bank, and had to increase its interest rates
on deposits from 4–5 per cent (and lending rates from 5–6 per cent) in
order to stay in business.[46] Later on, the banks increased their deposit rates
to 5 per cent, which put real pressure on the savings banks, which could
not increase their lending rates beyond the maximum permitted 6 per cent,
whereas the banks could more easily keep up their earnings from their discounting of bills, which was forbidden business for the savings banks, and
for which interest ceilings did not apply.

Other banks dating from this period include Postsparebanken, 1887 (later
renamed Postipankki, Leonia Bank, and Sampo Bank, taken over by Danske
Bank in 2007), and SKOP Bank, 1909, the bank jointly owned by the savings
banks, and which collapsed in 1992, and OKO Bank, the commercial bank
jointly owned by the co-op banks.

---

[46]A. Hästesko "Helsingfors Sparbank 1826–1926", *Helsingfors*, 1926, p. 20.

The banking Acts of 1866 and 1886

Finland's first banking Act,[47] passed by the Senate in 1866, was largely copied from the corresponding Swedish regulations. The main stipulations were that permission to form a bank would have to be obtained from the Senate based on an application containing i.a. descriptions of the intended share capital and plans for the building up of reserves. The share capital would have to be at least 1.5 million mark silver. Banks were forbidden to trade in anything but gold, silver, bills of exchange, and interest bearing paper (cfr. Chapter 6, Schedule 6.1).

The 1886 Act[48] made few, but important changes:

First, the Act made an attempt, however primitive, to define "banks". A "bank" was defined as a business ("företag"), which is engaged in borrowing from the general public by means of deposits or bond issues. Not a word on lending.

Second, the fundamental view of the Committee, which had prepared the Act, was that banking would best develop to the benefit of the country if it were least constricted by firm regulations (... "bankverksamheten ... utveckla sig till största fromma för landet, om densamma så litet som möjligt bindes av faste lagbestämningar)".[49] Therefore, the formal requirement for a minimum capital was scrapped. This point of view is in some contrast to opinions generally held in the early 21st century.

Third, the note-issuing rights of private banks was abolished. Only the UBF had ever made use of this right, and only to a limited extent.

4.4   The size of the financial sector

As everywhere else, Finland's financial sector grew more rapidly than the rest of the economy, but in the mid-19th century it started from almost scratch (cfr. Table 4.6).

4.5   The stock exchange

Inspired by what was happening in Stockholm in the early 1860s, a number of Helsingfors merchants led by H. Borgström (the Younger) organized a sort of "stock exchange" in 1862. It proved to be premature.

---

[47]"Förordning av 15. jan. 1866 angående enskilda banker med sedelutgivningsrätt samt om vilkoren för inrättande av enskilda banker i allmänhet".
[48]"Förordning av 10. mai 1886 angående bankrörelse som bedrivas av aktiebolag".
[49]As quoted from "Kommittébetänkande nr 8/1884", by R. Erma (1964) *Affärsbankernas soliditet – deponentens skydd enligt lagstiftningen* in *Affärsbankerna och Näringslivet* (Bankföreningen i Finland, in celebration of the 50th anniversary of the Finish Bankers' Association) p. 114.

Table 4.6   Relative Composition and Growth of the Credit Stock, 1860–1914

	BoF & government	Commercial banks	Savings banks	Bonds	Insurance & pension	Total	Total, million Marks	Index	Total in % of GDP
	Per cent of total credit stock								
1860	80		7		13	100	46	100	16
1870	37	22	7	22	12	100	82	178	24
1880	28	26	11	15	20	100	124	270	29
1890	25	34	15	8	18	100	261	567	50
1900	15	43	12	14	15	99	620	1,348	76
1910	10	44	17	12	17	100	1,293	2,811	
1913	9	40	19	13	19	100	(1,582)	(3,349)	(117)
	Per cent of GDP								
1860	13		1		2	16			16
1870	9	5	2	5	3	24			24
1880	8	7	3	4	6	28			29
1890	12	17	8	4	9	50			50
1900	11	33	9	11	12	76			76
1910									
1913	11	(46)	22	16	(22)	(117)			(117)

Sources: Pipping (1961 and 1969) *Från Pappersrubel till Guldmark*, p. 513, and *I Guldmyntfodens Hägn*, p. 433 (both BoF, Helsinki).
Government Funds: K. Vattula, ed. (1983) *Suomen taloushistoria*, Vol. 3 "Historical Statistics" (Helsinki) p. 340.

Note: BoF figures include government funds, although these were managed by the BoF after 1874.
Figures in brackets are partially SEA's estmates, based on interpolations and extrapolations.
For 1910, no GDP figures available.
Comments to Table 4.6:
1. The modest size of the total stock of credits (compared to Sweden and Denmark) is clearly seen. There was, however, not much difference compared to Norway.
2. Like in Sweden, the growth in the financial sector was very much concentrated on the banks, which developed as a centralized system of large banks with nationwide branch networks, in stark contrast to Denmark and Norway. Also like in Sweden, the savings bank sector remained relatively smaller than in Denmark and Norway.
3. Mortgage institutions never really got off the ground. The main issuers of bonds were the government and a few municipalities. The commercial banks also set up their own bond issuing departments to finance residential and commercial construction (included in the column "bonds").
4. Insurance companies and pension funds emerged as large-scale suppliers of long-term capital. Presumably, most of the lendings by these institutions financed residential and commercial construction, but this is difficult to document. In no other Nordic country did the insurance companies play a similarly large role as direct lenders.

Facilitating the development of the "stock exchange, a new Broker Regulation was passed by the Senate to replace the 1720 Regulation, the first Finnish Companies Act was passed in 1864, and a newspaper was issued bimonthly quoting prices of five shares, two bond issues, shipping particulars, and a number of commodities, e.g. flour, sugar, iron plate, cognac, sherry, rum, and port.[50] Almost anybody could trade almost anything. Still, very little trade actually did take place on this "exchange", so in 1869 it was dissolved.

A second attempt was made in 1879, when an application for permission to organize stock exchange auctions for shares, bonds, and other securities was approved by the Senate on the condition that such auctions were conducted by sworn brokers. Four years later the "Reglemente" was amended to the effect that also wholesale commodities could be traded. By this time auctions were also held in Åbo, Viborg, and Tammerfors.

The auctions were to be held twice monthly, but were often cancelled because of lack of business. Sales varied between ca. 413,000 marks in 1901 and ca. 1.3 million in 1907 (the top year), dropping off to around 620,000 in 1911.[51]

In 1911, a group of securities traders, i.e. "banquiers", who had by now emerged on the scene, decided to publish a joint price list for concluded stock exchange transactions (but not offer and bid prices). The first of these lists included six bank shares, two industrial shares, one shipping company, and two others. Hardly an impressive list. Substantially more trading probably took place outside the "stock exchange".

Because of the thin trading, the lack of information on bids and offers as well as the scarcity of information on the financial substance of the traded shares, auction prices were erratic and probably only by coincidence indicative of the prices obtained outside the auctions.

Under these "market" conditions there would be plenty of opportunities for Shylocks as well as for Antonios and Bassanios to cut a nice pound of flesh for themselves.

Therefore, new initiatives were taken to establish a "real" stock exchange.

In 1910, Aktiebolaget Börs was formed with a paid-in share capital for the purpose of erecting a regular stock exchange building on a site in Fabiansgatan acquired from a consortium, who had bought the place a couple of years earlier for precisely this purpose. Simultaneously, Börsklubben i Helsingfors was formed by 176 members with the intention of promoting a "real" stock exchange. Most of the shareholders in Aktiebolaget Börs were, of course, also members of the Börsklubben i Helsingfors.

---

[50]G. Stjernschantz (1987) *På Börsens Berg- och Dalbana. Helsingfors Fondbörs 1912–1987* (Helsinki Fondbörs) pp. 10–11.
[51]G. Stjenschantz (1987) *På Börsens Berg- och Dalbana*, p. 16.

This time, however, the matter was not left solely to private initiative. Civil servants from the Department of Commerce ("handelsfullmäktige") also discussed the matter, and a committee was formed consisting of representatives from the handelsfullmägtige, the merchants, the private banks, and the City of Helsingfors. The inclusion of the banks was probably an inspiration from Stockholm, where banks had been admitted to the stock exchange a few years earlier (cfr. Chapter 6). The Committee was chaired by J.O. Wasastjerna, General Manager of Föreningsbanken (UBF).

The Committee's proposed Regulation for the Helsingfors Stock Exchange was approved by the Governor General on April 25, 1912, which has since been considered the birthday of the Helsingfors Stock Exchange ("HEX"), arguably 104 years later than the birth of the Copenhagen Stock Exchange, and 93 years and 46 years later than the official birthdays of the Oslo and Stockholm stock exchanges respectively.

Legally, the Helsingfors Stock Exchange was an association of members who conducted their business from premises hired from the Aktiebolaget Börs, which owned and operated the building constructed in Fabiansgatan and completed in 1912.

The main points of the 1912 Regulation for the HEX were:

1. The Exchange was to be directed by a 12-member Board with representatives from the City of Helsingfors, the merchants, the banquiers, and the banks. In 1919, the City renounced its membership of the Board. The costs were to be covered mainly by annual subscriptions from members and fees from issuers. If that did not suffice, the city would cover half of the deficit, and the banks and the Chamber of Commerce would share the other half.
2. The assets to be traded on the exchange would consist of financial securities, foreign exchange, and commodities (the trading in commodities never materialized). By the end of 1912, 33 shares had been registered for trading (including ten banks, seven insurance companies, two shipping companies, five industrial companies, and a number of various trading and service companies). Tammerfors Linne & Jern Manufaktur Ab was the only major industrial company on the list. The largest industrial companies (Ahlström, etc.) showed no interest.
3. Only members could make bids and offers on the Exchange, but the proceedings were open to the general public. Membership was not particularly restricted. Non-bank members were to put up collateral for their commitments in amounts decided by the Board. The commissions were fixed at 0.5 per cent of the value of share transactions, and half of that for bond transactions.

Already prior to the opening of the Exchange for business, 17 members had been registered (five banks, and 12 individual banquiers or banquier firms).

Initially, the new Stock Exchange was no great success. In 1913, the number of share trades totalled 898 with a value of 2.5 million marks, and the value of bond trades was less than 18,000 marks.[52]

The low level of activity on the stock exchange cannot be explained by any absence of company formation. Although Finland's first Companies Act, passed in 1864 and largely copied from the first Swedish Companies Act (1848), was rather vague on many points, it did clarify the hitherto highly tricky question of limited liability for the shareholders. The 1864 Act stipulated that approval of a company's articles of association by the Senate was required if the shareholders were to enjoy the principle of limited liability.[53] A number of companies resembling joint stock companies had existed already before the passing of the Companies Act, but following the passing of this Act the number of joint stock companies grew rapidly, primarily through conversion of existing enterprises into joint stock companies. This did not necessarily raise much capital.

---

[52]Stjenschantz (1987) *På Börsens Berg- och Dalbana* (Helsinki Fondsbörs) pp. 28 and 162–3.
[53]For a discussion of the 1864 Companies Act and the ensuing amendments, see P. Schybergson (1964) *Aktiebolagsformens Genombrott i Finland. Utvecklingen före 1895 Års Lag*, in *Bidrag till Kännedom av Finlands Natur och Folk* (Vetenskaps-Societeten, H 109, Helsinki), 1964.

5

Norway, 1814–1918: From Province to Nation

"But ships are but boards, sailors but men;
There be land-rats and water rats, water thieves and land thieves
...
and there is the peril of waters, winds, and rocks."

("The Merchant of Venice", Act I)

5.1   An overview: Sailing towards independence

The land and water rats which finally broke up the nearly 440 years of union between Denmark and Norway came in the shape of inept diplomats[1] on both the English and the Danish side, landing Denmark-Norway on the losing side of the Napoleonic wars. The Congress of Vienna finally approved that Norway was to enter into a personal union with Sweden. Karl 14. Johan, Sweden's newly appointed king, became king of Norway as well.

Politically, the new situation gave the Norwegians substantially more autonomy than they had had in the union with Denmark. The relatively liberal "Eidsvoll Constitution" of 1814 provided for the legislating "Storting" consisting of members elected by a (limited) electorate, and a separate government appointed by the king.

Under the personal union with Sweden, Norway was allowed full "home rule" in economic and financial matters. Foreign affairs, however, would be taken care of exclusively by the Swedish government. The arrangement was, in fact, similar to Finland's position in the Russian empire (cfr. Chapter 4) except that the position of a Swedish governor general in Christiania, re-

---

[1]England had become suspicious of Denmark's Association of Neutrality with Russia and Prussia, and attacked Copenhagen with a superior force under admirals Parker and Nelson (Battle of Copenhagen, April 2nd, 1801). This pushed Denmark-Norway into Napoleon's camp.

named Oslo in 1925,[2] was abolished in 1873, and Finnish financial matters were decided in St. Petersburg (cfr. Chapter 4). Much of the time, however, the Storting was heavily leaned upon by the king, who took a keen interest in financial matters.

Towards the end of the 19th century there was a growing feeling in Norway that Sweden neglected Norway's foreign interests. Norway asked the Swedish government for permission to establish her own representations abroad for the purpose of negotiating shipping rights, fishery contracts, etc, which were all-important for Norway's economy and subject to restrictive foreign treaties, even if the lifting of the English Navigation Act in 1849 had been a great help. A decade of heated negotiations failed to produce any results, so Norway declared its independence in 1905. Sweden grudgingly accepted in return for some minor concessions. So, in the autumn of 1905, Oscar II, the Swedish king (1872–1907) who had learnt to speak fluent Norwegian, abdicated his Norwegian throne. Military conflict was narrowly averted.

In the late 1880s, the Norwegian GDP was lower than in the early 1870s. The reduction measured in fixed prices was, however, smaller than it would appear from Table 5.1 below, since the general price level was dropping in that period.

Table 5.1   **Gross Domestic Product, Gross Savings, and Gross Fixed Investments, 1865–1916**

Annual average	GDP million NOK	Gross savings, % of GDP	Gross fixed investments, % of GDP	Annual average	GDP million NOK	Gross savings, % of GDP	Gross fixed investments, % of GDP
1865–1868	503	13	13	1893–1896	833	13	16
1869–1872	570	17	13	1897–1900	1,024	13	14
1873–1876	772	17	18	1901–1904	1,088	13	17
1877–1880	721	15	16	1905–1908	1,214	15	18
1881–1884	743	16	15	1909–1912	1,490	17	20
1885–1888	679	15	14	1913–1916	2,560	25	21
1889–1892	788	15	17	1917–1920	5,808	20	27

Source: Statistisk Sentralbyrå (1965) *NOS XII, 163, Nasjonalregnskabsstistik*, 1865–1960 (Oslo). Figures prior to 1877 have been restated in NOK, by Statistisk Sentralbyrå, from original speciedaler amounts.

---

[2]Between 1624 and 1925 the town's name was Kristiania (before 1877 spelt Christiania), named after the Danish king Christian IV (1588–1648), who had the ancient hamlet of Oslo rebuilt a short distance from its original location. In this chapter the names Christiania, Kristiania, and Oslo will be used in accordance with the practice at the time.

National accounts for the 19th century should be read with a great deal of caution, but the figures in Table 5.1 indicate that that real growth in the years 1875–1890 was flat, and in many years negative. It also appears that savings and investments ratios increased sharply just before and after WWI. The absolute increase in the post WWI figures is, however, to a large extent the result of inflation, which was faster in Norway than in Sweden and Denmark in those years, although not as wild as in Finland.

During the 19th century, Norway's urban population increased from about 5 per cent of the total to some 18 per cent, which was a lower rate of urbanization than in most of Europe, including Denmark (38 per cent by 1900), but not much different from Sweden (21 per cent) and Finland (15 per cent) cfr. Chapters 3, 4, and 6.

Table 5.2   Norway's Population 1801 and 1900

	Christiania	Bergen	Trondhjem	Rest of Norway	Total
1801	9,200	16,900	8,800	ca. 870,000	ca. 900,000
1900	229,000	33,000	38,700	ca. 1,910,000	2,240,000

Sources: F. Hodne og O.H. Grytten (1994) *Norsk økonomi i det nittende århundre* (Fakbokforlaget, Oslo) p. 250.
Statistisk Sentralbyrå (1994) *Historisk Statistikk*.

In 1900, Kristiania still had little more than half of Copenhagen's number of inhabitants and only 60 per cent of Stockholm's. In both 1800 and in 1900 the total population was about the same as in Finland and Denmark.

In 1873 the Storting decided to replace the speciedaler (spd), its currency since 1816, with the Norwegian krone (one spd = four NOK) over a two-year transition period, and to join the gold standard. As from January 1, 1877, Norway joined the Scandinavian Currency Union with one NOK equalling one SEK and one DKK (cfr. Chapters 3 and 6), and with all three currencies accepted as legal tender in each of the three countries. In this chapter, all pre-1873 amounts have been restated in NOK.

5.2   The problems

Three aspects should be pointed out: First, there was not much of a monetary economy outside a few coastal towns before the mid-19th century.[3] Secondly, it is crucial for the understanding of the development of Norwegian society

---

[3]Cfr. Å. Egge (1972) *Trekk ved Sparebankvesenet og Sparebanklovgivningen i Slutet av Forrige Århundrede* in *Studier i Sparebankvesen* (Gyldendal Norsk Forlag) p. 103, where the author notes that a monetary economy had started to appear in the rural districts during the 1850s and 1860s.

and the Norwegian capital market to realize the significance of the relatively small population scattered over a vast territory, and the difficulty of communicating over these large and mountainous distances in the pre-telephone era. The first telegraph line was not installed until 1855. The consequence was an extremely fragmented country, socially, economically, and financially. The individual regions and towns had virtually no economic or financial links to each other. It was, e.g. easier to transfer money from Christiania to London or Hamburg than from Christiania to Bergen.[4] Before WWI banks did not open branches outside their own turf, or have accounts with each other. People had no wish to see their savings being invested outside their own villages or counties.[5] The result of this was that interest rates and credit availability could differ quite sharply between different regions, and that large amounts for major projects could not be raised. The battles over the Kongeriget Norges Hypotekbank in 1851 and the Savings Bank Act of 1887 were clear demonstrations of the opposing interests of the major towns versus rural districts, and of conflicts between the government and the Storting, as well as between central government on one side and the distant municipalities on the other.

Third, the Napoleonic wars had severed most financial and commercial ties between Denmark and Norway. Before 1814, many Norwegian merchants had their bills of exchange discounted at Copenhagen merchant houses, but after 1814 this could not continue, partly because new tariffs and customs barriers had now reduced the trade flows between Denmark and Norway, and partly because the Copenhagen merchants no longer had the resources to discount anybody's bills. With all these problems, it is small wonder that industrialization, railways, and a capital market came rather late to Norway.

Given Norway's mountainous nature, railways were, of course, expensive to build. Norway's first railway, a stretch of only some 70 km between Christiania and Eidsvoll, was not completed until 1854 and was the subject of much controversy and heated debates in the Storting. Nationalistic elements wanted the project to be purely Norwegian built and financed, but more realistic circles advocated the acceptance of a proposal from an English consortium offering both technical and financial aid. "Those who are against this offer are against the project being realized at all", they said.[6]

The construction costs were estimated at around NOK 8 million. There was, of course, no chance that an amount of this size could have been

---

[4]Cfr. Å. Egge (1978) *Kredittvesenet i Norge under industrikapitalismens gennombrudd* in G. Authén Blom (ed.) *Utviklingen av kreditt og kredittinstitusjoner i de nordiske land ca. 1850– 1914* (Trondhejm) p. 9.
[5]Cfr. F. Hodne og O.H. Grytten (1994) *Norsk økonomi i det nittende århundre* (Fakbok-forlaget, Oslo) p. 169.
[6]Cfr. E. Østvedt (1954) *De Norske Jernbaners Historie*, I–III, (Oslo), vol. I, p. 72.

raised on the Norwegian market for a single project, even when spread over the four years period of construction. Total annual gross capital formation in the 1850s hardly exceeded NOK 40–50 million.[7] It would have "crowded out" too many other investments. The end result was that the English offer was accepted, and the railway was built with a combination of English technical support, and English and Norwegian shareholders, including the Norwegian government.

In the years 1851–1920, the amounts spent on railway construction totalled NOK 760 million,[8] or 5–6 per cent of gross savings in this period. The individual railway projects in the latter half of this period would typically have construction costs of NOK 50–75 million, equal to 20–30 per cent of the combined balance sheets of the commercial banks.

Investments in shipping absorbed a large share of the nation's savings, but the investments and their financing largely by-passed the organized credit system until the last 5–10 years of the 19th century. Most pre-1890 shipping enterprises consisted of one-vessel outfits created by local carpenters, trades people, forest owners, farmers, etc, who formed these enterprises, mostly as joint liability partnerships. It was not until very late in the century that steamship companies were formed which needed capital on a scale far beyond what the local communities could supply, just as it was beyond the capacity of the Norwegian banks.

The fact is that by 1900, Norway could still not be considered an industrialized country, and Norway's financial infrastructure was too fragmented to be able to mount the sums required for any major projects in either steamshipping, railways, or major industrial undertakings. Until 1910, it was only in exceptional cases that any Norwegian bank would lend more than NOK 1 million to a single borrower.[9] The Norwegian banks played only a minimal role in the industrialization of Norway.[10] A number of banks in Denmark, Sweden, and Finland played much more active roles in this process in their respective countries, (cfr. Chapters 3, 4, and 6).

The industrial breakthrough came in the years 1905–1915 with i.a. the construction of the hydropower plants in Telemarken (Rjukan) for the

---

[7]Investment figures are not available for the 1850s, but according to Statistisk Sentralbyrå (1978) *Historisk Statistikk*, gross capital formation was NOK 60–65 million annually in the 1860s, cfr. Table 5.1.

[8]Cfr. E. Østvedt (1954) *De Norske Jernbaners Historie*, vol. III, p. 547.

[9]Cfr. P.H. Castberg, general manager of Cristiania Bank og Kreditkasse, in a speech (1910) *Bankernes betydning som støtte for industrien*, published in *Statsøkonomisk tidsskrift* (1910) pp. 121–39.

[10]Cfr. S. Knutsen (1990) *Norske Forretningsbankers Rolle i Industrialiseringen 1850–1913, med Hovedvekt på Perioden 1890–1913* in H.W. Nordvik & S. Knutsen *Bankenes rolle i norsk industriell utvikling 1850–1914* (Norges Råd for Anvendt Samfunnsforskning, NORAS) p. 13.

nitrogen production which came to be Norsk Hydro. The amounts invested in Telemarken in the years 1905–1910 totalled around NOK 100 million, which was clearly far beyond the capacity of the Norwegian financial system.[11]

The exploitation of hydropower started in the 1890s and because of the size of the capital needs, contacts were established with the Wallenbergs, who picked up 76 per cent (financed with a loan from Stockholms Enskilda Bank) of the shares in Det Norske Aktieselskap for Elektrokemisk Industri (Elkem), est. 1904, which proceeded to lay the foundations for Norsk Hydro. In fact, Elkem acted as a "venture company", adding Norsk Industrihypotekbank to its name in 1913.

The Wallenbergs eventually used their international connections to secure financing for the huge investment required. Banque de Paris et des Pays Bas was brought on board, and in 1905 Norsk Hydro Elektrisk Kvælstof A/S was formed with the French bank as the dominating shareholder. The Wallenbergs gradually withdrew. Their main interest had been to ensure that the machinery for the hydro power plant was supplied by the Wallenberg controlled ASEA.[12]

5.3   Responses and actions

5.3.1   Norges Bank ("The Bank of Norway")

The history of banking in Norway before 1816 is brief and insignificant: Danmark-Norges Speciesbank and the Depositokasse (est. 1791 and 1799, respectively, cfr. Chapter 2) had set up three branches in Norway (Christiania, Bergen, and Trondhjem), but their lending activities in Norway were minimal.

One of the top priorities of the newly created Storting (1814) was to plan a new national currency and banking system. After two years of heated discussions, a set of laws was passed on June 14, 1816. The three most important of these laws were:

1. "Loven om pengevesenet" (the "Money Act"), whereby the currency system in the new Norway was to be based on the speciedaler coin (spd) with a silver content of 25.281 gr (i.e. equal to the "old" Danish speciedaler). The circulating money would consist of notes to be issued by a new bank, Norges Bank. As from 1818, this currency was Norway's only legal tender.
2. "Loven om Norges Bank"[13] (the "Norway's Bank Act"), which provided the charter ("Fundation") for Norges Bank, today Norway's central bank.

---

[11]As for fn. 9.
[12]As for fn. 10, p. 41.
[13]The Lov om Norges Bank was amended many times during the 19th century. Most of the changes concerned the metal coverage of the note issues.

The most important of the Fundation's 73 paragraphs can be summarized as follows:

- The Bank was to have a capital of 2 million spd to be raised as share capital from private investors. Since voluntary subscriptions raised less than half of the target amount the rest had to be collected as forced subscriptions from all over the country (in proportion to wealth). It took nearly three years, and much agony, to collect.
- The Bank would be the only issuer of notes, convertible into silver[14] at the Bank's head office, and would offer loans, deposit, and clearing (giro) facilities. Loans were to be offered regionally in proportion to the forced capital contributions actually paid in. Loans could have a maturity of maximum six months, and could be offered up to certain percentages of the value of assets taken as collateral. Interest was not to exceed 5 per cent p.a., except that the Bank was free to discount bills of exchange at rates set by market conditions.
- The Bank's head office was to be located in Trondhjem, and branches were soon set up in Christiania, Bergen, and Kristianssand. By 1914, the Bank had 20 branches.
- Although the Bank was a private company, it was to be managed by a supervisory board ("representantskap") of 15 members, and a management group ("direksjon") of five members, all appointed by and reporting to the government and the Storting. Even the branch managers were government-appointed.

Until the 1860s, the Bank of Norway was, in spite of its declared purpose, mostly a mortgage institution. Mortgage loans made up 80–85 per cent of its total loans.

The statutory limitation to six-month loans was overcome by continuous prolongations. Norges Bank was not an easy bank to work with. It was very cautious in its valuation of collateral, particularly during the early years, when it had to build up its silver holdings. For its discounting of bills of exchange it required the bills to be endorsed by two people, one of whom had to be residing in a town where the Bank had a branch. This was time consuming and became a lucrative playing field for Bassanio-type middlemen.

The main structure of the Bank of Norway's balance sheet is seen in Table 5.3.

In the last third of the century, when other banks and financial institutions had emerged on the scene, the Bank of Norway increasingly restricted itself to the rediscounting of bills.

---

[14]Convertibility into silver was introduced in 1823, but at a discount of approximately 30 per cent. Convertibility at par value came in 1842.

Table 5.3   Norges Bank's Main Assets, 1820–1920 (Million NOK)

	Mortgage loans	Other loans	Other assets	Total assets		Mortgage loans	Other loans	Other assets	Total assets
1820	5	1		6	1880	13	21	34	68
1830	17	2		19	1890	8	26	41	75
1840	22	4		26	1900	4	48	47	95
1850	30	6	8	44	1910	2	51	75	126
1860	20	12	15	47	1915	1	86	147	234
1870	16	18	22	56	1920	1	27	699	727

Sources: H.I. Matre (1992) *Norske kredittinstitisjoner 1850–1990* (NORAS, rapport nr. 42), Table 3a.
Note: Liability figures before 1914 have not been published.

By its constitutional set-up, the Norges Bank had a number of similarities with and differences from other future European central banks. Like the Bank of England, the Banque de France, and the two years younger National-banken i Kiøbenhavn (but in sharp contrast to the Sveriges Riksbank and the Bank of Finland) it was a joint stock company fully owned by private share-holders and operating under a royal/government charter. It was, however, like the Banque de France, Sveriges Riksbank and the Bank of Finland, but in sharp contrast to the Nationalbanken i Kiøbenhavn and the Bank of England (until 1844), completely subjected to control by the government/parliament/Storting. All in all, the Bank of Norway appears in its constitutional set-up to be almost a replica of the 16 years older Banque de France.[15] The resemblance to the Banque de France is not mentioned in the official history of the Bank of Norway,[16] but given the French birth of King Karl 14. Johan, Norway's new king (born Jean Baptiste Bernadotte), who took a great interest in financial matters, some French influence is hardly surprising.

Norges Bank's "cleaning up operation" in 1900–1908 following the prop-erty and stock market "bubbles" in 1898–1899 and the subsequent wave of bank failures in Kristiania largely ended the Bank's role as a commercial bank.

In spite of strong opposition from the provinces against centralizing gov-ernment in Kristiania, it was decided to move the Bank's head office to Kristiania in 1897.

5.3.2   The savings banks: The first Savings Banks Act in the Nordics

Norway's first savings bank was Christiania Sparbank, formed in Christiania in 1822, i.e. about one year after the first Swedish savings bank, which had

---

[15]The parallel to the Banque de France was not complete, since it was not until 1848 that its note issuing monopoly extended outside Paris, and some remnants of share-holder rights did not disappear completely until 1936.
[16]Jahn, Eriksen, og Munthe (1966) *Norges Bank gjennom 150 År* (Norges Bank, Oslo).

actually served as a model. The initiative came from the Storting, which had been inspired by the Danish life insurance and pension fund of 1795,[17] which had been supplemented with a mechanism for the collection of minor savings. A five-member committee was formed with the task of proposing a pension fund, but it happened to give a higher priority to the formation of a savings bank. The five members of the committee, whose task it had been to propose a pension scheme, were all appointed general managers of the savings bank they had advocated. A "grunnfond" of NOK 4,000 was soon collected. The pension scheme was forgotten about.

Its by-laws stipulated i.a. that the purpose of the savings bank was to accept small deposits from persons of both genders primarily from the working and serving classes, to pay interest (4 per cent p.a.) on such deposits, deposits to be maximum 8,000 NOK per depositor, loss of interest if no deposits had been made during any two-year period, and maximum withdrawal of NOK 2,000 at a time. Not a single word on lending, investment of the funds received, or capital requirements.

In 1824 the Savings Bank Act[18] was passed, the first savings bank Act in the Nordic area (Denmark: 1880, Sweden: 1892, Finland 1895). The primary purposes of the Savings Bank Act were to protect and promote savings banks and therefore gave savings banks a number of privileges, e.g. permission to charge 5 per cent p.a. interest on mortgage loans (otherwise generally capped at 4 per cent until 1857), exemption from stamp duties, and preferential proceedings in cases of recovery of assets from bankruptcy estates, etc. The formation of a savings bank required the permission from the finance minister, who had to approve the by-laws and the capital base ("grunnfond"). This was, however, a mere formality. Those who supplied the "grunnfond" were entitled to interest on the capital supplied (maximum 5 per cent p.a.). Profits, if any, were to be retained as reserves or donated to charities.

From the 1840s, the formation of savings banks accelerated sharply. By the early 20th century Norway could boast of about 550 savings banks, i.e. some 100 more than in Sweden with twice Norway's population. The implication was that each of them was quite small and of little help for the collection of major amounts of savings. Their lendings were restricted to modest consumer loans and the acquisition of minor tools by local craftsmen and farmers, as well as small mortgage loans.

During the economic difficulties of the 1870s and early 1880s, a number of savings banks collapsed, or were subject to forced rescues by commercial banks, Norges Bank, and Kongeriget Norges Hypotekbank. This prompted the government to propose a new Savings Banks Act aiming at

---

[17]Cfr. B.R. Rønning (1972) *Norsk sparebankvesen inntil 1850* in *Studier i Sparing og Sparebankvesen i Norge 1822–1972* (Gyldendal, Oslo) pp. 12–14.
[18]Sparbankloven av 20.juli 1824.

a strengthening of their financial standing. The proposal was hotly debated in the Storting for several years, reflecting the opposing interests of urban versus rural Norway, and central control versus regional autonomy. The main bones of contention were partly the proposed control by public (municipal) officials as replacements for the local self-appointed boards, and partly the hated §8, which imposed requirements for placing 10 per cent of a savings bank's deposits in liquid assets. For urban savings banks this was no problem, but for the rural savings banks this implied "sending money to far away towns", since the only "liquid assets" (as defined by the law) were bonds issued by the government, or by the Christiania-based Kongeriget Norges Hypotekbank. The new Savings Bank Act was passed in 1887, but the rural savings banks kept fighting the §8, and in 1900 the 10 per cent liquidity requirement was reduced to 5 per cent, and completely scrapped in 1903.

5.3.3   The state banks

During the 1820s, when the Norges Bank had few branches and maintained a constrictive credit policy, discussion arose about how society's growing credit needs could be satisfied. This was a period, when also quite liberal moods were prevalent claiming that this was a matter the commercial world had to sort out for itself. Credits could be had bilaterally, i.e. from the "unorganized market", from Norges Bank, the emerging savings banks, or from a number of semi-official institutions and pension funds, like the Overformynderi ("Public Trustee's Office"), Enkekassen (the "Widows' Pension Fund"), Christiania Brandassurance-Casse (a mutual fire insurance fund dissolved 1827, with a fund of NOK 1 million), etc. The amounts lent by such institutions were not insignificant, e.g. loans outstanding from the Widows in 1830 were NOK 2.4 million,[19] but this "market" was not very transparent and did not extend much beyond the three largest cities (if at all outside the Christiania area). "Good" bills were discounted by private banquiers at around 12 per cent p.a., less good up to 24 per cent.

In 1820, the Storting succeeded in raising a foreign loan, albeit on strict conditions, and the proceeds were re-lent to private businesses at a rate of "only" 13 per cent p.a. (the NOK 1.4 million "Berlin loan"[20]). This initiated a long-lasting tradition in Norway for the government to support the private business sector with direct loans.

Since investors could obtain much higher returns from discounting bills, the supply of medium-term money (e.g. "vexelobligationer" with maturities up to five years) dried up. To ease this problem it was decided, in

---

[19]Å. Egge (1988) *Statens Diskonteringskommisjoner. Finansdepartementet som statsbank i det 19. århundre"* (Oslo Universitet, doctoral thesis) p. 33.
[20]As fn. 19, pp. 41 and 71.

1842, to make the vexelobligationer exempt from the interest rate ceiling, provided they had at least six months maturity and were not secured with mortgages over fixed property (in 1851, the interest ceiling was, however, re-introduced at the insistence of the farmers).

Diskonteringskommissjonerne

After much discussion in the Storting, including highly voiced opposition against the king's wishes to help out the business community through government loans when the discounting rates had hit 2 per cent per month, the Storting finally, in 1828, approved a decision to take up a foreign loan of NOK 1.2 million[21] mainly to be re-lent through a "diskonteringskommisjon" to be set up in Christiania. Its purpose was partly to discount bills (presumably at cheaper and less cumbersome conditions than those required by the Christiania branch of Norges Bank and the private markets), and partly to extend medium-term loans against good collateral. Over the next 30 years, a total of 11 such "diskonteringskommisjoner" were set up in various towns.

They were all strictly controlled and primarily funded by the Finansdepartement (the "Finance Ministry"), which would allocate a specific amount every year to each of these offices for re-lending. There was little market mechanism in the pricing or allocation of these funds. There were no deposits from the general public, and the lendings were also not meant for the general public, so they hardly fell under the definition of "banks" as proposed in the Introduction. They were regional organizations, which did not compete against each other, or against the savings banks. They did little for the development of a "capital market" in Norway.

At their height (in the 1850s) they accounted for about 9 per cent of total outstanding institutional loans (cfr. Table 5.4). In their individual locations, however, they had "market shares" which grew from around 22 per cent in the 1830s to some 34 per cent in the 1840s.[22]

The diskonteringskommisjoner were all dissolved during the 1860s, except for the one in Kristiania, which was kept alive until 1910 (primarily because the government wanted an alternative to the local branch of Norges Bank for various purposes).

---

[21]Obtained from London, and negotiated by Hambros Bank's Copenhagen office, cfr. Hodne & Grytten (1994) *Norsk økonomi i det 19. århundre* (Fakbokforlaget, Oslo) pp. 163–4, and Egge (1988) *Statens Diskonteringskommisjoner* (Oslo Universitet) pp. 82–3. Hambos Bank always had close relations to Denmark and Norway. In the shipping crisis of the early 1980s, the exposure of Hambros Bank to Norwegian shipping companies was a cause for some concern.

[22]As for fn. 19, p. 654.

Kongeriget Norges Hypotekbank, and the emergence of bearer bonds

During the 1840s, the Storting and the government discussed various means to increase the supply of medium- or long-term capital. Some favoured mortgage associations as proposed in Denmark, but the farmers pointed out that their farms were too small and scattered for this to work. Nobody wanted to be jointly liable with unknown people from the neighbouring valley on the other side of the mountain. Others advocated private note-issuing banks.

The end-result was the creation of Kongeriget Norges Hypotekbank, which had its by-laws approved by the king in 1852.[23] The main features were:

1. Its purpose was to offer mortgage loans to landowners at maximum 5 per cent interest, to be amortized with 1.5 per cent of the original amount semi-annually, and for amounts not exceeding 60 per cent of the fire insurance value (in Christiania), 40 per cent (in Bergen), and 30 per cent elsewhere.
2. The Storting would supply the institution with a permanent capital base ("grunnfond") of NOK 2 million, on which the Bank would pay 4.5 per cent p.a. interest (profits permitting).
3. The institution was to be managed by two Storting-appointed managers and one appointed by the king/government.
4. The institution was mostly funded with government guaranteed 4 per cent bearer bonds, i.e. a specific exemption from the 1754 prohibition against bearer bonds. The bonds would be redeemed in equal amounts over 30 years. The circulating amount of bonds could not exceed eight times the amount of the "grunnfond" and reserves.
5. In contrast to the Danish system, there was no requirement that the circulating bond volume should match the outstanding loans with respect to interest and instalments, and borrowers could choose between having their loans disbursed in cash or in bonds.

Operations started in 1852 with a torrent of loan applications, of which less than a third was approved (by amounts). During the years up to WWI, the institution's lendings fluctuated a great deal, but the institution's share of total institutional lendings was fairly stable (12–19 per cent, cfr. Table 5.4).

Having joined the gold standard and the Scandinavian Currency Union, the institution's bonds were increasingly sold abroad (70–80 per cent of total issues), finding their main markets in Hamburg and Copenhagen. In some years (1887, 1893, and 1900–1912) even 100 per cent was sold abroad.

---

[23]The 1851 Act and by-laws as well as those in force in 1952 are reprinted in Kaartvedt & Hartsang (1952) *Kongeriket Norges Hypotekbank 1852–1952* (Oslo) which also contains an exhibit with the main financial figures.

A certain volume was sold in Paris, until Norway slammed high import duties on French wines and spirits. The French government retaliated by banning Norwegian bonds from the Paris stock exchange[24] (Denmark had a similar experience, cfr. Chapter 3).

In 1966, the Hypotekbank and a number of other government banks were merged to form Statens Landbruksbank. In spite of the names, neither the Hypotekbank nor the Landbruksbank hardly ever qualified as "banks" according to the definition proposed in the Introduction. They never took deposits or offered current accounts.

Table 5.4   Lendings by Government Institutions, 1820–1920

	Government & government funds, % of total institutional	Norges Bank, % of total institutional	Kgr. Norges Hypotekbank, % of total institutional	Other state banks, % of total institutional	Total government sponsored, % of total institutional	Total institutional, million NOK
1850	20	40		9	69	75
1860	16	21	12	5	54	150
1870	13	16	15	1	45	230
1880	10	10	16	0	36	351
1890	9	8	19	0	36	446
1900	8	5	14	0	27	931
1905	9	5	13	1	28	1,143
1910	7	4	12	2	25	1,476
1915	6	4	9	2	21	2,315
1920	9	7	3	1	20	7,532

Sources: Government & state funds: H. Skånland (1967) *Det Norske Kredittmarked siden 1900* (Statistisk Sentralbyrå, Oslo) p. 75 and Tables VIII and IX.
Norges Bank: H. Skånland (1967) *Det Norske Kredittmarked siden 1900*, p. 75, and Table I. Excluding holdings of bonds and deposits with other banks.
Kongeriget Norges Hypotekbank: 1860–1900: Statistisk Sentralbyrå (1994) *Historisk Statistikk*, Table 24.5 (p. 622). 1905–1920: *Kongeriget Norges Hypotekbank 1852–1952* (Oslo, 1952) pp. 570–80 (total assets). Loan volumes have been assumed (by SEA) to be 87 per cent of total assets, which was the average for the previous 15 years. The inaccuracy caused by this assumption cannot affect any of the conclusions or observations made.
Other state banks: The difference between "State Banks" as given by Skånland (op. cit. p. 75) and Statistisk Sentralbyrå: "Historisk Statistikk", 1994, p. 622. Also Matre, op. cit. Table 2.a. and Norges Hyp.bank.
Insurance & social funds: Skånland, op. cit., Tables V and X.
"Other state banks" are: The Diskonteringskommisjoner (1828–ca. 1865), Den Norske Arbeiderbruk- og Boligbank (1903–1915), and Den Norske Stats Småbruk- og Boligbank (1915–1966).
Banks and savings banks (1994) *Historisk Statistikk* (Statistisk Sentralbyrå), except for 1820–1860 where Skå]nland's (op. cit.) figures have been used for the savings banks.
Bonds: Skånland (1967), *Det norske Kredittmarked siden 1900* (Statistisk Sentralbyrå, Oslo) pp. 310–12. The figures shown are those for bonds held inside Norway. A much larger volume was held abroad and has not been considered part of the Norwegian capital market in the present context.
Note: In the 1850s and 1860s. "Other state banks" include the diskonterings kommisjoner.

[24]Cfr. Kaartvedt & Hartsang (1952) *Kongeriket Norges Hypotekbank 1852–1952*, p. 327.

Later state banks

The very significant role played by government funds and government-sponsored institutions is quite striking, even if this role was gradually reduced from around 70 per cent of all outstanding institutional credits in 1850 to about 20 per cent in 1920 (it would grow again later in the 20th century).

Den Norske Arbeiderbruk- og Boligbank was created in 1903, and in 1915 reorganized into Den Norske Stats Småbruk- og Boligbank. Its purpose was to finance dwellings for the less affluent social classes and smallholders. It was funded by government contributions, bearer bonds, and deposits. In 1966 it was merged into Statens Landbruksbank, together with a number of other state banks.

Following the passing of a new Mortgage Institution Act in 1907, a number of semi-public regional mortgage associations were set up. They were essentially modelled after the Danish and Swedish systems, i.e. offering long-term fixed interest mortgages based on joint liability among the borrowers and bond issues which matched the underlying mortgage loans in terms of interest, amounts and maturities. The three largest and best known of them, based in Kristiania, Bergen and Trondhjem, soon (1909) merged into one institution, De Norske Bykredittforeninger.

Quantitatively, the mortgage institutions never played a very big role, with the exception of Kongeriget Norges Hypotekbank. Urban properties were primarily financed by savings banks and the commercial banks.

5.3.4   The private banks

Until 1924, there were no formal stipulations in Norway regulating the formation and operation of privately owned joint stock banks funded by deposits. Banks were regarded as normal commercial businesses.

The progress of the Norwegian economy during the 1830s and 1840s accelerated the need for bill discounting facilities – an activity not very eagerly pursued by Norges Bank, cfr. above. Bills were mostly discounted by a relatively small number of merchants and banquier houses,[25] as well as some of the savings banks and the above mentioned "diskonteringskommisjoner". There were, however, not many of these, and this scarcity of discounting facilities was reflected in the pricing. During the lean years before the 1840s, discount rates could easily be 3–5 per cent per month.[26] In the

---

[25]Among these, the best known were e.g. T.J. Heftye, an immigrant from Switzerland, W. Egeberg, an immigrant from Denmark, and N.A. Andresen, another Danish immigrant, whose firm was later transformed into Andresens Bank, which developed into a major Kristiania bank and merged with Christiania Bank og Kreditkasse in 1980, A. Grüning, a German immigrant, and E. Rohde, an immigrant from Riga, and banquier to the king. Cfr. E. Hoffstad (1928) *Det Norske Privatbankvæsens Historie* (A/S Forretningslivs Forlag, Oslo) pp. 23–34.
[26]Cfr. E. Hoffstad (1928) *Det Norske Privatbankvæsens Historie*, p. 33.

more prosperous 1840s, discount rates were still 1.5–2 per cent per month for good quality bills. The creation of new commercial banks, therefore, seemed tempting, provided stable sources of deposits could be found.

In most of the 20th century, the Norwegian banking scene was dominated by three banks, all originating from the mid-19th century, as in Denmark, Finland, and Sweden. A brief look at the origins of these three banks will be given below, together with a fourth bank which was, for a brief period, Norway's largest bank and had important foreign connections.

Christiania Bank og Kreditkasse, Norway's first private bank, 1848

The tight conditions for the discounting of bills prompted Christiania's leading business people, grouped in the "club" named "Selskabet Handelens Venner" (the "Society of the Friends of Commerce"), formed in 1841, to take the initiative to set up a committee with the task of making a proposal for a bank. The leading figure in the initiative was F.H. Frölich, a merchant of Prussian origins who had studied banks in Hamburg and elsewhere during his prolonged visits abroad. The proposal came in the spring of 1848 together with an invitation to subscribe shares in the amount of NOK 160,000, a very modest amount, of which half was to be paid in cash.

The invitation[27] quoted the Hamburg Kreditkasse (est. 1821) and the Kiøbenhavns Centralkasse (the bill discounting office essentially managed by Nationalbanken i Kjøbenhavn) as its sources of inspiration.

The invitation was successful, and thus Christiania Kreditkasse (since 1862 Christiania Bank og Kreditkasse) was born. F.H. Frölich became the new bank's first general manager.

The bank was a great success. It started very modestly, almost as a pawn-broker shop offering short-term loans against commodities and other goods. Mostly because of opposition from Norges Bank and the Storting, it did not start discounting bills in a major way until the early 1860s (hence the change of name).[28] As might have been expected, both Norges Bank and the Christiania diskonteringskommisjon strongly resented the arrival of a newcomer on the scene. Still, only twelve years after its foundation, its share capital had been increased ten-fold, and its deposits had increased from NOK 104,000 to 6.3 million. In the process, it had established branches in three other provincial locations, but these branches soon had to be sold. The Bergen Branch became the core of Bergens Kreditbank. There was no stomach in the provinces, not even in the ancient Hanseatic town of Bergen, to do business with "those Christiania people".

---

[27]Reprinted in Hoffstad (1928) *Det Norske Privatbankvæsens Historie*, pp. 46–7.

[28]Cfr. S. Knutsen (1990) *Norske Forretningsbankers Rolle i Industrialiseringen 1850–1913, med Hovedvekt på Perioden 1890–1913* in Nordvik & Knutsen *Bankenes rolle i norsk industriell utvikling 1850–1914* (Norges råd for anvendt samfunnsforskning (NORAS), Norges Handelshøjskole) p. 11.

Bergens Privatbank, 1855–1975. Bergen Bank 1975–1990

A generally felt shortage of credit in Bergen and close surroundings led the city's leading business circles to propose a local bank to be set up. The founding general assembly was held in November 1855. The share capital was to be NOK 200,000.

In contrast to the Christiania Kreditkasse, it started immediately to discount commercial bills.

In 1975 Bergens Privatbank merged with Bergens Kreditbank, originally the branch spun off from Kristiania Bank og Kreditkasse in 1876, to form Bergen Bank. In 1990, Bergen Bank merged with Den norske Creditbank to form Den norske Bank.

Den norske Creditbank (DnC), 1857–1990. Den norske Bank (DnB), 1990–

The difference between Christiania Bank og Kreditkasse and Den norske Creditbank was mostly timing and scale. In 1856–1857 a group of distinguished business people[29] had decided that there was room for a real commercial bank in Christiania (at this point of time, the Christiania Kreditkasse had not yet embarked on full-scale bill discounting, cfr. above).

The timing was heavily influenced by the European financial crisis of 1857 caused by the failure of a number of Hamburg merchant-bankers, who used to discount Nordic bills of exchange. Norwegian merchants needed alternative financial sources.

The bank was launched with an invitation to a subscription for a share capital of NOK 8 million, an unprecedented amount at that time, and more than twice the amount of equity held by Christiania Bank and Kreditkasse. In spite of the metropolitan flavour of the bank, subscriptions came from some twenty different towns all over the country, and the invitation was over-subscribed. To what extent this success was obtained out of sheer necessity in the face of the collapse of the Hamburg merchant-bankers, or out of enthusiasm for the project, appears to be an open question.

From its very start, it was always Norway's dominating bank – apart from a brief period when this position was held by the Centralbanken for Norge.

Centralbanken for Norge, 1899–1929

This bank was planned as a central consortium bank, where as many as possible provincial and foreign banks would join forces in order to counter the fragmented banking structure and the dominating position of the existing Kristiania banks.

After a few years of fighting against the Kristiania banks, it counted more than 40 Norwegian provincial banks and a handful of foreign banks among

---

[29]The group included i.a. N.A. Andresen, the banquier, and T.H. Heftye, the well-known banquier from Switzerland.

its shareholders, including Den Danske Landmandsbank, Stockholms Enskilda Bank, Deutsche Bank, Banque de Paris et des Pays-Bas, and Hambros Bank. For a few years it was Norway's largest bank.

The idea behind the bank was fine, but in the end it could not survive the post-war crisis and the lingering animosity of the provinces towards Kristiania institutions. When in the early 1920s the bank needed support, its provincial shareholders did not lift a finger to help it.

It had become too much of a Kristiania institution, and its idea of developing a nationwide branch network, thereby competing against its owners, had not endeared it to its provincial shareholders.[30] So, it was wound up.

Table 5.5 shows that the ca. 73–6 other commercial banks existing in 1900 had a combined market share of approximately 70 per cent, or an average of about 1 per cent each.

A comparison with the development of the savings banks is seen in Table 5.6.

On the eve of WWI, Norway had about 50 per cent more banks and savings banks than Sweden, which had twice the population, but the number of banks, and the degree of concentration, did not differ much from Denmark in the late 19th and early 20th centuries. Finland, just as thinly populated as Norway, had a much more concentrated banking structure than any of the three other Nordic countries, whereas the savings banks structure was very similar to that of Norway, i.e. much more fragmented than in Sweden.

Table 5.5 **Structure of the Private Banking Scene, 1880–1900, Loan Volumes (Million NOK)**

	Christiania Bank og Kreditkasse	*Bergen Privat-bank*	*Den norske Credit Bank (DnC)*	*"Big Three", total*	*Private banks, total*	*Market share of "Big Three"*
1880	16.3	13.6	20.1	50.0	80–88	63–56%
1900	27.1	29.3	39.1	95.5	321–349	30–27%

Source: H.I. Matre (1992) *Norske forretningsbanker 1848–1990* (Norges råd for anvendt samfundsforskning (NORAS), Rapport nr. 41, Oslo), Tables 4 a–c.
Private banks, total: The lower figures are from Statistisk Sentralbyrå (NOS, 1994) *Historisk Statistikk*, p. 624.
For a description of the available statistical information, see H.I. Matre (1992) *Norske forretningsbanker 1848–1990, en tilbageføring av forretningsbankststistikken* (NORAS, Report nr. 41).

---

[30]Cfr. S. Knutsen (1990) *Norske Forretningsbankers Rolle i Industrialiseringen 1850–1913* in H.W. Nordvik & Knutsen *Bankenes rolle i norsk industriell utvikling 1850–1914* (Norges Handelshøyskole, NORAS) pp. 34–5.

Table 5.6   **The Development of the Banking and Savings Bank Sectors, 1850–1915**

Amounts in million NOK	Banks, excluding Norges Bank			Savings banks		
	No. of banks	*Total deposits*	*Deposits pr. bank*	*No. of savings*	*Total deposits banks*	*Deposits pr. savings bank*
1850	1	0.3	0.3	90	17	0.2
1870	8	40.0	5.0	262	82	0.3
1890	33	119.5	3.6	350	194	0.6
1900	76	367.0	4.8	413	306	0.7
1910	102	449.0	4.4	487	507	1.0
1915	122	856.6	7.0	527	724	1.4

Sources: Statistisk Sentralbyrå (NOS, 1994) *Historisk Statistikk*, p. 624.

5.4   The size and shape of the financial sector

Until the late 1840s, there was practically no difference between the development of the financial scenes in Norway, Denmark, and Finland. In all three countries there was, until the middle of the century – in Finland's case until 1862 – only one bank, the future central bank, and a large number of savings banks. From about the middle of the 19th century, however, the financial scenes developed quite differently in the four Nordic countries.

In Sweden, commercial banking had started some 15 years earlier than in Denmark and Norway, and overshadowed the savings banks already from the middle of the century.

Table 5.7 shows the growth and changing composition of the Norwegian financial scene between 1850 and 1915.

Table 5.7   **Relative Composition and Growth of the Credit Stock, 1850–1915**

	Government sponsored institution	*Commercial banks*	*Savings banks*	*Bonds (domestic)*	*Insurance & social security*	*Total*	*Total million NOK*	*Total, in % of GDP*
	Per cent of total credit stock							
1860	53	13	29		5	100	152	
1870	44	17	35		4	100	236	44
1880	35	24	36		5	100	369	51
1890	32	26	35		7	100	495	63
1900	24	34	27	7	8	100	1,034	93
1910	23	32	28	8	9	100	1,614	112
1915	18	38	25	11	8	100	2,612	101

Table 5.7   Relative Composition and Growth of the Credit Stock, 1850–1915
– continued

	Government sponsored institution	Commercial banks	Savings banks	Bonds (domestic)	Insurance & social security	Total	Total million NOK	Total, in % of GDP
			Per cent of GDP					
1870	19	8	15		2	44		44
1880	18	12	19		2	51		51
1890	20	17	22		4	63		63
1900	23	31	25	7	7	93		93
1910	26	37	31	9	10	112		112
1915	18	38	25	11	8	102		102

Sources: GDP: Statistisk Sentralbyrå (1965) *Nasjonalregnskabsstatistik 1865–1960* (NOS XII, 163, Oslo) pp. 341–3.
H.I. Matre (1992) *Norske kreditinstitusjoner 1850–1990* (Norges Råd for Anvendt Samfundsforskning NORAS, rapport nr. 42, Table 2a and 2b.
H.I. Matre (1992) *Norske forretningsbanker 1848–1990. En tilbageføring av forretningsbankstatistikken* NORAS rapport nr 41, Table 4a–c.
Statistisk Sentralbyrå (NOS, 1994) *Historisk Statistikk*, p. 616 ff.

Comments:
1. The volume of the total credit stock in the organized market was clearly smaller than in Denmark, but about the same as in Sweden and larger than in Finland, cfr. Table 3.9, 4.6, and 6.7.
2. The role of the government and government-sponsored institutions remained conspicuously high and much more so than in any of the other Nordic countries after the 1890s.
3. The bond market remained small, like in Finland, but it expanded after 1913, in contrast to Sweden where it started bigger, but declined. Until about 1900, at least 95 per cent of the bearer bonds were issued by the government, the Kongeriket Norges Hyp. Bank or major municipalities. In 1897, the issuing of bearer bonds was liberalized, subject to ministerial approval of the conditions, including collateral. A request from Elkem in 1913 resulted in an almost complete liberalization. This opened the way for a number of bond issues being made by Elkem, Norsk Hydro, and a few other hydro power companies as well as by commercial banks, shipping companies, and mortgage institutions.
4. The largest Norwegian financial institutions remained smaller than the largest institutions in Denmark, Finland, and Sweden, and the structure of the banking and savings banks system stayed more fragmented than in Sweden and Finland, but not much different from Denmark.
    The fragmented structure of the Norwegian financial scene seems mostly to have been caused by the widespread local "patriotism" of the individual municipalities, each of which wanted to have its own bank and savings bank.
    Compared to Denmark, Finland, and Sweden, another striking feature was that there were no dominating names or families. No Tietgen or Glückstadt, like in Denmark, nobody like the Finnish Borgströms, and a complete absence of anybody like the Wallenbergs or Louis Fränckel in Sweden.
    Between the turn of the century and the outbreak of WWI, the three largest Norwegian banks were not much smaller than Stockholms Enskilda and Stockholms Handelsbank, but considerably smaller than Den Danske Landmandsbank, Skandinaviska Kredit AB and the two Finnish main banks. More significant, perhaps, was it that the average size of all the other ca. 100 Norwegian banks was only a small fraction of the size of the ca. 70 Swedish and ca. 15 Finnish regional banks – but not much different from the approximately 140 Danish regional banks. (Average amount of assets in 1915 of the respective banks, excluding "The Big Three" in each country: Denmark ca. DKK 4.5 million, Norway: ca. NOK 3 million, and Sweden: ca. SEK 20 million).

Table 5.7   Relative Composition and Growth of the Credit Stock, 1850–1915
– continued

5. The figures shown for bonds are those for bonds held inside Norway. They were nearly all issued by the government and some municipalities, or by Kgr. Norges Hyp. Bank and held by the commercial banks, savings banks, and insurance companies. About 90 per cent of the bonds issued by these issuers were held abroad[31] and have, for the present purpose, not been considered part of the Norwegian capital market. These bonds were usually denominated in two or three different currencies, including NOK. After 1914, most of these bonds were sold back to Norway.

Summing up, it must be concluded that before WWI, there was no coherent national capital market in Norway. The banking "system" consisted of banks operating purely inside their local surroundings with little or no connections to neighbouring municipalities or provinces. The savings bank world was even more fragmented. Suppliers of long-term capital consisted mainly of one institution catering for agriculture and forest owners (the Kgr. Norges Hyp.Bank), and one which financed urban properties (Bykredittforeningerne). In addition, Norges Bank and various government funds as well as some insurance companies offered financing on a secured basis for a number of more or less specific purposes.

Although the interest ceiling was gradually liberalized, the fragmented institutional framework prevented a competitive and dynamic system from developing.

5.5   The stock exchange

In early 1818, N.A. Andresen, the above-mentioned Danish born banquier and Storting member, made a proposal in the Storting for the formation of a stock exchange. The proposal was approved by the Storting and a few months later signed into law by the king.[32] Thus, the Oslo Stock Exchange is one of the few exchanges, which did not grow gradually from an earlier informal meeting place. The "Exchange Act" stipulated (§1) that as soon as possible, an exchange was to be organized in Christiania as a meeting place for the merchants, where these could agree and decide on anything concerning their commerce. It opened in early 1819.

Legally, it may be seen as a "self-owning" institution with a certain degree of government control. It was managed by a stock exchange commission consisting of three merchants appointed by the Ministry of Commerce at the recommendation of the city's merchants, and a government-appointed commissioner. It was financed by fees paid by the merchants to the Exchange according to a scale laid down in the 1818 Exchange Act, including fees for shipping agreements depending on the tonnage of the vessels, and annual

[31]Cfr. H. Skånland (1967) *Det Norske Kredittmarked siden 1900* (Statistisk Sentralbyrå) p. 96.
[32]"Lov angaaende Oprettelsen af en Børs i Christiania", dated September 8, 1818, a one page document of 17 paragraphs.

fees payable by the brokers and merchants. Broker fees, if brokers were used, would come on top and be paid separately. The annual accounts would be submitted to the Ministry of Commerce for approval.

The Exchange Act also instructed the Exchange to erect a building for its use as soon as possible. The building was completed in 1828 and forms the core of today's Oslo Stock Exchange Building.

The Exchange Act allowed virtually anything to be traded on the Exchange, but it instructed the Exchange in particular (§3) twice weekly to set foreign exchange rates ("… notere Cours paa Udlandet.").

The nature of the Christiania exchange can be seen from the fact that in 1819, more than half of the income of the Exchange was derived from clearing vessels with foreign destinations.[33]

Access to the Exchange was reserved for brokers and registered merchants, for whom membership of the exchange was compulsory. This was a fairly large group of people consisting of three brokers and 234 registered merchants – compared to Copenhagen's approximately 10–15 brokers and 50 merchants. Apparently, Christiania was too small to distinguish between retailers and wholesalers, which was a crucial distinction in Copenhagen with about ten times Christiania's number of inhabitants in the early 19th century.

During the first 63 years of its life, the Kristiania Exchange was not really a "stock exchange". Most of what was traded on the exchange had some connection to shipping, including ships and ship participations. The rest was foreign exchange contracts, fish, timber, or some other merchandise.

By 1881, this state of affairs appeared unsatisfactory, and an initiative was taken, again by the firm of N.A Andresen, to persuade the Exchange to arrange auctions for securities and price quotations on a weekly or bi-weekly basis. Some observers have seen this as the real birth of the Kristiania Stock Exchange.[34] It did, however, take nearly 15 years before there was any noticeable activity in this market, and prices were quoted only once a month. Until the mid-1890s, stock-trading was so irregular that an organized and systematic price list was hardly conceivable. There was no reliable secondary market at all.

Initially, prices were quoted for some 40 issues, of which 16 bonds and 23 shares, mostly issued by financial institutions, municipalities, and railways. Matters did not get a firm shape until 1897, when the exchange commissioners prescribed rules and conditions for allowing securities to be introduced on the exchange, and a joint price list had been agreed upon to replace some more or less informal lists produced by brokers or banquiers.

Since 1908 the price list was issued weekly, almost 100 years after weekly price lists started appearing in Denmark.

---

[33]"Kapitalkilde for Næringslivet. Oslo Børs gjennom 175 År" (1994) (Bedriftsøkonomens Forlag) p. 35.
[34]This explains the publication in 1931 of R. Due: "Et historisk tilbageblikk ved Oslo Fondsbørs' 50 års jubilæum", commissioned by Oslo Børs.

6
Sweden, 1814–1916: First Banking Act in the Nordics

> "What a piece of work is a man?
> How noble in reason! – How infinite in faculty!
> and yet, … what is this quintessence of dust?"
>
> ("Hamlet", Act II)

6.1   An overview: A changed identity

By 1814 Sweden was but a shadow of its former self. Finland had been lost, and Norway did not become a Swedish province as Finland had been (cfr. Chapter 5). The quintessence of Sweden's financial condition was that its currency and government finances were close to dust – like in Denmark in those years. Yet, after half a century of slow growth Sweden managed, between roughly 1880 and 1915, to achieve a remarkable pace of growth and industrialization, which brought the standard of living in Sweden up to a level close to that of Germany, France, and Denmark.

Politically, the year 1809 brought a new system of government, under which the king lost most of his remaining powers to the Assembly of the Estates. The Estates had the sole right to impose taxes, and it retained its control over Sveriges Rijkes Ständers Bank and the Riksgäldskontor (the government debt office). Soundness in government finances was gradually restored. By ca. 1840 the government was debt free, and a deep animosity towards public debt had grown up.

Commercially, the 19th century was characterized by the fast discarding of any remaining mercantilistic ideas, and a general liberalization of restricting rules and regulations, not least at the initiative of Johan August Gripenstedt, finance minister 1856–1866. The new winds brought several reforms, including the Companies Act (1848), formally recognizing the principle of limited liability – one of the first European countries to do so.

With respect to *capital markets,* the most striking institutional innovations of the 19th century were the banking acts, which the king could enact if they did not involve the Riksbank directly, and which also reflected changing attitudes towards banking in the Estates during the century. This process made Sweden one of the first countries, along with England, to introduce general banking legislation.

Savings banks and stock exchange regulations came later in Sweden than in Denmark and Norway (cfr. Chapters 3 and 5).

6.2 The problems

While economic progress was generally good from the 1830s onwards, albeit from a rather dismal starting point, a number of problems had to be addressed.

The persistently rather low savings rate (cfr. Table 6.1 below) was a problem. It implied that in the second half of the century, large parts of capital spending were financed by foreign borrowings.

The rudimentary monetary economy and the currency system were other problems. Until well into the second half of the century, money circulation was basically reserved for the few major towns, including some towns on the shores of the big lakes, through which timber and iron trade was channeled.

In this respect Sweden was not much different from Finland and Norway, but probably behind Denmark, which was more densely populated and closer to Hamburg. The currency system remained confusing and unstable until the 1830 currency reform (cfr. 6.3.1 below).

In 1830, there was no "organized capital market", and it grew up only very gradually during the rest of the century. There was a certain short-term "money market" centered in Stockholm, where people with borrowing needs would issue IOUs to affluent individuals, trading and insurance companies, or charities. There was little competition or transparency, and

Table 6.1 Sweden's GDP, Savings, and Investments, Selected Years, 1861–1918

Annual average	GDP million SEK	Gross invest- ments % of GDP	Savings ratio, %	Annual average	GDP million SEK	Gross invest- ments % of GDP	Savings ratio %
1861–1863	811	7.9	7.4	1890–1892	1,486	8.9	6.8
1867–1868	853	6.0	5.3	1897–1899	1,980	13.1	11.0
1870–1872	991	10.8	10.8	1900–1902	2,208	12.4	9.6
1877–1879	1,287	11.3	10.3	1905–1907	2,752	13.6	10.7
1880–1882	1,324	9.7	9.7	1910–1912	3,430	12.4	12.3
1887–1889	1,306	9.6	7.5	1913–1915	4,232	16.1	16.1

Source: O. Krantz & C.-A. Nilsson (1975) *Swedish National Product 1861–1970* (CWK Gleerup, Lund) pp. 156–7. Current prices, factor costs.
(Pre-1872 amounts restated from original amounts in riksdaler banco or riksdaler riksmynt.)

there were no "rules of the game". Like elsewhere, maximum interest rate regulations were easily circumvented.

Merchants in Stockholm and Göteborg continued the practice of making advance payments to the iron manufacturers, and refinanced themselves with bills of exchange drawn primarily against their credit balances – export proceeds – in houses in London or Hamburg. Both Shylocks and Antonios had their opportunities – or lack of them – all depending on their resourcefulness or craftiness.

Large investments were difficult to finance because of the almost non-existing financial infrastructure prevailing until the 1860s. In 1830, Sweden had only one bank, just as in 1657. The two branches opened by the Riksbank in Göteborg and Malmö during the 1820s hardly represented a major development. Had the savings ratio in the 1840s and 1850s been higher, it would still have been virtually impossible to organize the collection of such savings in a way, which would have made the financing of much railway construction possible.

In the Assembly of the Estates, the construction of a railway network had been discussed already in the 1840s, but the idea had been shelved primarily because of a general consensus that the capital needed for such investments could not be raised in Sweden, and borrowing it abroad was unpalatable at that time.[1] The remembrance of the awkwardness and embarrassment of foreign debts was too strong.

For these, or perhaps other reasons as well, industrialization came rather late to Sweden compared to e.g. England, Germany, and France. Given Sweden's centuries old mining industry, this could seem odd.

From Table 6.2 it is seen that there was no industrial breakthrough in Sweden until the 1890s or even after the turn of the century, but at least by some standards earlier than in Denmark. In Denmark the GDP contribution from manufacturing did not overtake the agricultural contribution until the 1930s (cfr. Chapter 3), whereas in Sweden this happened before WWI.

6.3   Responses and actions

6.3.1   Currency reforms

Restoring order to the country's currency, including convertibility into silver, was a top priority for the new government under King Karl XIV Johan (1818–1844).

---

[1]"... framför allt rådde enighet om omöjligheten av att skaffa fram tillräckligt kapital inom landet för ett järnvägsbyggande av någon betydelse. Anmärkningvärt är att möjligheten att skaffa kapital genom utländska lån icke på allvar diskuterades ...", L.-E. Hedin (1972) *Finansiering av den svenska järnvägen 1860–1914* in R. Adamson & L. Jörberg (eds) *Problem i svensk ekonomisk historia"* (Gleerup) p. 123.

Table 6.2   Population and Indicators of Industrialization

Year	Total population '000	Stockholm '000	Urban pop. in % of total population	Value of industrial production in % of agricultural production	Length of Railways in service, km
1800	2,118	76	10		
1860	3,425	112	11	28	527
1870	3,629	136	13	28	1,727
1880	3,875	169	15	30	5,876
1900	4,032	301	21	85	10,882
1920	4,161	419	30	135	14,869

Sources: Population: Statistisk Sentralbyrå (1969) Historisk Statistikk för Sverige, I, Table 14.
Railways: Statistisk Sentralbyrå (1960) Historisk Statistikk för Sverige, IV, Table 44, p. 76.
Industrial and agricultural production: As for Table 6.1.

The currency reform of 1830 established the riksdaler banco (the notes issued by the Riksbank) as the main currency of circulation and legal tender at the rate of 37.5 per cent of the silver value of the old riksdaler species. The value of the Riksgäldskontor currency (the riksdaler riksgäld) was fixed at 25 per cent of the riksdaler species, or 66.6 per cent of the riksdaler banco, and was gradually withdrawn from circulation. The riksdaler banco was made convertible into silver in 1834.

In the 1855 currency reform, the riksdaler banco was replaced by the riksdaler riksmynt, with the latter equalling 66.67 per cent of the former, and in 1872 the riksdaler riksmynt was replaced by the krona at the rate of 1:1, implying a rate of one old riksdaler species = four kronor (SEK).

For the sake of facilitating comparisons over time, all amounts in this chapter have been expressed in kronor (SEK).[2]

In 1873, Sweden and Denmark formed the Scandinavian Currency Union making their respective currencies legal tender in both countries at the rate of 1:1.

6.3.2   Railway finance

In 1854 it was finally decided, in spite of the financing problems, to start building a railway network consisting of a number of trunk lines constructed, owned, and financed by the government, and feeder lines constructed, owned, and financed by private companies.

---

[2]This has also been done in some of the sources used for this chapter. Where the sources have used riksdaler banco or riksmynt, the amounts have been restated in kronor by SEA.

The Riksgäldskontor was entrusted with the task of organizing the necessary financing. Initially (1855), a domestic bond issue of SEK 3 million was tried. It flopped hopelessly, raising less than 10 per cent of the intended amount. The following year the Estates reluctantly empowered the Riksgäldskontor to seek the required loans abroad. With some difficulty, a loan of SEK 20 million was placed with German financiers in 1858.[3]

As indicated above, the foreign loans were not taken up with a light heart. The feelings towards the foreign borrowing were summed up in the saying at the time that "the champagne the Swedes could have had, they are now drinking in Hamburg".[4]

Between 1854 and 1914, government investments in trunk lines totalled about SEK 400 million, or 5–10 per cent of total capital spendings, cfr. Table 6.1. One of the first trunk lines to be completed was the Stockholm-Göteborg line (1862). Thus, the Göta Canal had become obsolete only 30 years after its completion at such heavy costs (cfr. Chapter 1).

Between 1890 and 1910, the government gross debts had more than doubled, from SEK 260 million to 537 million,[5] most of which had been spent on railway construction, but since GDP had grown even faster in those 20 years, government debt in proportion to GDP had actually declined from 18 per cent to 16 per cent, a modest level seen with the eyes of the 21st century.

The total amount invested the feeder lines was about the same as for the trunk lines, roughly SEK 500 million, but the private lines consisted of several smaller projects, which could more easily be financed from local sources in a combination of share issues, bond issues – partly placed abroad – bank loans, as well as government loans. Share capital and bond loans accounted for about 70 per cent of the total. About 50 per cent of the share capital was subscribed by municipalities.[6]

6.3.3   The banking acts and the slow growth of banks

The changing attitudes to banking during the 19th century were reflected in the fairly large number of banking acts passed in this period, and sum-

---

[3]Following arduous and prolonged negotiations with bankers in Hamburg, Frankfurt, Paris, and London (including Lionel Rothschild, and C.J. Hambros & Son), the loan was finally signed with a consortium of Frankfurt bankers led by the House of Raphael Erlanger, cfr. E. Söderlund (1963) "The Placing of the First Swedish Railway Loan", *Scandinavian Economic History Review*, XI, pp. 43–59.

[4]Quoted by L. Magnusson (2002) in *Sveriges Ekonomiska Historia* (Prisma, Stockholm) p. 263, from C. Agardh (1856) *Försök till en statsekonomisk statistik över Sverige*, II: 2 (Karlstad). Also see fn. 22.

[5]*Historisk Statistik för Sverige IV, Statistiska Översigstabeller* (1960) (Statistisk Centralbyrå, Stockholm) p. 214. No figures are given for years prior to 1890, and no distinction is made between domestic and foreign borrowings.

[6]Hedin (1972) *Finansiering av den svenska järnvägen 1860–1914*, in Adamson & Jörberg (eds) *Problem i svensk ekonomisk historia"* (Gleerup) p. 130.

marized in Schedule 6.1[7] below. While the 1824–1846 period represented a replacement of the old mercantilism with a new liberalism, the years 1846–1864 marked a sharp renewal of the preference for state interference and restrictions, while the following years were a mixture of both of theses attitudes.

Schedule 6.1   Overview of Swedish Bank Legislation, 1824–1911

1824	A four-paragraph Act[8] in principle allowing citizens to form banking companies on the conditions that the owners would be jointly and severally liable for the company's obligations ("en för alle och alla för en"), and that the company's by-laws would be approved by the king. Clearly stated that they would never receive any government aid or assistance of any kind whatsoever. Charters granted for ten years. Renewals would have to applied for. The 1824 Act said nothing about note-issuing rights.
	They all, usually in connection with the renewal of their charters, included the word "enskilda" ("private") in their names (this was later made compulsory).
	Approximately 30 "enskilde" banks formed between 1830 and 1886.
1846	New banking Act[9] requiring banks to have a share capital of minimum SEK 1 million, and making the granting of charters conditional of a convincing argument that a proposed bank would be useful to society (§1: "… prövning … huruvida Bankinrättningen kan vara för landet nyttigt", …). Note-issuing restricted to certain multiples of particular assets of cash or near-cash nature (later changed to multiples of the bank's equity). Quarterly balance sheets to be submitted for inspection by the king.
	Trading activities restricted to gold and silver. No banks formed the next nine years.
1851	Resolution passed for the creation of small banks (share capital maximum SEK 200,000) without note-issuing rights, but funded with subsidized loans from the Riksbank. In practice operating as branches of the Riksbank, and therefore known as the "branch banks".
	22 branch banks formed. All disappeared by 1874 through mergers or closures.

---

[7]Please note that Schedule 6.1 is not a complete list of the banking regulations introduced in this period. The regulations not mentioned in Schedule 6.1 mainly dealt with the nature and amount of cover the enskilde banks were required to have for their note issues, or were directed only at the Riksbank.

[8]"Kongl. Maj:ts Nådiga Kungörelse, Angående Inrättande af Enskilde Banker eller Diskonter" ("His Majesty's Gracious Resolution Regarding the Formation of Private Banks or Discount Houses"). Reprinted in S. Brisman (1924) *Sveriges Affärsbanker*, I+II (Svenska Bankföreningen, Stockholm) I, *Grundläggningstiden*, pp. 229–30.

[9]"Kongl. Maj:ts Nådiga Kungörelse, Angående Enskilda Banker, Hvilka Utgifva Egna Kreditsedlar", gifven Stockholms Slott den 9. Januari, 1846 ("His Royal Majesty's Gracious Resolution Regarding Private Banks which Issue their Own Credit Notes"). Reprinted in S. Brisman (1924) *Sveriges Affärsbanker* I, pp. 231–6.

Schedule 6.1   Overview of Swedish Bank Legislation, 1824–1911 – *continued*

1864	The Riksdag accepted that joint stock limited liability companies formed according to the 1848 Companies Act could choose to engage in banking, but only with royal approval of their by-laws, and without note-issuing rights. As for other companies, no capital or liquidity requirements, and no requirement to be "useful to society".
1886 SFS 1886: 84	First banking Act addressing limited liability banks. Minimum share capital SEK 1 million (as for enskilde banks). Charters given for 20 years. Reserves to be built up to 50% of the share capital. Banks can trade only in gold, bills of exchange, and interest bearing securities (as for enskilde banks), i.e. trading in shares and real estate forbidden.
1903 SFS 1903: 101	Four banking acts passed simultaneously addressing both enskilde banks and limited liability banks. End of the note-issuing rights of enskilde banks (end of a seven year transition period). The use of the word "bank" restricted to enskilde banks, limited liability banks, and savings banks. Trading activities restricted gold, bills of exchange, and interest-bearing securities. Charters given for only ten years for both enskilde and limited liability banks. Limited liability banks not required to be "useful to society".
1911 SFS 1911: 74	New banking Act (comprising 260 paragraphs) giving limited liability and enskilde banks the sole right (besides the Riksbank) to engage in banking, and defining "banking" as business which includes deposit-taking from the general public on current accounts as normally done by banks.[10] "Investment banks" ("emissionsbank"), the postal savings bank, savings banks, and mortgage institutions each covered by separate legislation. Main points: Equity, minimum SEK 1 million share capital + 50% of share capital as reserves (unchanged since 1846/1886), new bank charters given only if such banks were deemed useful to society (new for limited liability banks), charters given for ten years, activities restricted to money-lending and deposit-taking, trading in gold, foreign exchange, bills of exchange, checks, etc., including bonds, and a limited right to trade shares for the bank's own account. Total amount of deposits limited to five times equity (first use of any balance sheet ratio). Cash and liquid assets to be at least 25% of demand deposits (first use of a liquidity ratio, apart from the note-covering regulations for the enskilde banks before 1903).

SFS: "Svensk Författnings-samling", the official publication of Swedish legislation.

---

[10]"Med bankrörelse förstås i denna lag sådan verksamhet, i hvilken ingår inlåning från almänheten på räkning, som af bank allmänneligen begagnas." Lag om bankrörelse, 22. juni, 1911, §1. It is unlikely that the somewhat circular nature of this definition has caused problems in real life. It was repeated in the Finnish Banking Act of 1933, cfr. p. 198.

About 255 of the 260 paragraphs concerned formalities regarding the formation, registration, and dissolution of banks together with rules for the keeping of records of board meetings, meetings of shareholders, changes of share capital, reporting, and auditing, etc.

Comments:

The 1824 Banking Act was the first banking Act to be passed in Northern Europe,[11] for the first time making it clear that private individuals could, in principle and generally, obtain permission to form banking companies subject only to royal approval of their by-laws and lending regulations.

The reason for the simplicity of the 1824 Act was the fear that too many specifications would end up involving or implicating the government in the fate of the banks, which would be a violation of the §4, i.e. the resolve never to have to contribute in any way or by any means to the existence or running of the banks.[12]

The main reasons why, much to the annoyance of the government, it took six years from 1824 before anybody tried to set up a bank were probably the insignificant privileges compared to the risks, some uncertainty about note issuing rights, and the unstable currency conditions prevailing before the 1830 currency reform.[13]

Eventually, Skånska Privatbanken was formed in Ystad[14] on the Baltic coast, funding itself with assignations against its deposits with the Riksbank, issued to bearer. These assignations circulated as money. Soon after, other enskilde banks were born issuing similar kinds of money, but not necessarily having the legal form of assignations of claims against the Riksbank.

The Estates allowed this infringement on the presumed monopoly of the Riksbank, because these notes were, after all, not legal tender. People did not have to accept them in settlement of obligations, and they could not be used for settlement of public obligations like e.g. taxes and duties. Because of the limited circulation of Riksbank money, the notes from the enskilde banks were, however, generally accepted, and the enskilde banks developed the practice of cashing each other's notes.

---

[11]The Swedish 1824 Act preceded by two years the first English Banking Act, which permitted note-issuing joint stock banks with joint liability to be formed outside a radius of 65 miles from London, where they were not supposed to compete with the Bank of England. In southern Europe, bank laws were known since the 13th century, e.g. Venice where bank licences were issued since 1270, cfr. R.C. Mueller (1997) *The Venetian Money Market* (John Hopkins University Press) p. 42, and Spain, where bank owners were beheaded if their bank could not repay deposits on demand, like the unfortunate Francesch Castello, who was beheaded in front of his bank in Barcelona in 1360, cfr. A.P. Usher (1943) *The Early History of Banking in Mediterranean Europe* (Cambridge, Mass) pp. 239–42.

[12]Cfr. S. Brisman (1924) *Sveriges Affärsbanker*, I, "Grundläggningstiden", Svenska Bank-föreningen, Stockholm) p. 77.

[13]Cfr. J. Grönstedt (1917) *Svenska Bankernas Historia*, I+II (Stockholm) I, *Solidariska Bankbolagen*, p. 18.

[14]Originally, the bank was planned to be placed in Malmö, but this was denied because the Riksbank had a branch there. The liberal attitudes prevailing in this period did not stretch so far as to allow competition to the Riksbank. In this respect, Sweden did not differ from England, France, Denmark, Finland, or Norway.

By 1916 most of them had gradually built up networks of 10–20 branches each. The creation of these 200–250 bank offices by 1916 did not, however, imply much competition among these banks. They were all strictly regional banks. The thinking at the time was that competition among these banks would lead to an excessive issue of bank notes and was, therefore, to be avoided. Consequently, the charters for these banks normally allowed them to operate only inside their home region ("län"). However, towards the end of the century, several of these banks opened branches also in neighbouring counties, and some also in Stockholm.

Their modus operandi was quite primitive. They did not, at least initially, make any efforts to attract deposits, and their lendings rarely had formal maturities exceeding six months. Overdraft facilities did not become widespread until the 1870s.

Stockholms Enskilda Bank, undoubtedly the best known of the enskilde banks, was founded in 1856 at the initiative of André Oscar Wallenberg (1816–1886). It was the fourth bank to be formed in Stockholm in nearly 200 years (Palmstruch, 1656, Rijksens Ständers Bank in 1668, and Diskont-kompaniet, 1773, having been the first three, cfr. Chapter 1). By now, Gripenstedt's influence and acquaintance with Wallenberg had overcome the Riksbank's resistance to competition.

A capital of 1 million kronor was subscribed by 72 shareholders. Wallenberg, having subscribed 5 per cent himself, became the bank's first general manager. Thus, Stockholms Enskilda Bank was founded a year before Privatbanken i Kiøbenhavn, with which it had certain similarities. Neither planned to have any branches, and both strove to form close alliances with the new industrial companies and with provincial banks. Stockholms Enskilda Bank also played a central role in the development of the Swedish bond market by arranging a number of bond issues for both private companies and municipalities – a line of activity which was, eventually, to cause a decisive split in the bank's board, cfr. below.

The restrictive period and the branch banks, 1846–1855

By the mid-1840s, general attitudes towards banks had changed in the Assembly of the Estates and in agricultural circles, not least under the influence of Carl Otto Palmstierna (1790–1878), finance minister 1851–1856. The banks were thought to be too powerful and to meddle too much in local politics. Their profits fostered envy. They had become seen as Shylocks.

The requirement that new banks had to be "useful to society" was no mere formality. An application to form a bank in Lund was declined because the presence of a bank in a university town might tempt the students to engulf themselves in excessive debts.[15] An application from Malmö was

---

[15]Cfr. S. Brisman (1934) *Sveriges Affärsbanke, II. Utvecklingstiden* (Svenska Bankföreningen, Stockholm) p. 12.

turned down because there were already two banks in the county of Skåne (Skånska Enskilda Bank in Ystad and the Riksbank branch in Malmö), and that was enough for Skåne, a fairly large and populous county.

The 22 branch banks set up in the 1850s and 1860s according to Palmstierna's 1851 Resolution[16] were too small to be of any quantitative significance.

The renaissance of the enskilde banks, and birth of the limited liability banks, 1864–1903

The growing financing needs of railways and industrialization could not be satisfied under Palmstierna's restrictive attitude towards banks, and in 1856 Palmstierna was replaced by Johan August Gripenstedt, a member of the Estates 1840–1873, and finance minister 1856–1866. Over the following 30 years more than 20 new enskilde banks were formed.

From 1863 onwards banks could choose between a status as "enskilda bank" with joint and several liability and note-issuing rights, or "kreditaktiebolag" ("credit company") with limited liability, but without note-issuing rights.

The first "kreditaktiebolag" to be formed was the Skandinaviska Kreditaktiebolag (SKAB), later known as Skandinaviska Banken. It was a perfect example showing how "the best-laid schemes o' mice and men gang aft a-gley".

In the early 1860s, C.F. Tietgen, general manager of Privatbanken i Kiøbenhavn (cfr. Chapter 3), approached Wallenberg about the possibilities for doing something about the underdeveloped Swedish banking market. Together the Nordic region's two most prominent financial figures of the 19th century organized a group of investors for the purpose of forming a large international bank centered in Göteborg and with branches in Stockholm, London, Paris, and Amsterdam. The share capital was to be an unprecedented, formidable, amount of SEK 15 million, of which 5 million was to be placed in Sweden, and the rest in London, Denmark, Norway, and elsewhere on the Continent. The intention was to create a "credit mobilier"-type of bank, floating industrial companies, arranging bond issues and taking stakes in commercial/industrial enterprises. Initially, there was plenty of interest from prospective investors, who convened in Göteborg in the summer of 1863, and so the Skandinaviska Kreditaktiebolag (SKAB) was born.

---

[16]The Resolution of the Estates, "Om Ersättende af Upphörd Privat-bank samt Penninge-Rörelsens Underlättande i Allmänhet" is reprinted in S. Brisman (1924) *Sveriges Affärsbanker*, I, pp. 240–3. It should be noted that this Resolution did not have the character of a "Kongl. Maj:ts Nådiga Kungörelse" as the 1824 and the 1846 banking acts had. The Resolution of the Estates can be seen as part of a power struggle between the Estates and the king, cfr. U. Olsson (1997) *I utvecklingens centrum. Skandinaviska Enskilda Banken och dess föregångere 1856–1996* (Sebanken, Stockholm) pp. 14–15.

When Swedish assistance in the threatening war between Denmark and Prussia proved unrealistic,[17] it became impossible to place the planned SEK 10 million shares outside Sweden, and the plans for foreign branches had to be abandoned. Without its international flavour, Tietgen and the bank lost interest in each other. None of the original grand plans materialized, but through a number of mergers, including Skånska Enskilda Bank (1910), Skandinaviska emerged before WWI as Sweden's largest bank.

In 1917, Skandinaviska took over Sveriges Private Centralbank, a bank founded in Stockholm in 1912 by 14 of the enskilde banks as their joint representative to undertake transactions, which were beyond the capabilities of the provincial banks. Fifteen years later, this bank proved to be poisoned to an extent, which nearly killed Skandinaviska (cfr. Chapter 10).

From Table 6.3 below it is seen that the two periods of significant expansion of the banking sector were the 1860s and the 1890s:

Table 6.3   Commercial Banks, Summary Balance Sheet, 1835–1916 (Million Kronor)

Year	No. of banks	Assets		Liabilities			Total
		Loans	Other	Capital	Deposits	Other	
1835	2	2	1	2	0	1	3
1850	8	15	18	16	2	15	33
1870	27	113	75	55	74	59	188
1890	43	478	173	107	352	192	651
1900	67	1,073	297	255	772	343	1,370
1910	80	2,114	412	585	1,465	476	2,526
1915	66	2,601	771	671	1,999	702	3,372
1916	59	3,091	1,022	717	2,497	899	4,113

Sources: S. Brisman (1918–1931) *Sveriges Riksbank 1668–1918*, I–V (Sveriges Riksbank) bd. V, pp. 172–87.
Note: Loans include discounted bills. Most of "Other" assets were bond holdings.
Deposits are deposits from the general public. Inter-bank borrowings and note-issues are included in "Other".

A.O. Wallenberg continued, in the meantime, to develop Stockholms Enskilda Bank to his taste. He had developed a particular liking for bonds issued by the government, municipalities, and the mortgage institutions. By 1870, approximately one-third of the bank's assets consisted of such

---

[17]Karl XV, the Swedish king (1859–1872), had indicated that Sweden might send an expeditionary force to help Denmark in case of war, but this was prevented by Gripenstedt.

bonds, and that share kept growing.[18] In 1871 a strong disagreement erupted between Wallenberg and the majority of the board members over this strategy. Eight out of 12 board members, including the chairman and the vice chairman, left the board. Most of the leaving board members represented Stockholm's merchants, who had so far not enjoyed much attention from the bank.

The leaving board members immediately set about creating a new bank, Aktiebolaget Stockholms Handels-Bank – later re-named Svenska Handelsbanken – as a "kreditaktiebolag" with a share capital of SEK 2 million.

Table 6.4 shows that the "Three Big" had a combined market share of some 25 per cent in 1910 and around 30 per cent in 1916, i.e. much less than the combined market share of "The Big Three" in Denmark (cfr. Table 3.7), but it would soon increase (cfr. Chapter 10).

Table 6.4   Market Shares of the "Big Three", 1910–1916

Million kronor	Stockholms Enskilda		Skandinaviska Kredit AB		Handelsbanken		Total bank assets
	Assets	% of total	Assets	% of total	Assets	% of total	
1910	146	5.8	367	14.5	150	5.7	2,526
1916	339	8.2	524	12.7	416	9.9	4,113

Source: K.-G. Hildebrand (1971) *I omvandlingens tjänst. Svenska Handelsbanken 1871–1955* (Stockholm, 1971) p. 395. SKAB and SEB: Lundström (1999) *Bank, Industri, Utlandsaffärer* (Stockholm) p. 154.

The 1897 Riksbank Act

The main points of "Lagen för Sveriges Riksbank av 12. maj 1897" were, first, to give the Riksbank a monopoly of note-issuing as from January 1, 1904, and, secondly, that the Riksbank would discontinue to offer interest bearing deposit accounts to the general public, and would, therefore, no longer compete commercially with the private banks.

One of the results was probably to strengthen the concentration on the banking scene, since the large "kreditaktiebolag" had never depended on note-issuing rights.

---

[18]K.-G. Hildebrand (1971) *I Omvandlingens Tjänst. Svenska Handelsbanken 1871–1955* (Svenska Handelsbanken) p. 3.

6.3.4   The savings banks

In 1819, C.D. Skogman (1786–1856), the Finnish born economist and father of the Swedish savings banks (cfr. Chapter 4) presented his report,[19] produced at the request of the Estates and based on studies of the English and Scottish savings banks. It included a proposal for by-laws for a savings bank to be formed in Stockholm.

In 1820, fast action by E. Ludendorff, a Prussian merchant, born 1790, who had settled in Göteborg in 1812, lead to the formation of the Göteborg Sparbank, Sweden's first savings bank. With a few modifications, the by-laws and regulations were copied from Skogman's proposals. Stockholms Sparbank was born early the following year with by-laws copied almost directly from the Göteborg Sparbank.

The main characteristics of the early Swedish savings banks were not much different from savings banks elsewhere. A group of 10–20 founders would provide a small capital base, and volunteers would do the practical work with administration, keeping the savings bank open for a few hours weekly. The management was amateurish, sloppy, and sometimes even

Table 6.5   **The Development of the Banking and Savings Banking Sectors, 1840–1916**

Amounts in million SEK	Banks, excluding the Riksbank			Savings banks		
	Number of banks	Total deposits	Deposits per bank	Number of savings banks	Total deposits	Deposits per savings bank
1840	6	0	0.1	60	5	0.1
1860	12	18	1.5	151	27	0.2
1880	44	246	5.6	341	146	0.4
1900	67	772	115.2	388	494	1.3
1910	80	1,465	183.1	436	855	2.0
1915	59	2,497	423.3	444	1,113	2.5

Source: Banks: Brisman (1918–1931) *Sveriges Riksbank 1668–1918*, Bd. I–V (Stockholm), Bd. V (Bilagor) pp. 172–87.
Savings banks: Statistisk sentralbyrå (1960) *Historisk Statistikk*, IV (Stockholm) pp. 99–103.

---

[19]Skogman's report: "Underrättelse om så kallade besparingsbanker" had a strong resemblance to a similar report ("En kort beretning om de i Stor-Britanien oprettede Spare-Banker, med vedføjede Forslag til lignende Bankers Oprettelse i vort Fædreland") dated 1816 and produced by F.H.A. Clauswitz, a Danish diplomat at the London embassy. Several phrases in the two reports are almost identical, but it is, of course, possible that both of them were based on a common source. Cfr. E. Sommarin (1940) *Grundlägningen av vårt Sparbanksväsen* (Stockholm) pp. 40–1.

fraudulent. Most of the lending consisted of mortgage loans in the local communities, and the rest was consumer loans against solid collateral. Ceilings were imposed on single deposits and on the maximum amounts on which interest would be paid, and deposits would normally be accepted only from low-income people living in the local parish or town. Branches were very rare before the 20th century.

Table 6.5 shows the over-all development of the savings bank sector compared to the banking sector, and clearly demonstrates the fragmented nature of the savings bank world. Although the combined deposits of the savings banks exceeded those of the banks until the mid-1860s, these deposits were so widely scattered among hundreds of savings banks that they were of little use for the purpose of financing major projects.

In 1875, a regulation was passed addressing a few of the most urgent problems, including a general supervision by county officials. In 1892 it was followed by Sweden's first Savings Bank Act, which showed some inspiration from the Danish 1880 Savings Banks Act, but with 30 paragraphs it was substantially more detailed. The main points of the 1892 Act were:[20]

1. The purpose of savings banks was defined as accepting interest bearing deposits, which could be withdrawn with some time of notice. Not a single word on lending.
2. Only savings banks could use the term "savings bank" in their name, and savings banks could only do "savings banks business". No current accounts, overdraft facilities, or discounting of bills, although this was not mentioned directly. Nearly as in Denmark.
3. Ten per cent of deposits was to be held as liquid assets – as in Denmark.
4. Savings banks, which had lost their reserves and 5 per cent of the deposits, were to be placed under administration – as in Denmark.

Needless to say, these changes met with much resistance from the hundreds of tiny parish savings banks, which had few possibilities to cope with all the extra "bureaucracy", particularly the accounting and auditing regulations also stipulated by the Savings Banks Act.

Also inspired by England, a postal savings bank was created in 1883. Its deposits were to be placed only in Riksbank deposits, government bonds, or bonds issued by the Sveriges Allmänna Hypoteksbank (cfr. below). It soon became by far the largest Swedish savings bank.

---

[20]Reprinted in Sommarin (1942) *Grundlägningen av vort sparbankväsen* (Stockholm) pp. 313–24.

6.3.5   The mortgage institutions

The proposal[21] made in 1815 by Count Frederik Bogislav v. Schwerin for the creation of a mortgage association based on the principles known from the Prussian Landschaften did not have any practical results until 1833, when Carl Adolf Agardh (1785–1859), professor of botany and economics, published a pamphlet[22] proposing the establishment of a mortgage institution in the southern province of Skåne, based on the principles suggested by Schwerin.

Action was taken immediately by members of the Skåne nobility. By-laws and management regulations were prepared and approved by the king, and in 1836 the Skånska Hypoteksförening ("Skånska Hyp") was formally established by 187 founders, each having signed up for an amount of their respective borrowing rights or intentions. Membership was open to all owners of rural property in Skåne valued at minimum 3,000 kronors, i.e. small-holders were avoided. Loans could initially be had for maximum 50 per cent of the value of the property, later increased to two-thirds. One per cent of the ownership share/borrowing right was to be paid in immediately and every following year as capital contributions.

In the years 1845–1851, six other similar mortgage institutions were set up in other Swedish provinces, differing from each other only in small technical details.

The mortgage bonds were increasingly sold abroad, mostly in Hamburg. However, even in Hamburg the appetite for Swedish paper had its limits, particularly following the financial crisis of 1857, and it became problematic that the mortgage associations could not, or at least did not, co-ordinate their foreign bond sales among themselves, or with the raising of government loans. Thus, the placing of the first railway loan (cfr. 6.3.2) was hampered by the more or less simultaneous "flooding" of the market with Swedish mortgage bonds. So, after much discussion in the Estates, it was decided to centralize the bond issues in a new independent but government controlled institution.[23]

So, Sveriges Allmänna Hypoteksbank[24] was created by royal decree, Förordning av 26. april, 1861. The intention was that bonds issued by the Hypotekbank should resemble government bonds as much as possible. The

---

[21]F.B. v. Schwerin (1815) *Om förlägenheten i allmänna rörelsen, ordsakerne dertill och botemedlen deremot* ("On the difficulties of the general business conditions, their origins, and remedies against them") (Stockholm).

[22]C.A. Agardh (1833) *Om möjligheten af hypotheksinrättningar för provinserne och synnerligen för Skåne*. Agardh had previously been involved in the setting up of a fire insurance company and a savings bank. Also see fn. 4.

[23]A similar idea had been proposed in Denmark, but was rejected.

[24]The use of the term "bank" is definitely misleading in this case. Sveriges Allmänna Hypotekbank had none of the characteristics of a "bank" discussed in the Introduction.

government injected a modest capital ("grundfond"), and any future profits were to be retained as reserves. The regional associations became "members" or "co-owners" of the Hypotekbank.

In return, the Estates decided that the Riksbank should discontinue its mortgage-lending activities as from 1865.

The relationship between the private regional associations and the Hypotekbank was copied directly from the relationship between the ultimate borrowers and the private associations. The private associations were jointly liable with all their assets for the obligations of the Allmänna Hypoteksbank in proportion to their respective shares of its combined lendings.

The Allmänna Hypotekbank only took care of the funding, and had no relation or contact to the ultimate borrowers. This was always taken care of by the regional associations. Thus the idea and system of a centralized government regulated mechanism of bond issues grew up.

As the 19th century progressed, the accelerating urbanization required huge investments in residential construction, and it was tempting to copy the agricultural mortgage system to finance it.

However, the contemporary view was that, while agricultural property represented a permanent value, urban properties could burn, fall into disrepair, or be vacated. Therefore, no agricultural mortgage institutions would accept being mixed up with the financing of urban properties. This was the background for the creation in 1865 of the Allmänna hypotekskassan för Sveriges städer ("Stadshypotekskassan").

In principle, the mechanism was identical to that of the rural mortgage system, i.e. automatic borrowing rights, and borrowers who were jointly liable with all of their assets for the obligations of the local associations, and the local associations were, in turn, jointly liable with all of their assets for the obligations of the Stadshypotekskassa.

The Stadshypotekskassa started its operations in 1871, but early in the new century there were still few cities with stadshypoteksföreningar.

Against this unsatisfactory background a proposal was made "to do something", and after several debates in the Riksdag during 1908–1909, the king signed two decrees,[25] which were to form the framework for the financing of urban property for the next 85 years. The "förordning" concerning the formation and operation of local föreningar (associations) established that competition among the associations was to be avoided. The centrepiece of the system was a new central "Konungariket Sveriges stadshypotekskassa"

---

[25]Kungl. Maj:ts förordning angående Konungariket Sveriges stadshypotekskassa, and Kungl. Maj:ts förordning angående grunderna för stadshypoteksföreningars bildanda och verksamhet, both signed on June 5, 1909.

supplied with a perpetual government "loan". In principle, it was a private institution owned by the local hypoteksföreningar, but this fact was camouflaged as much as possible. It was intended to look as much as possible as a government institution, and its bonds were designed to look as much as possible as government bonds. The purpose was to stimulate the foreign appetite for the bonds.

The new Konungariket Sveriges Stadshypotekskassa (KSS) took over the existing assets and liabilities of the old and entirely private Allmänna hypotekskassa för Sveriges städer, which was wound up.

The KSS was a perfect example of the hybrid private/government type of institution, which permeated the Swedish capital market since the formation of Palmstruch's Bank in 1658, and the "diskonter" of the late 18th century.

Finally, a number of private companies (the "inteckningsbolagen") had earlier obtained licences also to offer mortgage loans. The oldest of these was Stockholms Inteckning Garanti Aktiebolag (1869). Five others were formed later in the 19th century. Their combined market share remained less than 5 per cent. Whether these "inteckningsbolagen" ("mortgage companies") should be considered part of the "organized capital market" is a matter of taste and definition.

Table 6.6 below shows the structure of the Swedish mortgage market, i.e. those in favour of whom mortgages had been registered, 1880–1920:

Table 6.6   Market Shares of Registered Mortgage Lenders, 1880–1920

	Insurance companies, %	Savings banks, %	Com. banks, %	Hyp. bank, %	Stads. hyp., %	Others %	Total %	Total million SEK
1880	–	6.0	2.7	20.0	0.6	(70.7)	100	1,123
1890	5.3	9.6	3.6	17.7	0.8	63.0	100	1,619
1900	6.4	11.4	7.7	12.7	0.6	60.2	100	2,098
1910	6.8	12.6	13.7	7.5	2.3	57.6	100	3,917
1920	5.3	15.1	17.9	4.7	3.5	53.5	100	6,486

Source: Cramér & Fredericsson (1942) *Svensk Fastighetskredit* (Stockholm) pp. 34, 44, 45, 56, 76, 97.

The extent of the changes in market shares over the 1880–1920 period is quite striking, and explanations for them are not easy to find. It has been suggested[26] that the strong growth in both absolute amounts and in market share of the commercial banks represented mortgage financing of industrial and commercial investments in plant and equipment in connection with the growing industrialization.

---

[26]E.g. K. Kock (1932) *Svenskt bankväsen i våre dagar* (Kooperativa Förbundets bokförlag, Stockholm) p. 84.

"Others" represent what is here defined as the "unorganized market", which include the "inteckningsbolag" referred to above as well as private individuals and companies investing in mortgage bonds.

The main similarities and differences between the Swedish and the "Alte Fünf" Prussian – and Danish – mortgage institutions can be summarized as follows:

Similarities:

1. Legally, they were "associations of borrowers". In most cases of a non-profit nature.
2. Borrowing rights were "automatic" for all owners of rural property exceeding a certain size and in proportion to the value of the property, regardless of the "creditworthiness" of the owner.
3. Borrowers were jointly and severally liable with all their assets for the association's obligations.
4. Very little initially paid-in capital.
5. Funded by fixed interest bond issues with maturities and coupons essentially identical to the underlying mortgages. Thus, the associations did not, in principle, have any liquidity management problems – unless they chose, like Skånska Hyp, to disburse loans in cash rather than in bonds.
6. The associations were strictly regional, and did not compete against each other.
7. Mortgage institutions for urban properties came later and were separate from the agricultural associations.

Differences:

1. Loans were amortizing, in contrast to the original Prussian and Danish systems. Maturities usually up to 40 years.
2. The bonds could be called only after ten years (in Prussia, at any time).
3. Because of the increasing practice of cash disbursements, the principle of identical terms of the bonds and the underlying mortgages with respect to coupon and maturity became less strict than in Prussia and Denmark. As from 1890 all loans were disbursed in cash.
4. In Sweden, the associations were subject to the maximum rate of interest as decided from time to time by the Estates, in contrast to the Danish 1850 Mortgage Act.
5. Neither in Sweden nor in Prussia was the idea of splitting the bond issues into separate series with joint liability only among borrowers in the same series introduced, as provided for in the Danish 1861 Mortgage Act.
6. Neither in Prussia nor in Denmark was any central government institution introduced to take care of the joint funding of the regional associations.

Table 6.7 Relative Composition and Growth of the Credit Stock, 1860–1915

	Riksbank	Commercial banks	Savings banks	Mortgage institutions	Insurance companies & pension	Total	Total, million SEK	Index	Total, in % of GNP
Percentage of total credit stock									
1861	29	24	14	32		99	187	100	24
1870	13	29	15	41	2	100	387	207	42
1880	9	37	18	32	4	100	828	443	64
1890	8	38	22	25	6	99	1,254	671	87
1900	7	49	23	14	7	100	2,169	1,160	96
1910	6	54	22	10	8	100	3,923	2,098	119
1915	7	53	23	8	9	100	4,895	2,616	102
Percentage of GNP									
1860	7	6	3	8		24			24
1870	6	12	6	17	1	42			42
1880	6	24	11	21	2	64			64
1890	7	33	20	22	5	87			87
1900	7	48	22	13	7	97			96
1910	8	64	26	12	10	120			119
1915	7	54	23	8	9	101			102

Sources: GDP: As for Table 6.1, pp. 156–7. Otherwise as for Tables 6.3, 6.5, and 6.6.

Note: Since no lending figures are available for the savings banks, their deposit figures have been used as a proxy, which probably overstates the lendings by 5–10 per cent.

Comments:

1. Apart from the overall growth of the financial sector, one of the most striking features revealed by Table 6.7 is the relatively small absolute size of the "organized" capital market in Sweden as defined in Table 6.7. The total amounts are almost identical to the total amounts in Denmark (cfr. Table 3.9), although Sweden's population was almost twice as large.

2. The relative decline in the Riksbank's role as commercial lender was quite similar to the developments in Denmark and Finland. After the turn of the century the Nationalbank, Bank of Finland, and Norges Bank increasingly acted like central banks e.g. as guardians of the gold reserves of their respective countries, sole banker to their respective governments, and masters of discount rates (except the Bank of Finland), but it was not until after WWI that this role became the dominating one.

3. In Sweden, like in Finland and Norway, the commercial banks were dominating the capital markets. Less so in Denmark, where the mortgage institutions built up a larger combined market share than the banks, but where, on the other hand, the largest three banks were bigger than their counterparties in Sweden, Finland, and Norway.

4. Like in Finland, Denmark, and Norway, the savings banks in Sweden were numerous, but in contrast to Denmark, their combined lendings never reached the level achieved by the banks.

5. The reason why Denmark had the largest capital market per capita (and in absolute terms roughly equal to the Swedish), was the growth of the mortgage associations, which overshadowed even the banks, and which resulted in a secondary market for long-term fixed interest bonds, ultimately becoming one of the world's largest markets for such bonds. No simple explanation seems to offer itself for the difference between the size and growth of the Swedish and Danish mortgage systems.

6.4   The size and shape of the financial sector, 1861–1915

Like everywhere else, the capital market grew much faster than the economy as a whole between 1860 and 1915 (ca. 6.1 per cent p.a. against only 3.4 per cent p.a. for GDP). Also like almost everywhere else, the structural changes in these years were quite noteworthy. Some of the structural features seen from Table 6.7 are very similar to developments in Denmark, Finland, and Norway, but some are markedly different.

6.5   The stock exchange

Before 1863, there was no way the Stockholm Exchange could be considered a "stock exchange" or part of an organized capital market in the sense of the definition suggested in the Introduction.

A letter from C.G. Hierzéel,[27] one of Stockholm's authorized brokers, dated April 5, 1861, probably expressed a generally held opinion on the need for improvement.[28] At least, the letter had the intended effect. The letter was addressed to Stockholms Handelsförening ("Association of Stockholm Merchants"). The following abstracts will suffice to convey its gist (SEA's translation): "Since in recent years many different sorts of shares, participations, bonds, and similar securities have emerged ... a facility for fast and cheap disposals and trading of securities, so far missed, will be evermore needed ... So far, the only way to liquidate the ... securities has been to sell them through the City's auctions, but since the cost for this ... is one per cent ... and in addition it may take 14 days to receive payment ... it is clear that this is burdened with too high costs and trouble ... without in any way stimulating a brisker trade ...".

Naturally, Hierzéel's proposal ran into stiff opposition from the City of Stockholm, which wanted to preserve its monopoly and income from the auctions, which were conducted in the exchange building on the Stortorg, put up by the City for that purpose (cfr. Chapter 1).

---

[27]C.G. Hierzéel (1806–1894), descending from a family of Dutch origins, was primarily a highly successful commodities broker specializing in grain, spirits, and tar. When he withdrew from business in 1871 he left the firm to a colleague, J. Håkansson, who, in turn, passed it on to Alfred Berg, the stockbroker, in 1901. The firm still operates under the name of Alfred Berg, one of the largest Nordic stockbroker/investment banking companies, cfr. S. Algott (ed., 1963) *Stockholms Fondbörs 100 År* (Stockhols Fondbörs) pp. 17–18, the official history of the Stockholm Stock Exchange.
[28]The letter is reprinted in S. Algott (ed., 1963) *Stockholms Fondbörs 100 År* (Stockholms Fondbörs) pp. 6–7.

The lengthy discussions in the Assembly of the Estates finally resulted in a Royal Decree dated December 20, 1862[29] with ten short paragraphs. The main points were:

§1: Auctions for the sale of bonds, participations, shares and similar securities were to be held on the ground floor of the Exchange Building on the first Wednesday of every month.

§2: The auctions were to be conducted by such of the City's sworn-in brokers ("stadsmäklare"), who would take upon themselves to do it.

§3: The proceedings were to be overseen by a City representative, who was to keep records of the business.

§4: Sellers of securities were to address a "stadsmäklare" in writing with their intended business prior to the auction.

§9: The seller was to pay a commission of 0.2 per cent of the sales proceeds, to be split evenly between the auctioneer and the City of Stockholm.

The first auction under these rules was held on February 4, 1863, which date has since been celebrated as the birthday of the Stockholm Stock Exchange.

On the first auction, 22 transactions were done – against only ten in the 1853–1860 period.[30]

The 1862 Royal Decree represented a big step forwards in the creation of a "real" stock exchange as part of an organized capital market. It restricted the access to the trading floor to the sworn-in brokers, and it ensured that records were kept of the business done.

However, a number of aspects were still missing. There was no requirement for "bid" and "offer" prices to be posted, and still not much transparency. The records kept by the City representative seem mostly to have been made to ensure that the City received its half of the commission according to §9. There was no obligation to publish the records, or even to make them available for anybody else, and there was no official price list or list of quoted securities. Also, it does not appear that the Exchange was a

---

[29]"Kungl. Maj:ts Nådiga Reglemente för auktioner till försäljning av obligationer, lottbrev och actier m.m. å Stockholms börs. Givet Stockholms slott den 20 december 1862." Reprinted in *Stockholms Fondbörs 100 År* (Stockholms Fondbörs) pp. 235–6.

Five years later, a set of "Ordningsregler" ("Rules of Conduct") were adopted. Among the stipulations were that the Stock Exchange would be open on all weekdays between one and two o'clock, that tobacco smoking was not allowed, and that dogs were not to be admitted in the Stock Exchange building ("Ordningsregler för Stockholms Börs", fastställda den 27. jan., 1868), reprinted in *Stockholms Fondbörs 100 År*, p. 237.

[30]Cfr. *Stockholms Fondbörs 100 Å*, p. 29.

separate legal entity, which could sue and be sued. The management board did not seem to have the authority to enforce very much. Finally, the brokers who acted on the Exchange were not specialized stockbrokers. In most cases, stock broking was a minor part of their business, since auctions were held only once every month. It was not until 1895 that auctions were held weekly.[31]

Compared to Copenhagen, Stockholm and its stock exchange had several problems in the late 19th century. First, Stockholm was not a commercial and industrial centre in Sweden of the same relative importance as Copenhagen's position in Denmark, and Sweden had exchanges also in other cities, notably in Göteborg, Gävle, and Malmö. Secondly, telephones came rather late to Sweden. Denmark had a fairly countrywide telephone system already around 1870, but in Sweden this did not happen until the late 1890s. Stockholm had telephones in the 1880s, but there was no connection to other cities. Also, by the 1880s, trading in foreign bills of exchange, which had for many years been a prerogative of the brokers, had mostly been taken over by the banks, which "... sold foreign exchange bills like pastry sold from bakers' shops".[32]

From the mid-1890s, the banks also took up trading in securities, bypassing the stock exchange. Against this background it is, perhaps, small wonder that the number of brokers in Stockholm dropped sharply. From 15 in 1852, the number of Stockholm brokers grew to reach 20 by 1860. The number stayed at roughly this level until 1884, when it started to drop. Around the turn of the century, there were only five.[33]

Therefore, efforts were set in motion to reorganize the stock exchange.

Finally, in 1901 a new Broker Decree[34] was issued, which largely followed the wishes of the Stockholms Handels och Sjöfartsnämnd (HSN, a semi-official organization consisting of representatives from the business community and the municipality, and entrusted with i.a. the authorization of brokers). One of the aspects making this Decree noteworthy is that this was the first time the word "fondmäklare" ("stockbroker") was used in any Swedish piece of regulation. This makes it a milestone in the history

---

[31]Cfr. *Stockholms Fondbörs 100 År*, p. 244.
[32]"... affärerna i utrikes växlor ... flyttade från mäklarne ... till bankdiskerna, der man sålde utlandske valutor liksom man säljer kringlor i bagarbodarna ...", letter from J.H. Zethraeus, a prominent broker, here quoted from *Stockholms Fondbörs 100 År*, p. 5 (n. 9).
[33]Cfr. *Stockholm Fondbörs 100 År*, p. 48 and p. 234.
[34]Kungl. Maj:ts Nådiga Kungörelse Angående Fondmäklare i Stockholm, 8 February 1901 ("His Majesty's Gracious Decree on Stockbrokers in Stockholm"), reprinted in Svensk Författnings-samling, nr. 13, 1901.

of the Stockholm Stock Exchange and justifies a few quotations from its eight brief paragraphs (SEA's translation):

§1: "Brokers in Stockholm, who assist in that capacity with sales and purchases of bonds, shares, and other similar securities, must be specially appointed as stockbrokers by the City's Handels-och Sjöfartsnämnd ...".

Thus, the power of the HSN over the Stockholm Stock Exchange was cemented. They would decide, i.a. if the City was sufficiently endowed with brokers, and, if not, who should be authorized as such – much like the role played by Grosserer-Societetets Kommite in Copenhagen (cfr. Chapter 3).

§4: "... the Stock Exchange committee will ensure that records are kept on the Stock Exchange not only of the prices obtained for securities actually traded, but also for securities for which offers and bids have been made ... Following each Stock Exchange (session) the prices are to be made public in a suitable way".

The implication was clearly a much improved transparency, even if the stipulated publication of prices in a suitable way ("lempligt sätt") gave rise to several years of battles and squabbles, cfr. below.

According to the official history of the Stock Exchange, the 1901 Act represented the real transformation of the Stockholm Exchange into a "true" Stock Exchange. It did, at least, create an official organization centered around the Fondbörskommission with certain powers, including the powers to accept or reject securities qualified for being traded on the Exchange.

Membership of the exchange was restricted to authorized brokers, but their numbers had declined severely, and they were not necessarily specialized stockbrokers (somewhat in contrast to the Danish 1808 Broker Decree, cfr. Chapter 3). Also, securities trading was increasingly handled by banks outside the exchange, and the Stock Exchange was close to becoming irrelevant. Therefore, in 1907, the banks were allowed to become members of the Stockholm Stock Exchange. Soon 15 banks accepted the invitation (in respect of shares, they could, however, only trade as pure brokers for the account of clients, since the Banking Act of 1886 had forbidden banks to own shares). Thereby the membership became institutional, like in Germany, Norway, and Finland, rather than personal like in Copenhagen and London (until "Big Bang").

The battle of the price lists

Between 1863 and 1911, a large number of different price lists were circulated. Some were produced by various brokers as advertisements, others by newspapers for similar purposes.

One called itself (SEA's translations) "The Official Price List", another one "The Only Complete and Official Price List", although it was neither complete nor official.

Finally, in 1911, an agreement was reached between the Exchange Commissioner and the members of the Exchange to produce a single, co-ordinated official price list starting as from January, 1912.

In 1919, this agreement was replaced by legislation making it illegal to publish other price lists than the one produced or sanctioned by the Fondbörskommission.

By this time, the list comprised approximately 25 bank shares, a similar number of shipping company shares, 30–40 railway stocks, industrial and commercial companies, and a number of bonds issued by the mortgage institutions, municipalities, and the government.

Table 6.8 shows the development in the turnover of bonds and shares on the Stockholm Stock Exchange:

Table 6.8   Turnover of Bonds and Shares on the Stockholm Stock Exchange, 1863–1918, Selected Years (SEK '000)

The auction period, 1863–1901				After the 1901 reform			
1863:	240	1888:	2,250	1902:	1,302	1912:	318,246
1865:	504			1903:	2,524	1913:	180,018
				1904:	6,324	1914:	51,598
						1915:	50,919
1871:	627	1892:	3,441	1907:	36,500		
1873:	1,069	1894:	5,134			1917:	1,321,858
1878:	676	1897:	18,920	1909:	38,662	1918:	1,586,059
		1898:	21,129				
1880:	4,241						
1881:	1,924	1900:	6,378				
1886:	2,516	1901:	3,905				

Source: S. Algott (ed., 1963) Stockholms Fondbörs 100 År (Stockholms Fondbörs) pp. 244–5.

As always on a stock exchange, turnover was rather volatile, as confirmed by the figures shown in Table 6.8. The dizzying turnover figures seen in 1917–1918 "bubble" were not reached again until the 1960s (in current prices).

The leap in the turnover figures seen in 1897–1898 was mainly caused by the introduction on the Exchange of "Trafikaktiebolaget Grängesberg-Oxelösund" (TGO, or "Grängesberg"), a combined mining and railway company, which dominated the turnover on the Exchange until the 1930s.

Before 1915, TGO's share of the Stockholm Stock Exchange turnover was never less than 24 per cent. In some years it was nearly 50 per cent. Between 1907 and 1915, 50–55 per cent of the turnover was accounted for by the shares of only two or three companies.[35]

---

[35]Cfr. S. Algott (ed., 1963) Stockholms Fondbörs 100 År, pp. 363–4.

7
Denmark, 1918–2010: Towards Financial Abyss and Back

"Something is rotten in the state of Denmark"

("Hamlet", Act One)

7.1   An overview: A study in financial excesses

In Denmark, the 90-year period following the end of WWI can be divided into three sub-periods, each with distinctly different characteristics and implications for capital market developments:

1. The inter-war period of financial rot. First, waves of bank failures in the 1920s, mostly caused by excessive speculation and over-sized exposures of individual banks. Second, a cut-off from international markets in the 1930s.
2. An interlude, the post-war period of financial rot, 1945–1986. First, chronic foreign exchange shortage. Second, excessive spendings, mounting government debts, foreign debts, inflation, soaring interest rates, and devaluations.
3. Towards new horizons, 1986–2010. Gradual elimination of inflation, capital market and foreign exchange restrictions, and foreign debts. Stabilization of the currency against the DEM and the euro. In 2005–2007 excessive speculation in the stock and property markets, with associated bank failures, much like in the early 1920s, and much like elsewhere but of limited lasting consequence.

However, neither capital market regulations nor speculative excesses ever went so far as in Finland, Norway, and Sweden in the 1950–1992 years. Therefore, the scrapping of the restrictions in 1985–1986 did not have the calamitous effects seen in the other Nordic countries, where some banks found it difficult to handle the freedom won by the fast dismantling of intricate systems of detailed quantitative restrictions and regulations.

On the negative side, Denmark, having joined the EU in 1973 as the first Nordic country to do so, refused in two referendums, 1992 and 2000, to join the Economic and Monetary Union and the euro.

7.2 The inter-war period

7.2.1 The problems

Denmark, like the other Nordic countries, escaped The Great War, but not the economic and financial consequences of the peace. These included double-digit inflation until about 1919 followed by alternating periods of falling prices and renewed inflation caused by various combinations of tight monetary policies and strongly fluctuating prices of imported commodities.

In the early 1920s, speculative commodity transactions led to the collapse of numerous trading companies. A large number of banks suffered heavy losses from failed trading companies and from rash, speculative stock exchange transactions. About one-third of the nearly 200 banks existing in Denmark in 1920 lost some or all of their share capital between 1920 and 1930.[1] In 14 cases not only the shareholders, but also depositors lost money. In most of the cases the direct reason for the problems was excessive exposures to a small number of failed borrowers. In some cases managers or directors of a bank had been directly involved in speculative commodity or stock exchange transactions financed by the respective banks.

No doubt the most spectacular of these bank failures was the crash of the Landmandsbank in 1922. Under the leadership of Emil Glückstadt, the son of the bank's first general manager, the bank had grown rapidly and had been the largest bank in the Nordic region for some years with assets totalling DKK 1.5 billion[2] in 1920, almost a doubling since 1916. Unfortunately, the equity had expanded by only 20 per cent to 160 million, and unfortunately much of the growth in lendings had been concentrated on a few large customers, including a trading company which crashed with DKK 201 million[3] of loans from Landmandsbanken, out of a total loan portfolio of ca. DKK 775 million, and about 25 per cent more than the bank's booked equity. A substantial part of the Landmandsbank's expansion had been financed by loans from the Nationalbank. In September 1922, the

---

[1] A full list of the approximately 70 bank failures together with a brief explanation of the background for the failures and the position/action taken by the Nationalbank is given in Sv. A. Hansen et al. (1968) *Dansk Pengehistorie*, bd. I–III (Danmarks Nationalbank) bd. III, Bilag v/ K. Mordhorst, pp. 114–55.
[2] Danmarks Statistik (1969) *Kreditmarkedsstatistik* (Statistiske undersøgelser nr. 24) p. 33.
[3] Cfr. P. Nyboe Andersen (1947) *Rentepolitik og renteudvikling efter 1914* in P. Nyboe Andersen (ed.) *Lånerenten*, (København) p. 187.

Landmandsbank owed the Nationalbank DKK 240 million, nearly half of the Nationalbank's total loan portfolio.[4]

Three more of the large banks also found themselves in deep trouble in the 1920s, including Privatbanken, Copenhagen's oldest purely private bank, which had to suspend payments in 1928 because of losses from over-sized exposures to a limited number of collapsed commercial and industrial companies.

In the 1930s, there were only few and isolated bank failures in spite of a surge in unemployment in the first half of the decade. Credit cards and consumer finance had not yet been invented.

Some of the mortgage institutions, however, had difficulties because of problems in the agricultural sector. In the case of one of the second priority agricultural mortgage institutions, the bondholders had to agree to a prolongation of the maturity by two years, and a reduction of the interest payments by half also for two years. This was – and remains – the only case since 1860 of a Danish mortgage institution not being able to honour its obligations in full and on time.

7.2.2   Responses and actions: Legislation and rescues

The banking crises of the 1920s, and the banking acts of 1919 and 1930

Neither the government nor the Nationalbank had any clear policy for the handling of the many bank failures. Approximately half of the cases were solved privately through mergers, take-overs, or liquidations, and in the other half of the cases the Nationalbank was involved in various ways, and usually in consultation with the government. In some 20 cases the Nationalbank made contributions of share capital, and in about 15 cases the contributions consisted of straight loans, subordinated loans, guarantees, or a combination of all of these. In four cases the Nationalbank was asked to contribute, but refused. The stance taken by the Nationalbank was usually motivated by the failed bank's perceived importance for its local region, by the prospects for the bank's continued existence, or by the size of the bank. The Landmandsbank and the Privatbank were both considered too big to be allowed to fail. The Privatbank was reconstructed fairly easily with a write-down of the share capital by 80 per cent, and an injection of new share capital, of which nearly 30 per cent was supplied by the Nationalbank.[5]

The rescue of the Landmandsbank was a considerably more complicated and long drawn-out affair involving several reconstructions with the help of the Nationalbank, the government, and two commercial companies (GN Store Nord and the East Asiatic Company). Eventually (1927) the bank became fully state-owned, the government having previously guaranteed all the bank's obligations. The government re-introduced the Landmands-

---

[4]As for fn. 3, p. 188.
[5]As for fn. 1, pp. 146–52.

bank on the Stock Exchange in 1936, but it was not until the early 1950s that the government had sold its last shares.[6]

Schedule 7.1   The 1919 and 1930 Banking Acts Compared

	The 1919 Banking Act (Lov af 4. Okt. 1919) 23 paragraphs.	The 1930 Banking Act (Lov nr. 122 af 15. apr. 1930) 23 paragraphs.
Definition of "banking"	Only such joint stock companies which are engaged in "banking" may, and shall, call themselves "banks". "Banks" may engage in "banking" only, which generally includes receipt of deposits, offering credits, trading of precious metals, foreign exchange and securities, and offering assistance with setting up companies, depending on circumstances. By-laws to be approved by the minister of Commerce. A Banking Inspector appointed.	Minor technical amendments. Only "banks" and "savings banks" may solicit deposits. Issuing guarantees, making payment transfers and collections added as banking activities.
Capital requirement	Minimum DKK 200,000, and minimum 10% of total obligations.	DKK 300,000, and minimum 10% of total obligations, including guarantees.
Liquidity Requirement	Liquid assets to be minimum 15% of call deposits.	Minor technical amendments. Larger requirements for larger banks.
Exposure limitations	None.	Single exposures maximum 35%, and combined guarantees maximum 75% of equity.

Comments:
1. Approvals of by-laws routinely given. Foreign banks were, however, not allowed until 1974.
2. The wording "assistance with the setting up of companies, depending on circumstances" ("efter omstændighederne") reflected a very limited enthusiasm for "Gründerbank"-activities, a distaste, which was made stronger during the 1920s as reflected in the limitation imposed by the 1930 Act on share ownerships (maximum 50 per cent of a bank's equity could be placed in shares).
3. In the 1930 Act, senior bank staff were forbidden to engage in any way in any other business, or to make "speculative" transactions.

---

[6]Almost half of the shares sold by the government were picked up by the A.P. Møller shipping companies (now A.P. Møller-Mærsk). Through the mergers with the Kjøbenhavns Handelsbank in 1990 and Den Danske Provinsbank, the A.P. Møller ownership was diluted to the present ca. 23 per cent. A.P. Møller was chairman of the board between 1928 and 1952.

The bank failures in Copenhagen in 1907–1908 had persuaded the Rigsdag ("Parliament") that some sort of bank regulation was needed. The legislation was delayed by other priorities during the war, but Denmark's first banking Act was finally passed in 1919, together with an amended savings banks Act and Denmark's first stock exchange Act. The many bank failures during the 1920s caused the 1919 banking and savings banks Acts to be amended in 1930 and 1937 respectively.

Table 7.1 below illustrates the capital requirement compared to actual solvency ratios for ten banks which collapsed with losses for depositors, and for the rest of the banks:

Table 7.1   Solvency Ratios for Ten Banks Collapsed 1920–1922 with Losses for Depositors, Compared to the Rest of the Banks

	Equity in % of loans (approx. Basel I and II)	Equity in % of deposits (approx. 1919 Act)	Equity in % of total obligations (approx. 1930 Act)	Total booked equity, DKK million
Ten collapsed banks				
1918	10	11	9	130
1919	12	14	13	216
1920	13	12	9	222
All banks, excluding the Ten				
1918	14	13	12	330
1919	14	13	14	371
1920	15	15	14	383

Sources: Sv. A. Hansen et al. (1968) *Dansk Pengehistorie*, I–III, (Danmarks Nationalbank), bd. 3, Bilag v/K. Mordhorst, pp. 114–54.
Danmarks Statistik (1969) *Kreditmarkedsstatistik* (Statistiske Undersøgelser nr. 24).

Note: The ten collapsed banks include the Landmandsbank, which would have caused substantial losses for depositors had it not been for the rescue operations.
The solvency ratios are unweighted, i.e. averages of percentages for each of the banks.

The solvency ratios shown in Table 7.1 can only be approximations, since a precise calculation would require adjustments for a number of details only available from the internal accounts of the individual banks. The figures do, however, give a rough impression of the order of magnitude of the actual solvency ratios compared to the 10 per cent requirements in the 1919 and 1930 Acts. As for Basel II, no adjustment for "risk weighting", a cornerstone in that regulation, can be made. Since a large part of the bank loans had some sort of collateral, the solvency ratios shown above would definitely have been higher if calculated according to Basel II, unless there were substantial amounts of unsecured guarantees. There is no doubt that Basel II, which was intended to end all bank failures, was a substantial relaxation of capital requirements compared to the Danish 1919 and 1930 Banking Acts, and also compared to the 1974 Banking and Savings Banks Act, cfr. below.

It will be noticed that the solvency ratios for the collapsed banks, as measured before their collapse, did not differ significantly from those of the other banks. The reason is, of course, that the losses for the coming year are difficult to foresee, and that therefore insufficient provisions had been made.

Schedule 7.2   The 1919 and 1937 Savings Bank Acts Compared

Capital requirement:	Limitation on the distribution of profits unless reserves equalled 15 per cent of deposits. 1937: Tightened to 15 per cent of total debts.
Liquidity requirement:	Liquid assets (e.g. mortgage bonds) to equal minimum 5 per cent of deposits. 1937: tightened to 8 per cent.
Exposure limitations:	Maximum 10 per cent of assets to be placed in a single commercial bank. Detailed list of the type of collateral savings banks could accept. Anything else had to be prudent ("betryggende") and could not exceed seven times the guarantee capital and reserves. Blanco credits were scarcely permitted. 1937: Unchanged, except that "grandfathered" rights to discount bills of exchange were withdrawn.
Other:	A savings bank was to have minimum 25 guarantors, who could receive interest of maximum 1 per cent more than time deposits on their paid up guarantee capital, but who could otherwise not participate in the profits. Savings banks required to, and had the sole right, to call themselves savings banks and use the term "savings" in any public material. Savings banks expressly forbidden to do "banking business". Savings banks forbidden to invest in shares. The Inspector could close a savings bank if 5 per cent of the deposits was considered lost (repeated from the 1880 Act). By-laws of all savings banks to be approved by the Minister for Commerce. 1937: Essentially unchanged.

The Mortgage Institutions Act of 1936

The main changes were to bring the secondary institutions (the ("hypo-tekforeninger") under the same inspection as the first priority institutions, and to limit the maximum maturity of the mortgage bonds/loans to 60 years.

The Nationalbank Act of 1936

One of the conclusions to be drawn from the history of the 1920s is that the Nationalbank at this point of time certainly considered itself a "central bank" in the "modern" sense, although this expression was still not used. It was sole banker to the government – since shortly before WWI – it consulted the government on bank rescues, it was the guardian of the foreign exchange reserves, it had stopped competing with the commercial banks, and it was very close to being a lender of last resort to the commercial banks and savings banks. Its decisions were no longer taken from motives of commercial profitability. Its discount rate was set mainly from considerations relating to its foreign exchange holdings or the exchange rates. Its discount rate changes were increasingly followed by similar changes of the main interest rates of the commercial banks and savings banks.

After three years of negotiations between the Nationalbank and the government, the expiring 1908 Charter was replaced, in 1936, with a new Nationalbank Act. The main bones of contention had, of course, been the relative distribution of power between the Bank and the government.

Main points in the 1936 Act[7]

1. The legal status of the Nationalbank was changed from that of a privately owned joint stock company to a "self-owned" institution. The shareholders had their shares replaced with long-term 4 per cent amortizing bonds in twice the nominal amount of their shares. The last bonds were redeemed in 1961. It is not easy to see whether this was a "fair" deal.

2. The purpose of the Bank was stated to be to maintain a stable domestic monetary system and to facilitate and regulate money circulation and credit ("... at opretholde et stabilt indenlandsk pengevæsen og at lette og regulere pengeomsætning og kreditgivning", §1). The wording of this paragraph was essentially unchanged from the combination of §§3 and 5 of the 1818 Charter, repeated in 1908, and not much different from the spirit of the preamble to the 1736 Charter for the Kurantbank (cfr. Chapters 2 and 3).

3. The Bank's future profits would accrue to the state.

4. The Board of Representatives was supplemented with members of the Rigsdag, and a new Board of Directors was created, elected by various business organizations, trade unions, and the government. The chairman of the Board of Governors was to be appointed by the government, and the two other governors by the Board of Representatives. Neither

---

[7]Lov af 7. april 1936 om Danmarks Nationalbank.

the Board of Representatives nor the Board of Directors has any say on monetary policy. Both serve mainly as communications links, apart from their role in the appointment of two of the three members of the Board of Governors.

The Bank will, however, inform the government in advance of any discount rate changes, and it is generally assumed that the Bank cannot deny credits to the government, although this is not stated anywhere and has never been tested. Domestic state borrowings have been made through bond issues arranged by the Nationalbank, and foreign loans have been arranged by private banks as either syndicated loans or bond issues.

5. The name of the Bank was changed from Nationalbanken i Kjøbenhavn to Danmarks Nationalbank (the "Nationalbank").

The battle over the degree of government influence over the Nationalbank was mostly won by the Bank. From a purely formal point of view, the Bank has nearly full freedom of action. The nature and degree of co-operation with the government will, of course, to some extent depend on the personalities in question, but ultimately the government can try to have the 1936 Act changed. The governors remain in office until they reach retirement age (or retire voluntarily).

Danmarks Nationalbank remains the most independent central bank in the Nordic region, and is formally almost as independent as the Deutche Bundesbank.

7.2.3   A profile of the capital market, 1920–1940

One inevitable effect of the ravages of the 1920s was that depositors shifted their deposits to the savings banks. Since the savings banks were more restricted in their lending policies than banks, financial intermediation, and the growth of the financial sector slowed, probably with negative effects on real economic growth – just as it has been argued during the 2008–2010 financial crisis that the reduced lending capacity of the banking sector intensified the recession and delayed the recovery.

Table 7.2 shows that in the whole of the inter-war period, the relative size of the financial sector was smaller than in the 1910–1915 period, cfr. Chapter 3. The many bank failures of the 1920s caused the banking sector to shrink considerably both relatively and absolutely.

The savings banks had difficulty finding lending opportunities for their increased deposits and placed them mostly in mortgage bonds or government bonds.

The dominating role of the mortgage institutions is clearly seen.

In Table 7.2 no figures are shown for insurance companies, because they did not act as direct lenders in any significant way. They invested in mortgage bonds and in real estate as owners, rarely as lenders.

Table 7.2   Relative Composition and Growth of the Credit Stock, 1918–1940

	Commercial banks	Savings banks	Mortgage institutions	Insurance companies	Total	Total, million DKK	Index	Total, in % of GDP
	In % of total credit stock							
1918	49	16	35	–	100	6,319	100	133
1920	52	16	31	–	99	7,092	112	96
1924	37	19	44	–	100	7,663	121	117
1930	26	21	53	–	100	8,435	133	148
1936	23	20	56	–	99	9,390	149	140
1940	23	18	58	–	99	9,788	155	114
	In % of GDP							
1918	65	22	46		133	4,766	100	133
1920	50	16	30		96	7,396	155	96
1924	43	23	51		117	6,566	138	117
1930	38	31	79		148	5,705	120	148
1936	34	27	79		140	6,690	140	140
1940	26	21	66		113	8,620	181	113

Sources: GDP: Danmarks Statistik, Nationalregnskabsstatistik (Statistisk Årbog).
Banks: 1918–1920: Danmarks Statistik (1969), *Kreditmarkedsstatistik*, and, 1921–1940: Statistisk Årbog.
Savings banks: E. Hoffmeyer (1960) *Strukturændringer på penge og kapitalmarkedet*, (Sparevirke) p. 159.
Mortgage institutions: Danmarks Statistik (1969) *Kreditmarkedsstatistik*.

In spite of the upheavals in the banking sector, the relative market shares of the "Big Three" remained surprisingly stable, even if the Copenhagen Handelsbank gained a bit of market share at the expense of the Landmand-bank, cfr. Table 7.3:

Table 7.3   Market Shares of the "Big Three", 1920–1940, by Total Assets

	1920	1924	1930	1940
Privatbanken, million DKK	577	548	337	505
% of total	11%	15%	11%	14%
Landmandsbanken, million DKK	1,483	1,008	706	813
% of total	27%	27%	23%	22%
Handelsbanken, million DKK	736	652	533	638
% of total	14%	17%	18%	17%
"Big Three", million DKK	2,756	2,208	1,576	1,956
% of total	51%	59%	52%	52%
Total, million DKK	5,443	3,751	3,032	3,730
Number of banks	196	186	180	162

Source: Danmarks Statistik: *Statistisk Årbog*, relevant years.

7.3   An interlude, 1945–1985

7.3.1   The problems: Perennial foreign exchange shortage

Between 1945 and the mid-1980s, the chronic foreign exchange shortage was the overriding consideration behind most aspects of economic policy and capital market regulations. Inevitably, this had consequences for the structure and workings of the capital market and for the financing of private enterprise.

Until the second half of the 1950s, the balance of payments had to be kept in equilibrium, because borrowing abroad was not an option. This was partly because dollars were generally in short supply, and partly because the Danish government had defaulted on some earlier dollar loans. Denmark just did not have the foreign exchange required to service these loans in the early 1950s.[8] Until this was regularized in 1955, foreign capital markets were closed to Denmark, to the extent they existed at all.

From the late 1950s onwards, it was the other way round. Dollar shortage had turned into dollar glut, the "euro-dollar" market had been created, and Denmark took full advantage of the ample borrowing opportunities, running balance-of-payments deficits every single year until 1987 (except 1963). As a result, Denmark's net foreign debt rose from about 10 per cent of GDP in the late 1960s to 40 per cent in the mid-1980s.

The oil price hikes in 1973 and 1979 did not make life easier for Denmark, but fiscal policies were lax most of the time, and it fell on the Nationalbank to find ways to secure the necessary inflow of capital from abroad.

7.3.2   Responses and actions: Restrictions and reforms

The problems were dealt with in several ways:

First, strict controls on the use of the scarce foreign exchange reserves were maintained until the second half of the 1980s. Most types of cross border capital movements required permissions from the Nationalbank, whose permission policy was quite restrictive, except in respect of direct investments.

Second, the National Bank tried to curb the growth of lending by the financial institutions. It recommended that banks, savings banks, and mortgage institutions restricted their lendings for private consumption purposes and introduced quantitative measures when recommendations proved ineffective. The quantitative steps included forced deposits by banks and savings banks in low interest Nationalbank accounts (1965–1970), restrictions on bond issues by the mortgage institutions (the "bond-rationing", 1965–1968), and the ceiling imposed on DKK lendings by banks and savings banks, the most

---

[8]Cfr. E. Hoffmeyer (1968) *Perioden 1931–1960* in Sv. A. Hansen et al., *Dansk Penge-historie*, I–III (Danmarks Nationalbank), bd. II, p. 280.

long-lasting of all these measures.[9] The ceiling lasted from 1970 to 1980, and would be adjusted upwards annually by a percentage slightly smaller than the nominal growth rate of GDP. Apart from curbing the borrowings by households for consumption purposes, the ceiling had the intended effect of forcing companies to borrow in foreign currencies, i.e. helping the capital inflow. These foreign exchange loans were arranged and guaranteed by the larger banks, and supplied by foreign banks, which had no direct contact to the ultimate borrowers, except in the case of a dozen of the very largest companies.

This mechanism had certain negative side-effects, which were deeply resented in commercial and industrial circles at the time. The problem was that the continuous slide in the exchange rate of the DKK implied unpredictable and potentially large exchange rate losses on the foreign currency borrowings. By 1980, the DKK had lost roughly half of its 1960 value against the DEM and the CHF, the two most widely used currencies. On the other hand, interest costs were lower in these currencies than in DKK. Intended as a short-term, temporary system, it lasted from 1970 to 1980.

These measures resembled those used in Norway and Sweden, but in Denmark they were not nearly as rigorous and did not last as long as in the other Nordic countries.

The accelerating internationalization of the Danish banking system must be considered among the beneficial side-effects. The intermediation of the foreign exchange loans was a highly lucrative business for the handful of banks, which had the necessary network of foreign correspondents. It also meant that Danish banks set up offices abroad in order to bypass the foreign banks, and that foreign banks set up branches in Copenhagen in order to bypass the Danish banks. In 1974, Denmark opened up for foreign banks (branches, not subsidiaries), the first Nordic country to do so. In the early 1980s, Copenhagen boasted the presence of 6–8 foreign banks, including four Americans.

In the meantime, the managers of the largest savings banks had become bored by being just savings banks, leaving the lucrative business to the commercial banks. Also, the distinction between savings banks and commercial banks had always been sharper in Denmark than in the three other Nordic countries. So, in the early 1970s, the savings banks started lobbying for a change in the Savings Banks Act.[10]

---

[9]For a description of the details of these measures and the tricky negotiations between the National Bank and the government, and between the National Bank and the banks, savings banks, and the mortgage institutions, see R. Mikkelsen (1993) *Dansk Penge-historie 1960–1990* (Danmarks Nationalbank) pp. 73–170.

The trick was to put sufficient pressure on the financial institutions without having to ask the government for legislation, which would have been anathema for both the Nationalbank and the private financial institutions.

[10]For an analysis of the transformation of the savings banks, see professor P.H. Hansen (2001) *Da sparekasserne mistede deres uskyld* (Odense Universitetsforlag).

The Banking and Savings Bank Act of 1974

The amendments made in 1956 and 1959 to the respective 1930 and 1937 Acts on banks and savings banks were minor. Capital requirements were unchanged, but liquidity requirements for savings banks had been changed to conform to those for banks. The 1974 Act, on the other hand, was a revolution.

The revolution brought about by the 1974 Bank and Savings Banks Act can be summarized as follows:

1. For the first time the legislation on banks and savings banks was combined in a single Act, and the distinction between "banking business" – hitherto forbidden to savings banks – and "savings banks business" was scrapped. The definition of banks and savings banks was stated as "Banks are defined as companies, and savings banks as selfowned institutions, which conduct bank and savings banks business."[11] The definition of "banking and savings bank business" was simplified to read: "Bank and savings bank business is defined as the undertaking of activities in connection with the turnover of money, instruments of credit, and securities, and services in that connection."[12] The previous definition of banking business contained more than twice as many words.

   Henceforth, the difference between banks and savings banks was solely one of ownership and governance.

   In this connection, savings banks were also made subject to normal company taxation, a point understandably insisted upon by the banks. Savings banks had now been changed from non-profit, benevolent tax-free institutions into profit-maximizing business organizations. Still, the guarantors of a savings bank could only receive interest on their paid-up guarantee capital at a rate to be approved by the now combined Bank and Savings Bank Inspectorate.

2. The solvency ratio was changed to 8 per cent of total debts and guarantee obligations. For banks, this was a reduction (from 10 per cent), but for the savings banks it was a steep increase.

3. The liquidity requirements were slightly reworded, which probably meant a tightening in most cases: Cash to be at least 15 per cent of deposits at less than one month's notice, and liquid assets to be at least 10 per cent of the bank's/savings bank's total debt and guarantee obligations.

---

[11]"Ved banker forstås aktieselskaber, ved sparekasser selvejende institutioner, der driver bank- og sparekassevirksomhed." Lov om banker og sparekasser af 2. april 1974, §1, stk. 2.

[12]"Ved bank-og sparekassevirksomhed forstås varetagelse af funktioner i forbindelse med omsætning af penge, kreditmidler og værdipapirer og dermed forbundne serviceydelser." Lov om banker og sparekasser af 2. april 1974, §1, stk. 3.

4. It was made possible for banks and savings banks to merge and to transform themselves into joint stock banks. The savings banks were generally slow to take advantage of these opportunities.
5. Foreign banks were allowed to establish branches in Denmark – but not subsidiaries.

SDS and Bikuben, the two largest savings banks, were quick to exploit the new opportunities and quickly transformed themselves into banks with active trading of foreign exchange and securities. This eventually meant the death of Fællesbanken A/S, the commercial bank set up jointly by the savings banks.

The bond market and the reforms of the mortgage institutions, 1958–1985

Uncertain about the development of property values in the aftermath of WWII, the mortgage institutions were very cautious in their property valuations until the late 1950s. This made the government, reluctantly, step in with supplementary property financing at subsidized interest rates. Between 1948 and 1958, 90 per cent of all Danish residential construction was partially financed with government loans.

By the end of the 1950s, the government and the Nationalbank decided that this mechanism had to end. Therefore, in 1959–1960 four new third mortgage institutions were created by law and based on capital supplied, in different combinations for each institution, by the Nationalbank, private banks and savings banks, and various business organizations. Three of these institutions were for residential construction in various regions, and the fourth was for agriculture. They differed fundamentally from the traditional mortgage institutions by not being associations of borrowers, but "self-owned" institutions, and by not having joint liability among the borrowers. Otherwise, they operated just like the other institutions, i.e. the cash flows on their bonds matched precisely the cash flow from their loans.

This brought the total number of mortgage institutions close to 30.

Also in the late 1950s, the idea had come up that medium-term finance was in short supply for small- and medium-sized businesses in manufacturing industries. A "Macmillan Gap" was perceived, particularly by the National Bank, to exist also in Denmark.[13] The commercial banks were less

---

[13]The thinking in the Nationalbank on this subject seems to have been influenced by the contemporary and similar debate in the UK. The problem had first been raised in the report of the Macmillan Committee, London 1929–1931, identifying the "Macmillan Gap" as the perceived lack of access to medium- and long-term capital by companies not big enough to tap the market for stocks or corporate bonds. The issue was raised again by the Committee on the Working of the Monetary System, the "Radcliffe Committee", 1957–1959: "While the larger companies are well catered for, the smaller companies are less happily situated." (p. 81). At least one practical result of the Radcliffe Committee was the creation by the government of the Finance for Industry, intended to bridge the perceived "Macmillan Gap".

convinced, but accepted the creation in 1958 of Finannsieringsinstituttet for Industri og Håndværk A/S (FIH), when a special legislation allowed bank managers to join its board of directors.

Its purpose was to supply 5–8 years fixed interest finance to minor industrial companies secured by mortgages over their plant and equipment, and funded by short- and medium-term bonds. It was created as a joint stock company, with share capital supplied by the Nationalbank, the private banks and savings banks, and a few business organizations. For many years it remained a very small company, because the bank managers sitting on its board prevented it from doing business they thought their respective banks could do themselves.[14] It had no difficulty selling its bonds, partly because the volume was small, and partly because it was, originally, the only issuer of short- and medium-term bonds. Later, it broadened its range of services to include most types of commercial banking activities, except retail banking.

In 1990, the Danish owners sold the FIH (now FIH Erhvervsbank A/S) to Swedbank. Swedbank sold it to the Icelandic Kaupthing Bank in 2005, from which it was later taken over by the Icelandic government.

Finally, the Ship Credit Fund was formed in 1961 as a "self-owned" institution offering shipping finance on internationally agreed (subsidized) conditions. The Nationalbank, the private banks, and certain business organizations supplied the capital. In 2005 the Ship Credit Fund was transformed into a limited liability company, Dansk Skibskredit A/S, with the Nationalbank as its largest shareholder (19 per cent). The shares have been freely transferable since July, 2010.

Neither the legislation nor the by-laws of any of the six institutions created in 1958–1961 (nor for the existing mortgage institutions) specified any particular solvency or liquidity ratios to be maintained. These matters were considered subjects for ordinary management decisions. Funded by bonds matching their underlying lending, their cash flows are automatically matched, and their capital and liquidity requirements consequently minimal. Since the above-mentioned case in the early 1930s, the loss history of the mortgage institutions has not caused serious problems.

Since the above-mentioned "bond-rationing" (1965–1968) was only a temporary measure, two committees were set up to propose more long-term solutions and structural improvements to the bond market and its institutional framework. Both committees reported in 1969,[15] which resulted in the new Mortgage Institutions Act of 1970.[16]

---

[14]The first 20 years of FIH have been described by E. Mollerup, FIH's first general manager, in "Finansieringsinstituttet for Industri og Håndværk A/S, 1958/78".
[15]Betænkning nr. 52, 1969/70, afgivet af Realkreditkommissionen af 1966, and Betænkning nr. 541: "Redegørelse fra udvalget vedrørende obligationsmarkedets forhold", November 1969.
[16]Lov om realkreditinstitutter af 10. juni, 1970.

The main points were:

1. Reduced maturities (down from 60 to 30 years for single family houses, ten years for summer houses, etc);
2. Reduced maximum percentages of property values acceptable as collateral depending on type of property according to a detailed schedule (maximum 80 per cent of single family homes);
3. Scrapping of the distinction between first, second, and third priority mortgage institutions;
4. The concept of a solvency ratio was introduced. For the old institutions enjoying joint liability among the borrowers, a solvency ratio of 2.5 per cent of the remaining debts/obligations was introduced. For the 1959 institutions, which did not have joint liability, 5 per cent was stipulated;
5. The 1970 Act provided for mergers of the institutions. The Act did not force anybody to merge, but mergers had been recommended by the commission reports of 1969, and behind the scenes a lot of arms were twisted to achieve the final result. In the end, the nearly 30 institutions were reduced to four residential institutions, and five specialized institutions (one for agriculture, one for shipping, two for industrial properties, and one for municipal properties);
6. No new mortgage institutions could be formed.

Institutional changes, however, rarely change underlying problems. The imbalances in the Danish economy continued, leading to the appearance of government bonds in massive volumes from the mid-1970s onwards.

7.4　Towards new horizons, 1985–2010

7.4.1　Problems solved? – Or new challenges?

The mini-crisis of 1985–1993

By the mid-1980s, the problems of the 1979 oil price hike had faded away, and optimism permeated all aspects of economic activity. The DKK had been stabilized. Property and stock prices soared.

Small banks wanting to become big had financed a lot of investors acting in the firm belief that asset prices would keep going up. In some cases, banks had speculated in the markets for their own accounts. In all of these respects, Denmark in the second half of the 1980s was not much different from the years 1900–1908, the early 1920s, the early 1970s, or 2005–2008, or from what happened simultaneously in other countries. In some cases, savings banks, now having the formal freedom to act like banks, ventured into types of business of which they had little or no experience.

In any case, 47 Danish banks and savings banks (out of a total of approximately 225) were closed involuntarily between 1985 and 1994, more than in all of the previous 40 years combined. Seven of them went bankrupt.

Compared to the other Nordic countries, however, the Danish problems were small. The failures were spread over a longer period, and all the failures happened to small institutions, none of which had a market share exceeding 1 per cent by total assets.[17] The combined assets of the worst-hit eight banks were less than 2 per cent of the total assets of all banks and savings banks.[18]

Between 1980 and 1993, the lendings by all banks and savings banks were generally smaller than their deposits (80–90 per cent).[19] This implied less "systemic" risk than elsewhere and less than 15–17 years later, when this ratio had generally increased to more than 100 per cent. For these reasons, the Danish banking "crisis" of this period was not nearly as severe as that of the 1920s and those of the other Nordic countries in the early 1990s.

In nearly all cases, failed banks were absorbed by larger banks and/or wound up without the use of any taxpayer money, although the National-bank did step in with guarantees in a few cases, and in one case with a loan and the formation of a "bad bank", which was wound up over the following 10–12 years. The general public did not notice very much.

For the mortgage institutions, the recession of the early 1990s caused unusually large losses. As a result, they discarded the original and funda-mental principle of automatic borrowing rights. They now started the prac-tice of supplementing valuations of the collateral with evaluations of the debt servicing capacity of prospective borrowers. Since 1992, loan applications could be declined regardless of the valuation of the collateral.

The banking crisis of 2007–2009

In July, 2008, it became clear that the crystal balls available to bank super-visors are not necessarily clearer than those available to bank managers or external analysts, but also that concentration of risk is the absolutely dead-liest of all bank poisons.

Between July, 2008, and May, 2010, 60[20] of Denmark's approximately 100 banks and savings banks were subjected to various degrees and variations of reconstructions, recapitalizations, forced mergers, closures, or bankrupt-cies. A handful of banks were beyond rescue and were wound up in bank-ruptcy. The predominant reason for the problems were too big exposures to limited numbers of real estate development projects.

---

[17]Cfr. Økonomiministeriet (1995) *Redning af Pengeinsitutter siden 1984*, pp. 24–5. This investigation by the Ministry of Economic Affairs and the Banking Inspectorate also concluded that the accounts of the failed or "sick" banks did not differ systematic-ally from those of other banks: "Det konkluderes, at de ophørte institutters regnskab-sudvikling ikke systematisk har afveget fra udviklingen i de øvrige pengeinstitutter." p. 23.
[18]Cfr. Økonomiministeriet (1994) *Den Danske Pengeinstitutsektor*, p. 41.
[19]Cfr. Økonomiministeriet (1994) *Den Danske Pengeinstitutsektor*, p. 50.
[20]According to Finansiel Stabilitet, the government owned bank rescue vehicle.

What made the 2007–2009 crisis different from all the previous Danish "crises" was that previously there was little inter-bank lending and borrowing, but Danish banks had since the 1990s increasingly expanded on the basis of borrowings from other, mostly foreign, banks. In 2008, the Danish banking sector was estimated to have borrowed a total of some DKK 500–600 billion (EUR 70–80 billion) in the international inter-bank market. The higher gearing resulting from this practice had become possible by the lower capital requirements introduced by the authorities (Basel I and II). The higher dependence on inter-bank borrowings turned out to be a big problem when the international inter-bank market broke down following the collapses of first a number of UK banks (Northern Rock, RBS, Lloyds, etc) and then Lehman Brothers. Many Danish banks, quite regardless of their financial health, could not get their inter-bank loans prolonged as they would normally have been able to do. "Systemic risk" came into full action.

Thus, some of the bank failures can be ascribed to mismanagement – imprudent concentration of risk and poor credit handling (in at least one case close to criminal actions) – while others were caused mostly by the bad luck of the collapsed inter-bank market triggered by the collapse of a number of foreign banks. The tricky question is, of course, how much reliance on the inter-bank market constitutes "over-reliance". Retail deposits may also prove fickle, as demonstrated by Northern Rock and numerous other examples in the past. The latest "blip" on the inter-bank market since its re-emergence in the late 1950s, was caused by the collapse of the Herstatt Bank in 1974, and that "blip" lasted only a few weeks. There was not much reason in the early 21st century to doubt the reliability of the inter-bank market as a stable source of funding for reasonably well-managed banks.

Mortgage institutions, not being in the business of financing project developments, and not being in any way dependent on bank borrowings, were not much affected by the bursting of the "bubble" and the breakdown of the inter-bank market. They were, however, not entirely unaffected by the ensuing recession and rising unemployment.

7.4.2   Responses and actions: Mergers and rescues

The mergers

Between 1960 and 1992, the number of banks in Denmark was reduced from ca. 160 to about 70, and the number of savings banks dropped from nearly 500 to about 50. The reduction came about both through the taking over of small institutions by larger ones, and by the merger of small provincial institutions into larger regional banks or savings banks. In this process institutions like Jyske Bank, Midtbank, Sydbank, Den Danske Provinsbank, SDS, and Sparbank Nord, etc. were created.

Towards the end of the 1980s, it had become increasingly clear to the leading Danish banks that they were too small to service their largest customers professionally on a global basis, and that big structural changes would be to their advantage. Taking over more small banks would not solve any problems.

Consequently, Den Danske Bank of 1871 and the Copenhagen Handelsbank, the arch rivals, announced that they would merge with effect as from January 1, 1990, under the name of Danske Bank. It was soon joined by Den Danske Provinsbank, in which Danske Bank already had a large stake. Thus challenged, Privatbanken, Andelsbanken and SDS declared, a few weeks later, their decision to merge under the name of Unibank, also as from January 1, 1990.

These mergers among the biggest Danish banks were followed up in 1999–2000 with further big mergers. First, Danske Bank took over BG Bank, the result of an earlier merger of Bikuben, then the largest savings bank, with the privatized postal giro bank. Next, Realkredit Danmark, the largest and second oldest of the mortgage institutions, was merged into Danske Bank, thereby doubling its consolidated balance sheet.

Secondly, Unibank merged with Nordea, the result of the merger of the Finnish Merita Bank with the Swedish Nordbank. In 2001, Nordea was joined by Crisitiania Bank og Kreditkasse. Thereby, Nordea became the largest bank in the Nordic region, and the first truly pan-Nordic bank, although Danske Bank also has substantial Nordic operations, following its acquisitions of Östgöta Enskilda Bank (Sweden, 1997), Focus Bank (Norway, 1999), and Sampo Bank (Finland, 2006).

Nykredit A/S is the result of a 1984 merger of two of the four general mortgage institutions which came out of the 1970 reform. Following the take-over of Realkredit Danmark by Danske Bank in 1991, Nykredit A/S and BRF-kredit A/S are the only surviving independent mortgage institutions for residential property.

There can be no doubt that the professionalism, efficiency, and variety of services available from the Danish capital market institutions have all been enhanced by these mergers. It is less clear what the resulting concentration into a system with two absolutely dominating banks, only two independent residential mortgage institutions, and still about 90[21] minor and absolutely tiny institutions has done to competition in the fields of corporate and retail banking, and mortgage finance.

---

[21]This number includes about 30 tiny co-operative "banks" (andelskasser) with combined assets less than one-third of 1 per cent of the total.

The Capital Adequacy Directive of 1989,[22] and the Financial Institutions Act of 2003[23]

The increasing efforts of the EU to create a "level playing field" for financial institutions in the context of the Internal Market, as well as the Basel I and Basel II agreements, have had very direct and severe implications for the Danish capital market, in some respects positive, in others negative.

For *Danish banks and savings banks*, the main effect of Basel I and the 1989 Capital Adequacy Directive was to lower the prevailing solvency ratios (SEA's translation): "The new capital adequacy rules implied a significant relaxation of the regulatory capital requirements of the institutions, since the risk-weighted assets were about 30 per cent lower than the balance sheets."[24] The main reasons were, first, that the 8 per cent capital ratio introduced in 1974 was higher than in most countries, and, second, that the capital is measured on a group consolidated basis, so that Danske Bank's and Nordea's capital ratios are benefitting from property collateral of their respective mortgage finance subsidiaries, although in a hypothetical break-up situation that collateral would not be available to the bank creditors.

For many other countries, Basel I was a tightening. Basel II made no substantial changes, but just introduced certain cumbersome calculations, cfr. Chapter 11.

For the Danish mortgage institutions, the EU Capital Adequacy Directive of 1989 was a major blow.

As from 1989, Danish mortgage associations were to be considered "banks", although in contrast to British building societies, they have never taken deposits or offered current accounts, overdraft facilities, etc. Also, the EU directive did not accept the joint liability of the borrowers as "capital". Danish mortgage bonds issued after 1989 were, therefore, supplied with the stipulation that the joint liability could be abolished at the discretion of the issuer at any point of time. When new mortgage institutions were created, they did not have joint liability. Consequently, the old institutions announced that for bonds issued after 1989, the joint liability would no longer apply. Therefore, there are practically no more bonds in circulation with joint liability among the borrowers.

---

[22]The directive was transformed into Danish law by the Lov nr. 841 af 20. dec. 1989 ("Realkreditloven af 1989"), which also comprised a number of other stipulations previously embodied in separate laws, including the law on index loans, etc. The 1989 Act also stipulated that any future mortgage institutions should be organized as joint stock companies.

[23]Lov nr. 453 om finansiel virksomhed af 10. juni 2003.

[24]"De nye kapitaldækningsregler indebar en væsentlig lempelse af de lovfastsatte kapitalkrav til institutterne, idet de risikovægtede aktiver var omkring 30 pct. mindre end balancen." Økonomiministeriet: "Den Danske Pengeinsitutsektor" (1994), p. 40.

The 1989 Mortgage Institutions Act also provided that new mortgage institutions were to be established as joint stock companies. Existing institutions could choose to transform themselves, but did not have to. What was formerly private associations of borrowers now became taxable, profit maximizing companies, a transformation also experienced by the savings banks.

The Financial Institutions Act passed in 2003[25] implied a number of changes mainly harmonizing Danish legislation with the newest EU regulations in respect of all types of financial institutions. For banks and savings banks the changes were minor.

For mortgage institutions, one of the major changes is that foreign credit institutions can obtain permission to issue mortgage bonds in Denmark, provided their main activity is to offer mortgage loans funded with bond issues, and provided their lendings and bond issues satisfy the principle of balancing exactly the cash flows from their bonds and their lendings, as the Danish institutions have done since 1850.

Another change was the introduction of the "SDO"s ("særligt dækkede obligatrioner", or "specially covered bonds"), which are mortgage bonds with particularly good collateral. In case property values drop below certain thresholds, the bond-issuer will have to provide additional security for its bonds.

Otherwise, the traditionally rather staid mortgage world had been going through a good deal of "product development" since the early 1980s.

The first novelty was the index bonds introduced in 1982. They never became very popular, because inflations rates soon after receded quickly. In the 1990s, loans at variable interest rates began to spread. They were mortgage loans based on bonds with one, three, or five years maturity, so that the borrower could have the interest re-fixed annually, or every three or five years.

Finally, the 2003 legislation provided for mortgage loans with no amortization for ten years. After ten years, the lender would decide to what extent installments would have to be made for the remaining 20 years, assuming the original loan was for 30 years.

From a capital market point-of-view, this product development has been a great leap forward. It has increased the range of choices for borrowers as well as for investors.

It has, however, also been argued that the low-interest variable loans and the non-amortizing loans helped boost the 2005–2007 property bubble, but property bubbles have occurred before also without any newfangled financing mechanisms.

---

[25]Lov nr. 454 af 10. juni 2003 om realkreditlån og realkreditobligationer m.v.

The bank support and rescues 2008–2010

As the number of problem banks increased during 2007–2009, cfr. above, a framework for handling them was created.

The framework was formed in two steps:

1. "Bankpakke I" ("Bank Package I")
This "Package" was enacted in October, 2008,[26] as a direct consequence of the freezing of the inter-bank market following the collapse of Lehman Brothers. The main elements of this "package" was:

A: For a period of two years (i.e. until September 30, 2010), an unconditional and unlimited state guarantee was issued to secure that all simple claims against "banks" would be settled in full and on time (§1). Under a 2009 amendment, banks could apply for a three-year phased-out extension of this guarantee in respect of senior unsecured debts (other than retail deposits on individually negotiated terms and conditions).

B: The guarantee covered "monetary institutions" ("pengeinstitutter") which have applied for membership of "Det Private Beredskab til Afvikling af Nødlidende Banker, Sparekasser og Andelskasser" ("Det Private Bered-skab"), which had been formed already in 2007 in anticipation of future problems. Virtually all members of the Finansråd (the Bankers' Association) had applied for membership.

C: Any support under this arrangement would come from "Finansiel Stabilitet A/S", a state-owned company created for that purpose.

The Finansiel Stabilitet A/S is authorized to arrange for take-overs of distressed banks by other banks and to support such take-overs with injections of share capital.

Apart from a symbolic share capital paid in by the state, this company is funded primarily by two annual contributions of DKK 7.5 billion each from the members of the Private Beredskab, and if this does not suffice, from up to DKK 20 billion in further contributions from the Private Bered-skab, which collects this money from its members in proportion to their size. Thus, the private banking sector will bear the first DKK 35 billion cost of the rescue operation. Any cost above DKK 35 billion will be covered by the state. By the summer of 2010, it was clear that the DKK 20 billion would not be needed.

Any profits made by the Finansiel Stabilitet A/S will accrue to the state.

By the summer of 2010, it looks as if the Finansiel Stabilitet will make a handsome net profit.[27] The net profits for the two-year period expired in

---

[26]Lov nr 1003 af 10. okt. 2008 om finansiel stabilitet (the "Financial Stability Act").
[27]In the spring of 2010, opposition politicians (social democrats) have already made proposals for the spending of that money.

October, 2010 could be in the range of DKK 3–4 billion, but the final result will depend on how the outstanding loans, guarantees, and investments will be unwound in the future. The Finansiel Stabilitit A/S has taken owner-ship stakes in roughly 60 banks and savings banks, a handful of which have been fully taken over as bankrupt.

2. "Bankpakke II" ("Bank Package II")
The October 2008 "Bank Package I" addressed the liquidity crunch resulting from the freezing of the inter-bank market, but it did not address the solvency problem resulting from the deepening of the recession, or from bad credit decisions. Therefore, a new bank rescue package was enacted in early 2009.[28]
    The main elements in the "Bank Package II" were:

A: The creation by the state of a facility whereby the state (the Ministry of Economic and Commercial Affairs) can supply "hybrid core capital" ("hybrid kernekapital") up to a total amount of DKK 100 billion to credit institutions and/or underwrite new issues of share capital or "hybrid core capital" by credit institutions.
    "Hybrid core capital" is defined as "perpetual subordinated loan capital" ("… ansvarligt lån uden udløbsdato …") but the conditions will usually imply incentives for repayment as early as prudently possible, but earliest after three years. It was always made clear that it was not the government's intention to become a long-term bank owner, let alone bank manager (in contrast to Norway and, partly, Sweden).
    The conditions will be negotiated in each individual case. Interest will be somewhere between 9 and 12 per cent p.a., depending on the solvency ratio of the borrower. In principle, the capital could be con-verted into common stock, if both parties agree to it.
B: The facility was available only in 2009, and to all types of credit institu-tions (including mortgage institutions, in contrast to "Package I"). In addition, guarantees can be issued in respect of senior debt of monetary institutions which satisfy general solvency requirements.

Recipients are subject to certain dividend restrictions and limitations on the remuneration of top managers.
    The DKK 100 billion offered under "Bankpakke II" would have increased the total core capital of the credit institutions by roughly 22 per cent if fully utilized.[29] Approximately 65 per cent of the facility was committed when the curtain fell for new applications at end 2009.

---

[28]Lov nr. 67 af 3. feb. 2009 om statsligt kapitalindskud i kreditinsitutter.
[29]Cfr. the comments to the "Forslag til lov om statsligt kapitalindskud i kredit-institutter af 21. jan, 2009", the proposal for the capital injection by the state, which was passed by the Folketing unchanged two weeks later.

The end result of the bank rescue packages will probably be a good profit to the state. As indicated above, the DKK 15 billion collected from the banks and savings banks will probably turn out to be substantially more than what has been spent on the rescue or unwinding of the handful of collapsed banks and savings banks, and the interest (10–12 per cent p.a.) received on capital invested under "Package II" will constitute a nice net income. The final outcome will, however, depend on the future unwinding of the ca. DKK 65 billion guarantees or invested hybrid capital over the coming years.

The Danish banking crisis of 2007–2009, like the 1990–1992 "minicrisis", was not nearly as deep as the 1988–1993 crisis in the three other Nordic countries.

7.5   A profile of the capital market, 1950–2009

The result of 60 years of ever changing economic circumstances is reflected in Table 7.4. The table shows that, just like in the years following the end of WWI, the total stock of credits in the organized capital market had dropped considerably compared to the pre-war era, and to a level lower than the GNP (cfr. Table 7.2). However, the pre-war credit stock was re-established much faster after WWI than after WWII. The main reason was probably the very low growth rate of GDP in the 1950s compared to the 1920s, and the continued isolation of the Danish economy from the rest of the world necessitated by the shortage of foreign exchange and foreign borrowing opportunities.

7.6   The stock exchange

The framework

When Denmark's first Stock Exchange Act was passed in 1919 it was the biggest change since the Broker Decree of December 22, 1808 (cfr. Chapter 3), which it replaced (§12).

The main points of the 1919 Act[30] were:

§§1–2: Stock exchange activity required an approval from the minister of commerce, and if such activity took place in Copenhagen, it should be done in the Stock Exchange Building, and such exchange should have a board of directors with a chairman appointed by the said minister.

The exchange could accept any type of financial asset for daily quotation, which, in the opinion of the directors, would be of interest to the

---

[30]Lov Nr. 540 af 4. Okt., 1919 om Afholdelse af Fondsbørs.

Table 7.4 Relative Composition and Growth of the Credit Stock, 1950–2007, Selected Years

	Commercial banks	Savings banks	Mortgage institutions	Govern. bonds	Total	Total, billion DKK	Total, in per cent of GDP
	Per cent of total credit stock						
1950	23	15	37	25	100	20.0	91
1957	28	16	39	17	100	27.1	77
1963	28	15	49	8	100	51.7	88
1969	29	12	56	3	100	114.4	107
1978	21	8	61	10	100	436.5	141
1988		36	43	21	100	1,672.2	228
1998		34	45	22	101	2,745.1	236
2004		37	47	16	100	4,210.8	249
2007		47	46	8	101	6,198.0	367
	Per cent of GNP						
1950	21	13	34	23	91		91
1957	21	13	30	13	77		77
1963	24	14	43	7	88		88
1969	31	13	60	3	107		107
1978	30	11	85	15	141		141
1988		81	99	48	228		228
1998		79	105	52	236		236
2004		108	134	46	249		249
2007		171	168	28	367		367

Sources: Danmarks Statistik: *Statistisk Årbog*, relevant years.

Notes:
1. Bonds are recorded at face values. Market values would be 5–10 per cent lower.
2. Mortgage bonds include bonds issued by FIH, Kommunekreditforeningen (municipality bonds), and the Skibskreditfond. Collectively, these bonds account for approximately 10 per cent of the total amount shown.

Comments:
1. The dominating position of the mortgage institutions is clearly seen.
2. The government bonds circulating in the 1950s were older bonds issued in a distant past for more or less specific purposes unlike the bonds issued in large volumes between the second half of the 1970s and the mid-1980s, which were issued to finance of government deficits generally. They were normally long-term fixed interest bonds.
3. The credit stock/GNP ratio in 2005–2007 was probably among the highest in the world. This can partly be explained by Danske Bank's acquisition of other banks in Sweden, Norway, Ireland, and Finland, which may have accounted for approximately one-third of Danske Bank's outstanding credits in 2007, or some 10 per cent of the figure shown for commercial banks. Also, the property "bubble" of 2004–2008 and the widespread mortgaging of properties help explain the substantial increase in circulating mortgage bonds. The Danish bond market has for many years ranked among the five largest in the world. In other countries, much similar debt is represented by private mortgage deeds in formats not necessarily included in compilations or the "organized capital markets".
    Approximately 30 per cent of the government bonds and 10 per cent of the mortgage bonds were held abroad in 2007, but such holdings are, in principle, subject to substantial short-term changes.
4. Insurance companies and pension funds are conspicuously absent from Table 7.4. The reason is that their role as direct lenders is minimal, totalling less than 1 per cent of the total credit stock. Their assets mainly consist of bonds and real estate.

general public ("... saadanne Værdipapirer, om hvis Værdi i Handel og Vandel det er af Interesse for Offentligheden at være underrettet ... Afgørelse om ... Optagelse paa eller Udslettelse af Kurslisten træffes af Fondsbørsens Bestyrelse ...").

§3:   Only members of the Stock Exchange could make bids and offers on the exchange. Membership was restricted by certain criteria regarding net worth and experience, and the deposit of DKK 50,000. Authorizations would be given by the minister upon recommendation by the board of directors of the exchange, including – automatically – brokers authorized according to the 1808 Decree, provided they had made the required deposit.

§11:   A Stock Exchange Commissioner was appointed to ensure that all stock exchange activity was conducted appropriately.

No doubt, the Copenhagen Stock Exchange fulfilled the criteria for a stock exchange if not since 1808, then at least since 1876 (cfr. Chapter 3). Membership was regulated, limitations on what could be traded had been introduced, although in a vague form, and a controlling function had been installed. Probably, the Exchange could be regarded as a separate legal entity, which could sue and be sued, but this question remained open until 1972 when a new Stock Exchange Act[31] established the Københavns Fondsbørs as a "self-owned institution", and also conferred to it the sole right to act as a stock exchange in Denmark, thereby transforming a de facto monopoly to a formal one.

Its expenses were financed by annual contributions from the issuers of listed securities and from the stockbrokers.

In these respects, the 1919 Stock Exchange Act did not make much substantial change, but it did formalize and clarify some of the realities. In this connection, the distinction between "vekselmæglere" and "veksellerere" was abolished. All members of the Stock Exchange were now "fondsbørs-veksellerere" ("stockbrokers"), authorized by the Ministry of Commerce, upon recommendation by the Grosserer-Societetets Kommite.

The next major change was the Stock Exchange Reform One, introduced 1987. The problems were a fair mixture of practical difficulties with the execution of a growing volume of transactions, transparency, and the consequent limited use of the Stock Exchange.

The number of stockbroker firms, i.e. partnerships with a very limited number of partners authorized as members, was about 20. Each of them normally had their special expertise in particular securities.

---

[31]Lov Nr. 220 af 7. Jun., 1972 om Københavns Fondsbørs. The Stock Exchange Acts of 1930, 1951, and 1958 contained only minor technical adjustments to the 1919 Act.

The essence of the 1987 reform was to introduce the concept of "stock-broker companies" ("børsmæglerselskaber"), which replaced the stock-brokers as members of the Exchange. "Børsmæglerselskaber" had to be joint stock companies, and could be subsidiaries of banks and savings banks, or be formed by stockbrokers themselves if they could register with the required amount of share capital. The net effect was that over the following three to five years, all the former stockbroker names disappeared, e.g. Henriques, Hahns Enke, Brd.Trier, Vollmund, etc. The banks bought them and integrated them into their own securities departments, which used to be the clients of the stockbrokers. These integrated units now became bank subsidiaries. Stockbrokers disappeared.

The range of activities, which could be handled by the new stockbroker companies was a subject of intense discussions. In the end, it was agreed that stockbroker companies could, in addition to their pure stockbroker activities, act as advisers, portfolio managers, and market makers, and arrange new issues. In the latter connection they could not, however, act as underwriters, so bank services would still be required for new issues. As market markers it was, of course, necessary that the broker companies could trade for their own accounts, which was a major break compared to the 1808 Decrees. The 1919 Act was silent on this point, but the 1930 Act stipulated that brokers could not trade shares for their own account. The reason why bonds, but not shares, could be traded for own accounts was probably that the market for shares had been subject to much manipulation, speculation, and insider-trading during the feverish post WWI years. Such malpractices were less likely to happen in the standardized mortgage bond market.

Stock Exchange Reform Two happened in 1995[32] and was, perhaps, less revolutionary than Reform One. Its main purpose was to transform the formerly "self-owning" stock exchange into a joint stock company, with 60 per cent of the shares going to the members, 20 per cent to the issuers of the listed shares, and 20 per cent to the bond issuers. Secondly, the Fondsrådet ("the "Securities Council") was created, which was designed to oversee the general activities in the market and decide questions of general interest and uncertainty, including interpretations of the Stock Exchange Act and regulations. Finally, as a consequence of the EU Directive, membership of the Copenhagen Stock Exchange was opened to all EU securities dealers.

In 2005, the Copenhagen Stock Exchange merged into OMX, the Swedish stock exchange operator, and in 2008, OMX merged with NASDAQ.

---

[32]Lov nr. 1072 af 20. dec. 1995, as changed by Lov nr. 276 af 22. maj. 1996.

The substance

Until the early 1920s, bond trading was only a fraction of the dealings in shares, but during the 1920s these roles were reversed, and the Copenhagen Stock Exchange became primarily a bond market, cfr. Tables 7.5 and 7.6:

Table 7.5   Turnover of Listed Bonds and Shares, 1918–1950 (Million DKK)

	1918	1920	1922	1924	1930	1936	1950
Bonds	70	108	307	196	215	243	316
Shares	694	241	148	172	79	135	110

Source: Danmarks Statistik: Statistisk Årbog, relevant years.

The opposite directions taken by the trading in bonds and shares respectively are clearly seen. From the 1960s onwards, the bond trading became even more dominating not only because the market value of the circulating bonds outgrew the value of the listed shares, but also because there was a faster rate of turnover of the bonds in proportion to their market value, cfr. Table 7.6.

Table 7.6   Circulation and Turnover of Listed Bonds and Shares, Selected Years, 1971–2008 (Billion DKK)

	Bond circulation, market value	Bonds, turnover	Share circulation, market value	Shares, turnover
1971	97	6	4	0.09
1972	113	7	5	0.2
1981	500	24	45	0.4
1982	586	26	48	0.5
1990	1,237	1,923	264	77
1994	1,702	6,348	345	174
2000	2,017	5,611	896	455
2004	2,781	7,069	856	593
2006	3,071		1,598	
2008	3,480		1,036	

Sources: Copenhagen Stock Exchange: 1971–1982: Annual reports 1990–2004: Annual "Fact Books" 2000–2008: Statistisk Årbog.
Notes: Circulation figures are year-end figures.
Bond figures for 1971 and 1972 are nominal figures. The difference between nominal figures and market values can be estimated at 10–15 per cent.

By the 1980s, approximately 85 per cent of the circulating bonds were mortgage bonds, about 12 per cent were government bonds, and three per cent were "other". The number of companies listed on the Copenhagen Stock Exchange was fairly stable at 40–50 between the 1920s and the 1950s.

Between the early 1960s and the late 1980s the number grew to a little more than 200, but has since declined to around 180. The decline over the latest 15–20 years corresponds to developments elsewhere, and could be caused the increasing demands for information required by stock exchange authorities everywhere.

In comparison to other stock exchanges, the Nordic turnover figures for recent years look as follows:

Table 7.7   Turnover of Bonds and Shares on Selected European Exchanges, 1997–2008 (Billion Euros)

	Copenhagen	Helsinki	Oslo	Stockholm	Germany	London	Switzerland
Bonds							
1997	953	0	153	1,572	1,338		
2000	753	0	68	850	727	1,396	98
2003	926	0	119	1,097	401	1,914	158
Shares							
1997	41	32	43	156	947	1,777	507
2000	61	229	78	526	2,296	4,943	692
2003	56	145	68	269	1,140	3,174	550

Source: Copenhagen Stock Exchange: "Fact Book", relevant years. The "Fact Books" have not been produced in recent years.

8
Finland, 1918–2010: A Quick Adaptor

"Of all the wonders that I yet have heard
it seems to me most strange that men should fear
seeing that death, a necessary end,
will come, when it will come."

("Julius Cæsar", Act Two)

8.1 An overview: Through havoc to welfare state

Having finally gained their independence in late 1917, it seemed that the Finns had plenty of reasons to fear for their future. Internal strife soon led to most bloody civil war, hyper-inflation, and monetary chaos. The need for fast adaptation to new circumstances was glaringly evident.

Order was restored, for a while. The gold standard, re-introduced in 1925, had to be abandoned in 1931 like elsewhere, and the finmark (FIM) dropped sharply against most other currencies. This caused big losses from the large sterling and dollar-denominated foreign debts previously incurred, and the future looked threatening again.

Scarcely had a state of relative calm been restored in the mid-1930s, before Finland became a victim of the Molotov-Ribbentrop Pact, leading to the Soviet Union's attack on Finland in 1939 (the "Winter War" of 1939–1940) and the loss of the Karelia with the industrial town of Viipuri and 10–12 per cent of Finland's arable land. The German attack on the Soviet Union in 1941 was joined by Finland in an effort to re-take the Karelia (the "Continuation War", 1941–1944), but this just caused more losses, including huge war reparations.

The subsequent "Agreement of Friendship, Co-operation, and Mutual Assistance" (the "YYA Treaty") imposed on Finland by the Soviet Union in 1948 had, together with the war reparations, the effect of making large parts of Finland's industry and foreign trade directly dependent on the Soviet Union. Fear of the Soviet Union's reaction also made Finland decline the offer of financial assistance under the Marshall Aid Programme. Finland was, however, allowed to join the Bretton Woods institutions (the IMF and IBRD).

At the time of the civil war (1918–1919), Finland was still predominantly an agricultural country with clearly the lowest standard of living among the Nordic countries.[1] On the eve of WWI, Helsinki had just 100,000 inhabitants (Copenhagen 400,000). At the time of the "Winter War", half of Finland's population was still living in rural areas, even though Helsinki, Tampere, and a few other towns grew rapidly during the 1920s and 1930s.

Between 1940 and 1985, Finland had a second wave of strong inflation leading to at least eight devaluations between 1945 and 1991 and a currency reform with effect as from January 1, 1963, introducing the New Finmark, equal to 100 old FIM.

The breaking-up of the Soviet Union, and Russia's economic crisis in the 1990s, necessitated a fundamental re-orientation of Finland's exports and, again, fast adaptation to new circumstances.

In the longer run, however, the worst fears proved exaggerated. After much belt-tightening in the early 1930s, the 1940s, the 1950s, and again in the 1990s, growth accelerated, and any remaining difference between the Finnish per capita GDP and those of the other Nordic countries is now negligible. In spite of all difficulties, and against all odds, Finland's real rate of growth was faster than the rest of Europe between 1860 and 1985 (3.1 per cent p.a for Finland against 2.5 per cent for the rest of Europe[2]).

Table 8.1 shows the various periods of strong growth and inflation since 1913:

Table 8.1   Inflation and Real Rates of GDP Growth, 1913–1985

	GDP growth % p.a.	*GDP deflator, average annual change*
1913–1920	–1.4	38.0
1920–1938	4.7	1.2
1938–1946	0.8	23.3
1946–1960	5.0	9.8
1960–1974	4.8	7.8
1974–1985	2.7	9.7

Source: R. Hjerppe (1989) *The Finnish Economy 1860–1985* (The Bank of Finland) p. 43.

---

[1]It has been estimated that during the whole of the 1860–1913 period, the Swedish per capita GDP was about twice that of Finland, and about 1.5 times that of Finland during the first 30–40 years of the 20th century, cfr. R. Hjerppe & E. Pihkala (1977) *The Gross Domestic Product of Finland in 1860–1913. A Preliminary Estimate* (Economy and History, 1977, vol. XX: 2) pp. 62–3.

[2]Cfr. R. Hjerppe (1989) *The Finnish Economy 1860–1985* (Bank of Finland) p. 51.

In 1991–1992, Finland, like Norway and Sweden, went through a major banking crisis, which wiped out most of the savings banks sector, and sent the country into arguably the deepest recession since 1918, reinforced by the collapse of the Russian and Ukraine economies.

In 1995, Finland joined the EU and has since 2002 been the only Nordic member of the "Euro Club" (at approximately FIM 5.95 to the Euro).

8.2   The inter-war period

8.2.1   The problems

Against the general background summarized above it is hardly surprising that the development of the capital market would encounter a number of problems. These could briefly be listed as follows:

- A rudimentary network of few and relatively small banks and fragmented savings banks;
- The Bank of Finland's reserves depleted;
- Very limited domestic sources of long-term capital;
- Huge investment requirements for urbanization, industrialization, and infrastructure;
- A lob-sided economy, over-dependent on agriculture and timber;
- Foreign exchange shortage;
- Traditional export markets and customers (Russia, Germany, and the UK) disconnected and disrupted;
- Inflation, which left the price level in 1918 at six times its 1914 level, and which increased it six-fold again between 1918 and 1924,[3] caused by huge government budget deficits;
- A chaotic foreign exchange market. During the 1917–1924 period, the mark (FIM) fluctuated between FIM 9 and 80 to the dollar, before it was stabilized at FIM 40 in 1924, and the gold standard was re-established in 1925. After the breaking up of the gold standard in 1931, the FIM dropped further to about FIM 120 to the dollar in 1933.

8.3   Responses and actions

8.3.1   The banking scene

The Bank of Finland, which the new Finnish republic inherited from Russia in 1917, was an empty shell. The gold reserves had been used by Russia during the war, and the procurements bought from Finland, as well as the fortifications built by the Russians along Finland's borders, had all been paid

---

[3]Cfr. N. Meinander (1962) *Penningpolitik under etthundrafemtio år* (Finlands Banks Institut för Ekonomisk Forskning) p. 72.

for in rubles, which had accumulated in the BoF's accounts in St. Petersburg, and which proved worthless after 1917.

The new Finnish government "capitalized" the BoF with a loan of FIM 350 million as "cover" for its notes. This was, of course, just a book-keeping maneuver.

The BoF addressed the foreign exchange shortage by introducing strict rationing of exchange and tight import controls.

During the late 1920s and the 1930s, the BoF continued its activities as a commercial bank,[4] under the very active management of Risto Ryti,[5] the BoF's governor 1923–1939. The BoF was still not a "pure" central bank.

Table 8.2   The Number of Financial Institutions, 1918–1940

	Commercial banks	Savings banks	Co-op banks	Mortgage institutions	Posti- pankki
1918	22	443	607	6	973
1925	20	467	1,242	9	1,068
1930	18	479	1,428	10	1,173
1935	10	481	1,315	9	1,215
1940	10	485	1,094	8	1,213

Source: K. Vattula (1983) *Suomen taloushistoria*, vol. 3, *Historical Statistics* (Helsinki) pp. 325–7.
Note: "Commercial banks" include Skopbank and OKObank, the "central banks" for the savings banks and the co-operative banks respectively. The numbers given for the Postipankki are the number of its branches, essentially post offices. Mortgage institutions include the mortgage departments/subsidiaries of the three big banks.

In response to the accelerating credit demands from forest owners, saw mills, agriculture, embryonic industrial companies, residential construction, and feverish speculation on the stock exchange (1918–1920), 15 new banks were formed between 1918 and 1930, the Bankers Association was created (1914), and a few bond-issuing mortgage institutions were founded. In addition, savings banks and co-operative banks spread all over the countryside and provincial towns.

The purpose of the Bankers Association was primarily to restrict competition among the banks by fixing uniform prices, fees, and tariffs.[6] Since 1931, this co-operation was extended also to harmonization of interest

---

[4]Cfr. Meinander (1962) *Penningpolitik under etthundrafemtio år* (Finlands Bank) p. 76.
[5]Risto Ryti (1889–1956) was Finland's president 1940–1944. After the war, he and a few others were held responsible for Finland's initiation of the "Continuation War" and sentenced to ten years in jail. He was released in 1949.
[6]Cfr. *Affärsbankernas samarbete 50 år* in *Affärsbankerne och Näringslivet* (Bankföreningen i Finland, 1964) p. 7.

rates, at the request of the government, which feared that competition for deposits would otherwise lead to a harmful escalation of interest rates.[7] None of this did much to develop a capital market. All of the 15 new banks formed between 1918 and 1930 went either bankrupt, or were liquidated or taken over by the big Helsinki banks, except one, the Ålandsbanken. However, only in five cases did creditors make any losses.[8] The number of commercial banks (including SKOP and OKO) topped at 24 in 1919–1920, and kept falling until the late 1990s, when foreign banks started opening up in Helsinki.

Table 8.3   **Market Shares of the Main Banks (of loans to the general public), 1900–1961**

Per cent	1900	1913	1924	1938	1955	1961
UBF	28	26	40	36	41	42
NAB	27	20				
KOP	18	25	24	38	43	43
Others	27	29	36	26	16	15
Total	100	100	100	100	100	100

Source: H. Pipping (1962) *Bankliv Genom Hundra År* (Nordiska Föreningsbanken) p. 210.
Note: UBF = Föreningsbanken i Finland, merged 1919 with Nordiska Aktiebanken to become Nordiska Föreningsbanken or Union Bank of Finland. NAB: Nordiska Aktiebanken. KOP: Kansallis-Osaka Pankki (merged 1995 with UBF to become Merita Bank).

The savings banks and co-op banks were mostly tiny one-office outfits. In 1940, the 485 savings banks had a total of 75 branches, and only 10 per cent of the co-op banks had more than one office. The big banks dominated the scene already from the late 19th century. No other European country has had a banking market as concentrated as Finland.

Table 8.4 shows the overall solvency rates of the commercial banks, and their relative reliance on deposits and borrowings from correspondents.

The solvency ratio clearly dropped during this period, but it remained well above the levels contemplated for banks in the early 21st century.

The striking feature was that throughout the 1920s and 1930s, deposits and equity financed only some 80 per cent of the assets. Following the bank failures of the 1920s and the breaking up of the international financial scene after 1931, the reliance on borrowings from foreign correspondents declined

---

[7]In 1931, the Interest Regulation Act was passed, which would have forced banks to a government dictated interest rate agreement if a voluntary agreement had not been reached.
[8]Cfr. G. Åhberg (1942) *Strukturförändringar i affärsbankernas rörelse* (Ekonomiska Samfundets Tidskrift, Ny serie, Häfte 56, Helsingfors) p. 59.

Table 8.4   Solvency and Deposit Ratios of Commercial Banks, 1916–1938

Per cent of total Assets/liabilities	Share capital	Reserves	Equity	Deposits	Borrowings from domestic correspondents	Other	Total
1916–1920	10.9	5.5	16.4	61.4	5.3	16.9	100.0
1921–1925	11.2	4.2	15.4	55.6	8.8	20.2	100.0
1926–1930	10.1	5.5	15.6	63.0	8.2	13.2	100.0
1931–1935	9.0	5.9	14.9	67.0	9.2	8.9	100.0
1936–1938	6.5	5.0	11.5	69.1	10.2	9.2	100.0

Source: G. Åhman (1942) *Strukturförändringar i affärsbankernas rörelse* (Ekonomiska Samfundets Tidskrift, Ny serie, Häfte 56, Helsingfors) pp. 70 and 76.

noticeably. Part of this decline was replaced by domestic correspondents, including the savings banks, which had substantial deposit surpluses, and the BoF. Still, the equity/total asset ratio was high compared to what would be expected 70–80 years later.

It is, of course, now difficult to know to what extent the declining proportion of share capital illustrates the difficulties banks – and others – had placing new issues under the depressed market conditions of the 1930s, and to what extent it reflected a perceived lower need for share capital.

The 1919 Savings Banks Act

Independence, civil war, and hyper inflation made it clear that a lot of the existing legislation, including the 1895 Savings Banks Act, had now become hopelessly outdated. So, after fairly brief but intense discussions, a new savings banks act was passed on July 5, 1918, taking effect as from January 1, 1919. The essence of the new act was to enable the savings banks to conduct most of the types of business so far reserved for the commercial banks. Thus, savings banks were now permitted to offer current accounts, checking accounts, overdraft facilities, and even to discount bills and offer medium- and long-term amortizing mortgage loans.

These changes had not been requested by the savings banks. On the contrary, the opinion was wide-spread among the savings banks that such banking business was incompatible with the original social and rural nature of savings banks. The Savings Banks Association, which otherwise assisted the savings banks with working out standard documentation, deliberately omitted any paragraphs relating to the discounting of bills in its standard savings banks by-laws, so as not to encourage savings banks to engage in such hazardous and commercially oriented business. Even five years after the passing of the new Act, less than one-third of the savings banks offered bill discounting facilities, and less than half of them offered current accounts.[9]

---

[9] R. Urbans (1964) "Sparbanksväsendet i Finland 1822–1922" (Helsinki) p. 369.

The 1933 Banking Act[10]

In response to the many bank failures in the 1920s, a government committee was formed in 1926 to propose amendments to the 1886 Banking Act.
Its 1931 report[11] was the basis for the 1933 Banking Act, which was hardly
revolutionary compared to existing law. It did, however, define banking as
a credit institution ("kreditinrättning") which received deposits from the
general public on conditions generally used in banking ("... som allmänt
begagnas i bankrörelse", §1). If this definition appears somewhat circular, it
is almost identical to the wording used in the Swedish Banking Act of 1911,
cfr. p. 146. It also restricted the use of the word "bank" in a business name to
The Bank of Finland, commercial banks, savings banks, the postal savings
bank (Postipankki), and mortgage banks (§2), i.e. co-op banks could not use
the word "bank" in their names, and they were not subject to the Banking
Act. This illustrates the difficulty of defining "banks" and the precise nature of
financial institutions, which should be subject to general banking legislation
(cfr. the Introduction). The 1933 Act re-introduced a minimum share capital
(FIM 10 million), but did not follow the Committee's recommendation for
a minimum ratio of equity to total liabilities. That had to await the 1958
amendment (cfr. below). However, the 1933 Act did stipulate that a reserve
fund should be built up from retained earnings to an amount equal to at least
50 per cent of the share capital (§6), against only 25 per cent in the 1886 Act.

The co-operative banks

Until the 1920s, the co-op banks, which started appearing in 1903, were not
banks at all, but merely local associations formed for the purpose of chan-
nelling government loans and subsidies to the recipient farmers. Initially, they
were not allowed to receive deposits. In the 1920s this changed. A small
deposit-taking activity grew up, and they started working like savings banks,
but it was not until after WWII that their lending business began to take off
in a major way.

Eventually, the co-op banks developed a much stronger relative position
in Finland than in any of the other Nordic countries.

The mortgage institutions

The intention to copy the basic principles of the original Swedish (and Danish)
mortgage system (cfr. Chapter 4) could not be upheld in all respects, not least
because it proved impossible to sell long-term fixed interest bonds in sufficient volumes on the domestic market, particularly after 1914. This meant
that they could not maintain the principle of balancing assets and liabilities
with respect to maturity profile and interest. Since they borrowed substantial

---

[10]Lag nr. 87 av 17. marts, 1933.
[11]Kommittébetänkande nr. 14/1931.

amounts abroad, there was also a currency mismatch, which caused heavy losses when the mark tumbled on the foreign exchange markets. In most cases, the bond loans taken up abroad were guaranteed by the government – otherwise the bonds could not be sold – but the respective institutions had to bear the brunt of the exchange losses.

The earliest legislation on rural mortgage associations was enacted in 1925,[12] and on urban associations in 1927.[13] These acts did not stipulate any capital requirements, funding rules, or lending limitations, but concentrated on procedures for the foundation and administration of such associations. In 1969 a special Act[14] on "hypoteksbanker" was passed regulating the formation of mortgage institutions as joint stock companies, and these three Acts were combined into one Act in 1978,[15] which still did not prescribe any capital or liquidity requirements, nor any lending or funding limitations, in contrast to the Danish mortgage institution Acts of 1850 and 1861 (cfr. Chapter 3).

Between WWI and the 1990s, the main mortgage institutions were:

Finlands Hypoteksförening (cfr. Chapter 4) virtually stopped all lending between 1914 and 1925 because of foreign exchange losses, which also hurt it after 1931. The first 30 years after WWII it did not issue any bonds at all, but borrowed from the government, pension funds, insurance companies, and banks.

Finlands Bostadshypoteksbank, the other mortgage institution originally created with joint liability among the borrowers (like Finlands Hyp.) was formed in 1927 for the purpose of financing urban residential construction. Funded from the beginning with loans in dollars and sterling, causing heavy losses after 1931. Not very active after WWII. In 1979 it was merged into the above mentioned Hypoteksförening, and the joint liability was discontinued.

Fastighetsbanken i Finland Ab, formed 1907 by the savings banks and 80 per cent owned by Skopbank, the central bank of the savings banks. Its purpose was to offer mortgage loans against most types of real estate, except industrial properties and single-family houses. Funded primarily by selling bonds to the savings banks, which could hold these bonds as cash reserves, even if there was no secondary market for them. Dissolved in 1992–1993 in connection with the banking crisis, which resulted in the taking over of Skopbank by Svenska Handelsbanken and the breaking up of the savings banks (cfr. below).

Land-och Industribanken, formed in 1916 (with several later name changes) by the co-operative banks with Finlands Hypoteksförening as a major shareholder.

---

[12]Lag om hypoteksföreningar av 24. april, 1925 (130/25).
[13]Lag om bostadshypoteksföreningar av 8. januar, 1927 (1/27).
[14]Lag om hypoteksbanker (545/69).
[15]Lag om hypoteksföreningar av 8. december, 1978 (936/78).

Originally formed for the purpose of offering mortgage financing of agricultural properties, but later widened to other types of property as well. During the depression of the 1930s, it became majority owned by the government, which sold it to OKObank in 1941, but its activities were frozen until the 1950s. Funded primarily by bonds sold to the co-operative banks, but also by borrowings from insurance companies, pension funds, etc. Having had a few name changes, it was finally submerged into OKObank in 2000.

Finlands Industri-Hypoteksbank Ab, formed 1924 and owned 90 per cent by the three largest banks and 10 per cent by pulp and paper companies. As indicated by its name, its main purpose was to offer mortgage finance for industrial property. Originally funded by bonds sold abroad (dollars and sterling), it made heavy losses after 1931, and was therefore almost dormant until the mid-1950s. Following the acquisition of the Bank of Helsinki by UBF in 1985–1986, UBF became the majority owner of the Industri-hypoteksbank, which was later merged into UBF.

It seems that the weak development of the mortgage institutions can mainly be explained by the limited capacity of domestic banks, insurance companies, pension funds, savings banks, and co-operative banks to absorb long-term fixed interest mortgage bonds, and by the government's willingness to guarantee bonds sold abroad.

A bond market for non-institutional investors was not developed. The bonds issued by the above-mentioned institutions were not listed on the stock exchange until well after WWII.

The three big banks all set up their own mortgage finance departments already in the mid-1890s, but they never reached any significant scale, until they took over the above-mentioned institutions.

8.4   A profile of the capital market, 1920–1940

Three striking features are revealed by Table 8.5.

The most striking features is the small size of the financial sector compared particularly to Denmark, where the credit stock made up about 140 per cent of GDP in the 1930s, (cfr. Table 7.2), but also compared to Sweden, where the relative size of the organized capital market in those years was around 110–115 per cent of GDP (cfr. Table 10.8).

Second, the growth of the financial sector as a percentage of GDP was modest to the extent that there was any growth at all. The small growth between 1918 and 1930 was followed by a broadly similar decline over the next ten years. This was somewhat in contrast to what might have been expected in a country at this stage of its industrial and financial development. In both Denmark and Sweden, there was a clearly growing trend in the inter-war years, even if the development was quite bumpy.

Table 8.5   Relative Composition and Growth of the Credit Stock, 1918–1940

	State and BoF	Com. banks	Savings banks	Co-op. banks	Mortgage institutions	Insurance & pension funds	Total, million FIM	Total, in % of GDP
	Per cent of total credit stock							
1918	2	76	14	0	7	–	3,937	73
1925	4	58	17	3	7	11	11,139	51
1930	12	44	18	6	10	10	20,774	87
1935	12	35	21	7	9	17	20,823	76
1940	5	38	23	8	5	20	29,049	68
	Per cent of GDP							
1918	1	56	10	0	5	–		73
1925	2	30	9	1	3	6		51
1930	10	38	15	5	9	9		87
1935	9	27	16	5	7	13		76
1940	3	26	16	5	4	14		68

Sources: Credit stock: As for Table 8.2. GDP: As for Table 8.1, pp. 196–7.

Note: Figures for insurance companies and pension funds not available before 1927. The 1925 figure shown refers to 1927. The figures include the Social Security Fund.

The third striking feature is the relatively large role – compared to the other Nordic countries – played by the insurance companies and pension funds as direct lenders. In the other Nordic countries, the insurance companies and pension funds tended to act as direct investors in real estate rather than as lenders to property companies.

The strong growth in the absolute figures, particularly between 1918 and 1925, is mainly a reflection of the galloping inflation of the early years of this period.

The perennial shortage particularly of long-term capital prompted the state to take an active role as capital supplier, both as a shareholder and a lender. This started in the previous century with waterways and railroads, and it continued in the 1920s and 1930s with investments in forest industry companies (Enso Gutzeit and Tornator) and other industrial companies, e.g. Outokumpu, Rautaruukki, Kemira, Valmet, etc.).

In the 20th century, the general policy was, in principle, to restrict state lending to municipalities and other local authorities only, but in the inter-war period the number of private borrowers seems to have retained an almost equal share of the state lendings.[16]

---

[16]Cfr. Y. Blomstedt (1976) *Valtiokonttori 1875–1975* (Helsinki, 1976, the centennial history of the "Statskontor" ("State Treasury"), with a summary in English) p. 87. In 1899, the "State Treasury" was also instructed to start using the "Italian double-entry book-keeping system" (p. 186), an indication of the "advanced" state of Finnish financial management at that time.

The precise amounts of government lendings are not easily ascertained because of the several different channels through which the money was distributed (ministries, municipalities, co-op banks). Mostly, the government funds went to housing and agricultural subsidies. The funds were distributed according to purely administrative principles, and were scarcely part of an organized "capital market", since no "market" was involved. Since much of the money was distributed through the co-op banks, it is included in the lending figures for these institutions in Table 8.6, which implies a certain measure of double-counting.

The position of the Bank of Finland

Under Finland's 1919 Constitution,[17] The Bank of Finland was placed directly under the control of the Eduskunta (the directly elected "Parliament", just as it had been under the direct supervision of the Assembly of the Estates since 1868), just like in Sweden.

The significance of this arrangement has only been visible on few occasions. One such occasion was the "Cash Crisis" of 1955, when the government asked the BoF for a loan, which the BoF, then under the firm hand of the renowned R. von Fieandt, refused,[18] and the government actually defaulted on certain domestic payment obligations. Later (1957), the BoF officially reprimanded the UBF for having granted a credit to the government without having asked the BoF's for permission to do so.[19] Between 1962 and 1971 the BoF did not change any interest rates, because the BoF governors and the Parliament-appointed board members ("bankfulllmägtige") could not agree on the use of interest rates as a tool of economic policy.[20]

---

[17]Under the latest BoF Act, the chairman of the board of governors is appointed by the president of the Republic, while the other governors are appointed by the board of directors ("bankfullmägtige"). The bankfullmägtige generally meet once every month.

[18]Cfr. N. Meinander (1962) *Penningpolitik under etthundrafemtio år* (Finlands Banks Institut för Ekonomisk Forskning) p. 105. See also Chapter 4, fn. 45.

[19]Cfr. T. Vihola (2000) *Penningens Styrman* (Merita Bank) p. 43. Quite possibly, the problem was that the credit would have been granted in the form of a bill discounting facility, and the UBF planned to re-discount the bills with the BoF, so that the credits would ultimately end up with the BoF (SEA's speculation).

[20]Cfr. T. Vihola (2000) *Penningens Styrman* (Merita Bank) p. 35.

8.5   The long post-war era, 1945–2010

8.5.1   The problems: War reparations and inflation

In many ways, the problems facing Finland's financial system in the aftermath of WWII resembled those of the early 1920s. Thus, the financial scene was painted in the colours of:

- Depleted stocks and worn-down equipment, and therefore extraordinarily large investment requirements;
- Traditional trading connections and markets disrupted or cut off. In the inter-war period, the UK and Germany had absorbed about 50 per cent of Finland's exports; in the 1950s, nothing;
- The loss of Karelia meant the loss of important hydro-power plants and 10–12 per cent of Finland's population and arable land;
- Huge war reparations demanded by the Soviet Union (cfr. below);
- Acute shortage of foreign exchange, and very limited borrowing possibilities;
- Virtually non-existing domestic market for long-term capital, other than government bonds;
- Weak banking system. The largest banks much smaller than the largest Swedish and Danish banks;
- Limited political stability in the 1950s and 1960s (and occasionally later), leading to weak fiscal policies with continued government deficits, stronger inflation than elsewhere (cfr. Table 8.1), and several devaluations of the FIM;
- In the early 1990s, the Russian and Ukrainian economies, then Finland's largest export markets, collapsed.

Almost simultaneously, a financial crisis broke out in Finland (like in Sweden and Norway at the same time) stemming from severe losses by banks and savings banks (cfr. below).

War reparations

The armistice of 1944 between the Soviet Union and Finland, and the peace treaty signed in Paris in 1947, involved heavy war reparations with strong implications for the workings of the credit system.

The amount was fixed at USD 300 million, but the amount was specified in 1938 gold dollars, and additional demands in the final 1947 peace treaty meant that the bill eventually totalled between 600 million and 900 million 1944-dollars, to be paid over eight years ending in 1952.[21] The actual amount

---

[21]The description of the war reparation is based on an unpublished paper by the late professor Charles Kindleberger: *Finnish War Reparations Revisited*, presented at a seminar in Helsinki ("Wider") on August 15, 1986. The 31-page typescript manuscript is kept in the BoF's library, which kindly let SEA take a photocopy.

Other sources on this subject include J. Auer (1963) *Finland's War Reparation Deliveries to the Soviet Union* (Finnish Foreign Policy) pp. 66–83.

depends on the estimated values and prices of the goods, which had to be delivered. The difference between the Finnish war reparations and the war reparations demanded by the Prussians from France in 1871 and those demanded from Germany by the Treaty of Versaille was that whereas the two latter were monetary sums, the Finnish reparations had to be paid in kind according to a Soviet shopping list with prices set by a War Reparations Committee, on which the Soviet government had a dominating influence.

The ceding of the Karelia was not part of the reparations.

Several calculations have been made to estimate the real burden of the Finnish war reparations. The concensus[22] seems to be that the reparations amounted to annual deliveries averaging about 4 per cent of Finland's GDP, topping at 5–6 per cent in 1945–1948.

For comparison, Germany never paid more than 2 per cent of GDP under the Versaille Treaty and its subsequent amendments.[23]

A question discussed by Kindleberger and other historians is whether, at the end of the day, the reparations may not have been good for Finland's industrial development in the same sense that export orders from a developing country can stimulate industrial growth in that country. Kindleberger was not convinced in the case of Finland. Although Finnish shipbuilding has developed impressively in the post-war era, particularly with nuclear-driven ice-breakers and luxury cruisers, the vessels which made up most of the Soviet shopping list, consisted of quite traditional medium-sized vessels, river barges, even wooden schooners, and trawlers.[24]

The main effect of the reparations was probably that, because of the sheer volume and dictated nature of the deliveries to be made, the country's resources and investments had to be tightly controlled. Finland became close to a Soviet-style planned economy. Banks could neither grant loans for investment or construction purposes, nor for import financing without asking the BoF for permission. Credit was rationed both because of the general capital shortage (compared to immediate investment needs), and because of the need to allocate capital to purposes dictated by the war reparations. Bank loans to finance production or imports of consumer goods were given a very low priority.

---

[22]Kindleberger (1986) *Finnish War Reparations Revisited* (Unpublished working paper) p. 4.

[23]Kindleberger's unpublished paper, p. 5.

[24]Kindleberger's unpublished paper, p. 17. However, it has also been pointed out that the Finnish machinery and metallurgical industries (i.e. mainly Rautaruukki and Outokumpu) were stimulated by forced war reparation deliveries, cfr. F. Singleton (1998) *A Short History of Finland* (revised and updated by A.F. Upton, Cambridge University Press) p. 148, and N. Meinander (1962) *Penningpolitik under etthundrafemtio år* (Finlands Banks Insitut för Ekonomisk Forskning) p. 97.

In the early 1990s, the Finnish economy was still highly dependent on exports of forest industry products, and on the Soviet export market. The breaking-up of the Soviet Union and the subsequent economic crisis in Russia, etc, therefore necessitated a major re-orientation of the Finnish economy. The need for a reorganization of the financial system became acute in 1991–1992, when the "bubble economy" of the late 1980s burst, cfr. below.

8.5.2 Responses and actions

With respect to the general economic policies in the first 10–15 post-war years, and in some later periods, the main factor was that wages and salaries were kept at a much slower rate of increase than consumer prices.[25] This made private consumption drop and the savings and investment ratios increase sharply. Between 1920 and 1945, gross capital formation had averaged about 15 per cent of GDP, albeit with large variations around that average, but between 1945 and 1950 it increased to 20 per cent and averaged some 27 per cent between the early 1950s and the late 1980s. It dropped to 16–18 per cent in the 1990s.[26] The first 30 post-war years was a period of extreme "belt-tightening" and faster industrial growth than anywhere else in the western world except, perhaps, for West Germany.

The "belt-tightening" included foreign exchange rationing stricter than anywhere else in northern Europe.

With respect to more specific actions, the tight regulation of the credit market, mainly originating from the war reparation years, continued over the next decades, and the external value of the FIM was cut drastically. A total of six devaluations between 1945 and 1957 reduced the FIM from its pre-war level of about 40 to the dollar to 320 FIM to the dollar in 1957, and 420 in 1972, i.e. 4.20 new FIM (two digits having been slashed in the 1962 reform).

Other specific actions taken by the actors included indexation of various financial assets. The government was the first to do so, evidently not trusting its own anti-inflation policies, with indexation of government bonds. The savings banks followed with index-linked savings accounts, and then the commercial banks and insurance companies had to do so as well. In some cases there was 100 per cent indexation, in other cases only 50 per cent. Indexed assets continued to exist until the 1980s.

The main instruments employed by the BoF, apart from requiring banks to seek permission for making major loans to their customers, were interest

---

[25]Cfr. e.g. N. Meinander (1962) *Penningpolitik under etthundrafemtio år* (Finlands Bank) p. 93.
[26]Cfr. e.g. *Statistical Yearbook 2008* (Statistics Finland) p. 323, which shows the investment ratio for the whole 1860–2007 period.
Also R. Hjerppe (1989) *The Finnish Economy 1860–1985* (Bank of Finland) pp. 138–46.

and liquidity regulations, as well as lending policies. In many respects these regulations were reminiscent of those applied in Sweden, except that they were even more rigorous in Finland.

The interest regulations took their starting point in the 1931 Deposit Interest Agreement made at the BoF's initiative (cfr. fn. 7). With minor interruptions, it continued until 1986.

In 1959, the regulation of deposit interest rates was supplemented with ceilings over the lending rates banks could charge (tied to the BoF discount rate), and in 1961 a regulation of the average lending rates was added. The mechanism was that the maximum rate could only be applied to a certain portion (10–20 per cent of the portfolio, changed a couple of times) of a bank's loans, and the average rate was not to exceed the ceiling set by the BoF. Both the maximum rates and the average rates were lower for the commercial banks than for the savings and co-op banks, as were the deposit rates (until 1984). It was argued that the commercial banks had a wider range of services where they could make up for a lower net interest income.[27] The "average lending rates mechanism" had peculiar effects. Financially weak bank customers were often relieved of their interest obligations altogether, and the bank's missing interest income was then added to the rates paid by the customers who could afford it, so that the average rate could be fully used. That way, the most creditworthy customers who deserved prime rates, ended up paying the highest rates.[28] The BoF also advised that it preferred the maximum interest rates to be applied to credits financing the production, purchase and imports of consumer goods, i.e. without regard to the creditworthiness of the borrower.

The BoF had no difficulty enforcing its interest regulations. Between 1945 and the late 1980s, the banks (the commercial banks more than the savings and co-ops, cfr. Table 8.6) were always net borrowers from the BoF. The BoF made it very clear to the banks that if they did not "behave" it would have severe consequences for their borrowing facilities at the BoF. In addition, the BoF forced an agreement with the banks that they only changed their interest rates on deposits when the BoF changed its base rate[29] (a variation on the Swedish system, where interest changes by the banks had to be approved by the Riksbank, cfr. Chapter 10).

All tight regulations have a limited lifetime. Ways will be found to circumvent them. That happened in Sweden and Norway, and it happened in

[27]Cfr. T. Vihola (2000) *Penningens Styrman. Föreningsbanken och Merita 1950–2000* (Merita Bank) p. 34.
[28]Cfr. T. Vihola (2000) *Penningens Styrman* (Merita Bank) p. 36, where some cases of this nature are mentioned.
[29]Cfr. E. Letho (1984) *Korot ja korko-järestelmä Suomessa* ("The Interest System in Finland"), Bank of Finland, A:57, with a summary in English.

Finland (as it happened in the US with regulations Q and M, with inter-state banking, and with Glass-Steagall). In Finland, banks invented negotiated deposits ("market deposits"), which were not subject to the deposit rate regulations, and they started offering loans in foreign currencies,[30] which were not subject to the lending rate ceilings. Also – like in Sweden – they set up subsidiaries or associated companies offering leasing, factoring, receivables financing, etc, which were outside the reach of the BoF.

Legislatory changes, 1958–1993

The 1933 Banking Act was amended several times in the 1950s and 1960s, but not radically changed until 1969. The minimum share capital was kept nominally unchanged at FIM 10 million old, i.e. FIM 100,000 post-1962, but the required reserve fund was increased to 50 per cent of the share capital (1933: 25 per cent), and banks could now only have the form of joint stock companies (1933: also partnerships of at least ten persons or associations, "öppet bolag").

One major change was, however introduced in 1958. For the first time in Finland did a banking Act stipulate a specific ratio between a bank's equity (share capital + reserves) and another balance sheet item, in this case the bank's total liabilities. According to this 1958 amendment, a bank's liabilities could not exceed 15 times the sum of its equity and cash, claims on the government and municipalities, and on other banks. However, with the bank inspector's blessing, this ratio could be increased to 20 times, and with the permission of the finance minister, to 25 times.

In this calculation, guarantee liabilities counted only 50 per cent of their nominal amounts.

Depending on the amount of cash, deposits with other financial institutions, government bonds, guarantees, etc., a bank would have among its assets, and depending on use of special permissions from the inspector and minister, the 1958 capital ratio could be higher or lower than the Basel II prescription. Generally, it appears to have been lower. In addition, it will be seen that the more claims a bank would have against other banks, the more liabilities it could assume. In the early 21st century, this system would hardly seem prudent.

Neither the 1933 Act nor the 1951 and 1958 amendments contained any formal limitations on "large exposures".

Neither the 1933 Act nor its later amendments applied to savings banks and co-op "banks", whose activities were regarded as virtually risk-free (mostly "fully" collateralized mortgage loans, municipality loans, and the like).

---

[30]In 1985, foreign currency loans constituted 24 per cent of all commercial bank lendings. Between 1980 and 1985, 40 per cent of the increase in commercial bank lending took place in foreign currencies, cfr. *Statistical Yearbook*, Statistics Finland, 1998, p. 245.

When in the 1960s a committee was set up again to propose a new banking Act, there were strong forces in Parliament representing the savings banks and co-ops which wanted to scrap the traditional limitations on the activities of the savings banks and co-ops, in return for which they would have to accept certain capital requirements.

A new banking Act was passed in 1969.[31] Looked at with the eyes of the early 21st century, this banking Act was strangely old-fashioned. Its main elements were:

1. Banks were defined as joint stock companies engaged in banking (§1). Banks were forbidden to engage in non-banking business, including industry, construction, commerce, insurance, traffic, and real estate trading (§22). This included limitations on shareholdings in companies engaged in such activities.
2. Permission to form banks would be given if such new banks were deemed to be beneficial to society ("... tillgodoser ett allmänt intresse ...", §9, like in the Swedish banking acts of 1886 and 1911). Formation of branches would be subject to government approval (§10, like in Norway in the mid-20th century).
3. Banks would be required to hold equity of not less than 4 per cent of their total liabilities as reduced by the bank's holdings of cash and claims against other banks and public institutions.

   Depending on the structure of a bank's balance sheet, this could be either a tightening or a relaxation compared to the 1933 Act, but it was certainly less than required by the Danish 1930 Banking Act.
4. The novelty was that an "insurance fund" ("Affärsbankernas säkerhets-fond") was created, and that all banks were required to be members of this fund, whose purpose it was to ensure the solvency and deposits of the banks ("... att trygga affärsbankernas soliditet och insätternas tillgodohavanden ..."). A special management of this fund was to be appointed by the banks. Contributions to the fund would be between 0.1 and 5.0 per mille of the assets of each bank. Similar funds were set up for the savings banks and the co-op banks.

Simultaneously with the 1969 Banking Act, an almost identical new savings banks Act[32] was passed. The main difference compared to the Banking Act (apart from the formalities resulting from the different ownership structures) was the capital requirement, which was only 2 per cent for savings banks. The definition of their activities was close to that for the commercial banks. The earlier stipulation that savings banks were not supposed to engage in "more general banking activities" ("vidtstracktere bankrörelse") was replaced in 1969

---

[31]Lag om affärsbanker, Finlands författningssamling, 1969/540.
[32]Lag om sparbanker, Finlands författningssamling, 1969/541.

with the much broader wording that savings banks were entitled to engage in normal banking business within the restrictions otherwise laid down in the legislation ("... berättigat att bedriva till bankverksamheten allmänt hörande rörelse ...", §27). The restrictions included the §48 stating that savings banks could extend credits only against satisfactory collateral ("... må bevilja kredit endast mot betryggande säkerhet.")

Since the 2 per cent requirement could not be reached, this requirement was relaxed in 1979.

In fact, the savings banks and co-op "banks" (the "local banks") have been seen as being without capital at all, even if they satisfied the formal requirements. They developed the practice of giving each other deposits counting as "capital". If these deposits were netted out, there was no "capital".[33]

This was still the position when the 1990 Banking Act[34] was passed, effective as from January 1, 1991, which finally stipulated equal capital requirements and business areas for commercial banks, savings banks, and co-op banks.

It will be noticed that in the 1958–1990 legislation, capital requirements had been expressed as ratios related to liabilities (as in the other Nordic countries). This was radically changed in 1993,[35] in preparation of Finland's entry into the EU and the Basel I Accord, which defined capital requirements in terms of ratios measured against assets.

Table 8.6 intends to demonstrate actual capital ratios measured against credits and assets, reflecting the substance of the 1993 Act.

On the face of it, the figures look fine for the commercial banks, but dismal for the "local banks". However, the figures in Table 8.6 overstate reality, since the official source from which the equity figures are taken, include provisions for bad debts. There can be no doubt that savings and co-op banks were under-capitalized in the late 1980s and early 1990s compared to Basel I requirements, and this was probably also the case for commercial banks.

Mortgage institutions

The changes in legislation on mortgage institutions were, until 1991, of little significance. The 1978 Mortgage Association Act[36] defined a mortgage association as a credit institution whose purpose it was to provide long-term amortizing loans against mortgages, or to the state or municipalities against their guarantees, or other loans against satisfactory collateral, and

---

[33]Cfr. T. Vihola (2000) *Penningens Styrman* (Merita Bank) p. 31: "De lokale bankerna klarade formellt kapitaltäckningströskeln, men de facto var deras egna tillgångar i det närmaste illusoriska. Om insättningarna inom gruppan hade eliminerats, skulle kapitaltäckningen ha varit noll."

[34]Affärsbankslagen, Finlands författningssamling, 1269/90, Sparbankslagen, 1270/90, Andelsbankslagen, 1271/90.

[35]Kreditinsitutslag av 30. dec, 1993. Finlands Författningssamling, 1607/1993.

[36]Lag om hypoteksföreningar av dec. 8, 1978. Finlands författningssamling, 1978/936.

Table 8.6   Equity in per cent of Credits to the General Public and Total Assets, 1960–1992: Commercial Banks, Savings Banks, and Co-operative Banks Compared (Amounts in FIM million)

| | Commercial Banks | | | Savings Banks | | | Co-operative Banks | | |
| | | Per cent of | | | Per cent of | | Equity | Per cent of | |
	Equity	Credits	Assets	Equity	Credits	Assets		Credits	Assets
1960	195	6.2	5.6	65	4.2	3.2	25	2.3	1.8
1965	451	8.6	6.0	100	3.8	2.9	36	1.8	1.4
1970	821	8.6	5.2	132	3.0	2.3	57	1.7	1.3
1975	2,216	7.8	5.4	263	2.9	2.2	177	2.3	1.8
1980	3,236	6.7	4.0	495	2.6	1.9	451	2.7	2.1
1985	9,060	8.8	4.3	1,235	3.3	2.4	1,056	2.9	2.2
1990	32,967	13.5	6.2	6,880	8.0	5.6	5,327	7.0	5.1
1991	43,269	18.1	6.2	7,192	8.8	6.0	5,489	6.9	4.9
1992	37,509	17.1	7.2	4,129	5.6	3.6	5,536	6.9	4.8

Source: Statistics Finland: *Statistical Yearbook*, relevant years.
Note: Reserves include provisions for bad debts. In 1991 and 1992 reserves were negative by FIM 5,881 and 9,839 respectively, thereby reducing actual equity to FIM 37,378 and 27,670, respectively.

financed through bond issues or other long-term borrowings (§1), but nothing specific like in Denmark.

The 1978 Act stated directly (§3) that the membership of an association consisted of its borrowers and founders, and that the members were not liable for the obligations of the association, a strong contrast to the Danish mortgage associations until the 1990s (cfr. Chapter 7). There were also no requirements to match the cash flows of assets and liabilities.

The 1978 Act was made applicable also to the mortgage banks formed according the 1969 Mortgage Bank Act, with the modifications dictated by the different forms of ownership.

In 1993, Mortgage associations and mortgage banks were both incorporated into the 1993 Credit Institutions Act[37] according to which all types of credit institutions are, in principle, identical in terms of activities and capital requirements. The only differences were those dictated by differences in their legal forms of ownership.

Since 1993, mortgage institutions can only be created as joint stock companies. This is of little significance. The only remaining mortgage institution[38]

---

[37]Lag om kreditinstitut av 30. dec, 1993, Finlands författningssamling, 1993/1607.
[38]In 1989 two older municipality owned institutions combined to form Municipality Finance Plc, in principle a long-term lender to municipalities to help finance their investments in housing projects and other municipality infrastructure projects. It has about 300 shareholders, of which 272 are municipalities, and the state is the largest. It issues bonds, and borrows medium- and long-term money from other financial institutions. In the present context it is not considered part of the "organized capital market" because of its relatively limited scope. It does not address the general public directly.

is the Suomen AsuntoHypoPankki Oy (the Mortgage Society of Finland), which set up a banking subsidiary in 2003, and which is a member of the Finnish Bankers Association. Nobody expects any new mortgage institutions to be created, although in principle, it is possible.

Table 8.7   Relative Composition and Growth of the Credit Stock, 1950–2002

	BoF	Com. banks	Savings banks	Co-op banks	Mortgage institutions	Insurance & pension	Total, million FIM	Total, in % of GDP
			Per cent of total credit stock					
1950	10	44	19	17	2	7	1,840	34
1955	5	45	22	16	3	9	4,394	44
1960	3	44	21	15	6	11	7,241	47
1965	1	43	19	15	7	14	13,317	52
1970	1	37	18	14	6	23	24,517	56
1975	1	40	16	13	7	22	57,998	56
1980	2	43	17	15	6	(18)	113,000	59
1985	1	39	14	13	5	27	263,699	70
1990	0	44	16	14	4	22	533,513	104
1991	0	50	17	17	4	(11)	472,000	96
1992	0	49	17	18	5	(11)	444,000	93
1995	0	57	4	24	(6)	9	340,300	62
2000	0	56	6	19	(5)	(11)	433,000	52
2002	0	53	6	23	(4)	13	595,400	57
			Per cent of GDP					
1950	3	15	7	6	0	2		34
1955	2	20	10	7	0	4		44
1960	1	21	10	7	3	5		47
1965	1	22	10	8	3	7		52
1970	1	22	10	8	3	13		56
1975	1	22	9	7	4	12		56
1980	1	25	10	9	4	(10)		59
1985	1	31	11	11	4	21		78
1990	0	45	17	15	4	23		104
1991	0	48	17	16	4	(10)		96
1992	0	46	15	17	4	(10)		93
1995	0	35	2	15	(4)	6		62
2000	0	29	3	12	(2)	(6)		52
2002	0	31	4	13	(2)	8		57

Source: Statistics Finland: *Statistical Yearbook*, relevant years.

Note: Figures in brackets are SEA's (gu)estimates. The inaccuracies resulting from these (gu)estimates cannot be of an order of magnitude of any consequence for the observations made or the conclusions drawn. The (gu)estimates have been necessitated by changes in the time series in the sources used. The lending figures used are "credits to the general public", i.e. excluding credits to the government, local governments inter-bank credits, and credits to foreign entities. Pre-1963 amounts have been restated in 1963 FIM, i.e. two digits slashed.

8.6   A profile of the capital market, 1950–2008

8.6.1   The growth and composition of the financial sector

The Finnish capital market remained relatively under-developed compared to the other Nordic countries if looked at through the lenses of Table 8.7, which shows the growth and composition of the credit stock 1950–2002.

Structural changes in the banking sector, 1950–2009

During the late 1950s, the BoF gradually gave up its few remaining commercial banking activities, and finally became a "pure central bank".

Between the 1950s and the 1980s, the number of savings banks was reduced to approximately 86, and KOP swallowed a medium-sized commercial bank, but that was basically all.

From 1985 onwards, the Finnish banking scene changed rather fundamentally. The changes had their background partly in the deregulation going on everywhere in the late 1980s, including all the Nordic countries, partly in the feverish business cycle characterizing the late 1980s, and partly in the banking crisis, which engulfed the Nordic countries, particularly Finland, in the early 1990s.

The changes on the banking scene can be summarized as follows:

1985: UBF took a majority shareholding in the Bank of Helsinki. The two banks merged in 1986.

1988: Postipankki given the status of a joint stock commercial bank.

1991: Skopbank, the savings banks' central bank, taken over by the BoF because of mounting losses.

1992: Sparbanken i Finland formed by the merger of 43 savings banks all in various degrees of trouble. The other approximately 40 savings banks continued on their own. KOP took over the STS Bank Ltd, the bank transformed from the former trade union savings bank (it proved to be a highly poisoned pill).

1993: Sparbanken i Finland dissolved. The sound parts of the business sold to KOP, UBF, Postipankki (25 per cent to each), and the co-operative banks. The "sick" parts transferred to a "bad bank".

1995: The sound parts of Skopbank acquired by Svenska Handelbanken. The "sick" parts transferred to a "bad bank". KOP merged with UBF to become Merita Bank, the fourth or fifth largest Nordic bank at that time.

1997: Approximately 250 local co-op banks merged with OKObank to form the new OKObank. The remaining co-op banks combined under the umbrella of Aktia Sparbanken Oy. Merita Bank merged with the Swedish Nordbanken Ab to form Merita-Nordbanken Ab.

1998: The 100 per cent state-owned Postipankki merged with the 100 per cent state-owned Finlands Eksportkredit to form Leonia Bank Abp.

1999: Leonia Bank merged with Försäkringsbolaget Sampo Abp. The banking activities concentrated in Sampo Bank.

2001: The Danish Unibank A/S and the Norwegian Cristiania Bank og Kreditkasse AS merged with Merita-Nordbank to form Nordea Ab, the largest Nordic bank.

2006: Sampo Bank acquired by Danske Bank.

The process summarized above has left the Finnish banking market with the dominating (Swedish headquartered) Nordea Bank, about 40 savings banks, two co-op banking groups, and a handful of foreign or foreign-owned banks/bank branches, including Svenska Handelsbanken, Sampo, SEbanken, and DNB-Nor.

This structure, which also includes a single specialized mortgage lender, the Suomen AsuntoHypoPankki, is by far the most concentrated financial market among the Nordic countries.

8.6.2 The 1991–1995 banking crisis

In all four Nordic countries, the early 1990s witnessed a banking crisis of a magnitude not seen since the 1920s. The causes did not differ much between the Nordic countries, although Finland suffered more from the collapse of the Russian economy than did any other western country. Therefore, the financial crisis hit Finland worse than any of the other Nordic Countries. Denmark escaped substantially easier than the three other countries.

Over the four years shown in Table 8.8, credit losses swept away all of the equity of the commercial banks, twice the equity of the savings banks, and all of the equity of the co-operative banks. Operating income compensated for only a fraction of the credit losses.

Table 8.8 Credit Losses Recorded by Commercial Banks, Savings Banks, and Co-operative Banks, 1991–1994 (Million FIM)

	Equity at end-1990	1991	1992	1993	1994	Total, 1990–1993
Commercial banks	31,446	4,968	12,132	12,929	8,729	38,758
Savings banks	6,880	1,136	7,961	3,105	220	12,422
Co-operative banks	5,237	422	1,285	2,755	2,612	7,074
Total	43,653	6,526	21,378	18,789	11,561	58,254

Source: Statistics Finland: *Statistical Yearbook*, 2008, p. 283.

Note: The figures have been subject to some revisions over time. A memo from the Statsråd ("Ministerial Council") to Parliament, dated 16.11.99 ("Statsrådets Redogörelse till Riksdagen om Bankstödet"), stated the combined credit losses for 1991–1994 as FIM 65 billion (ca. EU10 billion).

It is easily seen that even if the Finnish banks, savings banks, and co-operative banks had been endowed with a good margin over the capital ratios required by Basel II or those considered for a Basel III, a wholesale government rescue operation would still have been necessary.

The reasons for these losses can be summarized as follows:

a) The collapse of the Russian and Ukrainian economies caused a wave of bankruptcies in Finland. In the 1980s, more than 20 per cent of Finland's exports went to Russia and Ukraine. In the early 1990s, it was almost zero.

b) Optimism brought about by the internationally surging business cycle in the second half of the 1980s, with soaring stock markets and property prices, like elsewhere (e.g. the London docklands). It would have been truly surprising if the developments in the rest of the world had not been mirrored in the recently deregulated Nordic countries.

   Office buildings, shopping malls, and luxury apartment blocks were built on huge scales, before any tenants had been found, and financed by banks and savings banks which shared the optimism of their clients.

c) Changes in banking regulations, which allowed savings and co-op banks to venture into more risky business areas, where they had little experience, and where they fought hard to gain market share. Commercial banks fought equally hard to defend their market shares.

When the markets had eventually topped, the ensuing decline was fast and steep, because everybody headed for the exit at the same time. The banks found themselves sitting with large loans, which could not be repaid, and which were secured with collateral now worth only a fraction of their earlier estimated values. The pattern was identical in most of the western world, in some places more acute than others, and it had been seen several times before (e.g. in the 1920s, around 1908, etc). It would be repeated in 2006–2008 in other countries, but not in Finland.

Deregulation has often been mentioned as one of the causes of the calamities. Depending on the extent and scope of the regulations, deregulation could be more or less earth-shattering.

In Finland, deregulation changed the world. Interest rates became a price mechanism and a competitive instrument. Capital was no longer rationed, and savings banks could compete with commercial banks for business they had earlier been more or less barred from doing. With booming stock markets, it was no problem for the commercial banks to raise more share capital enabling them to accommodate customer demand. Savings and co-operative banks also did not find it too difficult to raise additional funds. However, the capital raised in the late 1980s was wiped out by the losses of the first half of the 1990s.

As if directed by an invisible hand, investors decided in 1991 that the music was about to stop, and everybody stopped dancing[39] at approximately the same time.

The government and BoF rescue operation is summarized in Table 8.9. The table shows the amounts paid out as capital loans and under guarantees made under the Government Guarantee Fund Act of 1992[40] (which has been amended several times since).

Table 8.9   Government Support for Financial Institutions, 1991–1999 (Billion FIM)

FIM billion	Paid out	Repaid by 31.10.99	Net paid out, including outstanding guarantees
Commercial banks (excluding Skopbank)	7.4	4.7	2.7
Savings banks	88.1	42.7	45.4
– of which Skopbank	21.8	12.2	9.6
Co-op banks	1.5	1.5	–
Total	97.0	48.9	48.1
Per cent of 1992 GDP	20.3%	10.3%	10.0%

Source: "Statsrådets redogörelse till Riksdagen om bankstödet", November 11, 1999. ("The State Council's Report to the Parliament on the Bank Support")

In addition to the amounts shown in Table 8.9, the government supplied FIM 8 billion in new share capital to the commercial banks in 1992. All of this had been repaid by the end of 1998, except for the capital supplied to Skopbank (approximately half of the 8 billion).

Since 1999, approximately FIM 9 billion has been recovered, so that the end result was a loss of about 39 billion, or 8 per cent of the 1992 GDP.

The support was given by the "Statens säkerhetsfond" created in 1992 for this purpose, and funded mainly by government bonds and by foreign borrowings guaranteed by the Republic of Finland, after the "security funds" set up according to the 1969 Acts (cfr. 8.3.2) had been depleted.

Before the creation of the Statens säkerhetsfond, the BoF had to take over the Sparebanken i Finland and the sick assets of Skopbank. These assets

---

[39]"When the music stops, in terms of liquidity, things will be complicated. But as long as the music is playing, you've got to get up and dance. We're still dancing." Chuck Prince, Citigroup chief executive, July 9, 2007, as quoted e.g. in the Financial Times, December 9, 2009. This statement would have been an equally apt reflection of the mood in the Nordic countries in the early 1990s.

[40]Lag av 30 april 1992 om statens säkerhetsfond (379/1992).

were later placed in a "bad bank" ("Arsenal"), a model also used in Sweden ("Securum" and "Retriva", cfr. Chapter 10).

The BoF ended up with a loss of about FIM 4 billion, while the government (i.e. the tax payers) lost about FIM 35 billion.

The government support had conditions and strings attached to it, including board representation and dividend restrictions.

8.7   The stock exchange

Table 8.10 clearly shows the negligible turnover until about 1990, and the modest role played by bonds on the Finnish capital market. The surge in bond turnover in the late 1980s and early 1990s was, first, a result of the hectic atmosphere in the construction sector in the late 1980s, and, second, caused by the bonds issued to finance part of the bank rescues in the early 1990s, cfr. 8.6.2.

Table 8.10   Turnover on the Helsinki Stock Exchange, 1938–2007 (Million FIM)

Annual averages	Shares	Bonds	Total	Total in % of GDP
1938	2	0	2	0.5
1945	13	–	13	0.9
1950–1954	18	4	23	0.3
1955–1959	24	2	26	0.2
1960–1964	27	3	29	0.1
1965–1969	29	9	39	0.1
1970–1974	147	20	167	0.3
1975–1979	190	101	291	0.2
1980–1984	1,055	2,245	3,300	1.3
1985–1989	20,828	6,644	27,471	6.7
1990–1994	29,479	16,676	46,155	9.3
1995–1999	260,317	529	260,847	41.1
2000–2004	1,106,189	123	1,106,312	130.2
2005–2007	1,782,840	296	1,783,136	178.3
Million EUR				
2000–2004	189,092	21	189,113	130.2
2005–2007	304,759	50	304,809	178.3

Source: Statistics Finland, *Statistical Yearbooks*, relevant years.

On the merger of the Helsinki Stock exchange with the Swedish OM Group to form the OMX, see Chapter 10.

9
Norway, 1918–2010: Saved by the North Sea

"... it is very much lamented, Brutus,
that you have no such mirrrors as will turn
your hidden values into your eye,
that you might see your shadow."

(Julius Caesar, Act I)

9.1 An overview: Taking arms with a (North) Sea of riches

It is very much to be lamented that the Norwegian governments did not have a mirror that could make them see the nature of the dangers lurking in the shadows of their pursued policies.

Shipping rates, prices of timber, pulp, whale oil, and fish, exchange rates, and the balance of payments have all traditionally been the core of all financial debates in Norway during the last 200 years. Around the late 1970s, focus shifted from whale oil to North Sea oil. The trouble has always been that all of these elements are traditionally quite volatile, and that the prices and exchange rates of strategic importance for Norway, particularly the USD and the GBP, do not always move in harmonious patterns to Norway's advantage.

A few figures will illustrate the dimensions (see Table 9.1).

Norway re-joined the gold standard at the original gold parity as from 1928, slightly later than the other Nordic countries, and abandoned it again in 1931 like everybody else.

After WWII, the first 40 years were not much different in Norway compared to Denmark and Finland. Continuous foreign exchange shortage and a wish to expand public welfare services led to severe strains on monetary policies. Strict quantitative restrictions became important tools of monetary policy for extended periods in Norway, just as in Sweden and Finland.

Another peculiarly striking feature in Norway was the large number of special purpose state "banks" created in the first half of the 20th century. Even if a few such institutions were created also in the other Nordic

Table 9.1   Norway's Exports and Foreign Debts, 1920–1939

	GDP	Net foreign debts	
	NOK, million	*% of GDP*	*% of exports*
1925	5,633	24	81
1930	4,377	38	127
1935	4,362	36	136
1939	6,253	18	64

Source: Statistisk Sentralbyrå (NOS, 1994) *Historisk Statistikk*, pp. 532, 533, and 647.

Comments:

1. Between 1920 and the mid-1930s, GDP declined in nominal terms, but not in real terms. In real terms, the GDP growth rates were:[1]
   1920–28: 20 per cent;
   1930–39: 29 per cent (1931–39: 40 per cent. Unfortunately, there was a drop of about 8 per cent between 1930 and 1931.)

2. In the 1920s, Norway's export prices dropped faster than other prices (i.e. deterioration of the terms of trade), and Norway had deficits on the balance of payments. Foreign debts increased.

3. In the 1930s, Norway had surpluses on the balance of payments except for three years, and foreign debts declined. Still, it is evident that throughout the 1920s and 1930s, Norway was highly dependent on foreign sources of credit.

countries (e.g. for ship financing and long-term export finance), no other Nordic country formed so many governmental special purpose finance vehicles as did Norway. If they mirrored some problems, they failed to solve them.

Like the other Nordic countries, Norway had its banking crisis in the early 1920s, and several bank and savings bank casualties also in the 1930s.

By the mid-1980s things changed. First, the North Sea petroleum adventure was now yielding high dividends, freeing Norway from its perennial foreign exchange shortage, and secondly, the financial system was deregulated over a quite short span of time, like in the other Nordic countries. However, Norwegian governments still seemed to be short of the mirror which would have enabled them to recognize the dangers now emerging from the shadows.

In the late 1980s, a severe banking crisis erupted, and by 1992, the country's three largest banks[2] had ended up in state ownership. For Norway, state ownership of commercial banks was, however, not quite as controversial as in the other Nordic countries, possibly because Norway was used to having state "banks".

---

[1] G. Jahn, A. Eriksen, P. Munthe (1966) *Norges Bank gjennom 150 År* (Norges Bank, Oslo) pp. 262 and 286.

[2] DnC, Christiania Bank og Kreditkasse, and Bergen Bank.

In the meantime, Norway had rejected EU membership in two referendums (1972 and 2000), so Norway remains the only one of the four Nordic countries outside the EU.

Since 1931, the Norwegian currency (the NOK) has generally fluctuated in a range between 100 and 80 per cent of parity to the DKK (in 2010: 90–95 per cent).

9.2   The inter-war period

9.2.1   The problems

The ratio and composition of savings and capital spendings

The exceptionally high savings and investment ratios seen between the 1890s and 1920, cfr. Chapter 5, were lower but still fairly high in the 1920s, but increased again in the 1930s. Otherwise the growth rates indicated above would not have been realized.

The savings and capital spending ratios are shown in Table 9.2:

Table 9.2   Capital Spending and Savings Ratios, 1918–1939

Annual averages	GDP	Gross fixed capital formation		Gross savings	
	Million NOK	*Million NOK*	*% of GDP*	*Million NOK*	*% of GDP*
1918–1921	6,048	1,591	26.3	1,082	17.9
1922–1925	5,297	990	18.7	839	15.8
1926–1929	4,358	779	17.9	776	17.8
1930–1933	3,987	751	18.8	818	20.5
1934–1937	4,715	1,005	21.3	1,173	24.9
1938–1939	6,040	1,503	24.9	1,620	26.8

Source: Statistisk Sentralbyrå (NOS, 1994) *Historisk Statistikk*, pp. 532–4.

It is seen that during most of the 1920s, the investment ratio exceeded the savings ratio, while in the 1930s, this was mostly the other way round.

The structure of the savings did, however, differ from several other (industrialized) countries in a way, which has had important implication for the capital markets. The remarkable aspect was that a very large share of the savings was made by the central government, whose savings substantially exceeded its capital spendings. Table 9.3 shows the extent to which savings in the respective sectors exceeded net capital spendings in the respective sectors.

Table 9.3 shows that the central government was a net supplier of savings throughout the period, except in 1921–1926, and that Norway was a net borrower abroad in all years, except 1931–1939.

The "problem" with the net savings by the central government was to find a way to rechannel these savings back into productive capital spending. This was done by the creation of special purpose state banks, cfr. below.

Table 9.3   The Structure of Net Savings, 1915–1963, per cent of Net Fixed Capital Formation

Annual averages	1915– 1920	1921– 1926	1927– 1930	1931– 1939	1946– 1951	1952– 1956	1957– 1963
Central government	5.5	–10.9	14.2	13.9	31.9	17.2	23.9
Local government	–3.6	–6.5	3.7	–0.1	4.1	1.3	2.4
Private sector	–26.4	–53.0	–41.4	–5.2	–48.4	–25.4	–2.2
Total	–24.5	–70.4	–23.5	8.6	–12.4	– 7.0	–12.2

Source: H. Skånland (1967) *Det Norske Kredittmarked siden 1900* (Statistisk Sentralbyrå) p. 109.
Note: A minus means net borrowing. Negative totals equal net foreign borrowings.

The banking crisis of 1922–1924

The crisis, which culminated in 1923, had its roots in the final years of WWI, had deepened since 1920, when the "war bubble" punctured. Prices of strategic commodities fell sharply: By the end of 1921, the prices of timber, pulp, and whale oil had fallen to one-third or one-fourth of their 1920 levels, and the number of bankruptcies had increased from about 20–25 per month in 1920 to some 120 in the June 1921.[3]

Unsurprisingly, many banks suffered heavy losses.

The number of banks and savings banks, which went bankrupt, were placed under administration, or were liquidated, has been counted as shown below:

Table 9.4   Number of Banks and Savings Banks Rescued, 1921–1928

	1921	1922	1923	1924	1925	1926	1927	1928	1921–1928
Commercial banks	3	10	21	7	9	21	8	6	84
Savings banks	0	0	5	2	2	3	8	1	21

Source: H. Skånland (1967) *Det Norske Kredittmarked siden 1900* (Statistisk Sentralbyrå) p. 165.

The rescued banks included most of Norway's largest banks, e.g. Central-banken, Andresens Bank, Bergen Privatbank, Den norske Creditbank, and Norges Handelsbank. Some of the rescued banks survived after reconstruction, while others, like e.g. Centralbanken, failed permanently.

The effect on the number of banks and savings banks and their balance sheets are seen in Tables 9.5 and 9.6 below.

It would be a mistake to assume that the many bank failures were the result only of the malicious downturn of the international business cycle. Already in early 1922 had it been pointed out by Mr. Rygg, governor of

---

[3]Cfr. E. Engebretsen (1948) *Christiania Bank og Kreditkasse 1848–1948* (Oslo) p. 270.

Norges Bank, that many of the failed banks had concentrated too large exposures on too few clients, and that many of their transactions had been reckless or even violated the by-laws of the banks.[4] At the time he made these remarks he had seen only the beginning.

9.2.2   Responses and actions

Bank rescues and reorganizations

In the first stages of the banking crisis there was, of course, no "master plan" for the handling of collapsing banks. The initial reaction was, basically, to handle them as any other case of corporate bankruptcy, but widely dispersed compositions of creditors/depositors made it almost impossible for the creditors ever to agree on anything. Lack of agreement on reconstruction plans led to lost assets and bankruptcies. By the spring of 1923 the government and Norges Bank agreed that the repercussions of lost customer deposits and called in bank loans would be unacceptably destructive for the general economy. Therefore, and against much opposition, Norges Bank was empowered to place troubled banks under administration for a period of up to one year while long-term solutions were being sought. During the summer of 1923, 21 banks and six savings banks were placed under administration, representing about one-third of all bank assets,[5] and by 1928, when the Administration Act expired, a total of 46 commercial banks had been placed under administration. Only six of them survived as independent banks.[6] Approximately 40 other banks were reconstructed without having first been placed under administration.

The banking and savings banks Acts of 1924

The banking and savings banks Acts of 1924 did not spring directly from the banking crisis of the immediately preceding years. They were the result of concerns first aired in 1917 that the proliferation of banks in the feverishly speculative atmosphere prevailing around the end of WWI would lead to excessive competition among banks, and the financing of unhealthy transactions with the implied risk of losses for unwitting bank depositors. The short-term result of these concerns was the three-paragraph "Bank Formation Act of 1918", which introduced the requirement that no new banks could be formed, and no expansion of existing banks could take place, without a licence from the Ministry of Finance. This was a "stop-gap" measure intended to provide time for a solution to the more long-term issue of general banking legislation, which was being sorted out by a committee.

---

[4]Abstract from Mr. Rygg's speech to the Assembly of Representatives of Norges Bank, February 1922, as summarized by Engebretsen (1948) in *Christiania Bank og Kreditkasse 1848–1948*, p. 271.
[5]As for fn. 3, p. 280.
[6]As for fn. 3, p. 285.

The proposals of this committee resulted in the 1924 Banking Act, Norway's first "real" banking Act taking, effect as from January 1, 1925. For the substance of the 1924 Act, see Schedule 9.1 below, which compares it to the 1961 Banking Act.

The inter-war developments for the commercial banks are seen from Table 9.5.

Table 9.5   Commercial Banks, Summary Balance Sheets, 1915–1940

		Assets				Liabilities		
	No. of banks	Credits to the general public	Financial assets	Cash and other	Total assets & liabilities, NOK million	Equity	Deposits	Other
		Per cent of total assets				Per cent of total liabilities		
1920	192	74	18	8	5,461	17	68	15
1925	160	63	21	16	3,635	10	72	18
1930	151	54	22	24	2,401	12	78	10
1935	105	68	22	10	1,569	15	78	7
1940	104	50	43	7	2,222	11	80	9

Source: Statistisk Sentralbyrå (1994) *Historisk Statistikk*, pp. 624–5.

In the early 1930s, a number of banks (including Den norske Creditbank) and savings banks got into trouble and were subject to various forms of rescue operations by Norges Bank.

As in the other Nordic countries, the banking crises of the 1920s and 1930s had the effect of strengthening the market position of the savings banks at the expense of the commercial banks. Whereas total bank assets were about 200 per cent of total savings bank assets in 1920, it had dropped to about 100 per cent in 1940.

The development of the savings banks sector is seen in Table 9.6.

The many failures among the savings bank resulted in the formation in 1932 of Garantikassen for Sparekasser, a joint savings banks institution which offered guarantees in favour of member savings banks in difficulties. Membership was voluntary. Its funds were obtained from annual contributions from all the member savings banks plus a minor sum from the government. Several savings banks were rescued by this vehicle.

Interest rate regulation

During the 1930s, it was a general wish – in many countries – that interest rates should be lowered. Consequently, central banks reduced their discount rates. For Norges Bank – as for others – the problem was that commercial

Table 9.6   Savings Banks, Summary Balance Sheets, 1915–1940

	No. of savings banks	Credits to the general public	Financial assets	Cash and other	Total assets & liabilities, NOK million	Capital	Deposits	Other
		Assets				*Liabilities*		
		Per cent of total assets				*Per cent of total liabilities*		
1920	562	77	22	1	2,253	6	93	1
1925	584	65	33	2	2,768	6	93	1
1930	627	60	37	3	2,495	8	91	1
1935	614	59	38	3	2,288	11	88	1
1940	607	56	37	7	2,239	12	87	1

Source: Statistisk Sentralbyrå (1994) *Historisk Statistikk*, pp. 628–9.

banks set their own interest rates according to market conditions, which did not necessarily conform to political wishes.

Therefore, an interest act was passed in 1934,[7] which empowered the Bank- and Savings Bank Inspection to order banks and savings banks to lower their lending rates to the lowest levels applied by other banks. Interest rates as a tool of competition was hereby eliminated.

The state "banks"

As noted above (Table 9.3), the central government had substantial net savings (except in the 1920s), which had somehow to be channeled into capital spending. Once the first government sponsored special purpose mortgage institution had been founded (Kongeriket Norges Hypotekbank, 1852, cfr. Chapter 5), the idea seems to have stuck that government guaranteed special purpose "banks" was the way to manage and invest government savings, and thereby simultaneously to ensure that perceived "worthy" financing needs were satisfied. The foundation of a total of about 15 state banks took place over a period of nearly 100 years, with most of them born in the inter-war period.

They were not all of identical structure, and they seem often to have been the result of ad hoc decisions (like many other political decisions). Although official Norwegian statistics refer to them as "banks" ("statsbanker"), none of them satisfies any of the definitions of "banks" discussed in the Introduction. They neither took deposits from the general public, nor offered credits generally to the public.

---

[7] Lov av 29. juni 1934. Cfr. Jahn, Eriksen, Munthe (1966) *Norges Bank gjennom 150 År* (Oslo) p. 293.

These "state banks", whose intended purposes mostly emerge from their names, were, in chronological order (foundation year in brackets. Also see 5.3.3):

1. Kongeriket Norges Hypotekbank (1852). 1966 merged into Statens Landbruksbank
2. Den Norske Stats Smaabruk- og Boligbank (1917, a reorganization of a 1903 institution)
3. Den Norske Stats Fiskeribank (1921)
4. Norges Kommunalbank (1926)
5. Lånekassen for Fiskere (1932)
6. Lånekassen for Jordbrukere (1932)
7. A/S Den Norske Industribank (1936, jointly owned with private share-holders)
8. Driftskreditkassen for Jordbruket (1936)
9. Den Norske Stats Husbank (1946). Eventually the largest of the state banks
10. Statens Landbruksbank (1966). The result of a merger of Kongeriket Norges Hypotekbank (1852), Den Norske Stats Smaabruk-og Boligbank, and a few more of the above-mentioned institutions.

These institutions were created by Act of law to serve purposes given high political priority and perceived to be poorly served by the private financial institutions, including fishery, smallholders, students, the poor, etc.

They did not all exist simultaneously. Some were wound up at an early stage, and some were the result of mergers.

Table 9.7 shows their combined balance sheets. It will be seen that these state banks were not very large, and that they were almost fully funded by government guaranteed bond issues.

Table 9.7   The State Banks, Summary Balance Sheets, 1915–1940 (Million NOK)

	Number of institutions	Loans	Other assets	Total assets & liabilities	Bond issues	Other
1915	2	240	41	281	226	55
1920	3	310	53	363	301	62
1925	4	546	93	639	517	122
1930	5	821	169	990	796	194
1935	6	983	205	1,188	918	270
1940	9	1,104	231	1,335	1,019	316

Sources: Loans, bond issues, and number of institutions: Statistisk Sentralbyrå (1994) *Historisk Statistikk*, p. 622.
Total assets: H.I. Matre (1992) *Norske Kreditinstitutioner 1850–1990* (NORAS, Rapport nr. 42) Table 1a.

9.3 A profile of the capital market, 1918–1940

The banking crisis of the first half of the 1920s did not fail to leave its mark on the structure of the capital market, as seen from Table 9.8. The state banks took increasing market shares, and so did the savings banks, both at the expense of the commercial banks.

Table 9.8 Relative Composition and Growth of the Credit Stock, 1915–1940

	State banks	Commercial banks	Savings banks	Insurance companies	Mortgage institutions	Million NOK	Total in % of GDP
			Per cent of total				
1915	12	49	33	6	1	2,007	77
1920	5	64	27	4	0	6,363	85
1925	11	45	35	8	1	5,121	91
1930	19	30	36	13	2	4,264	97
1935	23	25	31	17	4	4,330	99
1940	23	23	26	22	6	4,817	
			Per cent of GDP				
1915	9	38	26	4	0		77
1920	4	55	23	3	0		85
1925	10	41	32	7	1		91
1930	19	29	34	13	2		97
1935	23	25	39	17	4		99

Source: As for Tables 9.2, and 9.5–9.7 (No GDP figures for 1940 available.)

Like in Finland, the organized capital market remained quite small compared to Denmark and Sweden (cfr. Chapters 7 and 10).

Norway was the only Nordic country where the market share of the savings banks surpassed that of the commercial banks, but after WWII, the commercial banks outgrew the savings banks again.

The strong growth of the state "banks" in this period is also conspicuous.

9.4 The post-war pre-oil era, 1945–1985

9.4.1 The problems

During the war, a vast system of controls, regulations, and rationings had grown up in response to shortage of almost everything, just like in Denmark. The shortages and rationings continued until the late 1950s.

During the first twenty post WWII years, changing governments, mostly social-democratic, chose to maintain the wide-ranging net of restrictions introduced during the war. In this policy,[8] Norway differed considerably from Denmark, where the general policy was to get rid of the war-time restrictions as fast as possible.

Like in Sweden, the Norwegian government saw residential construction, infrastructure investments, and the maintenance of low interest rates as the main objectives.

9.4.2   Responses and actions

Norges Bank nationalized 1949

Following a few years of discussions it was decided in 1949 to nationalize Norges Bank. According to the nationalization Act,[9] the state was to acquire the shares from the private shareholders at a price of 180 per cent of the face value,[10] paid cash.

The previous year, the bank governors had expressed strong reservations against the nationalization plans. They had argued, based on discussions with their foreign correspondents, that it would probably hurt Norway's precarious international creditworthiness.[11] Nevertheless, the government went ahead with the nationalization for the reason that it had found it right to establish also formally that Norges Bank was a government institution, fully and totally, like in the neighbouring countries of Sweden and Denmark ("... Regjeringa har funni det rett å slå fast, også rein formelt, at Norges Bank er en statsbank fullt og heilt, på same måten som i ... våre granneland som Danmark og Sverike."[12]). If Olav Meisdalshagen, the minister of finance, who made this statement to the Storting ("Parliament"), knew how fundamentallly different the position of Danmarks Nationalbank was from that

---

[8]Some historians have claimed that the chosen policy was a "necessity", e.g. P. Munthe (1966) in *Norges Bank Gjennom 150 År* (Oslo) p. 350, but surely it would have been possible to have a policy of dismantling the war-time restrictions "as fast as possible", but this objective was deliberately rejected. The restrictions were maintained largely as a matter of principle. See also Hanisch, Sölen & Ecklund (1999) Norsk økonomisk politikk i det 20. århundre (Höyskoleforlaget) pp. 150–4.

[9]Lov av 8. juli 1949.

[10]By end 1950, Norges Bank had a share capital of NOK 35 million and reserves of 65 million, giving it an internal value of approximately 285, so it looks as if the shareholders were short changed. In Jahn, Eriksen og Munthe (1966) *Norges Bank i 150 År* (Oslo) the official history of the Bank of Norway, no explanation is given for the calculation of the conversion price of 180.

[11]"Stiller en seg det spørgsmål om vi styrker vår utenlandske kreditt ved at Staten nå går til innløsning av aksjene i Norges Bank, bliver svaret ubetinget nej ... vår erfaring fra alle de ganger vi har vært i kontakt med med utenlandske kretser at en realisasjon av denne tanke vil være egnet til å svekke Norges kreditt." Statement from the majority of govenors of Norges Bank, April 8, 1948, as quoted in Jahn, Eriksen og Munthe (1966) *Norges Bank i 150 År*, p. 412.

[12]As quoted in "Norges Bank i 150 År", Oslo 1966, p. 411.

of Sverriges Riksbank, he at least found it opportune on this occasion to suppress any such knowledge.

The nationalization of the Bank of England and the Banque de France a few years earlier probably formed part of the psychological background. Given the original set-up of Norges Bank (cfr. Chapter 5), it appears unlikely that the nationalization ever made any material difference to any actions taken or policies pursued by Norges Bank.

The next major review of the status of Norges Bank took place with the 1985 "central bank Act",[13] which underlined the Bank's status as an operating arm for the government, at least as much as in Sweden if not more cfr. §2 (SEA's translation): "The Bank is to carry out its duties in accordance with the guidelines for economic policy as laid down by the government … In the Government Council ("Statsrådet") the King may decide on the activities of the Bank. Such decisions may constitute general regulations or instructions on specific matters."

The voluntary agreements

The continuation of the restrictions initially implied a principle of comprehensive and "voluntary" agreements between Norges Bank and the Finance Ministry on the one side, and each group of financial institutions on the other. Very much like in Sweden. A special organization, the "Samarbeids-nemnda" (the "Co-operation Committee"), was created in 1951 as a forum for discussing the "agreements" to be reached. However, some legislation was introduced, notably the 1953 Interest Act authorizing the government to set fixed ceilings over interest rates and fees charged by banks and savings banks, and the 1955 Act forcing banks and savings banks to invest certain minimum amounts in treasury bills ("statskasseveksler") in order to re-finance the government's loans to the state banks.

The banking and savings bank Acts of 1961

The banking and savings banks Acts of 1961 were the result of 11 years of deliberations in a special committee, which submitted its report on December 19, 1958.[14] Much of the thinking surrounding the formation of this committee was flavoured by the social-democratic government's taste for central control of the financial sector, which was also reflected in the nationalization of Norges Bank. In its parliamentary opening speech ("trontale"), December 1950, the government had declared that committees were to be formed, which would report on the possible nationalization of banks, breweries, and

---

[13]Lov nr. 28 av 24. maj, 1985 om Norges Bank og pengevesen m.v. ("sentralban-kloven"). Later amendments, latest in 2009, have changed only minor points.
[14]"Penge- og Bankkomiteen av 1950", formed by Royal Resolution dated March 24, 1950.

mines.[15] The instruction to the Banking Committee stated that consideration was to be given to the questions of both a qualitative evaluation of the credit policies practised by the banks and savings banks, and to the geographical distribution as well as the allocation of lendings by industry.[16] Rarely has the idea of "selective credit policy" to be pursued through government direction of private institutions been expressed more directly. The implication was that if the 50–60 commercial banks and 400–500 savings banks did not allocate their lendings, by industry and region, to the taste of the government, they faced the threat of nationalization. The instruction to the Banking Committee included a request that the Committee addressed the question of a nationalization of the banks,[17] referring to the remarks made in the "trontale". Nevertheless, the Committee's Report did not address this issue. Interest in this subject had faded away during the second half of the 1950s. Instead, the politically favoured objectives (housing, education, and regional development) were pursued through the state banks and other credit regulations. Most of the Committee's recommendations were adopted by the Storting. The main changes to the existing 1924 Banking Act can be summarized as shown in Schedule 9.1.

Table 9.9 shows the development of the main items of the balance sheets of the commercial banks between 1950 and 1992.

The very fast expansion of the assets, and the reduction of the solvency ratios during the 1980s are clearly visible. The increasing reliance on other sources of funding than customer deposits since the early 1980s is also clearly visible.

For the savings banks, the development was slightly different, possibly because of the strong concentration of the late 1980s, cfr. Table 9.10.

The state banks

In the 1960s, the government had decided that to expand the state banks was an easier way to pursue its goal of securing financing for low-income family housing, education, small-holders and regional development than through a nationalization of the banks (cfr. above).

Therefore, new state banks were formed, and existing state banks were merged and/or reorganized.

---

[15]Cfr. K. Petersen (1982) *Kredittpolitikken i Støpeskjeen. Forretningsbankenes historie i etterkrigstiden* (A/S Hjemmet-Fagpresseforlaget, Oslo) p. 217.

[16]"... det bør åpnes adgang til å undergi bankenes engasjementer skjønnsmæssig vurdering ... hvorvidt denne skjønnsmæssige vurdering hensiktsmessig kan omfatte spørsmålet om ... bankenes kredittgivning på en tilfredssillende måte imøtekommer kredittbehovet i de forskjellige landsdeler og næringer." The 1950 Banking Committee Report, dated December 19, 1958, p. 5.

[17]The 1950 Banking Committee Report, p. 6.

Schedule 9.1 The Banking Acts of 1924 and 1961 Compared

Subject	The Banking Act of April 4, 1924	The Banking Act of May 24, 1961
Definition of "banking", and allowed business	A bank is joint stock company engaged in banking business. Banks can do all kinds of business customary for banks. ("... kan drive alle slags forretninger som det er alminnelig for en bank å drive ..."	Banks ("forretningsbanker") can do all kinds of business transactions and services customary and natural for banks. ("... alle forretninger og tjenester som det er vanlig eller naturlig at banker utfører"). First time the term "forretningsbank" ("commercial banks") became the official term for deposit-taking joint stock banking companies.
Capital and solvency	Minimum NOK 400,000. Share capital + reserves to equal minimum 10% of total obligations. Total guarantees maximum 75% of equity.	Minimum NOK 1 million for new banks. Equity (defined as in 1924) minimum 8% of total obligations. Reduced to 6.5% in 1972. Total guarantees maximum 100% of equity. (Both in 1924 and 1961 with the possibility for dispensations in case of "safe" guarantees.)
Liquidity	Cash minimum 20% of call obligations, or 5% of total obligations except guarantees, whichever is higher. Cash included also certain bonds not guaranteed by the government.	Cash minimum 25% of call deposits from non-banks or 5% of all deposits from non-banks, but always minimum 10% of all deposits from non-banks. Cash defined as including short-term net claims on other banks, government and government guaranteed bonds.
Maximum single exposure	25% of equity.	One-third of equity. For borrowing associations with joint liability, up to 50% (e.g. associations of fishermen or forresters).
Share owner-ship	Maximum 20% of equity.	Maximum 30% of equity.
"Safety fund"		The creation of "Forrretnings-bankenes sikringsfond", a safety-net to which banks were compelled to contribute with 1 per mille of their assets until the Fund reached an amount equalling 2 per cent of total bank deposits.

Comments:
1. In principle, the 1961 Banking Act was identical to the Savings Banks Act passed simultaneously. The only reason why two separate Acts were passed, was the difference in the ownership structure. In terms of the substance of the business, there was no difference between banks and savings banks (in contrast to contemporary Danish legislation, cfr. Chapter 7).

Schedule 9.1   The Banking Acts of 1924 and 1961 Compared – *continued*

2. The definition of "banking" was circular. Banks are companies which do banking business, and banking business is defined as business done by banks (a similar circularity is found in Sweden and Finland). The Banking Committee gave up trying to define "banking". In its Report, it limited itself to the statement that banking "... has been, and can assumed to be, changing according to variations in economic conditions, in monetary and payment circumstances, and in customs and in the practice of law."[18] (SEA's translation)
   The implication was that any previous difference between "banking business" and "savings banks business" was formally abolished. This was very much in line with developments in Sweden and Finland, but in contrast to Denmark, where the distinction between "banking business" and "savings banking business" was not formally dissolved until 1974 (cfr. 7.3.2).
   No effort was made here to distinguish between "commercial banking", "retail banking", "savings banking", or "investment banking". Neither the private mortgage institutions (the "kredittforetak") nor leasing and factoring companies ("finansselskaper") were subject to the 1961 Banking Act.
3. Both the minimum capital amounts and the solvency ratio were controversial.
   In 1957, when the Committee completed its report, 34 out of Norway's 74 commercial banks had share capitals of less than NOK 1 million,[19] and very few of the banks and savings banks could satisfy the 10 per cent required by the 1924 Act. Therefore, it was reduced to 8 per cent in 1961, and to 6.5 per cent in 1972. The attitude was that if the banks could not meet the requirements, the requirements had to be reduced.
4. The liquidity requirements were soon made irrelevant by the 1965 Credit Act, cfr. below.
5. The limit on maximum exposures to a single borrower was controversial, because many of the small local banks had "big" local fishing, shipping, or forest clients. The end result was a compromise between local and central forces.
6. The increase of the share-ownership rights for banks and savings banks was mostly the result of some successful transactions by a few banks.
7. The creation of the "Forretningsbankenes sikringsfond" was the only really new provision of the 1961 Banking Act. It replaced an earlier voluntary guarantee organization comprising most of the banks. Membership of the new "sikringsfond" was compulsory.
   A similar "sikringsfond" was created for the savings banks by the Savings Banks Act to replace the voluntary Garantikassen for Sparekasser of 1932, cfr. 9.2.2.
   Both "sikringsfonde" were funded by a combination of contributions from the banks (one per mille of total assets) and government contributions. They had separate managements, and the banks and savings banks had no automatic or guaranteed right to receive assistance from the funds in case of need. The funds would decide each case on its own merits. In the 1987–1993 crisis, these funds were soon depleted.

Also, by comparing Table 9.7 with Table 9.11 it will be seen that the funding structure of the state banks had changed dramatically from the pre-WWII years, when bond issues financed roughly 90 per cent of the lendings from the state banks. After WWII, funding by bond issues became limited to the amounts the private financial institutions – including the insurance companies – were forced to absorb through "voluntary agreements" with the authorities (cfr. below). The remainder had to be provided by borrowings from the government or Norges Bank. The bonds could not

---

[18]"Den har vært, og antas å måtte være skiftende etter endringene i de økonomiske forhold, i penge- og betalingsforhold og i sedvaner og rettsregler." Report from the Banking Committee of 1950, p. 123.
[19]Cfr. K. Petersen (1982) *Kredittpolitikken i Støpeskjeen* (A/S Hjemmet-Fagpresseforlaget) p. 220. K. Petersen was the general manager of the Norwegian Bankers Association (Den norske Bankforening) 1961–1982.

Table 9.9   Commercial Banks, Summary Balance Sheets, 1950–1989

Year end or annual averages	No.of banks	Domestic loans to non-financial borrowers % of total assets	Total assets & liabilities, million NOK	Equity	Deposits from non-financial depositors
				Per cent of total liabilities	
1950	89	57	6,016	5.8	81
1955	76	67	7,489	5.9	88
1960	68	67	9,733	5.6	83
1965–1969	50–46	66	17,976	6.4	78
1970–1974	40–31	64	31,866	5.9	81
1975–1979	28–26	64	60,471	5.2	86
1980–1984	24–21	61	133,948	4.3	87
1985–1989	27–28	71	316,175	4.2	69
1990–1992	23–21	77	360,459	2.5	69

Source: NOS (1994) *Historisk Statistikk*, pp. 625–7.

Table 9.10   Savings Banks, Summary Balance Sheets, 1950–1989

Year end or annual averages	No.of banks	Domestic loans to non-financial borrowers % of total assets	Total assets & liabilities, million NOK	Equity	Deposits from non-financial depositors
				Per cent of total liabilities	
1950	606	45	5,021	5.6	94
1955	603	58	6,455	4.8	94
1960	597	63	8,510	4.3	95
1965–1969	540–509	66	14,109	3.9	94
1970–1974	493–418	66	24,298	3.1	94
1975–1979	390–345	66	46,113	3.6	93
1980–1984	322–227	64	91,491	3.8	90
1985–1989	198–151	76	214,055	4.1	77
1990–1992	142–134	82	240,684	4.7	84

Source: Statistisk Sentralbyrå (NOS, 1994) *Historisk Statistikk*, pp. 629–31.

be sold in the market on conditions acceptable to the government. Therefore, each of the state banks was made subject to "lending budgets" laid down by the Ministry of Finance and Norges Bank as from 1954.

"Kreditforetak" (private mortgage institutions)

In 1986, the oldest private mortgage institution, "De Norske Bykreditt-foreninger", cfr. Chapter 5, was split into its original three regional parts, each of which was soon swallowed by larger commercial banks in connection with the debacle of the early 1990s.

Table 9.11   **The State Banks, Summary Balance Sheets, 1950–1989**

Year end or annual averages	No. of state banks	Loans, % of total assets	Total assets & liabilities, million NOK	Capital	Bond issues	Borrowings
				Per cent of total liabilities		
1950	11	91	2,068		66	19
1955	11	94	4,683		25	65
1960	11	95	7,101		11	79
1965–1969	11–7	95	13,259	8	5	86
1970–1974	7–8	95	26,303	7	8	84
1975–1979	8	93	61,051	6	21	71
1980–1984	8–10	93	112,284	8	23	69
1985–1989	10	92	150,957	6	16	77

Source: Statistisk Sentralbyrå (1994) *Historisk Statistikk*, pp. 622–3.
1950–1960: H.I. Mattre (1992) *Norske kredittinstitusjoner 1850–1990* (NORAS, rapport nr. 42) Table 3b.
Note: The sources do not give figures for capital prior to 1960.

Between 1907 and 1940, approximately 15 other mortgage institutions ("kredittforetak") of various descriptions had been founded. They formed a mixed bag of bond-issuing institutions reflecting both the fragmented nature of Norway's financial fabric resulting from much regional "patriotism", and the importance of ship finance. They can be grouped in three different categories:

A: The real estate mortgage associations (De Norske Bykredittforeninger, and five others, including one for agriculture and forestry and two for urban commercial property);
B: The bank and savings banks related mortgage companies (Sparebankenes Obligasjonskasse A/S, A/S Næringskredit, A/S Forretningsbankenes Finansierings- og Eksportkredittinstitut, and A/S Låneinstituttet for Strukturrasjonalisering);
C: The ship-financing institutions, of which two were organized as associations (e.g. Den Vesten- og Nordenfjeldske Skibshypotekforening), and three were joint stock companies (e.g. Norges Skibshypoteksbank A/S, 1906). They were all associated with various shipping groups located in different parts of Norway.

There was no, or very little, competition or overlapping between these institutions. They all served particular purposes, some of them in particular geographical areas only.

Their general development is illustrated in Table 9.12.

Table 9.12   The Private Mortgage Institutions ("kredittforetak"), Summary Balance Sheets, 1960–1989

Year end or annual averages	No. of institutions	Loans, % of total assets	Total assets & liabilities, million NOK	Capital	Bond issues
				Per cent of total liabilities	
1960	13	92	1,953	6.4	86
1965–1969	15–17	93	4,025	6.0	88
1970–1974	17–15	91	8,030	6.3	89
1975–1979	17–16	90	20,556	4.4	91
1980–1984	15	90	46,160	4.4	89
1985–1989	15–14	86	126,544	4.8	73

Source: Statistisk Sentralbyrå (1994) *Historisk Statistikk*, pp. 632–3, and Mattre (1992) *Norske kredittinstitusjoner* (NORAS rapport nr, 42) Table 3i.

It will be noted that their loans were almost fully financed by bond issues. The rapid growth during the late 1980s was quite remarkable, and proved not to be healthy.

Den Norske Hypotekforening (1913) made heavy losses in the 1990–1992 banking crisis, and was taken over by Sparebanken NOR, Norway's largest savings bank, in 1993. Sparebanken Nor was the result of a merger of a handful of medium sized savings banks in the late 1980s.

In 1999, Sparebanken NOR merged with Gjensidige-gruppen, the mutual insurance and finance group, to form Gjensidige NOR, which merged with DnB in 2003 to become DnB NOR.

The 1965 Credit Act, and the 1984–1985 deregulation

The agreements, which Norges Bank had regularly made with the private credit institutions, were increasingly circumvented. The primary subjects of the agreements were the rate of expansion of the credit volume by the financial institutions, new issues of bonds and shares, the geographical distribution of the credit volume, the formation of new banks and bank branches, the volume of government and state bank bonds to be acquired by the financial institutions, and the rates of interest to be applied to deposits as well as lendings. Eventually (1965), the private banks and savings banks were made subject to "lending budgets" of the same nature as those applied to the state banks, and included in the annual government financial budgets.

Like in Sweden and Finland, the government wanted to control the price and the volume of credit simultaneously through an intricate system of credit rationing.

The increasing number of circumventions finally persuaded the government and Norges Bank that the system of voluntary agreements had reached its limits, and that legislation was necessary.

The 1965 "Credit Act"[20] was the result of these considerations, emerging from a committee formed in 1962 with a very wide-ranging instruction. The Committee's report, completed already in 1963,[21] closely followed a similar Swedish report,[22] on which the three 1962 credit Acts were based (cfr. Schedule 10.2).

The main points of the 1965 Credit Act[23] were:

1. Like in Sweden, it was an Act empowering the government to take certain actions if and when the Finance Ministry and the Norges Bank recommended such actions to be taken.
2. The nature of the actions which could be taken according to the Credit Act comprised regulations concerning liquidity reserves, foreign exchange reserves, additional reserves ("tilleggsreserver"), obligations to purchase certain securities ("plaseringspligt", the "placement obligation"), direct lending controls for certain lending institutions, maximum interest rates on lendings, and controls on new bond issues. (§1 of the Credit Act)

    Decisions regarding the various kinds of reserves would apply to commercial and savings banks, while regulations pertaining to interest rates and their placement obligations applied also to insurance companies, municipal and private pension funds, mortgage institutions, and other types of lenders. The direct lending controls would apply to banks, insurance companies and pension funds, and the new issue controls applied to bonds, whoever wanted to issue them.

It is easily seen that the scope of this Act was very wide-ranging. In fact, "Norway got a money- and credit policy Act more comprehensive than any other western country" (SEA's translation).[24]

The fact that the subjects previously agreed upon between Norges Bank and the financial institutions, or laid down in the above mentioned 1953 and 1955 Acts, were now embodied in the Credit Act demonstrated that the government had taken full control over monetary and credit policy, except that the government would consult Norges Bank on specifics before acting. In reality, Norges Bank had been reduced to an administrative arm of the government, as confirmed also in the 1986 central bank Act, cfr. 9.4.2. In this respect Norges Bank did not differ from Sveriges Riksbank

---

[20]Lov om adgang til regulering av penge- og kredittforholdene av 25. juni 1965, "kredittreguleringsloven", or the "Credit Act".
[21]Innstilling fra den penge-og kredittpolitiske komité. Bergen 1964.
[22]"Banklikviditet och kreditprioritering", SOU 1960: 16.
[23]The 19-paragraph Act has been reprinted in English in Norges Banks Skriftserie nr. 17: "Norwegian Credit Markets and Credit Policy" (Oslo 1989) pp. 95–8.
[24]"Norge fikk en penge- og kredittpolitisk lov mere omfattende enn noe annet land i den vestlige verden." K. Petersen (1982) *Kredittpolitikken i Støpeskjeen* (A/S Hjemmet-Fagpresseforlaget, Oslo) p. 154.

or from the Bank of Finland at the time, but the government's grip on the Sveriges Riksbank has since been loosened, cfr. Chapter 10.

Confident that the instruments made available by the Credit Act would produce the desired results, the government felt correspondingly free to run continuous budget deficits. This produced ample liquidity in the financial system, and accelerating inflation. Bank deposits and assets grew much faster than anticipated, and bank lendings continuously exceeded the targets set by the Finance Ministry and Norges Bank. In addition, ways were constantly found to circumvent the restrictions[25] since loan demand grew even faster than bank lendings. One of the ways developed to circumvent the credit ceilings was the use of "market loans" whereby banks would act as middlemen (Bassanios) between companies with temporary cash surpluses and companies with temporary cash deficits. Such "market loans" would usually be guaranteed by other finance companies with or without direct connections to the banks. The practice of shifting loans around between institutions with different reporting dates also became widespread.

Even though the "finansselskaper" (leasing, factoring, loan guarantors, etc) had been brought into the "controlled system", the sprawling net of "grey" credits, market loans, etc had become uncomfortable, and had distorted competition among the various credit institutions.

In late 1983, Norges Bank had reached the same conclusion as Sveriges Riksbank had reached almost simultaneously, that the restrictions did more harm than good. The quantitative restrictions did not work according to the original intentions. The authorities had lost grip over what was actually going on in the markets, competition among financial institutions had been completely neutralized or distorted, and neither "demand management" nor "selective credit policy", the ultimate purposes of the exercise, had succeeded. Norges Bank, therefore, recommended to the Finance Ministry that the direct controls and restrictions be dismantled.

Therefore, 1984 and 1985 saw the abolition or reduction of the placement obligation, the direct regulation of lendings by leasing and factoring companies (replaced by reserve requirements), as well as their guarantees for "market loans", the control over new bond issues by mortgage institutions, and ceilings over bank lendings as well as control over the establishment of new bank branches.

The 1965 Credit Act itself, and the interest rate regulation, on the other hand, remained in force. The rate of interest rates was a politically highly sensitive issue, because most home owners had loans with variable rates of interest – in sharp contrast to Denmark until recently, cfr. Chapter 7.

---

[25]"... det ble vist stor oppfinnsomhet i å kanalisere kreditt slik at reguleringene ble unngått." T. Johnsen et al. (1992) *Bankkrisen i Norge* (SNF prosjekt nr. 225, Norges Handelshhøyskole-Universitetet i Oslo) p. 25. (SEA's translation: "great ingenuity was demonstrated in the ways credits were channelled to avoid the regulations").

9.5   A profile of the capital market, 1950–1989

The two striking features revealed by Table 9.13 are, first, the surprisingly small relative size of the financial sector compared to Sweden and Denmark, and secondly, the remarkably big jump it took in the second half of the 1980s.

It is difficult not to reach the conclusion that the tight direct and quantitative regulations are the main explanations why the "organized" financial sector did not develop stronger than it did. Much of the credit expansion naturally connected to Norway's economic growth happened outside the "organized" capital market. Sweden also had a tightly regulated financial sector (cfr. Chapter 10), but it did not go to quite the extremes seen in Norway, particularly with respect to the long-lasting ceilings over lendings by banks, savings banks, and mortgage institutions and the forced investments in specific bonds at below market interest rates. Lendings by financial institutions did not form part of the Swedish national budgets, and in Sweden there were no state "banks" with politically decided lending strategies. On the other hand, the main reason why the financial sector in Sweden was larger than in Norway was the larger market for government bonds, cfr. Table 10.8. The relative size of the banking sectors was not much different in Norway, Sweden, and Finland. In

Table 9.13   Relative Composition and Growth of the Credit Stock, 1960–1989

Year end or annual averages	Commercial banks	Savings banks	State banks	Kreditt-foretak	Insurance companies	Total, million NOK	Total in % of GDP
	Per cent of total credit stock						
1950	50	33	17	–	–	6,866	42
1955	38	29	33	–	–	13,180	50
1960	28	23	29	8	12	23,118	64
1965–1969	28	22	31	9	10	42,429	64
1970–1974	26	20	34	9	11	79,288	70
1975–1979	24	18	38	11	9	164,625	86
1980–1984	25	18	35	13	8	319,476	79
1985–1989	32	23	21	15	8	709,205	127
	Per cent of GDP						
1950	21	14	7	–	–		42
1955	19	14	17	–	–		50
1960	18	15	18	5	8		64
1965–1969	18	14	20	6	6		64
1970–1974	18	14	23	6	8		70
1975–1979	20	16	32	10	8		86
1980–1984	20	14	28	10	6		79
1985–1989	40	29	27	20	11		127

Source: Statistisk Sentralbyrå (1994) *Historisk Statistikk*, pp. 622–41.

Denmark there were quantitative regulations on both bank lendings in DKK and on mortgage institutions, but these regulations did not last nearly as long as in Norway and Sweden, and were not nearly as comprehensive.

The explosive growth of the credit stock in the second half of the 1980s and the changing relative market shares of the different types of credit institutions seem quite noteworthy.

9.6   The oil era, 1985–2010

9.6.1   Problems solved? The 1988–1993 banking crisis

The scale of the crisis

By the early 1980s, revenues from the North Sea oil fields were a major source of income for the Norwegian government. However, oil revenues did not help the financial sector,[26] and fiscal complacency is rarely the solution to emerging problems. Severe headaches were developing.

Profitability and capitalization in most parts of the financial sector had been weak for several years, so neither the commercial banks nor the savings banks had strong resources available to withstand major shocks.

Table 9.14   Credit Losses Booked by Banks and Savings Banks, 1988–1993

	1988	*1989*	*1990*	*1991*	*1992*	*1993*	*Total*
Commercial banks, NOK billion	5.2	6.1	7.9	17.0	8.6	5.1	49.9
Per cent of loans	2.1	2.2	2.6	5.9	2.8	1.8	
Savings banks NOK billion	3.3	4.8	4.5	4.6	4.1	2.7	24.0
Per cent of loans	1.8	2.5	2.3	2.1	2.5	1.3	
Total, NOK billion	8.6	10.8	12.4	21.6	12.7	7.9	73.9
Accumulated credit losses in % of end 1987 equity:							
– Commercial banks	60	104	161	283	273		
– Savings banks	49	99	146	194	236		

Sources: Losses and per cent of loans: *Rapport til Stortinget fra kommisjonen som ble nedsatt av Stortinget for å gjennomgå ulike årsaksforhold knyttet til bankkrisen*, 29. juni 1998, p. 59 (Dokument nr. 17).
Equity: Statistisk Sentralbtrå (1994) *Historisk Statistikk*, pp. 622–42.

---

[26]Only two or three of the largest Norwegian banks had the resources necessary to participate directly in the financing of the development of Norway's off-shore oil and gas fields, and the side effects for the rest of the banking system were limited.

The headaches came in two waves, the first of which – 1988–1989 – initially seemed of manageable proportions and affected only minor provincial banks and savings banks.

The extent of the calamities is illustrated in Table 9.14.

The first problems surfaced in 1988, when a couple of provincial banks and savings banks[27] lost nearly all their capital, and the entire banking sector made an operating loss. The problems in this connection were "solved" by arranging for the collapsed banks to be taken over by larger and supposedly stronger banks. One savings bank was liquidated.

In the years 1987–1990, a total of 12 savings banks and three commercial banks had either lost all of their capital or so much of it that continued operation was impossible.[28]

The second wave, 1990–1993, revealed much deeper and more widespread problems involving also the three largest Norwegian banks.

There was, of course, no way other income could compensate for the magnitude of the credit losses shown in Table 9.14, even if the booked credit losses did not necessarily result in realized losses of identical amounts. Still, by end 1990 the entire capital of the commercial and savings banks was lost, but this, of course, did not necessarily mean that the capital of each and every one of the banks had been lost. However, in 1991–1992 the share capital of the three largest banks, accounting for about 80 per cent of total commercial bank assets, was written down to zero.

In one case, a bankruptcy caused minor losses for non-depositor creditors, but no depositors lost any money in any of these bank failures.

Table 9.15   Loan Losses in per cent of Loan Volumes, Nordic Countries, 1987–1993

	Denmark	*Finland*	*Norway*	*Sweden*
1987	1.1	0.7	1.3	0.5
1988	2.0	0.7	2.0	0.3
1989	1.6	0.7	2.6	0.4
1990	2.3	0.6	2.3	1.2
1991	2.7	1.7	4.3	4.0
1992	3.3	5.8	2.5	7.6
1993	3.2	5.6	1.6	6.3

Source: Rapport til Stortinget fra kommisjonen som ble nedsatt av Stortinget for å gjennemgå ulike årsaksforhold knyttet til bankkrisen (Dokument nr. 17) juni 1998, p. 66. This report will hereafter be referred to as the "1998 Stortings Report".

---

[27]Sunnmørsbanken, Sparebanken Nord, and Tromsø Sparebank.
[28]T. Johnsen et al. (1992) *Bankkrisen i Norge* (Norges Handelshøyskole/Universitetet i Oslo) p. 8.

Compared to the scale of the banking crises in the other Nordic countries, Norway's crisis differed by being stretched over a longer span of years (1987–1993, like in Denmark), and the losses were slightly smaller in relation to the loan volumes than in Sweden and Finland, cfr. Table 9.15.

The majority of the banks in all four countries survived this period in good shape. The losses were concentrated on relatively few banks, which had giant losses (e.g. SEBanken: 11.7 per cent of loan volume lost in 1990–1993, and Nordbanken and Gota Bank 21.4 and 37.3 per cent respectively).[29]

The background and causes for the banking crisis

With the benefit of hindsight it is almost easy to identify at least some of the factors leading to some of the collapses. Some common factors formed a general background paving the way for the crisis, but the individual bank failures were the result of decisions and business policies followed by the individual institutions.

The general background included:

- a strong upturn in the business cycle in the mid-1980s leading to a strong credit demand, which could be only partially satisfied before the 1985 de-regulation;
- a sharp reversal in the business cycle in 1986 with rapidly rising numbers of unemployed and bankruptcies, and a dramatic drop in stock market prices;
- the de-regulation, which suddenly made financial institutions compete against each other and set up branches wherever they wanted;
- a government policy of encouraging the banks and savings banks to accelerate their lendings, cfr. the following statement by Jan Syse, the minister for industry, on April 9, 1984 (SEA's translation): "We have noted a somewhat luke-warm attitude from the banks towards the acceptance of risks. Let's now have an effort which can show that there is yet courage and boldness in the banking palaces."[30;]
- a policy pursued by the Ministry of Finance and Norges Bank allowing a surge of bank borrowings from abroad and from Norges Bank. Before 1985, bank and savings bank lendings were more than covered by deposits, but from 1986 onwards loan volumes exceeded deposits by 20 per cent for savings banks and by some 40 per cent for commercial banks.

The individual failures were mostly caused by over-aggressive lending policies, particularly in connection with new branches set up in provinces, where the bank had no previous experience. In the general fight for market shares, some

---

[29]Cfr. the "1998 Stortings Report", p. 67.
[30]"Vi har registrert en noe lunken holdning fra bankenes side til å påta seg risiko-engagementer. La oss nå få en innsats her som kan vise at ennå er det mot og dristighet i bankpalassene." Here quoted from the "1998 Storting Report", p. 51.

branch managers were even given bonuses or promoted based, not on the profit of the respective branches or business, but on the growth in loan volumes, regardless of profitability.[31]

When the credit rationing ended, the demand for credit appeared almost insatiable, even though the direct interest ceiling had now been lifted, and a certain upward adjustment of interest rates had been allowed. Credit quality control, never a strong point because of the credit rationing, was relaxed and decentralized.

There appears to be a great deal of truth in the common saying in Norway that the crisis was caused by a combination of bad policies, bad banking, and bad luck.

9.6.2   Responses and actions

In the initial phase of the crisis, the problems could be taken care of by the Forretningsbankenes sikringsfond and Sparbankenes sikringsfond, the two funds set up according to the 1961 banking and savings banks Acts (cfr. 9.4.2). By 1990, the resources of these funds were, however, depleted.

Therefore, two government funds were created in 1991, the "Statens Banksikringsfond" (the "SBGF") and the "Statens Bankinvesteringsfond" (the "SBIF"). The first of these, the SBGF, was intended as a temporary measure for the purpose of providing liquidity to stricken banks so that no creditors would suffer any losses. The liquidity could come as share capital, loans, or through guarantees. It was initially funded with NOK 5 billion, later increased by an additional 6 billion, and was dissolved in 2002. The second fund, the SBIF, funded with NOK 4.5 billion, was designed to invest in banks and to invite private investors to join as co-shareholders, and eventually to dispose of its shares. It became the owner of Cristiania Bank og Kreditkasse and Focus Bank (until CBK joined Nordea in 2001, and Focus Bank was acquired by Danske Bank in 1999), and a 50 per cent owner of DnB/DnB NOR, until its ownership share was reduced to about 20 per cent through the sale of shares to the public and Nord LB, the Hannover-based Landesbank.

9.7   A profile of the capital market, 1990–2009

In the post-deregulation and post crisis era, the concentration trends intensified, but the financial sector as a whole did not grow in proportion to GDP. It is no surprise that the financial sector should take a severe dip during the crisis years of the early 1990s. That always happens during financial and economic downturns. However, a stronger rebound after

---

[31]Cfr. Norges Bank (2004) *The Norwegian Banking Crisis* (Occasional Paper no. 33, Oslo) p. 81.

1993 could very well have been expected. No easy explanation why this did not happen seems to offer itself.

In proportion to GDP, Norway's financial sector remains at approximately the same level as Finland's, but decisively smaller than those of Denmark and Sweden.

Table 9.16 shows the development.

Table 9.16   Relative Composition and Growth of the Credit Stock, 1990–2008

Annual averages	Commercial banks	Savings banks	State banks	"Kredit-foretak"	Insurance companies	Total, billion NOK	Total, in % of GDP
	Per cent of total						
1990–1993	32	24	22	14	9	821	114
1994–1997	36	30	20	7	6	858	88
1998–2001	73		15	10	2	1,216	90
2002–2005	75		11	13	1	1,709	101
2006–2008	68		10	20	1	2,648	112
	Per cent of GDP						
1990–2003	37	27	24	15	10		114
1994–1997	32	26	18	7	5		88
1998–2001	66		13	9	2		90
2002–2005	76		11	13	1		101
2006–2008	56		9	17	1		112

Source: Statistisk Sentralbyrå *Statistisk Årbok*, relevant years.

Note: As from the year 2000, the source does not distinguish between commercial and savings banks. "Commercial banks" include the Postsparebanken.

The striking features emerging from Table 9.16 are the flat development of the relative size of the "organized capital market", and the relative decline of the market shares of all types of financial institutions, except the mortgage institutions ("kredittforetak").

The mortgage companies, like the banks, suffered heavy losses during the early 1990s, but rebounded more strongly than the commercial/savings banks.

It remains a matter of taste and definition whether companies engaged in leasing, factoring, installment and credit card financing, counted in the official statistics as "finansselskaber" should be included in the "organized capital market", as presented in Table 9.16. During the credit restriction years, 30–50 such "finansselskaber" grew up, initially because they were outside the banking regulations. When in the late 1960s they were brought into the regulatory system, more such companies were still formed in anticipation of future restrictions on their formation. In the second half of the

1980s, when their relative size peaked, their total credit volume reached NOK 40 billion,[32] i.e. 5–6 per cent of the credit stock as presented in Table 9.13. The inclusion of these companies in the calculation of the size of the "organized capital market" would not affect any of the conclusions drawn very much, but their creation shows, just as in Sweden in the same period, that restrictions invite circumventions.

The number of financial institutions demonstrates a certain trend towards concentration, cfr. Table 9.17. It should also be noted that following the crisis of the early 1990s, several life insurance companies and mortgage institutions ("kredittforetak") formed close relations to the main banks in holding company structures.

Table 9.17   Number of Financial Institutions, 1950–2008

	Commercial banks		Savings banks	State banks	"Kreditt-foretak"	Finance companies
1950	89		606	11		
1975	28		597	8		
1992	22		134	10	13	52
2000	22		130	3	12	46
2003		152		3	11	48
2005		149		3	12	47
2008		148		4	18	50

Source: Statistisk Sentrakbyrå *Statistisk Årbok*, relevant years.

The reduction of the number of banks and savings banks seen from Table 9.17 was mainly the result of the taking over of provincial banks by the metropolitan banks, rather than mergers among the provincial banks as wished by the government. Some provincial mergers, however, did take place, e.g. the 1975 merger of two of Bergen's three banks to form Bergen Bank, and the merger of a number of provincial banks in the late 1980s to form Focus Bank, and the merger of an Oslo savings bank (Akershus) with a number of provincial savings banks to form the ABC Sparebank. Bergen bank was, however, merged with DnC in 1990 to form DnB, Focus Bank was bought by Danske Bank in 1999, and ABC Sparebank merged with the Oslo based Fellesbank, the umbrella bank for the savings banks, to form Sparebank Nor. This was later taken over by DnB, together with Postbanken, to create DnB NOR.

The increase in the number of banks in the 1980s was partly the result of an influx of foreign bank branches and subsidiaries, and partly a reclassification of certain other financial institutions, which obtained banking licences.

---

[32]Cfr. NOS, Statistisk Årbok, 2004.

The reduction of the number of state banks was the result of a government decision in the 1990s to wind down this kind of government activity. Norske Stats Husbank ("Husbanken") is by far the largest state bank, accounting for more than 90 per cent of the assets of the remaining state banks. Founded in 1946, it has financed or co-financed roughly 50 per cent of all owner-occupied dwellings built in Norway since 1950. Its main purpose is to provide sub-sidized financing for dwellings for low-income families. It is funded by a com-bination of government-guaranteed bond issues and direct borrowings from the state treasury.

The bond market

The Norwegian bond market was for many years completely dominated by government bonds. Since the 1990s, however, the volume of bonds issued by the banks and savings banks has grown faster than other types of bonds, cfr. Table 9.18.

The bond market has not been included in the calculation of the relative size of the capital market, because most of the bonds, including some of the government bonds, represent the financing of the lendings shown in Tables 9.13 and 9.16. Bonds issued by municipalities and government and municipality enterprises could, on the other hand very well have been included in Tables 9.13 and 9.16. It would have lifted the "capital market" in proportion to GDP by some 5–7 percentage points in the early 1990s, and by 2–3 percentage points in 2003–2006, but the capital market/GDP ratio would still have been in the 90–110 per cent bracket.

Table 9.18   Circulating Bonds, 1995–2003 (Billion NOK)

		Issued by					
	Government	*Municipalities & municipal & government enterprises*	*State banks*	*Mortgage institutions*	*Banks & savings banks*	*Others*	*Total*
1995	124	53	15	53	54	18	316
1997	137	56	17	42	86	21	359
1999	130	57	30	46	92	25	382
2001	150	62	0	72	114	46	424
2003	152	87	0	66	156	58	520

Source: Statistisk Sentralbyrå, *Statistisk Årbok*, relevant years.

Note: Year-end figures.

It will be noted that the circulating bond volume totals less than 25 per cent of the volume of mortgage bonds circulating in Denmark.

9.8   The stock exchange

Even if share trading took feverish proportions towards the end of the 19th century and in the early 20th century, and again in the aftermath of WWI, the Oslo Stock Exchange remained, until the early 1960s, primarily an exchange for commodities, shipping contracts, and foreign exchange. During the inter-war years, whaling contracts and whale oil accounted for nearly half of the turnover on the Stock Exchange.

Foreign exchange rates had been quoted daily on the Exchange since 1907, and shipping and whaling contracts since 1916. By 1922, the trade in securities had taken such proportions that daily price quotations were introduced for all kinds of securities accepted by the Stock Exchange Board. When the crowds thronging the Stock Exchange floor became intolerable, the stock Exchange Board decided to limit the access to one hundred. There were nearly 2,000 individual applications. Since 1915, banks were admitted as members. Membership had changed from personal to institutional – a change which in Copenhagen and London did not occur until the 1980s.

However, the post WWI "bubble" collapsed, and the ensuing banking crisis, economic slump, occupation, and post-war problems caused the Stock Exchange to fall into a 60 year slumber. By the early 1980s, the stock market capitalization reached a value of about 4–8 per cent of GDP.[33] In that period the Stock Exchange was sometimes referred to as a "dead horse".[34] The combined value of the 118 companies listed on the Oslo Stock Exchange amounted to about 75 per cent of the market value of Marks & Spencer on the London Exchange.[35]

The stock exchange was a playground for a very narrow circle of stock-brokers, shipowners, bankers, and perhaps a handful of industrialists.

In 1983 and the ensuing years, this changed dramatically. Stock prices as well as stock market turnover shot up 5–10 fold. A broadly similar development took place in the other Nordic countries.

Table 9.19 illustrates the development.

The reasons for the impressive growth in both market values and turnover are probably a mix of several factors, among which the deregulation of the financial sector generally, the up-turn of the business cycle, and

---

[33]1972 was an exceptional year, when the first commercial North Sea oil was landed, and the stock market briefly flared up, cfr. Table 9.19.
[34]Cfr. T.M. Bredal (1994) *Børsen og Omverdenen 1945–94* in *Kapitalkilde for Næringslivet* (Bedriftsøkonomens Forlag, Oslo) pp. 164 and 191.
[35]As for fn. 34, p. 124.

Table 9.19   Market Value and Turnover Rates of Shares on the Oslo Stock Exchange, 1969–2008 (Figures in brackets refer to the relevant year)

| | Market value, NOK billion | | Market value | | Turnover rate | |
	Lowest (Year)	Highest (Year)	% of GDP Lowest	Highest	Lowest	Highest % of market value
1969–1973	6 (69)	17 (73)	8	14	6 (69)	13 (73)
1974–1978	7 (78)	10 (74)	3	7	3 (77)	6 (74)
1979–1983	15 (79)	36 (83)	4	8	9 (79)	28 (83)
1984–1988	53 (84)	104 (88)	11	18	35 (88)	49 (85)
1989–1993	123 (92)	206 (93)	18	27	46 (90)	75 (93)
1994–1998	247 (94)	556 (97)	28	51		
1999–2003	502 (02)	689 (03)	33	47	86 (01)	98 (03)
2004–2008	913 (04)	2,157 (07)			110 (04)	157 (08)

Sources: Market values and turnover rates 1969–1993: Oslo Stock Exchange: *Kapitalkilde for Næringslivet, Oslo Børs gjennom 175 År* (Bedriftsøkonomens Forlag 1994) pp. 145 and 214. 1994–2008: Oslo Stock Exchange. GDP: Statistisk Sentralbyrå, *Statistisk Årbok*, relevant years.

Note: Market values are probably year-end figures. The sources are not specific on this point. Turnover rates are averages of annualized monthly figures. Highest and lowest market values in per cent of GDP coincide with the years of highest and lowest market values. This is not always the case with turnover rates.

the abolition of the turnover tax[36] all were important. At a slightly later stage, the admission of foreign investors also helped.[37]

Trading in shares, and new issues of shares, are what has traditionally caught the eye – and the statistics – but bond trading has always outpaced sharetrading, although not as overwhelmingly as in Denmark. A "true" bond market did, however, not emerge until the abolition in 1985 of the "placement obligation".[38] From the 1990s onwards, the turnover rate of bonds was at least five times the turnover rate of shares.

For the Oslo Stock exchange as a "self-owning" institution, neither the 1931 nor the 1988 Stock Exchange Act made major changes, although the 1988 Act introduced a new management forum for the Exchange. The "Børsråd", consisting of 27 members appointed by the finance minister upon recommendations from various business organizations, was to be the

---

[36]The original turnover tax on stock exchange transactions, a sort of domestic "Tobin tax", had been discontinued in 1970, but was reintroduced in 1974 with 1 per cent for both seller and buyer. This tax was abolished in 1978, but reintroduced in 1988, only to be scrapped again in 1989.

[37]Foreign portfolio investments in Norwegian bonds were allowed as from 1989, and in shares as from the early 1990s.

[38]A. Kigen (1994) *Den Nye Børsepoken – 25 turbulente År* in *Kapitalkilde for Næringslivet* (Bedriftsøkonomens Forkag) p. 115.

highest authority of the Exchange, and the objectives of the Exchange were specified to be to manage the market place, regulate and control the market, and to inform the participants of market conditions.

There is, however, no doubt that since WWI, the Oslo Stock Exchange fulfilled all the formal requirements defining a "stock exchange" as discussed in the Introduction, except that the membership admission was, perhaps a bit lax until 1931, and that the Exchange still dealt also with commodities.

This was, however, changed in 1963, when commodities – other than eggs (!) – were removed from the Stock Exchange. Thus, Oslo's Exchange was the last of the Nordic exchanges, which ceased to also be a commodities exchange.

In 1991, also foreign exchange rates ceased to be quoted from the Exchange.

In 1999, it was decided to float the Oslo Stock Exchange. Since then, it has been a public company which has, so far, refused an invitation to merge with the OMX Nasdaq, comprising i.a. the other Nordic and Baltic exchanges. OMX Nasdaq does, however, have a 10 per cent stake in the Oslo Stock Exchange.

10
Sweden, 1918–2009: Too Good to Be True

"Some there be that shadows kiss
Such have but a shadow's bliss"
("The Merchant of Venice", Act Two)

10.1   An overview: Big brother of the Nordics

Sweden escaped neither the WWI inflation nor the widespread depressions of the early 1920s and the 1930s, but the shaping of Sweden's capital market between WWI and the mid-1990s was more directly influenced by the neutrality upheld in both world wars, and the more than 50 years of social-democratic rule following the end of WWII. Great wealth was created from trading with both sides of the conflicts in the late 18th century, and this happened again in the first half of the 20th century. By 1920, the foreign debts accumulated since the 1870s had largely been repaid and remained insignificant until the mid-1970s.

During the first 20–25 years after WWII, the Swedish economy was no doubt the strongest in the Nordic region. Sweden had the largest industrial base with several internationally well-established companies (Volvo, Ericsson, Scania, ASEA, Atlas Copco, Electrolux, Saab Scania, etc., most of them formed in the 1875–1912 period). Sweden was the "Big Brother" in the Nordic region. Between WWI, when the Scandinavian Currency Union broke up, and the early 1970s, the SEK appreciated by 40 and 50 per cent against the DKK and the NOK, respectively.

After WWII, 43 years of social-democratic rule, broken only by a three-year interval 1979–1982, saw a rapid escalation of the welfare state. This led to 30–40 years of increasingly tight and detailed regulation of the capital markets. The intention was to reserve savings for the purposes favoured by the government, particularly residential construction and government expenditures.

Eventually, the resources absorbed by domestic consumption outgrew production. Inflation ran faster than elsewhere in Europe, and a major economic downturn hit Sweden in the early 1990s. Residential construction and real estate prices, having ballooned during the late 1980s, plummeted. The bubble burst. A wave of losses engulfed the banking sector, which lost virtually all of its capital. The international value of the SEK started a long downward slide. Too many shadows had been kissed.

If the crisis of the 1990s was agonizing, it taught everybody a lesson. It probably helped Sweden come through the 2007–2009 crisis much easier than many other countries did, including Denmark. In 2005–2007, people still remembered the early 1990s. A sense of realism had emerged.

Since the mid-1980s, deregulation of the financial markets became the order of the day, even to the extent that in 1999 the Sveriges Riksbank was given a measure of autonomy.

Between the early 1980s and 2009, the SEK dropped to about 0.70 DKK and 0.90 NOK, i.e. a halving against the other Scandinavian currencies over 25 years.

Sweden joined the EU as from 1995, but is unlikely to join the Single Currency before 2015, at the earliest.

10.2   The inter-war period

10.2.1   The problems

The "boom-bust" type of economy experienced all over Europe between 1918 and 1920 also hit Sweden. First, prices, the stock market, and real estate prices doubled or trebled, and then collapsed.

Between 1920 and 1922, Swedish exports fell by about one-third, and industrial production by one-fifth. Outstanding bank loans, having soared between 1918 and 1920, fell by 25–30 per cent over the next two years, and the banks made massive losses. The losses came from industrial credits as well as from shareholdings in industrial companies, or any combination thereof. Several banks foundered, although depositors did not lose anything.

The losses mainly hit the smaller banks, but Svenska Handelsbanken was also badly hurt.

In the 1930s, the Kreuger Crash was a disaster of unprecedented proportions. The losses revealed after Kreuger's suicide in 1932 totalled nearly SEK 1.2 billion.

Between 1908 and 1932, Ivar Kreuger had built up a vast and complicated industrial and financial empire in which he extended loans to foreign governments against monopoly rights to sell matches. He had loans from at least 30 different Swedish and foreign banks, and he formed banks abroad through which he channelled funds to foreign governments and to his own companies.

Early in this peculiar story, Kreuger had formed a close relationship with Oscar Rydberg, the general manager of Sveriges Privata Centralbank in 1917, when it was taken over by Skandinaviska Kredit AB (SKAB, later

Skandinaviska Banken AB). Rydberg joined SKAB and became responsible for its large customers, including Kreuger & Toll and Stockholms Tændstick AB (STAB), the two core companies in the Kreuger empire.

In 1932, when the party ended, STAB and its associated companies owed 24 Swedish banks a total of SEK 828 million, or 15 per cent of all credits extended by these 24 banks,[1] implying that only four of Sweden's 28 banks were not involved with Kreuger. Nearly half of this amount, SEK 407 million, was owed to SKAB, a credit representing 39 per cent of all loans extended by this bank at that time, and probably about twice its equity. STAB also had a portfolio of shares booked at SEK 800 million, which was sold over the following 20 years, fetching SEK 400 million. In 1952, the last of the shares were finally sold, and the Kreuger story was over.

Rydberg, who had always been considered a brilliant banker, was sentenced to ten months in jail for having concealed the true state of affairs of the Kreuger Group, where he had been chairman of the board during the final two years. Obviously, he had conflicts of interest.

On top of the Kreuger crash, Swedish banks were deeply affected by the general depression throughout the 1930s. In nominal terms, bank lendings did not regain its 1919–1920 level until after WWII, cfr. Table 10.1.

10.2.2   Responses and actions

Four main points seem particularly characteristic of the responses to the crises of the 1920s and 1930s:

First, the government, the Riksbank, and the commercial banks all agreed on the importance of avoiding any losses for depositors and foreign creditors of the banks.

Second, the Riksbank did not see itself as a "lender of last resort". Nor did anybody else.

Third, the problems were – as a consequence of the first two observations – handled in co-operation between the government, the Riksbank, and the largest commercial banks.

Fourth, successive governments displayed ambivalent attitudes to the question of direct government ownership and involvement in the banking

---

[1]Cfr. J. Glete (1981) *Kreugerkoncernen och Krisen på Svensk Aktiemarknad*, (Almquist & Wiksell och Sveriges Riksbank, Stockholm) p. 581. Glete's monumental work on the Kreuger debacle includes figures for the exposures of each of the 24 Swedish banks with Kreuger credits.

Kreuger had raised bond loans of more than USD 100 million. in the US market, on which he defaulted. According to F. Partnoy (2009) *The Match King* (Profile Books), this was one of the major reasons why the GAAP and the Securities and Exchange Commission were created. According to Partnoi, Kreuger could be considered the greatest swindler in history, even if 80 years after his death, the list of competitors for this position is getting longer.

sector. However, the trend was clearly towards tighter government control. This was reflected in several amendments to the 1911 Banking Act between 1917 and 1934.

The clearest and most important example of the co-operation among the government, Riksbank and the commercial banks was the formation in 1922 of the AB Kreditkassan av år 1922. It was majority owned and guaranteed by the government, but with substantial shareholdings by the Riksbank and the commercial banks (e.g. SEB: 9 per cent). Its purpose was to take over doubtful exposures from commercial banks which would otherwise have gone under, or to rescue such banks with capital injections or injections of "hybrid" capital ("förlagslån"), or guarantees. Apart from the share capital, the Kreditkassa was funded only by government loans.

The formation of the Kreditkassa sprang from the fact that the first bank having to be rescued (the Sydsvenska Kredit AB) needed more money than the other commercial banks were capable of supplying. It was a pragmatic solution, not an ideological one. The original plan was to close down the Kreditkassa in 1927, but this proved to be impossible.

When the Svenska Handelsbank[2] needed capital in 1922, this was provided or guaranteed by SEB and SKAB, which were otherwise its strongest competitors. No form of government assistance was employed.

Almost simultaneously, when SKAB had suffered heavy losses from various exposures, the Riksbank governor suggested that the state inject SEK 87 million into SKAB, thereby obtaining a 50 per cent ownership. This proposal was motivated by a wish to exploit the situation to gain a direct foot in the banking world for the social-democratic government.[3] The proposal was rejected by SKAB after two months of discussions. Instead, SKAB issued a SEK 100 million subordinated loan ("förlagslån"), which could only be placed because it was 20 per cent guaranteed by each of Kreuger & Toll, STAB, and Svenska Sockerfabrick,[4] i.e. 40 per cent by the Kreuger comglomerate, which did not make it any easier for SKAB later to refuse credits to Kreuger.

In 1930–1931, the SKAB credits to the Kreuger companies spiraled out of all proportions, and SKAB had to be rescued for a second time. This time, government help was unavoidable, but private banks also helped. The Riksdag approved a subordinated one-year loan ("förlagslån") of SEK 100 million, and the Riksgäldskontor extended a 12-year loan of SEK 112 million. A number of private banks collectively supplied SEK 40 million. The amounts involved in

---

[2]In 1919, Stockholms Handelsbank changed its name to Svenska Handelbanken, in connection with its acquisition of two major provincial banks.

[3]Cfr. U. Olsson 1997) *I utvecklingens centrum. Skandinaviska Enskilda Banken och dess föregångare 1856–1996*, (SEB) p. 138.

[4]Cfr. U. Olsson, as fn. 3, p. 139.

this case were too big for the AB Kreditkassan av 1922 to handle. The net result was that SKAB[5] had lost its position as Sweden's leading bank and never regained that position.

The legislative actions taken between 1917 and 1934 reflected the changing attitudes of successive governments, particularly with respect to safeguarding the interests of depositors and avoiding any domination of banks over industry.[6]

The main regulatory changes for banks between 1917 and 1940 are summarized in Schedule 10.1 below:

Schedule 10.1   Main Bank Regulations 1917–1940

1917	The maximum permitted "gearing ratio" imposed by the 1911 Banking Act (restricting total deposits to a maximum of five times equity, cfr. Chapter 6) lifted for banks with equity exceeding SEK 5 million. The wartime inflation had made deposits grow faster than banks' equity. Lifting this restriction only for major banks helped bank concentration.
1921 SFS, 310	Bank take-overs would be permitted only if such take-overs and mergers were not found to be detrimental to the interests of the general public. Royal permission required for banks to open branches outside the town of their head office. The reason was that nearly 40 minor banks had disappeared since 1908. The restrictive policy concerning the formation of new banks (introduced 1911) maintained.
1922	The right for banks to own shares in investment companies and property companies revoked, and the right to own shares in other types of companies restricted to banks with equity exceeding SEK 10 million (1911: 6 million).
1923	Temporary permission introduced to count subordinated loans ("förlagslån") as equity. First taken advantage of by Svenska Handelsbanken.
1933 and 1934 SFS, 18	New banking acts, first withdrawing completely the right of banks to own shares in other companies and, secondly requiring banks always to have satisfactory collateral. 1934: Joint liability banks ("solidariske") given the option to transform themselves into limited liability banks ("bankaktiebolag"). They all did so, but kept the word "enskilda" in their names.

Sources: M. Larsson (1998) *Staten och kapitalet* (SNS Förlag, Stockholm), and SFS (*Svensk Författningssamling*).

---

[5]In 1939, SKAB was re-organized and changed its name to Skandinaviska Banken AB.
[6]Cfr. the quotations referred to in footnotes 2 and 3 in the Introduction. The attitude of the Swedish government in the 1930s seems very parallel to Hilferding (1910) in *Das Finanzkapital*.

To a modern eye it could seem strange that this flurry of new bank regulations did not touch the question of capital ratios with a single word. After all, this had been introduced in Denmark in 1919 and (slightly) sharpened in 1930 as a direct consequence of the bank failures of the 1920s. The concept of "capital adequacy" had not yet been introduced in Sweden. The ceiling on the ratio between deposits and equity, introduced in 1911, had been abolished for major banks in 1917, and had not been replaced by anything else. However, a liquidity ratio had been introduced in 1911, cfr. Chapter 6.

The right for banks to acquire shares in other companies had been a hotly debated issue for many years. During the war years, several banks had made use of the limited rights given in that respect by the 1911 Banking Act in ways not foreseen by this Act. By forming share-issuing subsidiaries and investment companies, banks circumvented the limitations imposed by the 1911 Act.

The share-issuing companies disappeared once the wartime stock exchange frenzy had vanished, but some investment companies remained, and more were created. The largest and best known investment company from this era is no doubt Investor AB, formed 1916 by Stockholms Enskilda Bank and the Wallenberg family. The Wallenberg family owned approximately 38 per cent of Stockholms Enskilda Bank, and since the shares were distributed in proportion to the ownership of the bank, the Wallenbergs also became 38 per cent owners of Investor AB.[7] The companies in the Investor portfolio expanded faster than the rest of Swedish industry, so that in 1969, the Investor companies, including ASEA, Electrolux, Ericsson, SAAB, Alfa Laval, and Atlas Copco, etc., employed ca. 23 per cent of Sweden's industrial workforce.[8]

Similar investment companies were formed by Skandinaviska Kredit AB (Custos, 1937) and Svenska Handelsbanken (Industrivärden, 1943). However, these investment companies never reached the size of Investor, and had no dominating shareholders. The control by the respective banks was exercised through joint board members, many of whom were also shareholders in both the respective banks and investment companies.

The net result was a substantial concentration of ownership and influence among the owners and board members of the three largest banks and the 50 largest industrial companies.

---

[7]Cfr. R. Lundström (1998) *Bank Industri Utlandsaffärer, Stockholms Enskilda Bank 1910–1924* (Handelshögskolan I Stockholm) p. 57.
[8]Cfr. U. Olsson (1997) *I utvecklingens centrum. Skandinaviska Enskilda Banken och dess föregångare 1856–1996*, (SEbanken) p. 207.

10.3   A profile of the capital market, 1920–1940

The number of banks had peaked at 84 in 1908. The growth and concentration of the industrial sector brought a similar concentration in the banking sector, cfr. Table 10.1.

The decline in the amounts of loans and deposits between 1922 and the late 1930s was a product of the falling price level as well as a real decline resulting from the depression of those years. It was, however, also a result of a loss of market share to the savings banks, cfr. Table 10.3.

Table 10.1   The Balance Sheets of Commercial Banks, 1916–1940, Selected Years

		Assets		Liabilities			Total
	Number of banks	Loans million	Other SEK	Capital million	Deposits SEK	Other	SEK million
1916	60	3,059	1,148	717	2,497	993	4,207
1920	41	6,700	1,414	1,114	5,095	1,905	8,114
1922	35	5,338	1,368	983	4,325	1,398	6,706
1926	31	4,457	1,113		3,453		5,570
1930	30	4,757	1,148		3,631		5,905
1935	28	3,913	1,518		3,632		5,431
1940	28	4,468	1,553		4,321		6,021

Sources: Loans, deposits, total assets, and "Other": K.-G. Hildebrand (1971) *I omvandlingens tjänst. Svenska Handelsbanken 1871–1955* (Sv. Handelsbanken) pp. 394–6. Capital: 1916–1922: Brisman (1931) *Riksens Ständers Bank*, bd. V, pp. 185–6. 1926–1940: Hildebrand (1971) *I omvandlingens tjäns*. No combined figures available after 1922. Number of banks: Statistiska Centralbyrån (1960) *Historisk Statistikk*, bd. IV, p. 98.

It will be noticed that throughout the inter-war period, lendings by the Swedish banks exceeded their deposits, although the difference declined towards the end of the 1930s. This was never a problem, except for those banks, which got into trouble for quite different reasons in the early 1920s and 1930s. In most years, the difference was approximately of an order of magnitude corresponding to the banks' equity, but the amounts could change considerably from one year to the next.

Equity in per cent of total assets seems generally to have been around 14–17 per cent. A survey of bank balance sheets from 1916[9] showed that the equity/asset ratios of the 14 enskilde banks typically varied between 16 and 18 per cent. For the limited liability banks, the average ratio was close

---

[9] J. Grönstedt (1917) *Nuvarende Svenska Bankernas Historia*, I: *Solidariska Bankbolagen*, and II: *Bankaktiebolagen* (Stockholm) pp. 180–7 and pp. 156–63 resp.

to 20 per cent with a few cases in the 14–17 per cent bracket and some showing ratios of 22 or even 25 per cent.

To the eyes of a later age, these ratios look impressive, but they did not, of course, prevent many of these banks from getting derailed, when macro-conditions took an adverse turn.

During the process of concentration in the banking sector, the three "main banks" generally strengthened their position, cfr. Table 10.2.

Between 1916 and 1940, the "Big Three" increased their combined market share, as measured by total assets, from about 38 per cent to roughly 55 per cent. This increase can mainly be attributed to Svenska Handelsbanken. SKAB was still licking its wounds from the Kreuger affair, and SEB's expansion was hampered by its reluctance to establish provincial branches.

Table 10.2   Market Shares of the "Big Three", 1918–1940 (Million SEK)

	Stockholms Enskilda		Sv. Handelsbanken		Skandinaviska Kredit AB		Total bank assets
	Assets	% of Total	Assets	% of Total	Assets	% of Total	
1918	502	7.0	1,020	14.3	1,173	16.3	7,129
1920	510	6.3	1,614	19.9	1,570	19.3	8,114
1924	465	7.8	1,154	19.3	1,159	19.4	5,964
1930			1,394	23.6			5,905
1940			1,485	24.7			6,021

Sources: Sv. Handelsbanken and "Total": Hildebrand (1971) *I omvandlingens tjänst* (Sv. Handelsbanken) pp. 394–6. SEB and SKAB: R. Lundström (1998) *Bank Industri Utlandsaffärer. Stockholms Enskilda Bank 1910–1924* (Handelshögskolan i Stockholm) p. 154.

Table 10.3   Banks and Savings Banks Compared, 1916–1940 (Million SEK)

	Banks			Savings banks		
	Number of banks	Total deposits	Deposits per bank	Number of savings banks	Total deposits	Deposits per savings bank
1916	60	2,497	42	455	1,261	2.8
1920	41	5,095	124	485	2,108	4.4
1925	32	3,494	109	496	2,654	5.4
1930	30	3,631	122	482	3,299	6.8
1935	28	3,632	130	478	4,848	8.1
1940	28	4,321	154	472	4,245	9.0

Sources: Number of banks and savings banks, and savings banks deposits: Statistiska Centralbyrån (1960) *Historisk Statistikk*, bd. IV, pp. 98 and 103. Bank deposits: Hildebrand (1971) *I omvandlingens tjänst* (Sv. Handelsbanken) pp. 394–6.

As in Denmark, the problems experienced by the banks in the early 1920s and 1930s caused a noticeable amount of deposits to be moved from the banks to the savings banks. Whereas the deposits collected by the savings banks totalled only about one half of the volume collected by the banks in 1916, this ratio had approached 100 per cent by 1940, cfr. Table 10.3.

The average size of the savings banks, however, remained very small.

The savings banks figures include the government owned postal savings bank (Postsparebanken), established 1883 and by 1916 by far the largest of the savings banks. The average amount of deposits would have been around SEK 7 million in 1940 without the inclusion of the Postsparebank.

The savings banks were governed by separate legislation separating the nature of their activities fundamentally from those of the commercial banks. There were ceilings over the maximum amounts that could be kept in a single account, and on the amounts which could be withdrawn at one time and at short notice, and there were strict limitations on their lendings and the kind of collateral, which could be accepted. The Postsparebank could place its funds in very little but deposits with the Riksbank, government bonds, and municipal bonds. In these respects, the Swedish savings banks were, if anything, even more restricted than their Danish counterparts and do not appear to have played a role comparable to the role played by the Danish savings banks in the financing of dairies and slaughterhouses (cfr. Chapter 3).

10.4   The care-free post-war period, 1945–1980

10.4.1   The problems

The root of the problems haunting the Swedish economy and capital market in the last half of the 20th century was the policy initiated in 1946 to expand the welfare state rapidly and, included in the concept of the welfare state, to provide housing at prices below actual costs.

This policy led to a number of government actions blurring the distinction between monetary policy and regulation of capital market institutions. The policy implied the issuing of a fast increasing volume of bonds by the government, municipalities, and mortgage institutions. Industrial credit demands, including long-term credits through industrial bonds were given second priority. The problem was to find buyers for all these bonds, which could not be sold abroad. The world of free cross-border capital flows had died in the 1930s.

Consumer credit was tightly restricted. "Selective Credit Policy" became a reality.

All of this required changes to the existing regulatory framework. It also re-awakened earlier discussions about the merits of having a government owned bank to compete with the private banks, whose power was perceived to be too strong, and to help direct savings towards the "prioritized" purposes.

10.4.2   Responses and actions

The major legislative steps taken between 1946 and 1980 in relation to the capital market are summarized in Schedule 10.2 below. The regulations should be compared to the regulation of savings banks, co-operative banks, insurance companies, and pension funds, notably in respect of the obligation to invest in government and mortgage bonds (the "investment obligation").

The striking feature of the later banking Acts and regulations is the increasing inter-mingling of "pure" banking regulation with instruments of "pure" monetary policy, with the latter increasingly dominating the former. Some regulations, officially dressed up as banking regulations to protect depositors, were in fact designed to serve completely different goals of "selective credit policy" nature. This was particularly evident with the liquidity requirements imposed on financial institutions. Whenever the appetite for government or mortgage bonds appeared insufficient, thereby threatening a politically unacceptable increase in long-term interest rates, the Riksbank increased bank liquidity requirements, which could be satisfied almost exclusively by increasing holdings of these "prioritized" bonds, for which there was no real secondary market.

Schedule 10.2   Main Bank/Monetary Policy Regulations, 1945–1980

1946	The "gearing" of banks regulated by a complex set of rules limiting the volume of deposits a bank could take to various multiples of the bank's equity, the equity being calculated from the composition of assets. Large banks could take deposits up to ten times its calculated equity, smaller banks only six times equity.[10]
1951 SFS: 767	The Interest Rate Control Act passed, authorizing the Riksbank to request the banks to consult it on intended interest rate changes, and to ask for permission to arrange bond issues for customers, in reality permitting the issuing only of government and mortgage bonds, and a few issues to finance the expansion of hydro-power plants. On bond issues, the Riksbank would decide timing, amounts, interest, and maturities. In force as from 1952.
1955 SFS, 1955: 183	The most comprehensive banking Act revision since 1911. Banking would be allowed only to joint-stock companies, which had obtained royal permission ("oktroy") to operate as banks. Banking defined as deposit-taking on current account from the general public. The earlier requirement for a certain minimum size of share capital (1 million) replaced by a requirement that the by-laws stipulate a maximum and minimum amount. Banks could, for their own accounts, trade only gold, foreign exchange, bills of exchange, bonds, and similar securities. "Gearing" regulation simplified, but still limiting deposits to certain multiples of the equity, and differentiating between banks with equity capital of more than SEK 5 million and those with less.

---

[10]Cfr. M. Larsson (1998) *Staten och kapitalet* (SNS Förlag) pp. 152–3.

Schedule 10.2   Main Bank/Monetary Policy Regulations 1945–1980 – *continued*

	Blanco credits limited to SEK 75,000, and combined maximum 10 per cent of equity. Strict control maintained over the formation of new banks and bank branches. Combined amount of loans with maturities exceeding six months not to exceed 20 per cent of equity. Ceilings introduced on the growth of lending by all kinds of banks. Remained in force for 30 years.

1962 SFS: 257 and SFS 1962: 258	Insurance companies, savings banks, and pension funds could be forced to invest a certain percentage of the net increase in their assets in government, municipality, and mortgage bonds ("prioritized bonds"), if deemed necessary to provide sufficient long-term finance for the government and residential construction.[11]
	 The Riksbank mandated to decide minimum and maximum interest rates for deposits for all types of deposit-takers, as well as maximum lending rates if deemed necessary for the Riksbank to achieve its monetary policy goals.
	     The Riksbank mandated to block the issuing of bonds by others than the Riksgäldskontor.
	     On some points, the 1962 acts relaxed the 1951 Act, but it was also extended to cover more financial institutions than the 1951 Act.

1968 SFS, 1968: 601 (and others)	New Banking Act replacing the former "gearing controls" (deposits/equity ratios) with capital requirements relating minimum equity capital to four different classes of assets: 1. Cash and government bonds: Equity requirement: 0. 2. Other bonds and residential mortgages: 1 per cent equity. 3. Mortgages over 75 per cent of residential and 50 per cent of other property: 4 per cent. 4. Other: 8 per cent equity. Regulatory differences in the types of business allowed to banks, savings banks, and co-operative banks abolished. Controls of the formation of new bank branches abolished.
1974 SFS, 1974: 922	Credit Policy Means Act ("Lag om kreditpolitiska medel") passed. Mainly a concentration of the previous credit policy Acts into a single Act, with more precision, some modifications, and extension to cover more types of financial institutions. "Means of credit policy" defined to include control of lending and new bond issues, obligation of institutions to invest in "prioritized" bonds, and interest rate controls. The Riksbank authorized to impose regulations on financial institutions if it deemed it necessary to achieve its monetary policy objectives.

The numbers refer to the numbers given in Svensk Författningssamling (SFS), the official publication of Swedish legislation.

---

[11]In the late 1950s and the 1960s, "Prioritized" bonds would often yield interest rates 2–3 per cent lower than market rates, cfr. I. Nygren (1985) *Från Stockholms Banco till Citibank* (Liber) pp. 85 and 91.

Two factors formed the background for the interest rate and new issue regulations mentioned in Schedule 10.2:

First, the decision by the social-democratic government to aim for a construction volume of 100,000 new dwellings per year with the cost of a new two-room apartment not to exceed 20 per cent the income of industrial workers.[12] This required that large volumes of mortgage bonds could be sold without causing upward pressure on interest rates, which was unrealistic.

Secondly, the commercial banks unloaded the vast amounts of government bonds they had accumulated during the war. This, too, caused unpalatable upward pressures on interest rates. The Riksbank picked up these bonds together with new issues by the government, thereby quintupling the Riksbank's bond holdings by 1949, with corresponding effects on the money supply.

It was, however, not the intention of the social-democrat governments to let market forces interfere with their political plans.[13] They preferred to shroud the capital market in a cobweb of regulations. In 1948, a newly appointed chairman of the board of the Riksbank governors set out drawing up the draft for the 1951 "Interest Rate and New Issues Control Act".

The Riksbank supplemented its arsenal of weapons by designing the liquidity requirements of banks to include holdings of government and mortgage bonds, regardless of the almost non-existence of a secondary market for these bonds. So, bond-holdings increased from about 7 per cent of total bank assets in 1948 to about 23 per cent ten years later.[14]

The "system" consisted of monthly "discussions" between the Riksbank and the Bankers Association, the Savings Banks Association, etc. With the commercial banks, the atmosphere at these monthly meetings was not always amiable. The Wallenbergs, chairing the Bankers Association most of the time, and who had become billionaires from their banking and industrial investments, did not much like being told by Per Åsbrink, the social-democratic party functionary risen to Riksbank governor (1955–1973), how to set the banks' interest rates, and which bond issues to arrange or buy, in which amounts, and on which conditions, and which issues to abstain from. After such meetings, the Wallenbergs and the other bankers would,

---

[12]Cfr. P. Englund (1993) *Den gynnade bostadssektorn*, in L. Werin (red) *Från ränterägling till inflationsnorm* (SNS) p. 158.

[13]According to E. Wigforss, the finance minister in 1948 (SEA's translation): "... the social-democratic party should hold on to the right of the general public to limit the scope for private financial interests ('enskilde finansinteressen') to govern interest rates and monetary policies as they pick and choose ('efter sitt omdömme och sitt behag')". E. Wigforss (1948) "Frihet – för vem?", *Socialdemokratisk Skriftserie nr. 18* (Tidens förlag, Stockholm), here quoted from L. Werin, ed. (1993) *Från räntereglering till inflationsnorm* (SNS) p. 325. Note that Wigforss here identified the "general public" with the social-democratic party.

[14]Cfr. P. Englund (1993) *Den gynnade bostadssektorn*, in Werin (ed.) *Från räntereglering till inflationsnorm* (SNS) p. 163.

of course, immediately start thinking about how the agreements could be circumvented.[15]

When both government budgets and the balance of payments turned negative from about 1975, the sprawling network of controls and regulations not only failed to have their intended effects, but also did not fail to have unintended side effects.

Limiting deposits to certain multiples of equity caused banks to invent new types of deposits, which were not subject to regulations e.g. "certificates of deposit". This was part of the background for the 1968 reform changing the nature of the "gearing" regulation as shown in Schedule 10.2.

In retrospect, the capital requirements introduced in 1968 appear very low, but were probably designed not to increase existing capital ratios. In any case, the capital/ asset ratio dropped in the following years (cfr. Table 10.4 below). With capital requirements graded according to perceived risks of the asset composition, the system had a certain resemblance to the later Basel II.

The lending ceiling had the effect that by the late 1980s, nearly 300[16] leasing, factoring, and credit card finance companies had been created, which offered consumer finance rarely available from banks and savings banks because of the credit ceiling. Some of these finance companies had close links to specific banks, and some were independent.[17] The efforts made to circumvent the restrictions had made a mockery of the traditional distinction between what could be called the "organized" capital market and what was more like a "grey" capital market with limited transparency and few "rules of the game". In 1980, most of these finance companies were also subjected to the credit ceiling, but the holes in the regulatory framework became increasingly gaping, just like in Norway (cfr. Chapter 9).

10.5   Problems catch up, 1980–2010

10.5.1   Deregulation

Some time in the early 1980s, the Riksbank had concluded that its elaborate system of controls and "friendly" discussions with the banks had lost whatever effect they originally might have had. Therefore, the Riksbank initiated discussions with the government about a gradual dismantling of

---

[15]Cfr. L. Jonung (1993) *Riksbankens politik*, pp. 339–85, in Werin (ed.) *Från räntereglering till inflationsnorm* (SNS) pp. 339–85. Based on protocols from the meetings and interviews with some of the participants, Jonung gives several examples showing the nature of the negotiations.

[16]Larsson & Sjögren (1995) *Vägen till och från bankkrisen* (Carlssons) p. 135 and Statistisk Årbok.

[17]In the early 1980s, the Riksbank and the commercial banks made a common effort to work out the size of this "grey" market. They gave up, cfr. L. Jonung (1993) *Riksbankens politik 1995–90* in L. Werin (ed.) *Från räntereglering till inflationsnorm* (SNS) p. 333 (fn.).

the highly symbolic bastion of regulations built up by the social-democrats over nearly four decades. Kjell-Olof Feldt, the finance minister 1982–1990, understood the problem, but Oluf Palme, the prime minister did not.[18]

So, deregulation started cautiously in 1983 with a gradual relaxation of the control of new issues and interest rates. Interest rate controls were completely abolished by 1985, when also the lending ceiling on banks and some other financial institutions disappeared. In 1986, the obligation of insurance companies and certain other financial institutions to invest certain amounts in government and mortgage bonds was lifted, and the foreign exchange regulations were gradually abolished between 1985 and 1990.

The deregulation of the Swedish financial system cannot be seen totally in isolation from the wave of deregulations happening almost everywhere in those years, but it was primarily a recognition by the Riksbank that by the early 1980s, the elaborate cobweb of controls it had set up no longer served their original purposes, and were probably even counter-productive.

Table 10.4   Bank Balance Sheets During Regulation, Deregulation, and Crisis, 1964–2006

	Number of banks	Assets			Liabilities				Total assets & liabilities
		Credits	Bonds	Other	Equity	Deposits	Other	%	SEK billion
		% of total assets			% of total liabilities				
1964	16	58	19	22	5.3	75	20	100	36
1968	16	61	20	20	4.3	71	25	100	56
1974	16	52	22	26	2.3	68	30	100	133
1984	15	47	27	26	1.5	51	48	100	540
1987	25	50	14	36	1.8	42	56	100	692
1988	25	54	11	35	1.7	38	60	100	862
1991	16	56	13	31	5.0	44	51	100	1,596
1992	16	59	13	28	4.5	46	49	100	1,519
1995	29	44	26	30	5.5	48	46	100	1,585
2001	129	42	14	44	8.9	39	52	100	3,145
2006	125	39	15	46	9.4	36	55	100	5,089

Source: Statistisk Sentralbyrån: Statisisk Årsbok, relevant years.

Notes: Credits: Credits to the non-financial, non-central government general public. Bonds: 80–90 per cent long-term mortgage bonds. The rest mainly government bonds. Deposits: Deposits from the general non-financial public. The reason for the big jump in the number of "banks" after 1995 is that savings banks and co-operative banks were included in the statistics as "banks" as from the 1990s, cfr. Schedule 10.2 and Section 10.5.2 below.

---

[18]In 1985, Mr. Feldt discussed the issue with Mr. Palme. Towards the end of the discussion, Mr. Palme, highly irritated, said (SEA's translation): "Do as you please, I still don't understand anything." ("Gör som Ni vill. Jag begriper ändå ingenting"). K.-O. Feldt (1991) Alla dessa dagar – i regeringen 1982–1990 (Norstedts förlag, Stockholm) p. 260.

Two of the most striking features revealed by Table 10.4 are, first, the extremely thin capitalization of the banks, with equity/asset ratios around 2 per cent before deregulation and about 5 per cent in the mid-1990s after the hive-off of the bad assets. Secondly, the growing weight of the item "other" in the balance sheet. Among the assets, the "other" mainly consisted of investments in associated finance companies, which were largely financed by inter-bank borrowings accounting for much of the "other" among the liabilities.

10.5.2   Main institutional changes, 1951–2010

The commercial banks

In the late 1940s, there was much discussion in government and labour union circles about the desirability of creating a state-owned bank, partly to rationalize the multitude of small special purpose government lending funds managed by the Riksbank and the Statsgäldskontor,[19] and partly to compete with the private banks, which the social-democratic government regarded as too powerful. These deliberations, which continued for many years, resulted, first, in a reorganization in 1951 of the Kreditkassan av 1922 (cfr. 10.2.2), into Sveriges Kreditbank AB, a fully fledged state-owned commercial bank. It still nursed some bank relics from the 1922 crisis. Secondly, the Postsparebank and the Postgiro Office were merged in 1960 to form the AB Postbank. Third, Sveriges Kreditbank AB and the AB Postbank were merged to form the PKbank AB in 1974. In 1989, the PKbank absorbed Nordbanken, the result of a 1985 amalgamation of the Sundsvall Bank and Upplandsbank, and adopted the name of its acquisition. Thereby the state's ownership was diluted to 70 per cent, but in connection with the 1991–1992 banking crisis the Kingdom became Nordbanken's sole owner. In 1997, Nordbanken merged with the Finnish Merita Bank to form the Merita-Nordbank, which became Nordea AB after the 2000 merger with the Danish Unibank. Between 2000 and 2006, the government sold most of its Nordea shares. The plan was to sell the remaining 20 per cent, but this was – temporarily – prevented by the 2007–2009 financial crisis.

When Skandinaviska Banken (the former SKAB) and Stockholms Enskilda Bank merged in 1972 to form Skandinaviska Enskilda Banken (SEB), it was hardly a surprise, given the role of the Wallenbergs in the formation of both banks. Finally, Stockholms Enskilda had a branch network, and the Swedish banking scene would consist of the "Big Three" and 12–15 small- or

---

[19]In 1947, there were 61 government special purpose lending funds with an outstanding loan volume totalling SEK 840 million. Other government funds totalling SEK 625 million provided interest subsidies for homeowners, cfr. "Betänkande med förslag om inrättande av en statlig affärsbank", 1949, p. 21. The existence of special government funds continued into the 1980s.

medium-sized banks. The increase to about 25 in the late 1980s was caused by the arrival of a number of foreign banks.

The savings and co-operative banks

Also the savings banks went through a process of consolidation. In 1982, Första Sparbanken had been formed through a merger between two of the largest regional savings banks. In 1992, the problems suffered by Första Sparbanken and a number of other savings banks led to a major consolidation. Most of the savings banks, including Sparbankernas Bank, joined the holding company structure of Sparbanken Sverige, but some continued on their own. In 1997, Sparbanken Sverige merged with Föreningsbankernas Bank[20] under the name of FöreningsSparbanken. Following the acquisition in 2005 of the Hansa Bank in Estonia, it took the name of Swedbank, which now comprises most of the original savings and co-operative banks.

In 1962, the savings banks were allowed to do nearly all types of "banking" business, and the 1968 banking acts scrapped all distinctions between the types of business which could be done by commercial banks, savings banks, and co-operative banks. In 1987 the savings banks and co-operative banks were allowed to transform themselves into joint stock limited liability companies and operate completely like commercial banks. The 1987 Banking Act, the most comprehensive banking act revision since 1955, took the approach of regulating specific types of business rather than which type of institution did the business. Thus, there was one law regulating banking business (quite detailed paragraphs on capital ratios to be held against various types of collateral, etc,) and other laws regulating the formation, dissolution, etc of joint stock banks, savings banks, and other types of credit companies. Capital requirements became identical for all types of capital market institutions ("kreditmarknadsbolag"). This approach became even more pronounced in the 1997 Banking Act, which otherwise was mostly an incorporation into Swedish law of EU legislation, following Sweden's entry into the EU in 1995.

The mortgage institutions

After nearly 70 years of substantially unchanged structure, the world of Swedish mortgage institutions changed dramatically during the last decades of the 20th century.

The government policy of giving priority and subsidies to housing finance, and the Riksbank regulation that mortgage bonds were part of a bank's

---

[20]Föreningsbanken was the new name of the original "jordbrukskassor", a network of roughly 350 small agricultural co-operative thrift institutions, the first of which was formed in 1915. They catered only for members and were even smaller than the savings banks. At their peak, they numbered more than 700, but their combined assets never reached more than about one-third of the combined asset of the savings banks. In 1956, they were renamed "föreningsbanker", and Föreningsbankernes Bank, a central "umbrella" for the local institutions, was created.

liquidity requirement, induced banks and savings banks to engage themselves heavily in mortgage institutions (e.g. the taking over by Handelsbanken in 1955 of the Inteckningsbank, the formation in 1961 by the savings banks of Spintab Ab, and by 12 commercial banks of Svensk Fastighetskredit, and the later formation by the föreningsbanks of FBkredit). In 1997, Handelsbanken acquired the Stadshypotek AB, the mortgage institution created in 1910, transformed into a joint stock company and floated on the stock exchange in 1994.[21] Also Swedbank has a large mortgage subsidiary (Swedbank Hypotek), whereas the SEB's original mortgage subsidiary has been merged into the bank as a department.

SBAB ("Sveriges bostadsfinansieringsaktiebolag") was formed in 1985 to take care of the government housing finance activities. It now offers a broad range of financial services, and the intention is to "privatize" the SBAB "when the time is right".

Compared to Danish mortgage institutions, the main difference is the lack of conformity between the structure of assets and liabilities. Whereas Danish mortgage institutions – whether they are independent or bank subsidiaries – are required by law to maintain identical structures of assets and liabilities, this is left open to the discretion of the management of Swedish mortgage institutions. The difference is clearly seen from their balance sheets:

Table 10.5   The Balance Sheet of Mortgage Institutions, 1980–2006 (Billion SEK)

| | Assets | | Liabilities | | | Total assets |
	Loans	Other	Equity	Bonds	Other	& liabilities
1980	199	8	2	163	42	207
1990	906	252	9	702	447	1,158
2001	1,124	87	62	731	418	1,211
2006	1,662	134	78	1,182	536	1,796

Source: *Statistisk Årsbok*, relevant years.

It is seen that mortgage loans are covered only some 60–70 per cent by bond issues. The balance has been borrowed from banks. The Swedish mortgage institutions, in contrast to the Danish mortgage institutions (bank owned or otherwise), have a liquidity management problem, just like British building societies.

Their capital base is quite small (4–5 per cent of loans – like in Denmark). This has proved sufficient, even in the unprecedented property slump of

---

[21]Stadshypotek Ab was the 1994 replacement for the Konungariket Sveriges Stadshypotekskassa, cfr. Chapter 6.

the 1990s. The value of the collateral is of less importance than the ability of the property owners to service the debts.

The post WWII years witnessed a substantial rationalization of the numbers of financial institutions in Sweden:

Table 10.6   The Shrinking Number of Financial Institutions, 1960–2006

	Commercial banks	Savings banks	Co-op banks	Mortgage institutions	Other credit institutions	Total
1960	16	434	572	3		1025
1980	14	164	420	3	ca. 290	ca. 890
1990	21	104	373	ca. 10	179	687
2006	125			9	59	193

Source: *Statistisk årsbok*, relevant years.

Since the 1990s, all mortgage institutions are bank-owned subsidiaries, except in the case of the SEB, which has organized its mortgage finance as a department of the bank, and the state-owned SBAB.

The "Other credit institutions" consist mainly of leasing, factoring, and credit card financing companies created in response to the restrictions imposed on the banks before 1985.

10.5.3   The 1992 banking crisis and bank rescues

The first real sign of trouble was when Nycklan AB, a finance company, suspended payments in the autumn of 1990 and was declared bankrupt a few months later. Nycklan was one of a number of finance companies created in the 1980s to take advantage of the combination of the lending ceiling imposed on the banks, and the golden prospects which the property markets seemed to offer. Gamlastaden AB, a similar type of finance company, followed shortly after together with several other minor finance and property companies.

With a little bit of equity injected by their founders they borrowed from the banks, and paid the means thus raised into subsidiaries as equity. These subsidiaries then borrowed large amounts from banks and the general public, ending up with a gearing ratio of possibly 1:10 or more. Much of the funding took place in the shape of short-term commercial paper, often bought by banks and savings banks. Because of this "double gearing", the combined gearing of parent and subsidiary could well be 1:100. All the funds thus collected would be invested in fixed property.

In the 1980s, helped by economic growth and devaluation fuelled inflation, the Nycklan type of finance companies did very well, but about 1990 inflationary expectations had burnt themselves out, and property prices stagnated. When recession also hit, vacancy rates started climbing, and property companies found it increasingly difficult to service their debts, or sell their commercial paper, and had to start selling property, causing property prices to drop precipitously. Having very little equity, and having financed a disproportionate share of the fixed assets with short-term money, finance and property companies went bankrupt, and the banks, having bought their commercial paper, etc., made huge losses.

The extent of the Swedish real estate "bubble" of the late 1980s is seen in Table 10.7 below, which shows that prices of office property increased 14-fold over eight years, and doubled over two. The bubble of particularly office properties was probably bigger than anything seen before anywhere, with the possible exception of the London docklands in the same period, and Norway. The 2004–2007 property bubbles in the US, the UK, and in the rest of Europe were minor in comparison. The halving of Swedish property prices over the next three years was also more dramatic than the 2007–2009 decline in the US, UK, and the Continent, where property prices dropped "only" 30–40 per cent from their respective peaks.

Table 10.7   Property Prices and Bank Losses, 1980–1992

	Price index of apartment properties	Price index of office properties	Bank losses, billion SEK	Bank losses, per cent of loan stock
1980	100	100		
1986	300	700		
1988	550	1,100	3	
1989	540	1,450	4	0.4
1990	500	1,300	10	1.1
1991	350	800	34	4.0
1992	325	600	69	6.4
1993			45	6.2

Source: Price indices: A. Boksjö & M. Lönnborg-Andersson (1994) *Svenska finanskriser* (Rapport nr.2, Uppsala Universität, Dept. of Economic History) p. 43. Bank losses: Amounts: As for the price indices, p. 46. Per cent of loan stock: M. Larsson (1998) *Staten och kapitalet* (SNS) p. 214.

The combined relative size of losses suffered by Swedish banks, savings banks, and co-operative banks from the bursting of this bubble (and from other exposures) also exceeded what was seen elsewhere in 2007–2009, although there were individual cases of very big losses in several countries.

With approximately 14–18 per cent of the loan stock written off over just three years it is clear that by 1993, the equity of the entire Swedish banking system (SEK 70–80 billion, cfr. Table 10.4) had been lost, perhaps twice over, but the write-downs were, of course, neither equally distributed between all the affected institutions, nor necessarily identical to the final losses.

Anyway, the net effect was that the Swedish banks were totally paralyzed in the 1990s, and drastic measures were unavoidable.

The rescues

The bank rescues of 1992–1994 were neither the result of any pre-conceived "masterplan" nor an expression of any particular ideology. They sprang from the basic view that the chaos, which would result from bank collapses causing losses for depositors, would be unacceptably destructive not only for the domestic economy, but also for both private and public relations with the international financial world.

All banks and savings banks suffered heavy losses, but the largest losses were suffered by the institutions born during the structural changes of the 1970s and 1980s, i.e Första Sparbanken,[22] Gota Bank, and Nordbanken (cfr. 10.5.2), and a number of the savings and co-operative banks which had fought hard to exploit the opportunities opened to them by the 1968 banking Acts and the deregulations of the 1980s. They all struggled to gain a respectable market share and a foothold in corporate banking. They all went deeply into real estate financing, where the collateral looked fine in the light of the galloping prices.

Första Sparbanken, with 1991 losses twice the size of its equity, was rescued in 1991–1992 by interest free loans totalling SEK 7.3 billion[23] from the other savings banks, guaranteed by the government. In that connection the savings banks were reorganized into a holding company structure (cfr. 10.5.2). The government received 70 per cent of the shares in the savings banks as collateral for the guarantee.

When in 1991 it was clear that Nordbanken needed more capital, the share issue had to be picked up by the state, which thereby increased its ownership from 70 to 77 per cent. When this capital injection proved insufficient, the government bought the remaining circulating shares (for SEK 2 billion), and increased the share capital. The capital injections were, however, far from sufficient, and more drastic measures were needed. In September, 1992, the government issued a guarantee covering the obligations of all banks and certain other credit institutions.

In addition, Nordbank was relieved of its poisonous assets through the creation of Securum, a new state-owned "bad bank". It was given a share capital of SEK 24 billion together with loans from the Riksbank of 27 billion, which enabled it to buy ca. 49 billion of non-performing exposures[24] from Nordbanken at book value, and saving Nordbanken from very substantial

---

[22]The losses as per cent of their loan stocks were approximately 14.5 per cent (1990+ 1991), 23.9 per cent (1991+1992), and 16.4 per cent (1991+1992) respectively, Cfr: M. Larsson & H. Sjögren (1995) *Vägen till och från bankkrisen* (Carlssons Bokförlag) p. 141.
[23]Cfr. Larsson & Sjögren (1995) *Vägen till och från bankkrisen* (Carlssons Bokförlag) p. 142.
[24]Cfr. C. Bergström, P. Englund & P. Thorell (2003) *Securum and the Way Out of the Swedish Banking Crisis* (Center for Business and Policy Studies, SNS) p. 21.

write-downs. It was expected that a winding up of these exposures might take up to 15 years, but already in 1997 most of the credits had been wound up, either through liquidation of the respective borrowers or from sales of the companies or their assets to private investors, or, in a few cases, through flotation on the stock exchange.

When the dust had settled over Securum, the state had recouped about SEK 14 billion of the 50 billion originally supplied to it.

In the case of Gota Bank, the "Securum-model" was also used, this time with a "bad bank" named Retriva, but most of Gota Bank's losses were covered by Tryg-Hansa, the insurance company and Gota's main share-holder. Trygg-Hansa sold its Gota shares to the state, which later merged Gota into Nordbanken.

When the government will, eventually, have disposed of its remaining 20 per cent stake in Nordea, all of its costs in connection with the 1991–1993 rescue operations will probably have been recouped.[25]

The property bubble was mainly caused by inflationary expectations fed by the government's fiscal policies, with deficits producing annual inflation rates 2–3 percentage points faster than in the rest of the OECD countries. The large budget deficits created private sector liquidity, which the central bank regulations did or could not soak up, in spite of the ever-increasing liquidity requirements imposed on the banking sector. This liquidity would find its way to fuel the property bonfire, quite regardless of lending ceilings, controls on new issues, etc.

At the peak of the crisis, the autumn of 1992, the combination of recession, the bursting bubble, and severe balance-of-payments problems caused a massive capital outflow from Sweden. In defence of the SEK, the Riksbank increased its o/n rate to 500 per cent p.a., but the SEK still sank drastically on the foreign exchange market.

10.5.4   The 2007–2009 banking problems

Compared to the 1990–1992 meltdown of the Swedish financial sector, the problems of 2007–2009 hardly deserve the label of "crisis".

By 2007, property prices had recovered from their 1992 rock-bottom levels. Whether or not this recovery is seen as a "bubble", is mainly a matter of taste and definition. Share prices also rose fast in the 2002–2007 years, but the ensuing weakness in both property and share prices caused only manageable losses among financial institutions. However, banks with large exposures in the Baltics and Ukraine, e.g. the SEB and Swedbank suffered heavy losses from those exposures.

---

[25]According to the Svenska Bankföreningen. Any such estimates will, however, depend on the rates of interest applied to the government outlays over the ca. 25 years involved.

Against this background, a "Bank Support Act"[26] was passed in 2008, providing for

A: Liquidity support upon request, and
B: Capital injections in case of needs, and subject to specific agreements between the recipient and the capital provider, i.e. initially the Riksgäldskontor (the "Government Debt Office"), and
C: The building up of a "Stability Fund" through contributions from the financial sector itself.

The intention is that the "Stability Fund" is to be built up to an amount equal to 1.5 per cent of GDP by 2015, and that any future support for distressed financial institutions is to come from this "Stability Fund". Initially, the individual contributions to the fund will come from financial institutions in proportion to their relative size. As from 2011, the intention is that contributions will be levied in proportion to the "riskiness" of the individual institutions, but so far there are few indications how the insoluble problem of quantifying the "riskiness" will be addressed. The fund will be managed by the Riksgäldskontor. Seven institutions signed guarantee agreements with the Riksgäld, but only in one case (Swedbank) was the guarantee made use of through two bond issues in 2008. As of the summer of 2010, roughly half of these loans have been repaid.

10.6   A profile of the capital market, 1950–2008

Slow economic growth in the mid-20th century, combined with capital market restrictions in the 1950s–1980s, meant that by the mid-1970s the relative size of the capital market was no larger than just after WWI, cfr. Table 10.8.

If the hundreds of leasing, factoring, and credit card finance companies fostered by the 35 years of quantitative regulations had been included in the calculation, the conclusion would have been only slightly different. The total credits from these finance companies grew from around SEK 50 billion in the early 1980s to some 170 billion in 1990, i.e. about 10 per cent of the total credit stock as defined in Table 10.8 below, and about 7 per cent of GDP. Following the deregulation, the number of these finance companies dropped from around 300 to about 75.

It is also seen that the relative size of the banking and savings bank sector shrank considerably during the years of the lending ceiling. Instead, the relative size of the mortgage institutions and government bonds – the "prioritized bonds" – increased their respective shares, which is hardly surprising. This was, after all, a natural consequence of the priority given to residential construction and the public sector.

---

[26]Lag 2008: 814, om statlig stod till kreditinstitut.

Table 10.8   Relative Composition and Growth of the Credit Stock, 1916–2000, Selected Years

	Com. banks	Savings banks	Mortgage institutions	Insurance companies	Public sector bonds	Other bonds	Total, billion SEK	Total, in % of GDP
			Per cent of total credit stock					
1916	54	21	10		14		6	94
1920	63	19	5		12		11	87
1925	48	26	8		18		9	117
1930	46	28	10		16		10	112
1934	37	32	13		19		11	116
1950	35	27	12	12	15		26	84
1955	24	24	12	12	29		42	86
1968	27	23	17	6	18	9	127	95
1975	26	14	29	4	18	9	295	98
1985	21	8	25	0	31	14	1,214	141
1990	37		35	0	16	12	1,789	132
1992	39		33	0	18	10	2,336	162
1995	26		33	0	39	2	2,710	164
2004	37		18	0	31	14	3,770	144
2006	39		19		23	20	5,095	176
			Per cent of GNP					
1916	51	20	9		14			94
1920	55	17	5		10			87
1925	56	31	9		21			117
1930	51	32	11		18			112
1934	43	37	15		22			117
1950	29	33	10	10	13			85
1955	20	20	10	10	25			85
1968	25	22	16	6	17	9		100
1975	26	14	28	4	17	9		98
1985	30	12	36	1	42	20		141
1990	48		46	0	21	16		132
1992	62		54	0	29	17		162
1995	42		54	0	64	3		164
2004	54		25	0	44	21		144
2006	67		33	0	40	35		176

Source: *Statistisk Årsbok*, relevant years.

The relative share of the mortgage institution increased even more during the property bubble in the early 1990s, which is also no surprise. The explosion in the circulating volume of public sector bonds between 1975 and 1985 is truly remarkable and the main reason for the increase of the credit stock from about 100 per cent of GDP in 1975 to about 140 per cent in 1985.

The changes in the relative sizes of various types of lending institutions is probably not of much significance in the early 21st century, when all types of financial institutions are subject to nearly the same regulations, including identical capital and liquidity requirements, and when mortgage institutions like the government owned SBAB offers traditional savings banks deposit accounts, and when other traditional mortgage lenders, like e.g. Stadshypotek, are owned by commercial banks.

10.7   The stock exchange

Throughout the 20th century, the Stockholm Stock Exchange remained primarily an exchange for equities. The bond market existed as a primary market for the few centralized mortgage institutions and for corporate bonds, but no significant secondary bond market had developed. The bonds were acquired by banks, savings banks, and insurance companies, which mostly kept them to maturity.

In Sweden, the effects of the global stock market crash of 1929 were reinforced by the collapse of the Kreuger companies in 1932. Total market capitalization dropped from SEK 4,974 million in January, 1929, to SEK 1,552 million in May, 1932.[27] Two-thirds of the SEK 3.4 billion loss of market value was concentrated on the two Kreuger companies and L.M. Ericsson. The stock market remained paralyzed and nearly dormant until the 1970s, in terms of stock prices as well as new issues and trading volumes.

The dominance over the market by just three shares (and by Grängesberg-Oxelösund after the demise of the Kreuger companies) was, of course, possible only because of the small size of the market. The total market capitalization in January, 1929 when the market peaked, represented about 53 per cent of GDP, and just 20 per cent of GDP in 1932 (when GDP had dropped by 16 per cent in current prices). The development of the size of the stock market is illustrated in Table 10.9.

The growth in market values and turnover since the mid-1980s may seem explosive and appear like a 20-year "bubble", but they should be seen against the very low levels from which they came. They should also be seen against the background of the deregulation of the 1980s, including the abolition in 1990 of the "valpskatt", a turnover tax on stock market transactions introduced in 1987 as a sort of domestic "Tobin tax", which was found, after three years, to be counterproductive.

The average figures shown in Table 10.9 cover some wild gyrations. At the market troughs in 1992 and 2002, the market capitalizations were only 38 per cent and 72 per cent of GDP respectively, but 147 per cent at the top of the market in 2006.

---

[27]Cfr. S. Algott (1963) *Bidrag till Stockholms fondbörs historia* in S. Algott (ed.) *Stockholms Fondsbörs 100 År* (Stockholms Fondsbörs) pp. 175–8.

Table 10.9   Stock Exchange Turnover and Market Capitalization, 1916–2006 (Billion SEK)

Annual averages	Turnover			Market capitalization (shares)	Market capitalization in % of GDP
	Shares	*Bonds*	*Total*		
1916–1920	0.9	0.0	0.9	1929: 4.4	1929: 53
1921–1930	0.2	0.1	0.3	1931: 2.4	1931: 27
1931–1940	0.2	0.1	0.3	1932: 1.6	1932: 20
1950–1966	0.2	0.1	0.3		
1967–1971	0.9	0.2	1.1		
1972–1975	2.0	0.6	2.6		
1976–1980	3.0	4.0	7.0		1979: 10
1981–1985	55.5	9.7	65.2	198	28
1986–1990	117.8			545	48
1991–1995	392.8			831	55
1996–2000	2,231.8			2,713	133
2000–2006	3,637.5			2,905	112

Sources: Market capitalization 1929–1932: *Stockholms Fondsbörs 100 år* (Stockholms Fondsbörs, 1963) p. 176. GDP 1929–1932: Statistiska Centralbyrån: *Historisk Statistik*. bd. IV. Market capitalization 1981–2006 and turnover: *Statistisk Årsbok*, relevant years.
Note: Market capitalization figures are averages of year-end figures, except for the 1929 and 1931 figures, which are end-January, 1932, which is end-May, and 1979, which is end-year. Figures comprise both the A-list (80–90 per cent of the total) and the O-list.

Except for the second half of the 1970s, bond trading was small compared to the turnover of shares, and so insignificant that Statistisk Centralbyrån, the central statistics office, has not published the figures in the Statistisk Årsbok after the mid-1980s.

Between the 1920s and the mid-1970s, the number of stock exchange listed companies grew from about 25 to 75, and the number of stock exchange members remained fairly constant at roughly 20.

Since 1975, both the number of listed companies and stock exchange members has more than trebled. However, from a peak of 311 listed companies in 2000, the number has kept dropping.

Institutional changes

In line with the tightening controls of the 1970s, a new Stock Exchange Act was passed in 1979 i.a. conferring a monopoly on the Stockholm Stock Exchange as from January 1, 1980. The relatively insignificant exchanges in Göteborg and Malmö were closed. Soon after, the Stockholm Exchange was turned into a limited liability joint stock company owned by its former members.

A more substantial change occurred in 1998, when the Stockhom Exchange was taken over by OM AB, a broker firm established in Stockholm in the

1980s specializing in standardized options contracts (OM being short for "optionsmäklarna", the "options brokers"). In the following years, it merged with the HEX plc, the Helsiki Stock Exchange, to form OMX (2003), the Copenhagen Stock Exchange (2005), the Icelandic Stock Exchange (2006). It also took a 10 per cent stake in the Oslo Stock Exchange, and took over the Armenian Stock Exchange (2007), as well as the stock exchanges in Tallin, Riga, and Vilnius.

Finally, in 2008, OMX was merged into Nasdaq to become NASDAQ OMX.

11
Some Reflections and Conclusions

"If you prick us, do we not bleed?
If you tickle us, do we not laugh?
If you poison us, do we not die?"

("The Merchant of Venice", Act Three)

11.1 Why the fuss about definitions?

One of the most fundamental changes seen in the capital markets over the latest 50 years, is the disappearance of differences between various categories of financial institutions. Gone are the days of stockbrokers and jobbers, forgotten is the distinction between commercial bank business and savings bank business, and eliminated are the differences between investment banking and commercial banking. Nobody can anymore tell the difference between "Gründerbanken", "banques d'affaires, merchant banks, and commercial banks. Mortgage institutions have become deeply involved in ordinary retail banking, and banks have absorbed broker firms and insurance companies. Capital markets have become dominated by financial conglomerates rather than by specialists.

In some countries, this development has been less conspicuous than in others. In the Nordic countries, particularly Denmark, the transition has been more revolutionary than in the rest of Europe, because historically the distinction between the different classes of financial institutions has been sharper than in most other European countries. In Germany and France, Sparkassen and caisses d'epargnes have been doing regular banking for more than 100 years. In Denmark, "banking business" was formally forbidden to savings banks until 1974. In Sweden and Finland, savings banks were originally told not to engage in "more general banking". Until recently, mortgage lending was a world apart in all Nordic countries except Finland.

The gradual integration of all these different types of financial institutions and services into a single regulatory conglomerate mess of "monetary

273

institutions" has mostly happened as a response to wishes from the savings banks. Since the early 1970s, the argument was that since they would bleed from losses, laugh when times were good, and die from poisonous assets, they might as well be treated as all other "banks". Also since the early 1990s, the Danish mortgage system, probably the most stable and problem-free in the world, has been partly undermined for the purpose of creating a "level playing field" in the EU.

The question is to what extent this development has been sound, and to what extent it is healthy to administer the same regulatory medicine to all the different kinds of lips which drink from chalices with different kinds of poisons.

Schedule 11.1 below intends to capture some of these issues.

Schedule 11.1   Financial Institutions, Risks, and Capital Requirements

Type of financial activity	Risks		Capital requirement
	Funding (liquidity)	Counter party	
Retail banking	Moderate	Moderate, if widely spread	Lower than average
Commercial/ wholesale Banking	Dependent on interterbank market	Notable, because of large m/t and l/t lendings	Higher than average
Mortgage lending a) Traditional Danish (matched cash flows)	Limited in deep bond markets	Limited, if widely spread	Limited
b) Structured/ unmatched, and projects	Considerable	Depending on spreading of risk	Considerable
Investment banking (underwriting)	Limited, but subject to volatile markets	Limited, because risks are sold	Considerable, and subject to volatile markets
Pure stockbroking	Limited	Settle ment risks	Small
Stockbroking, including proprietary trading	Considerable and volatile	Market risks	Higher than average
Fund management	Limited	Limited	Lower than average

These are the diverse types of activities which are being regulated under the common "umbrella" of financial institutions legislation introduced by the EU and the Basel Committee. The different classes of risk are intended to be encapsulated in the "Basel II" risk calculations and capital requirements.

11.2 The intellectual hubris of Basel II

"If to do were as easy as to know what were good to do,
chapels had been churches, and poor men's cottages princes'
palaces."

("The Merchant of Venice", Act I.)

If the future had been predictable, and credit risks calculable, managing banks would have been easy, bank failures would not have happened, and poor men's cottages would have been princes' palaces.

Perhaps the most closely watched banking regulation is the solvency ratio. Historically, there does, however, not seem to be any measurable connection between the capital ratios seen in failed banks a year before the crashes, and those of surviving banks. The reason is, of course, that loans are booked at their face values until just before it can be seen that at least some of the money has been lost. The timespan between the day a bank feels seriously threatened by a loss till the loss turns into a near certainty is rarely more than a year, and can be as little as a few days.[1] The largest financial collapses have come as a complete surprise even to people very close to the situation. The Kreuger crash, Nordisk Fjerfabrik, Enron, and LTCM are certainly not the only cases in point. Six months before Lehman Brothers hit the wall, not even its own top management knew that it would happen (although they did suspect that it might, judging from some of the information which has since come to light).

It is understandable if bank regulators, of whatever description, think they can draw analogies between insurance accidents and banking/credit accidents. Credits – at least of the standard retail type – go into default with a certain statistical regularity, vaguely related to the business cycle, just as people die and cars crash with a certain regularity. On the face of it, this is just a question of feeding the computers with the right information. In life insurance, this has worked for more than 200 years, even without computers.

On the other hand, it is glaringly clear that for two very fundamental reasons, insurance analogies can be made applicable to banking only to a very limited extent.

The first reason is lack of sufficient and relevant statistical information.

Two of the fundamental corner stones used in the Basel II to calculate the amount of capital a bank will need to satisfy the 8 per cent "risk weighted" solvency ratio, are: 1) the "probability of default", and 2) "loss, given default". Both are supposed to be calculated from statistical data, just like in insurance

---

[1]This statement is, of course, difficult to substantiate statistically, but it reflects SEA's experience from about 25 years in the banking world.

business. The problem is that no bankruptcy statistics anywhere provides any information on the "mortality" rate of credits, and how that "mortality" relates to specific balance sheet characteristics during a prolonged period prior to a default.

The second reason is the absence of conceptual clarity. This means that not only do meaningful statistics not exist, but also that such statistics cannot ever, in principle, be produced. The reason is that the statistical incident, a "credit default", cannot be clearly defined. Many "defaults" are not officially declared, and therefore cannot be counted, because banks consider it better to renegotiate the credit and/or reconstruct the borrower. In life insurance, the calculation of mortality rates is fairly simple. Death is rarely renegotiated. Credits turned sour are often renegotiated. Weak credits are stretched, covenants are renegotiated, companies are merged and restructured, loans are swapped into equity, and everything is up for discussion. In any calculation of probability, what is needed is fractions with precisely defined numerators and denominators, and large numbers of clearly defined observations. In banking, none of this exists.[2] Everything depends on a more or less accurate prediction of the future, and on what is the good thing to do in a given situation. One needs only to ask the question how life insurance companies would have done their calculations if death had been subject to renegotiation or restructuring?

Yet, hundreds of people spent about 8 years to come up with Basel II, which is totally based on the assumption that the necessary calculations can be made from non-existing statistics and the opinions of a few rating agencies, whose ratings imply life or death to the rated banks either because of their effect on the funding costs of the banks, or because of the effect on their capital requirements. The faith placed in the rating agencies appears quite extraordinary, almost as if they were medieval doctors.[3] Those who assigned this extraordinary importance to the opinions of a few rating

---

[2]In the US, there is plenty of statistics relating defaults on corporate bonds to various credit ratings and credit profiles. Rating agencies, e.g. Standard & Poors and Moodys, have statistics dating back from the early 20th century. The problems are that most of these ratings apply to corporate bonds, and that bond defaults are different from bank credits, because they are more difficult to renegotiate, and that similar rating statistics are rare in Europe and almost non-existent in the Nordic countries for other than financial institutions.

[3]One is reminded of Lady Bracknel's response when she was informed that Bunbury had died:

Algernon Moncrieff: "... The doctors found out that Bunbury could not live, ... so Bunbury died."

Lady Bracknell: "He seems to have had great confidence in the opinion of his physicians."

Oscar Wilde (1895) *"The Importance of Being Earnest"*, Act III.

agencies seem to have disregarded the fact that such agencies are, like all other companies, staffed by ordinary human beings who have obvious conflicts of interest.

Obviously, the item "loss given default" is a purely individual, personal opinion, since also here no sufficiently meaningful statistics are available.[4]

In spite of the impossibility of measuring and quantifying "risk" in the banking world, Basel II stipulates that "monetary institutions", of whatever description, type or nature, shall have a "risk weighted" solvency ratio of 8 per cent. Nobody seems to know how the target of 8 per cent was ever decided upon. It has certainly never had anything to do with even semi-scientific statistics.

So, a lot of complicated calculations are made from non-existing statistics and American rating methodologies to hit the "mythical" figure of 8 per cent, for which absolutely no logical justification can be given.

Basel III seems to be strolling down the same path into wilderness. Whilst the Nordic banking crises of the early 1990s could happen because financial institutions over-exploited the possibilities opened to them by the deregulation of the previous years, and the sub-prime crisis in the US might not have happened if the investment banks had not been freed from Glass-Steagall, or if Glass-Steagall had been lifted at a different point of time, this does not necessarily mean that deregulation should not have happened. It does mean, however, that when regulations are designed and introduced, attention should be given to the question of what will happen when such regulations will eventually have worn themselves out and have to be lifted.

History shows that banking regulations have their limitations. The more restrictive they are, the more circumventions will be found, including all shapes of "grey" market activities and institutions. Sweden and Norway have provided plenty of proof of that. The "inventiveness" of the market participants should never be underestimated.

In addition, there is a risk that by issuing too detailed banking regulations and too strict solvency ratios, the banks will become less useful to society, and the authorities can be held co-responsible for the running and the fates of the banks.[5]

The question is, of course, if anything better than the unhelpful Basel II and III can be conceived. Admittedly, this is not easy, since any regime will necessarily reflect human deficiencies, short memories, limited foresight,

---

[4]In very large and homogenous credit portfolios, such as those of the Danish mortgage institutions, some useful statistics could, in principle, be made. For commercial banks or integrated institutions like British building societies, this is more difficult.

[5]Cfr. Some of the considerations behind the Swedish Banking Act of 1824 (6.3.3), the Finnish Banking Act of 1886 (4.3.4), and the Danish Second Priority Mortgage Act of 1897 (3.3.4).

and political compromises. The proposals made here, should, however, be taken into consideration:

I. Capital requirements, if they are used at all, should be applied to specific financial activities (e.g. defined as shown in Schedule 11.1), not to consolidated conglomerates. The present (and proposed) regulation implies e.g. that banks with mortgage finance subsidiaries benefit from the collateral of such mortgages, although in a break-up situation this collateral is not available to the bank's creditors. Nordea, Danske Bank, Swedbank, and Svenska Handelsbanken are all parent banks which satisfy the regulations with less than 4 per cent equity ratios, because in respect of Basel II they benefit from the collateral in their mortgage finance subsidiaries and therefore meet the 8 per cent requirement on a consolidated basis. This is hardly logical, even if the proposed "gearing" limitation goes some way to mitigate this absurdity.

II. If "banks" decide to engage in other than "general banking" (e.g. mortgage lending, project finance, etc., cfr. schedule 11.1 above) such activities should be organized in specific subsidiaries of holding companies, each separately capitalized. Mortgage lending, in particular, should be kept in separate companies, which could be owned by bank holding companies or the other way round, and they should be required to match their assets and liabilities and their cash flows, as in the traditional Danish mortgage institutions. Several British building societies, savings banks, and investment banks round the world illustrate the dangers of not observing these principles.

III. Since history has shown risk concentration to be the main bank killer, the main regulatory lever should not be a solvency ratio, but a risk diversification ratio. The present limit on individual exposures should be substantially reduced, e.g. from 25 per cent of the lender's equity to maximum 5 or 10 per cent, but it is, of course, difficult to argue logically for any particular limit. If a 10 per cent limit had applied to Danish banks in the 1920s and in the early 21st century, the bank mortality would have been a small fraction of the actual numbers.

The question whether any specific solvency ratios should be imposed, is not nearly as obvious as it is mostly taken to be. If the frequency of bank failures following the introduction of solvency requirements during the 1920s or 1930s has been less than before the introduction of such requirements, it could very well be due to the many involuntary mergers and takeovers of weak banks. This makes the counting of "bank failures" somewhat hypothetical.

It should not be entirely unthinkable to envisage a banking system without formal solvency requirements, and where banks compete on solvency ratios. Banks with low ratios would lose deposits to banks boasting of better solvency ratios. Choosing a solvency ratio would be a management decision taken against the background of the business composition of the bank, the perceived cost of capital, and the capital ratios of competitors.

In any case, even if 10 per cent is better than 8 per cent, the difference is minor. Virtually all of the Nordic banks which failed in the early 1990s and in 2007–2009 (Denmark) would still have failed if two years prior to their end they had booked a 10 per cent solvency ratio.

11.3 The latest banking crisis: A few questions and observations

11.3.1 Are central banks omnipotent, and could the crisis have been averted?

During the 2008–2009 banking crisis, the argument has frequently been advanced from all kinds of observers and politicians looking for scapegoats that central banks should have acted early to "prick" the "bubble", which they failed to see was coming. By raising interest rates faster and stronger in 2004–2005, particularly in the US and the UK, so the argument goes, the respective central banks could have stopped the accelerating real estate and stockmarket prices in 2005–2007, thereby preventing the collapses of 2008–2009.

This line of argument raises at least four questions:

1: To what extent do central banks decide interest rates?
2: To what extent do which interest rates influence property and stock prices?
3: Is it a "natural" task for central banks to try to "influence" property and stock prices?
4: Are the "crystal balls" available to central banks better than those available to other mortals?

Some brief answers are suggested here,[6] based not only on the experience of the Nordic countries:

1. Central banks do, of course, decide their own interest rates, which are usually ultra-short, i.e. usually over-night rates, and rarely longer than three months, applicable to other financial institutions. These other financial institutions set their own interest rates on a large number of different types of accounts, ranging from very short-term types to very long-term pension and savings accounts. To these other financial

---

[6]These questions have been discussed with Jesper Berg, until recently Head of Department, Danmarks Nationalbank, now in charge of regulatory matters in Nykredit, Denmark's largest mortgage finance provider.

institutions, the central banks are marginal suppliers of funds. The extent to which other financial institutions follow interest changes by the central banks depends on the extent to which financial institutions have to use this marginal source of funds, which is usually very little and only very short. Therefore, central banks cannot dictate neither the structure nor the level of market interest rates as they please, except to the extent that agreements between the central banks and the private banks (or legislation) work to this effect (as it did in certain periods in the Nordic countries). At best, they can delay or accelerate interest changes, which would have come anyway through market forces. The link between central bank interest changes and changes in medium- and long-term interest rate changes is weak and unpredictable.

2. Property and stock market prices are probably, and probably much of the time, partially influenced by interest rates, but probably mainly by medium- or long-term rates, and less by short-term rates, since property and stocks are long-term assets.

3. Central banks have traditionally been given the task to maintain a sound and stable monetary system internally and externally, generally taken to mean keeping inflation as low as possible, and controlling exchange rates.

   Central banks have long ago had to give up controlling exchange rates. According to several recent suggestions by a number of observers, central banks should now be asked to control "asset prices" in addition to the general price level. If central banks are asked to control the prices of IT stocks, share prices in general as well as real estate prices, quite regardless of their imagined ability to do so, it is difficult to see where the responsibilities of central banks would end. Commodity prices, such as gold, oil, other metals, or maybe potatoes? Copper, zinc, and cereal prices also went through the roof in 2004–2007. Also, the logic of conferring such responsibilities on central banks would be that central banks should also support those markets, whenever they were appearing to drop too steeply. This does, however, not seem to have been suggested by anybody.

   Even if it as accepted that central banks have some sort of responsibility not only for the development of general price level developments, but also for the movement of specific prices, it does not appear quite clear when and how a central bank should do precisely what. To the multitude of stock market analysts and traders, and to the real estate agents, it would probably seem odd or inappropriate if the central banks tried to move their respective markets in one way or the other.

4. If the crystal balls available to central banks had been of a superior quality than those available to governments and other analysts, chapels would have been cathedrals. Their computers have been programmed by ordinary mortals, and their econometric models are based on statistics which can show only the past. Those who blame central banks for not having

predicted the 2008–2010 recession precisely already in 2004–2005, should ask themselves why nobody in 2009–2010 is expecting the central banks to confidently coming up with precise predictions for the pattern of the 2011–2015 recovery.

The problem with forecasting is that it is not good enough to predict the turning points of a trend, though this has always been the most difficult part of forecasts. What is required is to predict what comes after the turning point. Everybody knows that no "bubble" will last forever. What nobody, including central banks, could know in 2006, was whether the top of the "bubble" would come in early or late 2007, or maybe even later, and whether it would be succeeded by a period of stagnating asset prices, slowly dropping prices, or precipitously falling prices. That is also why economists in 2009–2010 kept discussing whether the coming upturn will be V-shaped, U-shaped, or a W. There is no way of knowing, or there would have been a lot more billionaires and palaces around.

Presumably, central bankers are fully aware of their limited powers as briefly discussed above. They are, however, never heard to admit to these limitations in public. Maybe they fear that such confessions would have undermined the respect in which they are generally held. On some occasions central bankers[7] seem to prefer to admit having taken an afternoon nap back in 2004–2005 rather than admit that they were, in principle, unable to see what was coming, and that even if they had seen or suspected what was coming, there was not much they could do about it. Those central bank governors who are up for periodical re-appointments, e.g. the FED chairman, the Bank of England governor, and the governors of Norges Bank and Sveriges Riksbank, might not get re-appointed if they admit to such inabilities. Others would be found who would express more confidence in their own forecasting powers and action abilities.

In the Nordic countries, nobody ever suggested that the respective central banks could or should have done anything to prevent the banking crises

---

[7]Cfr. Alan Greenspan, FED chairman until 2006, who, when testifying in a Congressional hearing in October 2008, admitted that he had been partially wrong on the benefits from deregulating derivatives, and that there were flaws in his model of how the financial world worked, and still had not fully found out how the crisis got so deep. As if a little more thinking by Mr. Greenspan and a slightly better model would have prevented the unfolding of the delusions and madness of the crowds. It probably would not. Even though Mr. Greenspan was no longer up for reappointment, he still felt he had to defend the reputation of the institution he had once represented. It would have seriously undermined the position of the FED and Mr. Bernanke, his successor, if he had told the truth.

of either the early 1990s or during the 2005–2009 bubble (except for a few remarks in a Norwegian government report, cfr. Chapter 9).

11.3.2   The wonderland of property finance

The property markets and property financing have widely been pronounced the sources of the latest banking crisis, just as it happened in Norway, Finland, and Sweden in the early 1990s, and on several earlier occasions. The conclusion from this is not that property financing is inherently poisonous, but that distinctions should be made between, on the one hand, mass mortgages undertaken by specialized mortgage lenders with matched cash flows, good spreading of exposures, and no project risks, and, on the other hand, project financings with associated off-take risks and un-matched cash flows, undertaken by commercial banks, occasionally and unfortunately with excessive concentration of exposures.

The former captures the essentials of the traditional Danish mortgage system, which has demonstrated a remarkable robustness over 200 years, while the latter characterizes what happened in the London Docklands in the late 1980s, and in Sweden, Norway, and Finland at about the same time, and in Denmark in 2005–2007. That was unfortunate, not particularly clever, and much influenced by the extraordinary popular delusion that property prices would keep going up. Such is the madness of crowds, and several banks shared the delusions of their customers.

11.4   The issue of "over-indebtedness", and the size of the financial sector

Table 11.1   Organized Capital Markets in per cent of GDP in the Nordic Countries, 1980–2006

	Denmark	Finland	Norway	Sweden
1860	40	16		24 (1861)
1880	72	29	51	64
1900	134	76	93	96
1920	96	73 (1918)	85	87
1925	117 (1924)	51	91	117
1930	148	87	97	112
1939/1940	113	68	99 (1935)	116 (1934)
1950	91	34	42	84
1970	107 (1969)	56	70 (1970–1974)	95 (1968)
1980	141 (1978)	59	79 (1980–1984)	141 (1985)
1990	228 (1988)	104	127 (1985–1989)	132
2000	236 (1998)	52	101 (2002–2005)	144 (2004)
2006	367 (2007)		112 (2006–2008)	176

Sources: As for Tables 3.9, 4.6, 5.7, 6.7, 7.2, 7.4, 8.8, 9.8, 9.16 and 10.8.

Table 11.1 compares the relative size and growth of the organized capital markets in the four Nordic countries since 1860.

Minor differences are, of course, of no significance, but it is clearly seen that the relative size of the organized capital market in Denmark has almost constantly been substantially larger than in the other Nordic countries, and that the Finnish capital market is the smallest. The two main reasons are probably first, the large role in housing finance played by the central and regional governments in Finland, Norway, and Sweden bypassing the capital markets in contrast to the Danish mortgage institution system, and secondly, the extensive capital market restrictions maintained in the three other countries for a prolonged period.

It could be added that a monetary economy seems to have developed earlier in Denmark than in the three other countries, probably both because of a higher density of population and the proximity to Hamburg, both of which helped Denmark to a good headstart in the mid-19th century. Denmark has also had the highest GDP per capita among the Nordic countries, apart from the first 30-odd years after WWII, when Sweden could boast of that position, and apart from Norway including the off-shore economy since about 1980.

In relation to the latest as well as earlier financial crises, it has frequently been argued by various observers and analysts that the "general indebtedness levels have been too high", and that "there is too much debt around".

Such arguments are not entirely convincing. They raise the intricate question of the size of the "appropriate" amount of "general indebtedness" or "amount of debt around".

Is it "appropriate" for the size of the "organized" capital market to be 50 per cent, 150 per cent, or 350 per cent of GDP?

Nobody seems to have had any suggestions.

Also, for any cent, dime, or krone of debt, there is a corresponding asset. Nobody seems ever to have complained that there are too many assets around.

There are plenty of examples of individuals, companies, and even countries, which have over-indebted themselves. The distribution of assets and debts can be a problem, but that problem can exist regardless whether the aggregate amount of assets and debts are ten or 400 per cent of GDP.

As indicated by Table 11.1, and the tables on which it is based, the aggregate amounts of assets and debts generally increase as GDP increases. Since the Industrial Revolution, fixed assets and corresponding savings have grown faster than income. This has, however, never been a smooth process. In connection with wars, recessions, and financial crises, capital markets tend to contract. In budding booms and bubbles – and following deregulation – they expand.

When business cycles weaken – which they do with intervals of 4–6 years – capital markets contract because both supply and demand for capital weaken. In that process, some financial institutions will stumble, quite regardless of financial regulations.

So, banks will continue to fail until the last syllable of recorded time.

Index

General note

The main references to cities which have changed their names in the course of history will be their modern names, but there will be cross references from older names if both old and new names have been used in the main text, whish is usually the case (e.g. Oslo is found under Oslo with cross references under Christiania and Kristiania).

In connection with names of institutions, old spellings are generally used (e.g. Kjøbenhavns Handelsbank instead of Københavns Handelsbank).

Names of Finnish institutions are generally found under the names used in English, unless their original Finnish or Swedish names are normally used outside Finland (e.g. Föreningsbanken i Finland, or Suomen Yhdyspankki (SYP) is found under Union Bank of Finland, while references to Kansalis Osake Pankki are found under KOP, and Suomen Pankki is found under Bank of Finland).

DISCARDED
CONCORDIA UNIV. LIBRARY